JOHN BAILEY'S
Fishing Bible

JOHN BAILEY'S
Fishing Bible

Everything You Need to Know About Fishing

NEW
HOLLAND

This edition published in 2013 by New Holland Publishers
Some original material first published in 2001, 2003, 2004 and 2009 by New Holland Publishers (UK) Ltd.
London • Cape Town • Sydney • Auckland
www.newhollandpublishers.com

Garfield House, 86-88 Edgware Road, London W2 2EA, UK
Unit 1, 66 Gibbes Street, Chatswood, NSW 2067, Australia
Wembley Square, First Floor, Solan Road Gardens, Cape Town, 8001, South Africa
218 Lake Road, Northcote, Auckland, New Zealand

10 9 8 7 6 5 4 3 2 1

A catalogue record of this book is available at the British Library.

ISBN 978 1 78009 4090

Senior Editor: Sally McFall
Designer: Kimberley Pearce
Production: Olga Dementiev
Publisher: Simon Papps

Printed and bound by Everbest Printing Co Ltd (China).

ACKNOWLEDGEMENTS

Firstly, I'd like to thank the great tackle makers in the UK for all the help that I've received from them over the years. I have cherished working with Hardy and Greys for over a decade and also my relationship with Shimano that dates back to the late 1980s. I'd particular like to thank people like Ken Brewster, Lucy Bowden, Howard Croston, John Wolstenholme, Richard Sanderson, Jan Porter, Kevin Nash, Alan Blair along with Peter Drennan and Gary Barclay.

I'd like to mention other professionals in the angling game who have provided me with so much help and inspiration. These names would include Nick Hart, Henry Gilbey, Johnny Jensen, Jan Porter again, John Wilson, Tim Knight, David Hall, Steve Martin, Dean Macey and many others sadly too numerous to mention.

I believe very much in the phrase, 'brotherhood of the angle' and my work wouldn't be possible but for the support of so many friends. Thank you Ian Miller, Tim Ellis, Neill Stephen, David Lambert, Simon Clark, John Gilman, Simon Ratcliffe, Ian Rotherham, Phil Humm and so many others. I would also include Andy Steer and, of course, my great friend Rob Olsen. To both of you, thanks for your friendship, ideas and wonderful artwork.

I'd like to thank even longer term friends who have made my fishing life as profound as it is. Thank you Shirley Deterding, Subhan, wherever you're resting, Bola and others who will know who they are.

Special thanks also to the team that put this book together, notably Sally McFall, and Carol, who still sorts my life out for me. Thank you especially to Sarah for love, encouragement and bankside picnics.

CONTENTS

FOREWORD

Throughout my career in athletics, I've always been aware of the central importance of coaching. You can't do without the best, whether you're competing on the track, on the field or even in that bobsleigh, where I spent some pretty hairy moments indeed, believe me! And it's exactly the same with fishing, another of the sports that I've simply adored since my childhood.

This is where John Bailey enters my life. I used to read his work more years ago than either of us would like to remember, first of all in that legendary partwork, *Fisherman's Weekly*, that he contributed to for several years. After that, John went on to write shoals of angling books, all acclaimed but some more practical than others. These books might not have had the glamour of some of the travel and adventure works but the fact remains that A-Z knowledge is a vital part of this sport, just as it is any other one.

That's why *John Bailey's Fishing Bible* is such a landmark. It's great to have a real treasury of knowledge brought together into one volume. 'The Bible' consists of the best advice distilled from several of John's past New Holland works and put together to provide a real hands-on guide to every aspect of angling – fly, bait or lure, 'The Bible' covers it. Game, coarse or sea fish, it doesn't matter what your discipline is, you will find pointers in this book. River, sea or stillwaters? Float or lead? Winter or summer? Everything to do with angling you will find in 'The Bible'.

Recently, John has become even better known as the 'new Mr Crabtree.' His love of teaching and his love of angling have come together in these cracking TV series that recreate the iconic Bernard Venables' cartoon book of the post-war years. Since the programmes, there has been a surge of interest amongst kids everywhere, all keen to get into angling and that's super for them, for society and for the sport.

And upsurge of interest in angling is also important for the environment. Without fishermen, fisheries will suffer. There is no one who cares for the aquatic environment like anglers and that's a fact. Fishing gives kids, all of us, a connection with the natural world that you just can't get any other way. Fishing, too, gets kids and all of us out there, in the real world, facing real challenges, catching real fish. That's providing you know how to do it, of course.

John's 'Fishing Bible' is one of the great leg-ups. Like the real Bible of old, if you take all the lessons on board, you won't go far wrong and you won't find yourself facing many situations when you feel alone. Having this book on your side gets you off to the sprint start in angling that I always aimed for in my athletic career.

Dean Macey

INTRODUCTION

I'm delighted and rather honoured that this selection from my books of recent years is being put together. I like to feel that this compendium represents a real body of knowledge to take anglers from the A to the Z of angling experiences. Obviously, here and there, I've updated the original writings because fishing itself moves on. More especially, I find that I learn each and every time I go out on the bankside. That's fishing, or how I feel it should be. Fishing never stands still for you and that is its lifelong appeal. The angler who believes that he knows everything probably, in truth, knows next to nothing!

I'm showing off a stunning, fly-caught Scottish brown trout. The dog is more interested in looking for rising fish.

The Aware Angler

So why do I feel that fishing is so all encompassing and what justification do I have for putting forward this book as a so-called 'Bible', a reference book for years to come? Well, first, I believe in the 'Aware Angler'. By this, I believe in the angler who understands and supports all manner of conservation work. In this modern age, it's not simply enough to know how to catch fish, you also have to know how to help preserve fish. I find that half my time these days is spent discussing the threats to fish and to fisheries and how to circumvent these. Once upon a time, fishing was so much more simple. Not today. Along with conservation goes the care of fish that you catch. Never, under any circumstances, must you stress any capture and, today, I'm the firmest believer in catch and release unless you take the odd fish, humanely killed, for the pot. The Aware Angler also shows sensitivity to the waterside. He or she will leave it exactly as it was, hopefully pristine. The Aware Angler will show a sensitive approach to fishing methods, always being careful not to spook the fish. The Aware Angler knows his impact at the waterside must be minimal. It's the cycles of the fish and the fishery that are the important considerations.

The 'All Species' Angler

This new collection reinforces my belief in the 'All Species Angler'. For generations it's been the norm for anglers to limit themselves to one or two species. Perhaps anglers have been salmon fishermen or trout men. Perhaps they have just wanted to catch carp or predators. Perhaps they're beach anglers only or simply enjoy match fishing for relatively small silver fish. All these pursuits are tremendous in themselves, but I have never felt that they should be exclusive. For me, the angler who fishes for all species throughout all the seasons of the year is the angler who has got it right. My own belief is there are more of these all-rounders each and every day. Increasingly, anglers are beginning to realize that every species of fish has something to offer, some individual excitement. From what I've witnessed, the All Species Angler has the richest time of it,

There is a real art just in choosing the right float.

sampling pretty well every thrill there is to be found in this sport of ours.

The 'All Method' Angler

Closely linked to the All Species Angler is the 'All Method Angler'. I'll agree that some methods probably require more skill than others, but each and every method demands attention and respect. Of course, putting out a salmon fly 27 or 37 metres (30 or 40 yards) with a rhythmically controlled spey cast is a magnificent skill in itself. So is flicking out a dry fly or a nymph, but let's not overlook the equally high-octane skills of the man who trots at distance for grayling or roach. How about the lure angler, working his spinner or plug with pinpoint accuracy and endless imagination? Let's not forget the bass fisherman on the rocks battling with the surf, casting a bait into the wind to land on a ten-penny bit. All these methods are absorbing. They're all there to be learnt and enjoyed on waters around the globe.

The 'All Venue' Angler

The 'All Venue Angler' is likely to be the angler who knows the most about watercraft, one of the most

It's on rivers like these that watercraft plays a huge part.

bone-juddering cold of winter you begin to question your sanity, but there is always something to rescue the day, to make it memorable. Perhaps, at last light, even as the snowstorm is clearing, you will see a barn owl hovering over the fields. Perhaps you'll catch a beautifully blue-scaled roach from a steely-grey river. All the suffering will instantly be worthwhile. Perhaps it's tench on a summer morning or salmon as the leaves begin to fall. Perhaps you're out fishing the mayfly for a spring brown trout. Perhaps it's an early summer bass off the beach or perhaps a cod when the northerlies begin to rage. Think of a cold, misty dawn in November when the pike are beginning to feed for the first time properly in the year. Or perhaps you're fishing for carp on a lazy, hot summer afternoon when

Why let a bit of snow come between you and your enjoyment!?

vital considerations there is in fishing. Watercraft has, recently, tended to come well back into fashion after a period when it was somewhat overlooked. Watercraft is simply that ability to read the water, to understand it and to make sense of all its varying moods and subtleties. Water speaks to some anglers. It shouts out, it demands to be studied. And of course, without watercraft, you will never totally understand why the fish are where they are at any particular time. The real All Venue Angler will look at a piece of water of any type, anywhere in the world, and begin to search for all the important features. Any water type will be like an open book to him, quick to surrender its secrets. Watercraft is a massive skill within itself and you will read a lot about it in the coming pages.

The 'All Year' Angler
I've always been an 'All Year Angler'. If I could, I'd fish every day of the 365. Sometimes, in the

My Fishing in the Footsteps of Mr Crabtree *protegé Tadhg and I show off his prize catch of a ravishing roach.*

the fish are in the surface layers, idly sucking down surface baits. There's not a second of any day in any year when it's not great to be out fishing.

Sharing wisdom

I also believe completely in teaching, in wisdom being passed down, handed on from generation to generation. That's how I was taught by so many anglers throughout my life from childhood and even into the present day. This is one of my strongest certainties. Unless wisdoms are not passed on like this, we will literally forget more than we actually know. Angling is unlike any other sport and you've probably picked that up from the words so far in this introduction. It's simply so multifaceted. There is simply so much to learn if you are going to be a master of the sport that you've got to benefit from help and advice at every single step of your way.

Through 2012 and 2013, I was heavily involved in the TV series *Fishing in the Footsteps of Mr Crabtree*. The series was based on the legendary 1940s' *Daily Mirror* cartoon strip that featured Mr Crabtree taking his son Peter fishing throughout the year, fishing for all species, using all methods and having a simply fantastic time. That is how fishing should be. It should be all about passing on the torch of knowledge and understanding. I'll be proud if anything I have done in a long career in angling measures up in the smallest degree to what Mr Crabtree's legacy has left us.

This is why I'm pleased with this particular book. The knowledge in it is in small part mine but in large part what I've been told and shown by so many generous anglers through so many long years. My life has been changed and bettered by the angling wisdoms of others. What I'm trying to do here is simply to repay the debt.

Get fishing and enjoy it all your life. You'll never regret it.

John Bailey

CHAPTER 1

THE BASIC SKILLS

Make no mistake – angling is a sport, not a hobby. Moreover, it's a sport that demands the utmost in physical and mental skills. Sport fishing is, then, a very apt term, and the accomplished sports angler will have a deep knowledge of the fish, the waters, the tackle and the methods available. He or she will develop scores of skills as the years pass, and the experience bank will build up until a real and satisfying level of expertise is reached.

Learning the Basics

There is no more diverse sport in the world than that of angling. With most sports – football, for example – it doesn't matter whether you're a professional player or you just like to kick a ball around in the park. The rules are the same: you are essentially trying to score goals, or keep them out. The same holds true for baseball, basketball, cricket, and most other sports that you care to name – except fishing.

At its best, fishing is both active and skilful. Here I've waded out mid-river from where I can better control the float as it trots down the stream to roach, dace, chub and grayling.

100 sports in one

An angler on a wild, winter coast hurling heavy leads way out into angry seas could not be fishing more differently from the man stalking a delicately rising trout on a crystal river. There's just no comparison between what the two anglers are doing. Similarly, twitching a popper back along the surface for a black bass is a totally different sport to casting 100 yards plus for a carp or wreck fishing for conger eels.

Shared skills

This variation in species, waters and techniques is one of the joys of angling, and there will never be anybody who is totally expert in every aspect of the sport. There is always more to learn and more to try. That said, there are basic skills that are common to every angler, whatever he or she is doing. For example, you've just got to make sure that the knots that you use don't pull apart under pressure. Equally, you've got to be able to read the water in front of you, and it doesn't matter if it's the Atlantic shoreline or a tiny upland river. Wherever you are fishing, you have to know which features will hold fish and where you are likely to find them. When you catch a fish, whether it's a cod, a carp, a catfish or a Chinook salmon, you must know how to play that fish successfully, land it and then deal with it as humanely as possible once it is yours.

Shared courtesy

Another thing we should all have in common, wherever we fish, is courtesy towards other anglers. Even fishing somewhere as large as the sea, you still don't cast over or near another angler's bait. You should always give a fellow angler room and never crowd his or her space. Give advice if requested or if it is obviously needed.

John is showing the many facets of fishing – not only is he crouching low and camouflaging himself so as not to alert the fish to his presence, he is busy eyeing the river for areas, such as overhanging branches, where fish will congregate and where he is therefore most likely to feel that welcome tug on this reel.

Practical philosophy

In large part, the basic skills can be taught from a book, but they can only really be put into effect through actual practice on the water. The more you practise, the greater your experience and the better everything will become. Even techniques that once seemed all but impossible soon become easy. Little by little, frustrations get ironed away and the basic skills become more like a stepping stone to your fishing than a millstone around your neck. An important basic skill, therefore, is to accept the problems that you are bound to face with a good spirit.

Pike are particularly susceptible to stress. Get them back in the water as quickly as possible and cradle them there, holding them until they are capable of swimming off.

Essential qualities

There are some basic skills that you can't really begin to describe, but it's good to look out for them and start to recognize them. I've been very lucky over the years that I've fished in the company of some great anglers, and the factor that unites them all is, for want of a better word, comfort. Perhaps this is the most essential, fundamental skill of all: to be comfortable in whatever branch of angling you are enjoying. Your approach to any fishing situation should be unhurried, relaxed, inconspicuous and confident. Take time to work out a strategy and then have the confidence to stick with it and see it through.

Physically, the really excellent angler will always (or as often as possible) be in control. You won't find many really experienced fly anglers wrapped up in their lines like a Christmas parcel and you won't find many expert lure fishermen falling off rocks or spending all their time snagged up in trees.

individuality and personal interpretation. I've known some pretty non-textbook fly anglers, for example (myself included), but they can certainly whack out a line any distance they want. Fishing is very much a living, breathing sport and one that is developing with every year that goes by. Collectively, as world anglers, we're learning absolutely all the time, and there isn't a year that passes without me, personally, making at least half a dozen different discoveries that totally change the way I look at what I'm doing. However, hold on to your basic skills, work on them, improve them and you will have all the tools you need for your entire fishing life.

Guidance, not rules

Basic skills like casting are not set in stone. There are guidelines to follow that have been developed often through centuries of experience and observation. That doesn't mean, however, that there isn't room in every branch of the sport for

◀ ▲ ▶ *All the skills – These three photographs (clockwise from the left) say it all. Look at the balance and co-ordination that Mike Atherton, the one-time cricket captain, shows as he punches out a salmon line. And then, the focus and accuracy of Juan Del Carmen's casting as he approaches a wild fish in a crystal stream. Finally, there's big Mitch Smith, a world-champion carp angler, showing the cerebral side of fishing: how to construct a rig that will outwit even the most cautious carp.*

Understanding Fishing

If you're going to start fishing, to some degree you need a helping hand. I say, 'to some degree' because you should remember that what you experience and learn by yourself is invaluable. A perfect balance in your learning career is what you should be aiming for. I'd like this book to be your fishing friend, a constant companion, and a source of inspiration, advice and confidence. If, sadly, I can't be out on the bank with you, well, this book is a substitute and, I hope, a really good one.

Lending a hand – Here I am guiding, hopefully bringing pleasure to a young friend who is just about to land a very serious fish indeed.

An active sport

There's a huge misconception about fishing that, somehow, it's a relaxing sport, and not a taxing one. But once you really get into fishing, you'll find that there are just as many physical skills to learn as you need for soccer, baseball or golf.

You'll want to know how to cast an imitation fly 20yd (18m) or more, sometimes into a wind, and so lightly that it hardly disturbs the water as it settles. Learning how to work a lure – an imitation fish of wood, plastic or metal – so that it looks exactly like a living, struggling fish can be quite a challenge. You'll also learn to trot a float – that is, letting it drift with the current a hundred yards or more – yet remain in complete control. You'll experience the excitement of feeling the line for a biting fish, and interpreting all the signals that are transmitted. In short, fishing is an active, mobile sport, and the 21st-century angler is somebody who really goes with the flow, fishes actively, and is a long way from the stereotyped image of a sandwich guzzler rooted to his basket.

Fishing as a challenge

The methods that you will begin to pick up are mind-consuming and fascinating. Fishing is like a huge chess game, always demanding new approaches. Every water, every lie, every day brings a new challenge. You'll soon find that if you approach every situation in the same way, your successes will begin to falter. It's vital to think, to experiment, and to stay one step ahead of the game. You'll also find that often the most important lessons revolve around the smallest of things.

In order to meet these challenges, slow down and don't be in too much of a hurry as you set out in the sport. Watch, take your time and work things out. Develop confidence in yourself, because that's essential. And remember that angling is a sport, something to be enjoyed and not something that should cause you heartache. You are on the threshold of a magical new departure in your life, so try to enjoy every privileged and thrilling moment that you spend by the waterside.

Andy Murray shows the alertness and agility needed to be an angler, as he fishes in the Spey River.

Taking in the scenery

Above everything else, fishing gets you into some wonderful environments. I look back through the 40 years that I've been a passionate angler and I think of the beautiful places that I've been fortunate to visit. Lakes of total peace and serenity. Gushing rivers, full of vitality and life. Lonely marshes. Streams running fresh from snow-capped mountains. Heart-stopping sunrises and sunsets. I think too of the amazing wildlife I've seen – kingfishers actually perching on my rod, badgers taking bread almost out of my hand as dusk begins to fall. An otter whistling downriver

Fishing really is about loving your environment. The aquatic world is perhaps the most beautiful of all. Scenes such as these, on the opposite page, say it better than a thousand words possibly could: above left, taken in the very early morning on a Scottish loch, and below right, at sunset on a beach in Gambia.

in the dawn light. And when I've been travelling and fishing abroad, the rumble of a bear, the bellow of an elephant, or the swooping displays of fish eagles.

Enjoying the tools of the trade

You will find, too, that fishing tackle itself, the tools of your trade, can be extremely beautiful. There's a lot to appreciate in exquisite workmanship. Modern rods are breathtakingly feather-light. With luck, if you choose properly, you'll build a relationship with your rod, reel and floats, and a real intimacy will begin to flourish.

A bucket brims over with the enticing tools of the lure fisher.

The physical satisfaction of using the gear properly will bring you much pleasure. You might find artificial flies fascinating, or you might even begin to tie your own, and suddenly the long cold winter evenings become golden times when you feel that you can smell the warm summer evenings to come.

Fish appreciation

But, perhaps above all, the modern angler appreciates the fish themselves. The creatures that we pursue are fascinating. Each species has its own habits and idiosyncrasies, and to succeed as an angler, you have to immerse yourself in their natural history. There is a whole aquatic world waiting to be discovered. Fish are absolutely, achingly beautiful. Moreover, it's a secret beauty, a loveliness that's only really appreciated by the fisher. You will surely come to marvel at the wonder of the fish that you catch.

Look carefully at each and every one of them. Note how their scales all have different patterns and sheens. Admire the shape of the fish; consider how it is perfectly adapted to its own particular environment. Examine the fins – see how delicate and yet strong they are, and how they are streaked with the most vividly coloured rays. Fish are priceless creatures, not some commodity that you buy in your weekly shop from a superstore.

Friends for life

Fishing also breeds comradeship, and I have an address book absolutely crammed with the very best of companions from the past and present. Men – and women – with whom I've shared some of the very best times of my life, out in the open, by the side of water, often under the stars, around a campfire. Stories swapped. Theories presented and ideas hammered out. Laughter. Shared successes. Mutual, passionate interests. There's an old phrase about the 'brotherhood of the angle', and it couldn't be more true: it doesn't matter where you fish, either home or away, you'll find friends that you never forget.

Opposite right: Good fishing is all about good friends.

Below: All fish are different and unique. This is especially the case with very big carp like White Tips here. The white fringing on this magnificent fish's fins is a complete giveaway and this is a target for many ambitious carpers.

THE FISHING CODE

Most thoughtful and experienced anglers have their own personal codes, as well as those imposed upon them by clubs and organizations.

- It's a good idea to collect other people's litter up at the bankside, as well as your own. Take a bin liner with you so you can clean up your own little patch of other people's refuse. This might sound like a chore, but many foresighted anglers are now doing this; litter breeds litter and the less there is around the waterside, the less the likelihood of it being dropped in the future.

- Make sure that you always take any discarded nylon line home with you. There used to be a school of thought that you could burn it at the bankside, but there's little point in that. Simply bin it.

- Shut all gates; and if you are driving across fields, keep to the tracks. It's important that anglers and farmers get on well together. I know through bitter experience that lack of co-operation can lead to tears. Remember that straightforward-looking grass is the beef farmer's crop just as much as a field full of cereal, so take great pains to avoid harming it.

- Watch out for anybody who might be poaching. Illegal sales of big fish are now big business, and, as most of us have mobiles now, a quick call to a club secretary or even the police does not come amiss if you have real suspicions – though, of course, don't put yourself in any danger.

- Most vital of all, do watch out for any sign of pollution. This is particularly likely after heavy rain, when streams can overflow and push all manner of toxic substances into watercourses. A poisoned fish (such as the one in the image above right) is just about the saddest sight any of us can see. If you see the water becoming tainted or, even worse, fish in distress, then make an immediate call to the club secretary or the local Environment Agency. Remember that anglers are the guardians of the countryside, so take this vision of yourself seriously from the beginning.

Getting Started

It's very hard to say which part of this book you'll find the most interesting – fly fishing, bait fishing or even sea fishing. Naturally, a lot depends on where you live. If you're in a mountainous area with fast-flowing streams, then you'll probably be destined to fish for trout. If your home is in a lowland, urban environment, it's very probable that you'll do more bait fishing. Obviously, you've got to make a start somewhere and the most obvious places are close to home.

Sport for all – Fishing really is a sport for everybody, young and old, male and female. If you are a real beginner, it makes sense to fish in the nicest possible weather: undoing tangles is never fun, but it's all the worse in wind and rain.

What style of fishing?

It's best to start out somewhere local, so the type of water bodies that are most prevalent in your area will probably determine the type of fishing you start out doing. But is your interest in fishing grows, you'll probably do more travelling, spread your wings and begin to appreciate all the styles of fishing that are available to you.

I personally think it's a great shame when anglers become blinkered into one discipline. For example, it's very common for an angler simply to pursue trout all his or her life and totally ignore the interest in pike, say, or carp. Equally, the carp specialist often overlooks the delight of fishing a roach river with a stick float. Only by fishing for as many species as you possibly can, in as many water types, and using as many different methods, will you become a truly rounded angler.

In the know – *There is an old phrase 'the brotherhood of the angle', and it's true that most anglers welcome beginners to the sport or visitors to a new water with helpful advice. Just don't be afraid to ask.*

Rules and regulations

First, you've got to serve your apprenticeship. Where do you begin? You've got to check that your chosen water is actually in season. Traditionally, waters worldwide have had closed seasons to allow fish to spawn in peace. Different types of fish spawn at different times, and the closed seasons have been designated to protect them all. So, before you begin to fish, you need to do your research. Remember, though, that wherever you live, there's likely to be some kind of fish in season that you can target, whatever the month.

Whatever part of the country you choose to fish, it is likely that you will need at least one, if not two, licences. As a general rule, you will have to buy a national or state rod licence and, very frequently, you will then require permission from the owner of any

A wild brown trout – Although trout are nearly always caught on a fly, there are times when they may respond very well indeed to a float-fished worm. This is especially true when the water is very coloured, and you want to fish for them at long range. Always check the local rules, though.

specific water. It sounds confusing, but don't worry, any tackle shop will give advice.

It really pays, though, to think about joining a local angling club. You won't have any difficulty locating these – the world is honeycombed with them. The

Young Billy has really landed a monster, but it is honestly wise not to aim too high when you're starting out. Billy might be young, but he's been a carper now for many, many years. A wise head on young shoulders, if you like.

club will have a good sprinkling of waters within easy radius of your home and, above all, it will probably have outings and evenings that will help you to develop confidence and knowledge.

As you progress, you might want to join a syndicate; groups of anglers come together to pay large amounts of money to a landowner in return for access to desirable waters. However, these can be costly, so it's generally best to wait until you've got more experience.

Wherever you begin your fishing, always check the local rules and regulations. Every different water and each different club imposes its own rules. Some, for example, will not allow live baiting, night fishing, or whatever takes the committee's fancy! Don't worry too much. This isn't bureaucracy gone mad, it's simply a way of protecting the water, the fish themselves and the enjoyment of those that fish there.

Purchasing tackle

Now for equipment. It's important to build up a relationship with a tackle dealer. If you live in a large urban area, there will probably be quite a choice. Tackle shops can seem forbidding places at first –

there will be gear in every corner, and you probably won't have a clue what any of it is for. There'll be muttered conversations at the counter, which sound like nothing but gobbledygook. But don't worry, I know exactly what it's like, and there's nobody alive who is expert at everything. My advice is to visit all the tackle shops and see where you get the friendliest welcome. Do you think the tackle dealer is going to advise you impartially, or will he try to get you to buy an expensive rod that has been on his hands for quite a while? The wise tackle dealer will know that a beginner like yourself could easily become a valued customer in years to come and, if he's got any sense, he'll do his very best to make sure that you start off on the right footing.

The variety of tackle available can confound a beginner, so ask advice from your tackle dealer. Dave Lambert, braving freezing winter conditions for river grayling, makes sure he has a wide selection of fly patterns to choose for this very demanding fish.

Mail order is, however, a quickly growing branch of the tackle trade. Some mail order companies aren't particularly fantastic – their stocks are limited and their service is slow. However, the biggest and best mail order operations are very slick indeed. It's a really good idea to get hold of their catalogues at the very least, as this gives you a really good overview of what tackle is available and also what it's for. Before you put in an order, speak to someone about the tackle that you are considering buying and see if his or her advice is detailed and considerate.

The right clothing

Think very carefully about your clothing; it's likely that you'll need at least a few bits of specialist gear.

Things aren't too difficult in the summer – all you'll need is a lightweight waterproof, in case a sunny day turns into a thundery one. The real problem comes in the winter. If you're cold, you can't simply

just concentrate on your fishing. You'll feel miserable and it won't be long before you set off for home. Winter clothing has, however, come along in huge strides over the last ten years or so. Thermal boots and gloves mean comfort for the extremities. Multi-layered, synthetic underclothes are also a boon, especially topped by fleeces and 100%-effective waterproofs. Many of the manufacturers now claim that you can fish out in temperatures to -40°C (-40°F) and still feel warm… mind you there'd be some 2m (6ft) of ice over the fastest flowing river by that time, wouldn't there?!

When it comes to buying your winter clothing, it really does pay to buy the best that you can afford. If there's any weakness or any vulnerability in your gear,

Always make sure you've got the right clothing. In the depths of winter, this might not be glamorous but it's effective. Notice how Simon and I both wear snug, warm beanies, waterproof jackets and, in my case, almost impenetrable chest waders! You could fall in and not get wet…though I don't advise it.

you can guarantee a cold, snow-bearing northerly will show it up.

Footwear is also vital. In the summer, if the money is available, I don't think you can do better than lightweight Gore-Tex chest waders. These allow you to get out into a river or over a firm lakebed without fretting over wet feet. They also provide a great deal of protection from heavy dew falls and, if it should come to rain, all you'll need is a lightweight top to make sure you stay as dry as a bone. Gore-Tex is breathable, which means that you can walk for miles in hot temperatures and not experience any perspiration whatsoever. Try that in traditional rubber chest-waders and you'll create your own little pond in each boot.

In the winter, you can either keep your lightweight Gore-Tex chest waders and wear warm thermals underneath, or buy neoprene waders. These really do keep you very cosy indeed, and the elements can hardly reach you at all – even when you're seated on a wet and muddy riverbank.

THE COMFORTABLE ANGLER

It's very important to realize that unless you're comfortable and at peace with yourself, you just won't be able to concentrate properly on your fishing. In fact, you'll pretty soon make an excuse to pack up and go for home, and you won't catch many fish that way! Here are just a few pointers to help you feel comfortable at the waterside, so that you can get on with the job of enjoying your fishing.

1. Don't drink alcohol – it acts as an initial stimulant but leaves you cold in winter after the first flush of euphoria. In the summer heat, it is far better to take soft drinks, mineral water or juices.

2. In the winter, supply yourself with plenty of hot drinks to maintain inner warmth. The early and late summer months can also prove to be very chilly.

3. Don't stint on energy-producing food, especially if you're fly fishing, lure fishing, or any style of fishing that demands physical activity. If you're feeling hungry, then you'll soon be thinking of home.

4. Even if you don't wear it, always take a hat with you. Remember that in winter a great deal of heat escapes through your head and, even in summer, if your head gets wet, you'll soon begin to feel chilly.

5. Unless it's a baking summer's day, always make sure that you keep your body and, in particular, your hands and feet, bone dry. Once your fingers become wet and icy, then all chance of effective fishing will disappear.

6. Be especially careful of riverbanks in icy winter conditions or even in wet, slippery summer ones. Believe me, there is absolutely nothing worse than falling in when temperatures are below freezing… I know, it's happened to me on a couple of occasions and the second time I was lucky to escape with my life.

7. If there are mosquitoes or midges about, don't forget a net or insect repellent lotion – you just cannot fish if you're harassed by insects.

8. If you're planning a very long stay at a water – after carp, for example – make sure that you've got something comfortable to sit or to lie on. Once your body begins to ache, your concentration soon vanishes.

Don't Spook the Fish

Second only to the section on water safety, this is the most important of all the fishing skills. Scare the fish, and everything else you read in this book is absolutely academic. A scared fish will rarely, if ever, feed – no matter how good your bait, tackle or tactics – so don't shoot yourself in the foot before you've made a single cast.

When you're fish spotting on small waters like this, keep low, dress drab to merge in with the bankside undergrowth as much as possible, use Polaroids and sometimes shade your eyes to keep out unnecessary light.

The first approach

It's dawn and you're at the riverbank. Look hard in the dew or, if you're after grayling or pike in the winter, at the frost. Are there any footprints heading along the bank? If so, tread resolutely in the opposite direction. You're not being antisocial, but the probability is that if you're not the first on the river, someone else has already blown your chances clean away.

The noise factor

Whatever you do, bear in mind that sound is intensified by a factor of about five under water, so watch your footsteps. Don't tread heavily, and don't hurry to the waterside. Be controlled and patient, and keep the disturbance down. If you can, choose a grass or mud bank rather than gravel, on which it is almost impossible to tread quietly.

It's the same with your voice. Speak in quiet tones or not at all. Remember that fish are especially sensitive to sound in shallow water, or when lying in the surface layers.

Visibility

Consider what you wear. The colour and texture of your clothing do matter. Think drab and soft. A hat is good for shielding the flash thrown when the sun strikes a pale face – or a shiny pate.

Walk upriver so that you are approaching fish from behind, and think about how you walk. Be aware of your shadow, and know that it lengthens as the sun sinks. Don't point at a fish, as this abrupt gesture will always spook it. Be particularly careful to avoid scaring small fish in the margins, or they will flee and trigger off a chain reaction of fear. Don't be proud – realize that if the water is clear and shallow, it's best to creep and crawl and make yourself as tiny as a mouse.

On the fly

If you're fly fishing, make the first cast count. If you've got a guide, listen to him. Watch the lie and take your time until you've worked out a strategy. Remember that the more casts you put over any piece of water, the further your chances fall. Don't false cast more than you have to. Learn to cast lying on your back, from a crouching position or even on your stomach. Learn to roll cast (see pg. 77 and 173–174) and spiral cast so that trees are no problem. Cast slowly and

Lucy Bowden of Hardy and Greys crouches low to place a fly upstream to an unsuspecting trout.

Be careful of your reflection with the sun behind you.

close-in fish, so try to catch that one first.

Use everything that happens around you to your advantage. Learn to cast when there's a natural disturbance that will help mask your own unnatural intrusion upon the fish. For instance, fish close to a feeding swan – but not so close that you could run the risk of hooking it. If you see drinking cattle, get close to them and flick a fly immediately downstream. Use a floating weed to break up the silhouette of your fly line or to mask a float.

The subtle float

The considerations that apply to fly fishing are largely true for bait fishing, too. This is why holding back a float is so important when you're trotting for grayling or roach: this way, the first thing the fish sees is the bait and not the shot that, as often as not, will rap it on the nose. Floating weed or other debris will help to mask a float and avoid spooking wary fish.

methodically, and avoid jerky movements. Think about your silhouette all the time. Remember that you must strive for distance only when you've spooked the fish, and the more you strive, the more you will spook them. Don't become a human windmill.

Aim to cast one foot above the water so your line and fly fall lightly. On thin, clear water you'll need to cast a long leader if you're to avoid lining a fish. Put a fly line over a wild trout and you've said goodbye to it. Dull your leader down to avoid glint in bright conditions; rub it in dirt or clay if necessary. When you're spinning or fly fishing on a stillwater, don't be impetuous. Put a few casts down each margin before exploring the water. If you don't, you'll scare any

Think up your own tricks. For example, in crystal clear water, a carp could be afraid of a commercially made float. Providing you don't have to cast far, a discarded goose feather will cause it no concern. If you're grayling fishing in clear winter water, chances are that a strike indicator could alarm a wily shoal. Take it off and tie on a piece of twig or a sliver of reed. If wading is allowed, go a fair way upriver and kick up the bottom – the slight discoloration will increase your chances five-fold.

Feather your spool on the cast if you are bait or lure fishing, so that your tackle lands on the water with as little disturbance as possible. Remember that accuracy is more important than distance.

STALKING TIPS

1. It's always best to have the sun behind you as it will light up the water that you are looking into and there will be less light reflecting into your eyes from the water. Remember to wear a sun visor above your Polaroids to cut out unwanted light.

2. At the same time, bear in mind that your shadow can really ruin your chances of success as a fisher, so try to stand behind a tree (as in the image at right) or amidst reeds – this will break up your outline. Don't wear white or bright clothing.

3. To remain unnoticed, always move slowly. Vibrations travel well in water, so step gently.

4. In the summer, rub yourself well with insect repellent because fish watching often calls for long periods of immobility amongst mosquito-infested reed beds!

Know when to stop

Don't overcook a lie if you're fly fishing or a swim if you're bait fishing. Catch a fish and move on. This is good for the fish because you're not overstressing them and, as a result, it becomes good for the fishing. Play fair by the river and it will play fair by you.

Often, if you get out into mid-river and fish with as little disturbance as possible, you won't spook the fish but frequently attract them closer and closer towards you. In part, I think this is because the bait is actually dribbling out of your bucket and feeding the water as it trickles down with the flow.

Fish Watching

Learn to watch fish. It's an art that will stand you in great stead. Discover their patrol routes, feeding grounds and body language. You will find yourself entering into a fascinating and unique world and, of course, you'll improve your results as well.

Bridges give you a fantastic vantage point to see what is happening in the river beneath. Stay still, make sure the sun is not behind you to cast a shadow and always use good-quality Polaroids.

What you need

Polarizing glasses are one of the great boons of the modern age. Glare on the water's surface is minimized or obliterated, and suddenly the fish and the underwater contours become magically apparent. Good glasses give you a true gift of sight, so choose them carefully. Scratch-resistant lenses, tough but light frames and comfortable nose pads are all essential items. Wrap-round lenses also give enhanced glare protection. Grey and copper-coloured lenses are great for medium to bright conditions, while silver-flash mirror lenses are best for bright weather. Amber lenses are best in medium- to low-light conditions. Think carefully about which colour will suit the bulk of your fishing, unless you want to invest in several pairs.

Binoculars are also an essential tool for getting in close. Focus in tight to the fish and you'll be able to see the insects they are eating or what it is exactly about your end rig that is turning them away.

As mentioned in 'Getting Started', chest waders are invaluable. In clear, bright water you can get out and stand close to fish that are nowhere near as spooked around you as when you are on the bankside. A canoe, too, can be a very useful means of getting you close to where the action is taking place.

And then there is what nature can give you. In the previous chapter, I explained how the cover that vegetation, banks and rocks can provide might prove invaluable. This is a stalking game in which camouflage plays a vital part. Look out, too, for climbable trees or handy bridges that offer you the opportunity to get up above the waters and look down on them with maximum vision. Sunlight is, of course, a great boon, opening up the water to your polarized gaze.

Where to look

On still waters, the key areas for fish spotting are shallow bays, reedy margins, the fringes of islands, shallow plateaux or the broad backs of trailing gravel

Gotcha! – Gerry has spotted a fish and is pointing it out to cricketing hero Ian Botham. It might just be a gleam that has caught Gerry's eye, or the flick of a tail, or even a glimpse of white as the fish's mouth opens. In part, it's experience, almost a sixth sense calling out 'fish!' to him.

POLAROID GLASSES AND BINOCULARS

Polaroid glasses are essential for looking through the surface layer of the water and seeing how the fish are behaving. Binoculars are also a huge boon, allowing you to zoom in on a far distant carp or a close-up fly hatch.

Rule 1: Always buy the best that you can afford. Quality does count.

Rule 2: Ask advice before purchasing and, if possible, test at the waterside.

Rule 3: With Polaroid glasses, always choose strong frames and, if possible, scratch-proof lenses.

Rule 4: You'll find that different colour lenses are particularly suited to different light values. A good, general all-round colour is light bronze.

Rule 5: Attach your Polaroid glasses to a cord so that they hang around your neck. It's all too easy to lose several pairs during a single year!

Rule 6: Try to choose a relatively light pair of binoculars. If they're too heavy, you'll find that you leave them at home or in the car, rather than taking them to the bankside where they really make a difference.

Rule 7: Make sure that the binoculars offer adequate magnification and let in enough light – 8 x 32 or 8 x 40 are perfect models.

Rule 8: Always make sure that the binoculars you buy are waterproof for obvious reasons!

Carp and lily-beds almost invariably go together. Carp like the muddy yet firm texture in which the plants grow, and all manner of fish enjoy hoovering the stems and pads of the plant for aquatic organisms.

bars. Look out, too, for feeder streams and water sheltered by overhanging branches. In a river, check out the backwaters, weir pools, confluences and clear, bright water over sand and gravel.

Look for fish around sunken vegetation: underwater cabbages, ranunculus weed or lily pads. Check out submerged branches and fallen masonry. Remember that fish are concentrated in places where they feel safe from predators, sunlight and strong currents.

When to look

Get up around dawn and you probably stand the best chance of seeing cyprinids and predators feeding. Look out for strings of bubbles on a calm surface, and

It's dawn. The scenery is wonderful and you can bet that the fish are feeding hard in the slow-moving river. However, the world is really quiet and, if you're not careful, you're intrusion will be quickly noticed.

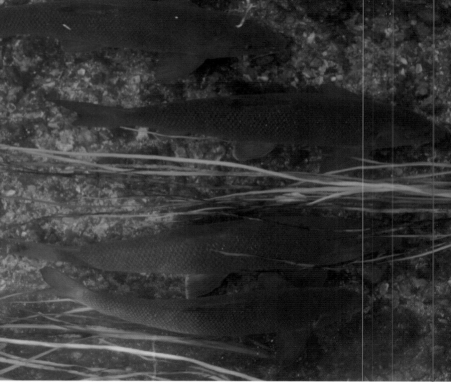

Be aware that fish blend perfectly into their natural environment. The dark brown bodies of these two chub are hugely difficult to pick up in even crystal clear water. You've got to slow down, take your time and watch for the signs.

This picture shows how very easy it is to overlook even big fish in the water. This shoal of barbel was photographed from above and even at just 2–3m (7–10ft), it's difficult to see the fish. It's so easy to think there is nothing in the swim when, in actual fact, there could be the fish of a lifetime.

for brown water where fish are feeding in the mud. Dusk, too, is great for many species, especially on still waters, where there are often big hatches of insects as the light fades.

For general fish watching, a clear, bright, calm day is the best. Good amounts of sunshine illuminate the water and the lack of breeze cuts down on ripple and glare. You can lose yourself in fish watching, so beware of dehydration and sunburn. Cover up well and take plenty of water on board.

How to look

First of all, have patience and take your time. This is not a job to be rushed. The fish can see you more easily than you can see them, so make sure all your actions are calm, controlled and, above all, slow. Actually, physically seeing fish can often be a problem until you get used to it. Fish are built to be as near invisible as possible, or they would be picked off by the many predators above and below the water. Fish, generally, move gently and subtly, and blend in

seamlessly with their surroundings, so your eye needs to be trained to pick up very diffuse images indeed.

So how do you actually, physically watch for fish? Look at a piece of water in soft focus for just as long as it takes. Let yourself fall into something like a trance and then, if there's a fish around, it will move and something about that movement will attract your eye. Something will stand out from the rhythm of the river, to which you have adjusted. You might suddenly see a glint or perhaps a shadow. Perhaps it will be just the flash of a shifting flank or the waft of a drifting tail, but something will make an impression and then immediately your gaze transforms into intense focus. Home in on these little telltale signs, and the chances are you'll begin to pick out a scale, an eye or the profile of a fin. Let your eyes really bore into the water where you've seen the telltale sign. Once you've done that, focus even more sharply and the whole fish will begin to come into view. Then do nothing at all until you've established exactly where the fish is lying and the extent of its feeding range.

Fish are like ghosts. They drift in and out of the shadows and depths, and you've got to expand your own consciousness to encompass their fluidity. Fish watching is an art and a pleasure in itself: it's a skill you'll be proud to master and will always treasure.

Study tips

If you can manage it, never go to a new fishing water with a rod in your hand, as this just makes you too eager to start. It's far better to make that first visit with Polaroid glasses, binoculars, a sketch pad, and an open mind. Give yourself time to relax and watch what is going on about you. The better you get to know a water, the more it will reveal its secrets to you.

The sketch pad enables you to make a rough map of the whole water and detailed sketches of particular areas. When preparing your fishing strategy at home, these will remind you where deep water lies, where there are shallows, which bays face north or west, and where there are reed beds. Never discard any single piece of information that you might pick up. Everything adds to your complete understanding of the water to be fished.

A thermometer is a very useful tool for the angler, because temperature plays a much more vital role in the life of a fish than it does for us. Being cold-blooded, they tend to adapt their entire life to the temperature of the water around them. As a rule, the colder the water, the more torpid the fish. As the water warms up, their body mechanisms kick-start, and they begin to feed again. A thermometer tells an angler how the fish may be behaving. For example, if river temperatures drop much below 6 or 7°C (42-46°F) in the winter, then it's unlikely you will find barbel feeding, and it's best to fish for pike. If water temperatures rise much above 30°C (86°F), then you are probably better off fishing in the cool of the dawn.

OBSERVATION EQUIPMENT CHECKLIST

1. Hat A broad brim keeps the sun off your head and out of your eyes.
2. Binoculars These allow you to scan the water surface for signs of fish topping.
3. Boots Always choose a pair that is warm, well-fitting and waterproof.
4. Polaroids Reducing glare, these are your windows into the fish's world.
5. Bread Many fish species adore the simple, ordinary shop-bought loaf.
6. Sketch Pad A simple map can prove invaluable when planning your strategy.
7. Pen and Thermometer These are essential aids. The water temperature is an important piece of information.

Chub can be difficult to spot in deeper, darker water, but when they do open their mouths it's always a dead giveaway. Look for that big gleam of white lips and you'll know you're in business.

The Angler Naturalist

Two of the great skills of fishing are to be able to read the water and the immediate aquatic environment, and to interpret what is going on around you. The angler with these skills reaps an enormous benefit. If you're conversant with plants and water-weed, birds, aquatic mammals, insects and all the other many forms of life that go to make up the world's waterways, then you simply draw more pleasure out of the fishing experience.

A heron doesn't survive by accident. Its camouflage, its eyesight, its reactions and its knowledge of its own particular water are all 100 per cent. We'd all do well to adopt the heron as our role model.

Locating fish havens

The first job of importance is to locate the fish within the water. This might sound blindingly obvious, but it's not always easy. You've got to remember that fish aren't scattered about like currants in a cake. Rather, they live tightly packed in closely defined areas. And there's always a good reason for it. In general terms, fish are looking to find homes that provide them with food and security. So, for example, small fish will nearly always hang around reed beds or areas of heavy weed. Such places give them bountiful food supplies as well as the opportunity to hide whenever a predator comes into view.

To take another example: imagine a huge, featureless pit that has just been excavated and filled with water. There are absolutely no contours or places to hide. However, if a dead tree falls into the water, within days a pike or group of bass will be lurking among its sunken roots and branches, using it as an ambush area. The message is clear: look for anything in the water that can provide the fish with a hiding place or an ample food supply. This may be a bed of freshwater mussels, or a colony of insects. The more you look, the more you'll see, and the better the picture of the water that you build up in your mind's eye.

In high water conditions, you've got to use your brain! Think exactly where the fish are going to be. They probably won't want to move far from their normal haunt, but they'll need just a little bit of protection from the main flow of the current. A stranded tree like this is perfect and the fish will often push into the very branches themselves.

These Spanish barbel are making use of the slack water behind this overhanging tree and feeding hard on tiny insects that have been blown from the branches. Remember that all fish are opportunists like this.

Practical benefit

The second motivation behind learning the skills of an aquatic naturalist are more prosaic: the more you understand about how waters work, the better you will be at predicting where fish live, how they behave, how and on what they feed and how best to catch them. The very best anglers of all don't just catch fish out of some sort of intellectual vacuum: the finest catchers of fish are always observing what is going on around them and interpreting the signs.

A skill like this is supremely visual, so let's look at the following sets of photographs and see what, if anything, can be learnt from them.

Companions on the riverbank – If you can get as close to otters (above) and water voles (left) as this, then there is absolutely nothing wrong with your stalking skills. Seeing wonderful creatures like these should make any fishing expedition worthwhile, whether successful with the rod or not. Keep in mind the fact that 90 per cent of anglers fail before they make their very first cast simply because of their approach. If you can fool the otter, then you can certainly fool the fish.

Up from the sea – If your approach is that of the heron, you will see a lot in shallow water – spawning sea lampreys in this case, which are especially interesting. Coming up many European and American rivers after spending most of their adult life out in the oceans, they team up with their sexual partners and excavate holes in the riverbed by moving stones and rocks using their limpet-like mouths. The eggs are then laid, fertilized and covered up again with smaller stones. As the adults drift helplessly back to the sea, dying on their way downstream, the baby lampreys begin to hatch out. This fascinating life cycle is of interest to the fish catcher. As the baby sea lampreys emerge, they are hugely attractive to big shoals of hungry salmonids, especially trout, and also to cyprinids such as barbel and chub.

A really good angler is totally in tune with his environment. This photograph shows one of nature's most effective baits – the caddis grub. These grubs live in places that they make out of sticks, stones, sand and tiny pieces of gravel. This gives them protection until they are big enough to hatch out into insects. You will find them under stones, where they cling to defend themselves against the current. Prised from their cases, they are absolute killers for virtually all fish species.

Above: Watch where ducks and other diving birds repeatedly work. The chances are that the bottom will be rich with foodstuffs that attract more than birds alone.

Below: Watch what's going on on the bankside. The animals around can frequently help your cause. You may see a group of cows gathered under a tree in the margins of a lake, and it's easy not to give the scene a second glance. Wrong. As these cows wade and snort and splash and drink, they are colouring up the water and digging deep into the mud, releasing all manner of insect life. Fish know that cattle drinking like this spell a food bonanza and will come close inshore to make the most of the feast.

Above: This 20lb pike has been eating waterfowl as the feathers of this coot, probably, confirm. Remember that all fish are opportunistic. They'll latch on to the most plentiful and most easily catchable food supply.

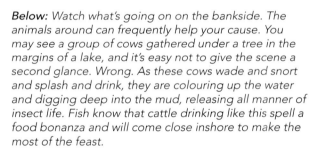

Bird clues – A swan and its cygnets present a gorgeous river scene as they progress upstream. However, as they feed they dislodge huge amounts of insects that have been hiding in the tresses of weed. Fish know this, and will often follow swans hoping for easy tidbits.

The feathered fisher – Birdlife can not only be enjoyed by anglers; it can also tell you a great deal about where fish might be lying. Cormorants and other fish-eating birds like these grebes obviously aren't going to be hunting in pools where there are no fish! Keep your eye on them and they will draw you to some of the best swims on the river.

Pond life – A typical European pond scene – the rudd in mid-water looking up to the surface for a struggling fly, perhaps, while the tench keeps lower, its mind set on a meal of bloodworms.

Getting to know fish

So what about the fish themselves? What of these creatures that we are pursuing, hoping eventually to catch? It's all too easy to imagine them as alien to us

A close-up of the head of a very big pike indeed. This head is all about survival. The eyes are placed at the top of the skull to give a tremendous view of anything approaching from the surface, either prey or predator. This head will also pick up the most subtle of vibrations around it so it will know if there are prey fish close or if a potential predator is approaching. The fish also has a highly developed sense of smell. Pike have been on the planet for millions of years and it's easy to understand why.

in every way – they're cold-blooded, they breathe through gills, have a scaly skin, and are covered in a protective slime.

In all these ways they are indeed different from us, but there are many similarities between fish and humans. It's important to realize that fish have very acute eyesight, that they can feel vibrations just as easily as we pick up sounds, that they have a very well developed sense of taste, and that they learn rapidly through experience. Fish are not fools – they are complicated packages of subterranean life. The

fisher who forgets this often ends up fishless.

It's equally vital to recognize that all fish species behave in slightly different ways. The experienced fish watcher knows that each and every species has its own distinctive characteristics that immediately mark it out as unique and individual. In Europe, for example, roach and rudd look alike and are both shoal fish. Rudd, however, tend to hang much higher in the water, frequently dimpling the surface for insects. Roach, on the other hand, generally work in mid-water, or towards the bottom. Bream, too, are

FISH SELF-DEFENCE

1. Many fish prey on the fry of other species – and even their own! Because it reduces their losses, small fish will come together in shoals, like the shoal of rudd on the right. By darting around, they confuse a predator and make it difficult for it to pick out a single target and home in for the kill.

2. Camouflage is another important weapon in the protective armoury. Many fish will adapt their colour to suit their background, and the individuals of any particular species can vary widely in appearance, depending on their habitat.

3. Hiding is another technique used, especially by prey fish. They will utilize any object in a water that gives them cover and security.

4. Experience is also vital. Fish do learn fast, and they'll recognize anglers as threats just as much as an otter, a kingfisher, or a pike.

shoal fish, but they are almost always lying deep. Carp will move together in small groups, not really shoals, and then break away for solitary feeding. One predator, the pike, is generally a loner, and yet perch, walleye, and zander, which are also fish eaters, tend to operate in packs. To make things even more confusing, brown trout generally have a territory all to themselves, whereas rainbow trout will frequently cruise together in large numbers.

We often talk about human beings having body language and the same is certainly true for fish. As your experience as a riverside observer grows, you will soon be able to distinguish between the distressed fish, the sulking fish, and, vitally for the angler, the fish that's very shortly going to be looking for food.

Reading the body language

As you become more adept at seeing fish, you'll soon find that there is more to learn from them than the simple fact that they are there. In no time at all, you'll discover how to interpret their body language. Take, for example, a carp that is barely moving, simply hanging under the surface film, occasionally stretching a fin out into the sunlight. This is a fish that is not feeding at all. It is simply browsing, half asleep, enjoying the sunshine, and no amount of effort on your part is likely to persuade it to take a bait. When, on the other hand, you see a carp moving purposefully, often dropping down toward the bottom, then you know this is a fish with food on its mind, one that's becoming catchable.

What about a pike, lying doggo on the bottom of a lake, with perhaps silt or leaves building up around it? This is a fish that's fed heavily and is lying comatose, digesting its prey. Once you see that pike rise a few inches from the bottom, however, often angled upward like a cannon, then you know it's ready to spring, ready to attack, and catchable once more if you make the right approach.

FEEDING TERMS

Fisher-people over the years have concocted all manner of terms and phrases to describe how fish feed. Here are some of the most common ones.

Bubbling – Many fish send up bubbles (as in the image on the right) as they root around on the bottom. Tench produce strings of tiny bubbles, whereas bream produce fewer, larger ones. In time, you'll get to know which bubble goes with which species.

Fry feeding – You'll often see whole carpets of tiny fish, or fry, lift from the surface, especially toward the late summer and autumn. These are almost certainly being harried by groups of predatory fish such as trout, perch, or even pike that have come together for the feast.

Nymphing – This describes fish, trout in particular, that are feeding on nymphs (see pg. 166) as they scuttle looking for cover, or rise to the surface to hatch. You will often just see the white of the inside of the mouth as the jaws open and close.

Smoke screening – Sometimes you'll see a vast area of silty mud rise to the surface. This will be made by a group of big fish, probably carp, rooting around in the mud for minute organisms.

Feeding or spawning?

It's fascinating to watch fish as they spawn. You get a good impression of the size and numbers that the water holds of any particular species. However, there are times when the fish aren't actually spawning at all but are offering you one of the great fishing opportunities of your life…

Running the river – These are definitely spawners above. Great numbers of trout are swimming up the streams of New Zealand's south island as the spawning season approaches. You wouldn't want to fish for these even if they showed any interest in your fly. Let them pass and allow them to do what nature intended.

On the gravels – Here's an interesting one. Are these chub in the image at right on the gravels to spawn, or have they already spawned and are they now cleaning themselves, hungry and quite possible to catch? In fact, it's the latter. The fish spawned just a few metres upstream four or five days ago, and now they are regaining their strength and feeding hard, often on the eggs they've just laid and fertilized.

The Psychology of Fishing

I'm well aware that mind-set isn't a skill in the physical sense, and it's a little out of the ordinary run of things, but that doesn't make a scrap of difference to its importance. Believe me, as a guide I have seen hundreds of days ruined for anglers who have simply failed to see the big picture, and have made themselves miserable over matters of very little consequence indeed.

The three amigos watch their rods on a Gambian beach. This laid -back attitude exactly suits this fishing situation. Remember sometimes you can be relaxed, and at others, you've got to be on fire like our heron.

The right attitude

Whether you enjoy the day or not is purely a matter of attitude. Frankly, it's quite stupid to ruin the best days of your life worrying about something as inconsequential as catching a fish! I mean it. To make matters worse, the more desperately you want to catch fish, the harder it becomes. You put pressure on yourself that stops you from fishing to your ultimate potential. I can't think how many times I've seen people hound themselves into demoralizing failure.

There's another aspect to this, too. It's often the fish you don't catch that you remember; and the worst trip; and the foulest weather. It might seem bad at the time but, providing you live through it, I'll guarantee you will look back on the tough times and they will be amazingly vivid in your mind forever, so don't discount any experience, however unpleasant it might seem at the time.

Obsession

Try to avoid all the dangers that come with obsessional fishing, and there are plenty of them. I know – I've been there. Believe it or not, I actually used to feel guilty if I wasn't out there on the bank, day and night, thrashing the water. I can barely believe it now, but 20 or 30 years ago the obsession was startlingly real.

If I lost a good fish, I'd be suicidal, and there'd be no comforting me. I couldn't get my head around the fact you can't lose what you've never had. A simple failed hook-hold was somehow life kicking me in the teeth. Talk about making your own life a misery for yourself!

Weights and records and personal bests meant everything to me. A pike would be worth nothing if it came in even a fraction of an ounce under 20lb, and somehow a magical creature if it flickered above that weight. I was absolutely blind to the beauty of what I was seeing, totally enslaved to what I now realize were false values.

I like these photographs because they show another aspect of fishing mentality – dogged determination. Ian just was not going to give up on this particular carp. He didn't want to see it tethered and he was determined to get the fish to safety. His prize of this exquisite carp was worth the perseverance! Fishing isn't always for the fainthearted but, of course, always take care.

Monarch of the River

I've fished with many people over the years who've wanted to be king – or queen – of the river at the end of each and every day's fishing. It's impossible. Remember that however good and skilful an angler is, there's still a massive element of chance. Fishing

Always see the funny side of the sport as well. One minute I'm posing in a professional way with a trophy chub and in the next second, Ian decides it's time to take things a little less seriously.

places, groups of fishermen have become fragmented, and there's been no semblance of the brotherhood and generosity that fishing should be all about.

This type of mental set is one that I absolutely abhor, and I fight it tooth and nail if I suspect its presence in one of my camps. I'm always on the lookout for a potential would-be king of the river, and I'm ready to remind him that if he celebrates the success of others, then they will celebrate with him when his turn comes, as it surely will.

Being there

The philosophy that I try to put across, and which I've now followed for 20 years, is simply 'being there'. You see, it doesn't matter who catches the fish, whether it's you, Don, Tom or whomever. It's the fact that you are there, that you're in a wonderful place with good company and you've had the massive good fortune to see a wonderful fish caught. Take on board that it is seeing the fish that's important, and not necessarily being the captor of it. In fact, in absolute, honest truth I can say that I would much, much prefer my clients and my friends to catch fish before I do. I'll do anything to make sure they have the best places, the best baits and the best chances.

Believe me, it's a relief when this philosophy takes hold of you. Just the desire to be there removes a colossal burden of expectation from your shoulders. King of the River? The thought never enters your head.

Fair to the fish

Once you've embraced this laid-back approach, you begin to find that you are becoming much fairer to the fish and this, I think, is of major importance. Once you stop being fish-hungry, everything begins to fall into place. For example, you won't use any of the dubious tactics or baits to catch a fish. Catching a fish is no longer the be all and end all of your existence, and you know there's no point pulling stunts to catch one. You also no longer have to subject each and every fish to the indignity of being weighed. Weights

is a wheel of fortune, and luck may be with you for a while before settling on your partners. That's the way it should be, although not everyone sees it like that. I've had clients sulk for days because they're not catching the biggest fish. Greed and jealousy has oozed from every pore, and their surly reaction to the success of others has soured the atmosphere. There's been competition for the supposed best

actually become less and less important to you. A fish is simply a beautiful creature, and you admire it for a second or two before slipping it back into the water. What are weights apart from artificial standards that we impose on wonderful living creatures? Of course, if a fish is particularly special to you, then weigh it carefully and kindly. There can be no problem with this but, hopefully, you will soon find that weights become less important as your fishing career progresses.

Make no mistake, fish don't like being caught. If you're on a shoal of feeding fish, it's all too easy to fall into a type of frenzy. This is your red-letter day and you've got to catch them all! Of course

I can appreciate that, but you've got to realize that this approach does a shoal of fish serious harm and subjects them to noticeable stress.

Once you start being fair to the fish, you will recognize a situation like this, perhaps catch a couple and then you'll move on to look for others. This way, shoals are not traumatized, stretches of river remain relatively unpressured, and you'll be treating the river and its inhabitants with total respect. You'll be happier and, importantly, so will the fish.

Friendship

When you reach this psychological state, you begin to discover what true fishing friendships are all about.

This is one of my dearest photographs. It shows me and Al cradling one of his very last, big fish. Sadly, shortly after this fish, Al passed away. The fish made his day, no, his very last season on earth. It's important to realize that fishing can bring this type of pleasure and that you've got to enjoy every session to its utmost.

You'll meet up with similar characters who would do anything for you, for their other friends, the fish and the environment. There's no jealousy in these friendships, no hoarding of secrets. Everything they possess is out there to be shared. You'll begin to enjoy total, implicit trust. You'll rejoice to see these people on the river and not inwardly curse because you fear they'll be on the best lies. Everything will become more relaxed. There'll be no rush for the best places, no thrashing of the water to catch the most fish. You'll be just as happy to brew up, have a cup of tea and discuss the meaning of fishing and of life.

Odds are that soon you'll enjoy rod sharing. There's no more civilized way of fishing than this. One rod and two or three friends, walking the river, watching fish, discussing challenges and working out solutions, taking it in turns to wield the rod or issue instructions, loads of leg-pulling and lots of genuine congratulations. Each fish is a shared fish, and the pleasure you are taking from your sport is enhanced as a result.

Smell the roses
Fishing is the most wonderful sport. It's a vast kaleidoscope of skills, and it can be practised virtually anywhere on the planet in wonderful places for wonderful species. Perhaps only mountaineers see nature as clearly as anglers do. Learn to appreciate sunrises, sunsets, storms and the endless play of light on the water. Learn the names of the waterfowl. Recognize water plants. Develop your interest in aquatic insects. Take binoculars with you so you can look at birds and wildlife. Push yourself to fish different places and catch different species. You'll meet new people, eat different food and learn fascinating customs.

Be disciplined with yourself and try out all the skills mentioned in this book. It's not just about becoming a better angler; it's about savouring new ways of fishing. You'll find very often that you don't actually have to catch a fish using a particular method in order to gain huge satisfaction from practising it. Take the spey cast, for example. I've seen anglers fish hour upon hour on rivers without a single salmon being present, but they've been spey casting and they've loved it, and the day has been a joy. Remember, even a bad day on the river beats a good day in the office. The wise angler learns to appreciate all the gifts of his or her sport.

◀ ▲ *See what I mean about fishing being a team effort and about celebrating the successes of others? The three of us are in a difficult, rapid swim on the River Wye. It's hard to get out to mid-river and you've got to be very careful. This is where comradeship comes in. Also, I just had to be there in order to net the fish. In a fast flow like this, you nearly always need to double up. It's a team fish and that's the joy of it.*

Water Safety

This is possibly the most important skill-set in this book. Water safety may not directly help you to catch fish, but at least you'll still be alive to keep trying. Remember, we're not fish, and water is potentially a lethal element for us. You will be trying to get close to the water, on it if you're boating, and even in it if you're wading, and you may well be on your own. In these circumstances, things can get dangerous.

The danger beneath – *This river looks wonderful at dawn, smoking as the sun begins to rise. But the currents are actually treacherous. The water is deep and cold. However picture-perfect the river might seem, make sure you don't mess with it.*

Learn to swim

No matter what kind of fishing you enjoy, you should learn how to swim and, especially, learn how to be proficient on your back. As a bank angler, if you should fall in, your best bet by far is to float down river on your back, shouting for help, gradually paddling yourself in towards a safe landing place. Don't panic. Keep your head (preferably above water!): it is panic that drowns most people. The human body is buoyant, especially with layers of clothing trapping extra air. It's important to keep your mouth shut should you unexpectedly hit the water's surface. Keep cool, don't swim against the current, don't wave your arms about, keep your mouth closed and you will survive.

Be wary of steep banks after rain, especially if there isn't much in the way of long grass or shrubbery. If you must fish in such places, a rope tied to yourself and a tree is a good idea. Be wary of undercut banks, which can collapse with heavy rain and swollen rivers, and be especially vigilant after dark. Whether you are bank fishing or wading, always make sure that your boots have an excellent grip and that they aren't worn smooth.

Wading

When you are wading, with chest waders in particular, there's a great temptation to push into ever-deeper water. Take care. Never wade in water that makes you uneasy, that is too deep and too fast for your safety, or that doesn't offer good visibility – you could easily step off a safe ledge into a deep hole. Be wary of wading in, or soon after, heavy rain – a river can suddenly rise, colour up and put you in danger. Just two extra inches of water can result in a tremendous increase of pressure – enough to throw you off balance.

Check you are not below any kind of water flow control system, such as a sluice. There are locations where water can suddenly rise by a matter of feet! Never wade between steep, impenetrable banks, only where there is easy access to and from the water.

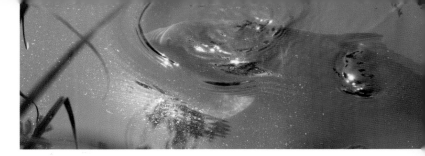

Ian and I are on a wonderful lake and see several big fish feeding off the surface. Ian decides to go for them.

He creeps out over a landing stage, which under his weight buckles, groans and collapses, throwing both him and me into the water.

But Ian hangs on in there. Although we both hit bottom in about 12ft of water, fortune has it that we bob up again and finish the job.

There's a bit of sorting out to do, like getting the water out of chest waders.

Job done and we can photograph the carp now, which weighed a fraction under 30lb. As you can see – a very successful and eventful piece of fishing. But it could have all gone very seriously wrong. It never, ever pays to take any chances at all and remember that danger never goes on holiday!

Always wear a personal flotation device when wading. Choose products that are certified to turn you over and keep your head out of the water, even if you are unconscious. Choose a lifejacket that automatically inflates within a few seconds of water immersion, and don't forget that most safety devices require annual servicing to ensure total reliability.

Don't neglect the use of a wading staff, preferably on a staff retractor that pulls the wading staff to your side when it's not in use. A wading staff really does act as a third leg and is of massive support in quick currents, as well as being useful to check the riverbed in front of you.

Boats on freshwater

Never go out in a boat that doesn't have a bailer, a spare oar and rowlocks. Even if you have an engine, don't forget the oars. Make sure the engine is reliable and that you have enough fuel. Always check weather forecasts and don't go out if there's any possibility of approaching storms.

Take care when stepping into a boat and always put your feet on the floorboards as near the middle as you possibly can. Always fish sitting down in a boat and don't stand up unexpectedly. If you need a pee, use the bailer bucket rather than risk standing up, and never succumb to the temptation to have a quick swim unless the boat is firmly anchored in shallow water.

An angler wades out to net a fine carp. Always be careful if you do anything like this. Make sure you've got adequate footwear to protect you against sharp stones and always keep an eye for an unexpected drop-off.

Neighbourhood watch – *When fishing with a partner in a boat, always be aware of where he or she is and what he or she is doing. Watch how you cast. Keep the boat balanced. Look out for rocks and other potential hazards.*

If your companion falls overboard, don't throw him a rope without first tying a bowline in it. The loop must be big enough for the man in the water to get his head and shoulders through it so that it can hold him underneath his armpits.

Be particularly careful when you want to up-anchor in a strong current. The current can swamp a boat if your weight is transferred forward too quickly. Take care and make every move a cautious one.

If your boat does capsize, keep your mouth shut when you hit the water. If the wind is blowing you towards the shore, then it pays to cling to the upturned boat or to oars. If the wind is blowing you away from the shore and there is no help in sight, you might decide to swim for it if the shoreline is close. Even if the shore is close, don't be tempted to take clothes off to make swimming easier – cold is going to be one of your major problems. If you tire, turn on your back but keep your arms and legs moving so you're still making progress. When you reach the shore, get on your feet quickly and move about to avoid paralyzing cold setting in.

Boats at sea

If you're a novice boat-owner, join your local club for some expert advice and tuition. Never go out on your own until you have complete confidence in your abilities.

If your engine dies, drop anchor and stabilize the situation. Make sure that you have sufficient anchor chain and rope to hold bottom. Keep calm. A breakdown is a mind-numbing experience, but gather your composure as quickly as possible and set about asking for help.

Don't rely on a mobile phone for talking to lifeboats or rescue helicopters. You need a properly installed VHF to get you through to the emergency services or neighbouring boats, and your boat should be properly fitted with the right radio equipment. Listen to the regular weather bulletins put out by your local coastguard every few hours. If there's a sudden change in the weather, head for shore. Don't be afraid to admit that you've got a problem. As soon as you sense danger, make that call. Act swiftly and don't let a crisis develop. Charts are useful, and always have a compass with you. Always try to give the coastguard your exact position in a crisis.

You might have to wait for help, so always take lifejackets, warm clothing, food, water and flasks along with you. Make sure that you have flares on board, particularly at night. Always tell somebody where you are going. If you change your plans, phone through the information. No matter how good the fishing is, don't leave it too late to return to port, as this can be very worrying for those on shore.

Familiarize yourself with your boat and its engine. Make sure you carry spares and know how to use them. It's also a good idea to have alternative means of propulsion. Stick an old outboard engine, for example, somewhere down in the boat's hold. Even a pair of oars can make a difference. Make sure everyone on your boat – you included – is wearing a lifejacket. Drinking alcohol is unacceptable out at sea, especially if you are the skipper. Keep a clear head at all times and make sure anybody fishing with you does the same.

Carbon and electricity

Nearly all modern rods are composed of carbon fibre, which makes them excellent at conducting electricity! You should thus be very careful in storms, and be especially wary of any overhead power lines. Keep in mind that a rod doesn't even have to touch a live wire for it to kill you – high-voltage electricity can arc across several feet. Don't cast over a power line, as this, too, can cause a shock, particularly when using a lead-core fly line.

Heading to sea – Howard is heading out to the open sea. There's a stiff wind and a strong tide running, and he and the crew will be constantly aware of any changing conditions.

If you're fly casting, it is always essential to wear either Polaroids or normal glasses.

A sharp reminder

Always wear polarizing glasses to protect your eyes and a hat to shield those vulnerable ears from high-speed hooks, especially when fly fishing, but even when bait fishing or spinning. Be particularly careful when fly casting in a cross wind – a tube fly thudding into the back of your skull is a most unpleasant experience as I, from painful memory, can tell you.

If you do manage to hook yourself, then there are obvious advantages in having a barbless hook. If the hook is not barbless, however, and you are anywhere within reach of civilization, get yourself to a doctor or a hospital rather than doing a botched first-aid job on the bank. In a worst-case scenario, nip the eye off and push the hook out point first – it hurts less that way! And make sure that you're completely up to date with your anti-tetanus jabs.

WATER SAFETY GUIDELINES

1. Never wade in water that is so cloudy that you can't see the bottom.

2. Make sure that you never wade in too strong a current.

3. Never wade so deeply that you begin to feel afraid.

4. Always have a wading stick with you (like the angler shown in the image below) – this third 'leg' can be a real lifesaver.

5. Wear Polaroid glasses when wading – you will gain a more secure foothold if you can see the bottom contours.

6. Always wear a buoyancy aid when either wading or out in a boat.

7. A whistle is good for attracting attention in case of an emergency.

8. When setting out in a boat, always make sure that you have a pair of oars and rollocks, even if you think your engine is reliable.

9. Always set off into the wind on a big water. If the engine should fail, it's easier to row home with the wind at your back.

10. Always let somebody on shore know where you're going on a large water and approximately what time you expect to be back.

11. Always check the weather forecast before setting out onto a big, exposed water. Dangerous conditions can whip up in a matter of minutes.

Glossary of Knots

It is essential for every angler to know how to tie a selection of knots. Knots are used to secure the line to the reel and to join a hook or lure to the line. Although there are thousands of different knots, the basic knots illustrated below will be sufficient for most angling purposes.

Half blood knot

The half blood knot is commonly used for joining hook to line. This type of knot, when tied in nylon line, will not come undone.

Step 1 Thread the free end of the line through the eye of the hook.

Step 2 Pass the free end underneath the line and bring it back over the line to form a loop.

Step 3 Continue to loop the free end over the line (as step 2) until you have approximately four turns.

Step 4 Pass the loose end between the eye of the hook and the first loop.

Step 5 Pull on the loose end to tighten the knot. Trim off the end.

Double overhand loop

Also known as the surgeon's loop, this knot can be used to create a loop at the end of a fly line, to which a looped leader can be attached.

Step 1 To begin, double the end of the line back against itself.

Step 2 Next, tie an overhand knot in the doubled line.

Step 3 The doubled end should then be tucked through the loop again.

Step 4 To finish, pull the knot as tight as possible and trim off the end.

Blood bight

This knot has similarities to the double overhand loop. If the end of the knot is not trimmed, several loops can be created to attach, for example, mackerel flies.

Step 1 Fold the end of the line back against itself (this is known as a bight).

Step 2 Cross the doubled end once around the line.

Step 3 Pass the looped end of the line back through the turn.

Step 4 Pull the knot tight. Trim off the end of the line to finish.

Water knot

This knot is also known as the surgeon's knot. The water knot is used to join two lines together, for example attaching a lighter hook length to the mainline. The bulk of the knot will stop a sliding bead, and can be useful when legering.

Step 1 Put the ends of the two lines alongside each other so that they overlap by about 15cm (6in).

Step 2 Take hold of the two lines and make a wide loop.

Step 3 Pass the ends of the line through the loop four times. Be sure to hold the two lines together.

Step 4 Pull the lines tightly so that the loop makes a knot. Trim the two ends.

Blood knot

The blood knot is also used to join two lines together. As in the water knot, begin by overlapping the ends of the two lines.

Step 1 Take one end and twist it four times round the other line. Then pass it between the two lines.

Step 2 Repeat with the other free end. Make sure that the first stage does not come undone.

Step 3 Wet the knot to lubricate it, then pull it tight. Trim off the two ends.

Needle knot

The needle knot shown here can be used to tie monofilament to a fly line.

Step 1 Push a needle through the end of the fly line, Heat the needle until the line begins to bend.

Step 2 When cool, remove the needle. Thread the mono through the fly line and five times around it. Bring the end back and hold it against the line.

Step 3 Take the large loop and bring it several times around the fly line, trapping the mono.

Step 4 Pull on alternate ends of the mono and when the knot is firm, pull it tight.

A Braid Loop

Although some fly lines are fitted with braided lines for attaching a leader, it is a simple task to form your own from braided mono.

Step 1 Push a large-eyed needle into the braid. Thread the braid through the eye.

Step 2 Push the needle through the braid until the loose end emerges. A matchstick will keep the loop end emerges. A matchstick will keep the loop from closing.

Step 3 Adjust the loop until it is the size you require. Cut the loose end until it lies flush, and seal using waterproof super glue.

Fly Life Recognition

As a fly angler, it's absolutely imperative that you recognize at least the four main groups of insects and food types that make up the bulk of the fish's diet. These are the items from the fish's menu that you are going to try to imitate, so recognition becomes a core skill.

Fish are quick to reap any harvest and at certain times may even capitalize on an imitation of a wasp.

Up-winged

Firstly, there are the up-winged flies, notably the olives and the mayflies (Ephemeroptera). These are recognizable by their tall, graceful, sail-like wings and their long, delicate tails. They begin life as a nymph and can spend years living in the sand and gravel of the riverbed. They then hatch into a dun, and then transform again into the spinner, the completed insect. It is now that mating takes place before the females return to the water to lay their eggs and die. All these life phases can be imitated by the fly tier and used by the angler.

Roof-winged

The next most important family are the roof-winged flies (Trichoptera). These fold their wings across their bodies in the form of a roof. The most common of the family are the sedges. Their life cycle goes through the different stages of egg to larva to pupa and finally, adult.

Flat-winged

The flat-winged flies (Diptera) are also important. This family includes hundreds of species, from tiny midges to the relatively goliath daddy-long-legs. However, all share some common features: six legs, a pair of short wings and a well-segmented body. The most common aquatic members of this family are the chironamids, often referred to as buzzers or, in Ireland, duck flies. The buzzer begins its life as a bloodworm before transforming into a pupa and finally hatching out to become the adult midge.

... and the rest!

Other food items include crustaceans, corixids, and the many terrestrial insects that alight on still and running waters. Common crustaceans include freshwater shrimps and snails. Corixids (Corixidae) are also known as water boatmen, and they look like small beetles, living in shallow water and grabbing bubbles of air from the surface. Common land insects found during autopsies on trout include alder flies, black gnats, hawthorn flies, reed smuts, moths and flying ants. The fact is, fish will target

Nymphs – Big nymphs like this will turn into dragonflies of one type or another. They are aggressive and eat a whole range of aquatic food items. However, they are prey as much as predator, and will often feed under the cover of darkness.

Mayflies – A mayfly has reached the end of its lifecycle and has collapsed to die on the surface of the river. It has drifted into the still water on the edge of a river eddy, where it will very possibly become an easy meal for a big, lazy trout.

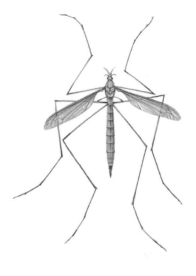

Daddies – Daddy-long-legs, or craneflies, come into their own in the late summer, when there's a good breeze blowing them off the land and onto the water. Trout and black bass in particular come to the feast.

virtually anything edible, and that includes wasps, grasshoppers, tadpoles, fry, fingerlings and even ladybirds.

Being able to distinguish between the main groups of insects mentioned above is just the beginning of a knowledgeable angler's education. For more detailed information on the many types of insects that appear on the fish's menu, see 'Food, Feeding and Flies', pgs. 164–171, in Chapter 3 of this book.

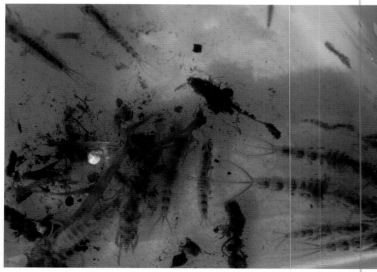

My great friend, Terry Lawton, is conducting a river fly-life survey on a quick stream.

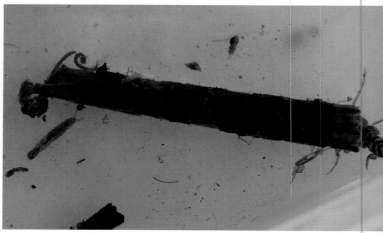

He takes his findings back to the table for analysis. It's unbelievable how much fly life a square metre of the riverbed yields.

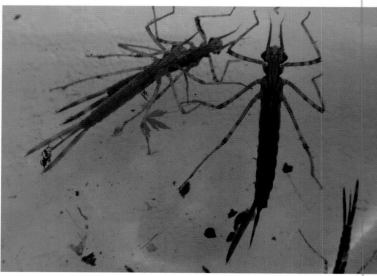

Macro shots of the wide variety of insects the survey has produced – no wonder the fish were so fat!

The rise as a clue

It's worth noting that you don't have to see the insect to get a clue as to what a fish is feeding upon. Trout, especially, will give the game away by the manner of their rise.

A slow rise, where you see the head, then the back, the dorsal fin and the tail, suggests a trout feeding on buzzers and dead insects in the surface film. Try fishing just subsurface and move your fly very slowly indeed, even letting it hang immobile for a minute at a time.

Sometimes you will simply see a boil on the surface with no sign of the fish itself. This is a trout taking food, often an ascending nymph, a few inches beneath the surface. Cover a disturbance like this with a quick sinking nymph or a buzzer weighted to get a couple of feet from the surface in quick time.

Audible hints

Sometimes you will hear rises as well as seeing them. In calm conditions especially, listen for a sip, a suck or a full-blooded slurp! These noises are made by trout consuming buzzers or spinners very close to the surface, often in the surface film itself. Try a dry fly or a buzzer pattern when this activity is taking place.

On other occasions, rises can be seen far off as explosive splashes. These often indicate trout hurrying after a big meal that they don't want to lose – for example, a mayfly on the point of lifting off into the air. Alternatively, these could be fish feeding on fry or even taking buzzers on their route to the surface if there's a big hatch on. Try a big dry fly, a small fish-resembling lure or a buzzer until you discover the key. If you don't immediately succeed in matching your imitation to what the trout are feeding on, then you've simply got to try one pattern, intelligently chosen, after another until you get there. So, read the clues, watch for the signs and you will be on your way to becoming the ultimate nature detective.

This dace was caught during a big mayfly hatch down on the River Avon in Hampshire. The fish had obviously been feeding on the naturals and could not resist an imitation.

Matching the hatch – On many waters, the advent of the mayfly in early summer signals the most exciting and frenetic fishing of the season. All fish – but trout especially – gorge on these beautiful insects.

Reading Rivers

Think of a river as your friend. Learn to live with it. Learn to love it. View your relationship with it with confidence. Rivers are beautiful places. While still waters can be beautiful, mysterious, awe-inspiring or beguiling, it's moving water that really stirs the blood, and pretty well every serious angler I know would pick a river over a lake nine times out of ten. But a river has its secrets. It's vital to understand what the river is telling you.

The well-oxygenated rapids of any river hold lots of food and lots of fish. The fish will lie in the deeper water through the day but come out to feed in very shallow water once the sun begins to sink.

Getting to know the river

Rivers don't always give up all their secrets easily. You've got to learn to read them, to recognize the clues and the signs that they give away, so let's take a walk down an imaginary river and see what we can learn. Remember that we are looking at the major factors of river reading – the strength and the direction of the current, the depth, the amount of cover and the make-up of the riverbed.

Most rivers are a series of deep pools and shallower, stony rapids. You'll often find fish feeding in the shallows before moving down to rest up in the deeper, slower, better-protected water. This is the basic structure of most rivers around the world, so learn to recognize when it's better to fish the shallower, fast water and when you should move down deeper.

There are certainly exceptions, but most species of fish like to hang where the current is neither too strong nor too slow, where there's enough water to make them feel secure and where they can find shelter from predators. Clean gravel or sand is also the bottom make-up that most species prefer, as this fertile structure harbours prolific stocks of food.

Moving water

First we come to a weir, or maybe a mill pool. Where the water tumbles over the sill, it's white and foaming, well-oxygenated and bringing lots of food from upstream. Fish love it. They also love the fact

*1 **The rapids** – Fish of all species move into the rapids to feed, especially at night or when oxygen levels are low.*
*2 **The point** – A place like this gives an angler tremendous access to the river.*
*3 **Into the distance** – It's always exciting to see what's round that next bend. Trees, in particular, always harbour fish.*

Weir fish go – Fish of all species are attracted to bridges and little weir pools like this. In part, it is the oxygen but there is also plenty of shelter and a lot of food gathering under the stones that almost always dot the riverbed in places like this.

An enormous fallen tree like this, brought down by the floods, almost invariably holds fish of every species that use it as a shelter against the current.

that this churning water has, over the years, created a big, deep pool and possibly an even deeper central channel. There are likely to be large rocks, too, providing some shelter from the current and predators.

As the pool steadies and shallows, there is more good water, about 6ft deep and pushing over a gravel bottom. Towards the end of the pool, the water shallows to perhaps 4ft, but again there is gravel and now there is more weed – ranunculus, which holds a lot of insects and is therefore hugely attractive to many fish species.

Food and shelter

Walking on down the meadow, we come to some fallen willow trees that have collapsed in a late winter storm. A raft of rubbish, dead weed, leaves and driftwood has built up around the branches, creating dark, still water beneath. Predators love areas like this, and so do fish species such as chub. They provide shelter from attacks by water birds like cormorants. The branches harbour insects, which fall into the water and provide an added food source. And fish like the darkness and the shade from sunlight.

Moving on a further 100yd, we come to an old road bridge, probably constructed some 200 or 300 years ago. It has a couple of arches and the river divides around a large, central buttress – a great place for fish. Over the decades the force of the water, where it has narrowed and deepened, has created a large pool downstream of the bridge, and it's full of food. Over the years, passers-by have thrown rocks into the pool, there's an old lorry wheel, the remains of a cart – all objects that have settled into the river and now provide a haven for food stocks and for the fish that feed upon them. Of course, bridges are also the most perfect vantage points for anglers, giving them the height to peer into the depths beneath.

Twists and turns

Now we are coming to a series of bends, and on a river a bend almost invariably means fish. Bends are attractive in winter and summer alike – in winter because the deeper pockets of water give protection from floods, and in summer because there is always depth on a bend however low the water level sinks. Food also tends to drop onto the bottom when the

Fishing a deep glide in winter as the sun sets. Places like this always hold fish, especially if there is tree cover on the far bank. The more cover the better as winter temperatures begin to fall.

flow begins to decrease over the deeper part of the bend itself.

Look out, too, for what anglers call the crease – that's where the current is separated from the slack water that all bends produce. You can see where the fast and slow water meet because there is a very visible dividing line there. Fish like to move backwards and forwards along this crease, slipping into the faster water to feed and then back into the slower water to rest and digest.

Rivers run ceaselessly, their currents pushing stones and gravel hither and thither as they run. Yet many fish can more than hold their own in even the fastest-flowing water.

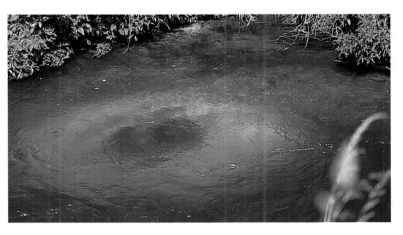

Shade and structure

Way downstream, we can see that the river enters a thick, unkempt wood, and both predators and prey fish love stretches of water overhung by trees and bushes. Areas like this offer security from overhead attack, shelter from the sun, protection from cold winds in the winter and added food sources in the shape of terrestrial insects falling into the water from the leaves and branches.

I happen to know that in the shade of this wood there lies the remains of an old stone boat jetty that disintegrated half a century ago. The rocks are now strewn along 50yd of the riverbed and have attracted a lot of fish. Once again, the rocks provide a haven for all manner of invertebrate life, and fish are attracted to the honey pot. You see, fish are exactly like us: all they really want from their home is comfort and security and a well-stocked kitchen. They don't like places that make them feel at risk and exposed, where the water is too open and shallow and where there aren't enough food stocks. Of course, until fish talk, we'll never know exactly why one piece of water is so attractive and another is shunned, and you will occasionally find swims that look exactly right in every way but that hardly ever hold anything. Experience counts for a lot, but you will always meet up with surprises.

Reading Stillwaters

Stillwaters aren't, at first sight, quite as easy to decipher as rivers. Large stillwaters, in particular, can be especially daunting, and yet the signs are nevertheless there if you keep a cool head, keep watching for them and keep trying to interpret them.

It's on massive stillwaters like this that watercraft is really hard. In fact, sometimes, what you are best doing is covering as much water as possible and try to locate the fish.

Depth and shade

Let's kick off with dams. The dam wall of a reservoir or estate lake is always a good starting point for locating fish. The depth is attractive to them and there are nearly always insects sheltering amongst the brickwork. Added attractions like water towers only increase the drawing power of these places.

Next, never ignore weed, reed or lily beds. Smaller prey fish will never stray far from the refuge of cover, and this is exactly what vegetation gives them. Where there are prey fish you will find predators, too, and larger, non-predatory fish like to browse among vegetation, reaping the benefits of plentiful food items. Lily pads, in particular, have magnetic qualities for fish, especially carp and tench, which love to graze on insects that inhabit the undersides of the pads and the stems that lead down to the bottom silt. Watch for the subtlest movements as the fish pass beneath and rock the stems. Reed beds are another major attraction, bulrushes probably being the most sought after because they like to grow on a hard, clean, gravely bottom – just the sort of place in which tench, for example, prefer to feed.

Islands are another key feature in any stillwater complex. They are particularly attractive when they are overhung by trees or lined by heavy reed growth. Islands are a prime location when there's no way onto them from the main fishing banks. When they are quiet and distant, they offer complete sanctuary, and fish are always looking to escape from noise and irritation.

Water supplies

Inflows and feeder streams are always real hotspots on stillwaters of any size or type. Fish tend to congregate where water enters, hoping to profit from food being washed from the fields around. This activity is particularly pronounced during periods of heavy rain, when lobworms are washed from the land. The incoming stream might also help colour up the lake and make fish feed with extra confidence. Always look for clouded water – another sure sign that fish are feeding.

Massive reed beds like this are a magnet for all fish species, especially at spawning time in the late spring and early summer. It's to the reed beds that most fish of the cyprinid family flock to lay their eggs.

Find your lilies and you'll find your fish!

Fortune favours the brave on a day like this. It's probably an underwater spring that keeps this tiny hole free of ice. You will find that this fractionally warmer water also attracts fish to it so sport can be good. Always pack up, however, if you have any feeling that you might lose fish under the ice. Never risk a break-off.

Springs frequently bubble up to the surface of lakes and pools. These can be very attractive to fish in hot weather conditions, when the water gets stale and begins to lack oxygen. Springs are usually cool and they bring hot summer temperatures down to more acceptable levels. Trout especially are attracted to springs.

Focus on features

Look carefully at the bottom contours of your stillwater. As an example, deep central channels often run down the middle of estate lakes. These are frequently the old streambeds that were dammed hundreds of years ago to make the lake in the first place. Fish will often congregate in this deeper water for the security and rich feeding that it offers. Look for plateaux, gullies and drop-offs close to your bank – especially if these are lined with reeds or overhanging trees. A stillwater may look like a large and featureless saucer, but in nearly all cases if you lift the veil and look under the surface, there will be all

sorts of clues to fish location. Look also for any man-made structures. Boathouses, for example, attract large perch shoals. The perch like to rub themselves against the submerged timbers and they enjoy the shade from bright sunlight. Piers and jetties are equally attractive, and fish will also congregate under temporary 'constructions' such as a moored boat. Perch, again, like to rub their bodies against anchor ropes.

Keep looking

Never settle at the first swim on any new stillwater, but walk as much of the lake's circumference as you can, watching carefully for any telltale signs; binoculars can be helpful. What are you looking for? As I've mentioned, clouded water, which is generally a sign of feeding fish. I've also talked about twitching reed stems and lily pads – they don't have to move much to indicate the presence of a very big fish indeed. Watch for clusters of bubbles hitting the surface: these may be just marsh gas, but more

*1 **Coves:** Fish of all species love to investigate coves and inlets on the lake shore.*
*2 **Points:** Areas like this catch the winds, which in turn blow food towards the fish and are highly attractive.*
*3 **Into the woods:** Many terrestrial insects fall off the branches of trees and end up in the water. The fish know this.*
*4 **The open water:** The middle of a lake might seem featureless, but you'll find some of the biggest fish here.*

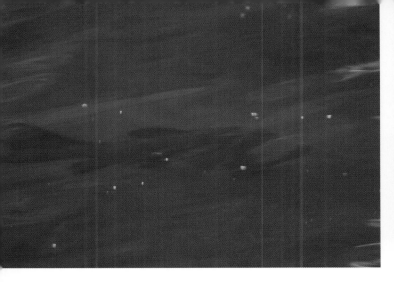

Even at distance, you will see things like this, when a carp erects its dorsal fin clear of the surface. A real giveaway.

Look very, very carefully indeed and you will see the shadow of a tench moving over a clear area of sand. This is a real giveaway. You will find that fish frequent these sandy, clean-bottomed areas above all others. In fact, it's probably their feeding that has made the bed clean here in the first instance.

likely they're being produced by fish feeding on the bottom. Look carefully at the water and see if you can spot any flat areas in patches of rippled water. These are caused by fish moving heavily just under the surface. Look, too, for fish physically breaking the surface: slow, steady porpoise rolls often indicate fish taking hatching midges just subsurface.

Pay close attention to the wind direction. Many, if not most, types of freshwater species tend to follow the wind, gradually moving towards the bank that it is hitting. In Europe, we are generally faced with westerly winds and this tends to mean that the eastern shores are a good place to start.

As ever, dawn is the time that you must be out on a stillwater to get the very best of it. Choose a mild, breathless daybreak and you will see what the lake has in store for you. Watch for fish rolling, bubbling or just topping. This is the time of the day when they are most active and most easily seen.

Fly Casting

Casting a fly is an art, but it's actually fairly easy to master even though it looks quite complex. Much like riding a bicycle, good fly-casting is all about technique, timing and balance. And furthermore, contrary to what many people think, good casting isn't particularly about physical strength; indeed, some of the best casters are women, children and slightly built men. The roll cast and the overhead cast are the two basic casts in any fly angler's armoury. They both have to be mastered before you can really fish with any proficiency. The double haul cast is the best tool for the angler on large stillwaters, while the single spey and the double spey are primarily casts to be used with double-handed rods intended for salmon or steelhead, or for fishing on large rivers where distance casting is necessary.

Fearless casting – Fergus casts fearlessly into the brisk Hebridean breeze. Perfect control, perfect focus, perfect technique.

The basic roll cast

The roll cast straightens an untidy line before you move into an overhead cast. It's also a very important cast in its own right, especially on small rivers or when there's no room to back cast because of tree cover. You can also use it for safety, especially in a boat when the weather is very windy. It's also the ideal cast to lift a sunken line out of the water.

1 Start with the rod tip touching the water and then lift slowly but smoothly.

2 When you get the rod to about 11 o'clock, you should pause. You'll have a lot of line off the water and the rest will be slowly moving towards you.

3 Now sweep the rod smoothly back in a wide arc, round and up until your thumb is level with your right ear (or left ear, if you are left-handed), and the rod is pointing back to 2 o'clock. Pause again. The loop of line should have formed behind the rod looking much like a perfect 'D'.

4 Now it's time for the hit. Drive your thumb forward in a flicking movement as if you were swatting a fly on the wall just in front of you. Aim straight at the target and stop the rod sharply at 10 o'clock.

5 You'll find this movement should flick the line off the water and push it through the air towards the target, landing straight and true.

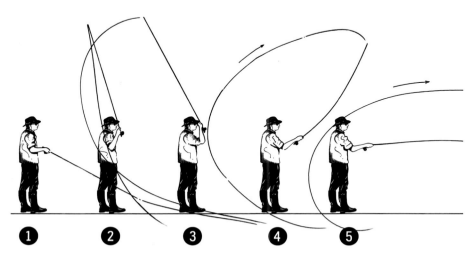

The overhead cast

This is the main cast in the fly fisher's armoury, and you must learn it before going on to other techniques. It's simple. There are only three basic movements – the lift, the back cast and the forward cast. So don't be intimidated.

1 Start with the rod tip just touching the water and the line straight out.

2 Lift slightly with the forearm and accelerate gently.

3 Your thumb should now be level with your right eye (or left eye if you are left-handed), with the rod pointing at about the 12 o'clock position. The inertia of the rod will have allowed it to go further back to about 11 o'clock. Don't let the rod go back further than this or the cast will fail.

4 You are now casting forward with your thumb driving the rod down. Stop at the 2 o'clock position in front of you. This movement feels like a tap with a small hammer or swatting a fly against a wall.

5 The line is now flying out in front of you, arrowing to its desired position.

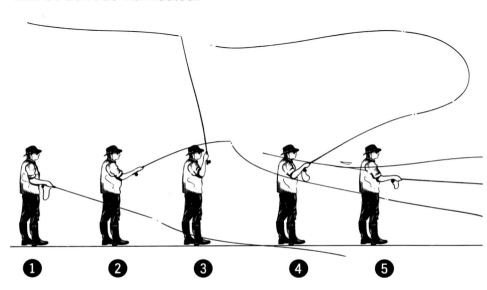

The double haul

The double and single haul casts are primarily to get distance, especially on stillwaters. They can also be used to increase the line speed and to combat wind.

1 Hauling is basically a technique where the non-casting hand tugs at the spare line being held between the butt ring and the reel.

2 This method increases the inertia and, therefore, the loading of the rod spring on the forward or back cast, or both.

3 The result is that everything works harder and faster, and it's possible to shoot extra metres of line that can prove to be critical.

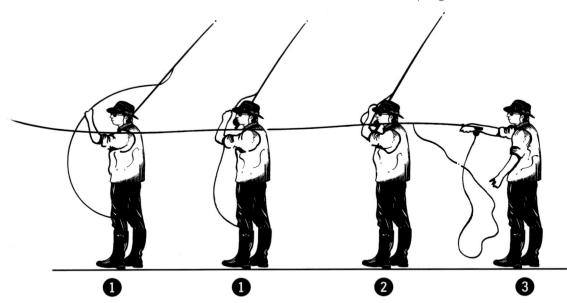

The single spey

The single and double spey casts are used on lazy rivers fished with double-handed rods. If there is an upstream wind, the single spey cast is used because the fly and the loop in the line are swept upstream before hitting out to the target.

1 Stand square onto the target. Leave the rod pointing downstream with the tip of the rod at the water.

2 Raise the rod by bending your upper forearm at the elbow slightly towards the near bank. Think of 10 o'clock on your rod clock.

3 Turn right with your upper hand and sweep away and out. Your right thumb comes round to the side of your shoulder to a position level with your ear. You will now have the 'D' loop formed behind the rod, facing the target.

4 Punch the rod smartly forward before stopping sharply at 10 o'clock in front of you. This flicks the loop of line out across and above the water. This is a wrist and forearm flick, not a shoulder heave.

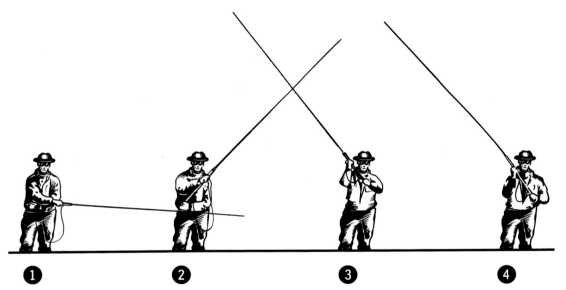

The double spey

If there is a downstream wind, you'll need the double spey cast, where the fly and the loop in the line are kept downstream before hitting out to the target.

1 With the rod across your stomach and your right hand uppermost, your hands will not be crossed.

2 Tow some line upstream, lifting the rod tip until your hands are crossed over like they were for the single spey. Leave the fly still downstream of you.

3 Lift as you did for the single spey, up to 10 o'clock and slightly in towards the nearside bank.

4 Sweep the rod around and back downstream, lifting back up until your hand is level with your right ear (or left ear if you are left-handed). The line will peel back and round and form the 'D 'loop.

5 Hit the loop out, as in the single spey. All these actions are done to a rhythm and not rushed or flustered.

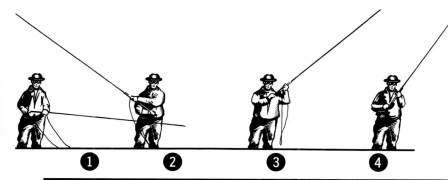

①   ②   ③   ④

SAFETY CONSIDERATIONS

1. You will already have picked up throughout this book that I'm a firm believer in anglers wearing polarizing glasses at all times, because you can see so much more through the surface of the water. This is especially important when fly casting, as you want to target your fish as accurately as possible. These glasses also help you to see the riverbed when wading, and may prevent you stepping into a deep hole!

2. The eye protection that glasses offer is vital. Remember that you have a hooked artificial fly travelling round your head and body all day long, frequently at great speeds. There is a real possibility that a gust of wind could blow it directly at your face. I've seen people with hooks in their noses and ears, and I've had one in my scalp. That's bad enough, but the thought of a hook in the eye… wear those glasses!

3. To avoid hooking yourself, always check wind speed and direction. Be very wary of a wind that is blowing the fly line actually toward you. If you're right-handed, this obviously means a wind coming from the right. Try to avoid such a situation, especially when you're a beginner.

4. Once again, as in nearly all forms of fishing, use a barbless hook or flatten the barb when you're fly fishing. Should anything go wrong, a barbless hook slips out with relatively little pain or fuss.

5. Always check above and behind you for any power lines. Remember how easily electricity is conducted through carbon.

6. When fly fishing, always be aware of anybody moving behind you along the bank. Never risk that quick cast before they arrive – you may have your timing wrong.

7. When changing position, always look behind you to see if there is any problematic foliage…or livestock. I've actually seen a bullock get hooked in the ear!

8. If you're wading on a river or stillwater, it's often tempting to go out just a bit further to reach rising fish. Do so carefully, always making sure you're within your depth. It's also sensible to bring a wading stick for balance and depth testing. Be extra careful if there is a rapid current.

The snake roll cast

Andy Sowerby is an expert caster and a leading member of the Hardy and Greys' team, perhaps Britain's premier tackle company. Andy is in the lucky position of fishing in the north of England and having access to some of the great salmon rivers of the Scottish borders. Here he discusses his snake roll cast technique for deep water. This cast is particularly useful if there's a downstream wind, especially if you are deep wading.

'Casting a double-handed rod in deep water has its own limitations,' Andy says. 'To overcome these, you need to make some small modifications to your casting technique. Deep wading presents many problems, and the snake roll cast is one of the easiest ways of putting out a fly line in this situation.

'My personal tips? Well, a net is a nuisance but it's better than dragging a fish up dry gravel and then releasing it. Often I net fish without moving into shallow water, as I find it is quicker and less stressful to net in waist-deep water. Notice how I always use a weighted stick with a rubber button attached. If you're not sure of the bottom, it is better to stay dry and comfortable. Finally, grease your reel regularly. As you can see in the photograph, my reels spend a great deal of their lives in the water, and it's surprising how quickly a reel loses its grease when immersed for long periods.'

2. 'The cast begins by drawing the fly line in a slow, progressive movement.'

3. 'As I'm drawing the rod back, I slightly lift it very quickly – just 5–8cm (2–3in). This creates a small "bump" that runs down the fly line from the tip of the rod. This lifts the line in a quiet, relaxed manner so it leaves the water with minimal disturbance. In the photograph you can actually see the "bump" running down towards the water, lifting the line as it goes. The rod has stopped at the 11 o'clock position, with my upper arm held at eye level.'

1. ' When starting the cast, I like to hold the rod away from my body.'

4. 'Now the rod is pushed forward with the upper hand and pulled in with the lower hand. This creates a roll cast following the same angle that the line has been drawn up from.'

5. *'I now want to face the target area rather than the area from which I have originally drawn my line, so I turn my body from the hips to change my angle of view.'*

6. *'I lift and draw the line with my upper hand higher than normal to compensate for the depth I'm wading at. This allows the line to run out behind me smoothly. I'm also allowing the line to key itself on the water no further than a rod length away from me. This acts as an anchor and creates the "D" loop every caster is trying to form.'*

7. *'That "D" loop is nicely illustrated here. A smooth push of the upper arm combined with a quick pull in of the lower arm towards the chest stops the tip of the rod high. This flexes the rod, storing up and then releasing its power.'*

8. *'With this power I can punch the line out over the water with minimal disturbance towards the target position. The fly turns over, settles and commences its swing round in the current.'*

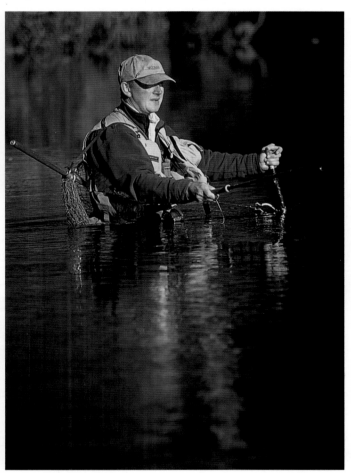

9. *'The cast is complete and the fly is fishing. Notice how I hold the tip up and follow the line round, watching the loop down to the water. I hold about an inch of line in my hand and allow this to go when I feel a fish take. I then lift the rod and tighten up into the fish.'*

Casting a Multiplier

If you're going to be serious about catching big fish, then at some
stage in your career you're going to have to learn to master a multiplier
reel. A multiplier will almost certainly hold a greater length of heavy line
than any fixed spool reel, so if you're after fish that can run off 230m
(250yd) of 30lb line, you're certainly looking at a multiplier. Also, the
clutch on a multiplier is generally stronger than that of any fixed spool
reel. This means that you can put enormous pressure on a big fish in
a fast current without the reel locking up or even exploding. Finally,
multipliers are built for the most rugged fishing situations imaginable.
If you're embarking on a real white-knuckle adventure, a multiplier of
reputable make is unlikely to let you down.

*Hard-core rods –
Multiplier reels are the
perfect tool for long-
range fishing in extreme
conditions when big
fish are being pursued.
They are especially suited
to heavy lines and heavy
weights. With reels like
this, it is possible to
cast well over 100yd
on both saltwater and
freshwater venues.*

Cast mastery

Playing fish on multipliers isn't particularly difficult. Of course, before setting out after big fish you should take as many hours as you need to familiarize yourself with the reel. That said, you can learn how to use the clutch and drag system blindfolded, but it's actually the casting that causes most people problems. Either they can't cast far enough, or the bait just whistles out and causes overruns. There's nothing worse than spending half a day fiddling around with birds' nests, those great tangles of line that bring your reel to a total standstill.

To demonstrate, we're going to India to look at the techniques of two master multiplier fishermen. On the subcontinent, fishing with multipliers is second nature and, as you can see, the guides there are brought up with them from childhood.

The start of the cast – The bait is a ball of ragi paste and there's a spiral Indian lead some 60cm (2ft) above it. Before the cast, Anthony likes to compose himself, look at his bait and look out over the water to where he is going to cast it. This is also the moment to check the tension of the reel. If he takes his finger off the spool now, the weight of the bait and lead should just slowly take off line. If line gushes out, the tension is too slack. If the spool doesn't give any line, then loosen it bit by bit until it does.

Ready to go – The rod is at about 45 degrees behind the caster with the bait 1.2m (4ft) beneath the rod tip. He holds that position for a few seconds to ensure his own personal balance, and to check that the reel is free and the cast is ready to go.

The cast winds up – Great force is put into the cast through the shoulders and down the forearms. At the 12 o'clock position (when the rod is directly overhead), Anthony will take his thumb off the spool and allow the line to follow the bait out on its course over the river.

Once the bait is on its way – Anthony watches its course, hawk-like, with his thumb on the spool ready to feather the cast as the bait drops towards the water.

As soon as the bait hits the water – Anthony's thumb will stop the spool completely to avoid overrun. This is a critical moment because if the spool keeps revolving once the bait has hit the water, there will be line everywhere! Notice how relaxed Anthony is at this stage in the cast.

Unlike the situation in which Anthony was casting, Mola is fishing a much narrower stretch of river, where accuracy is far more important. The cast is only going to go about 37m (40yd), but it has to be pinpointed behind a rock.

INCOMPARABLE MAHSEER FISHERMAN

Subhan is one of the greatest Indian mahseer guides in history and has been a guide with me for well over 25 years. He's probably the most famous name on the subcontinent in this line of work. His understanding of the river and the fish is second to none, and he has a serious list of big fish to his credit. However, it's in the fight that Subhan really proves his worth. He has endless tricks to beguile fish out of snags, and he'll even dive to free a fish if it's wound the line around underwater rocks or sunken trees. Mola (see images at right) is one of his sons, and he's learning the trade of river fishing from the master. Mola is showing every sign of being just as good.

Like Anthony, Mola keeps perfectly still before the cast. The bait, again, is about 1.2m (4ft) beneath the rod trip, but look how Mola is looking fixedly at the point in the river he wants to reach.

The cast begins. Once again, power comes from the shoulders, and look how his right foot lifts just a little to give added impetus. His left foot, however, is planted in the sand, giving him total stability.

At the 12 o'clock point, Mola's thumb comes off the spool and the line is free to run out. He still has his gaze fixed firmly on the bait's entry point.

The bait is well on its way and the rod is moving down towards its final angle. Still Mola is watching the bait in flight, and his thumb is just above the reel's madly spinning spool, ready to clamp down as soon as the bait hits the water…

…which it is doing exactly now. The cast has come to an end and you can see Mola still watching those very last stages. His thumb is now clamped down on the spool and he's about to turn the handle to re-engage the reel. Fishing can now begin.

Detecting the Bite

Not every fish drags the rod from your hand when it takes the bait. Takes to fly especially, but bait and lure as well, can be infinitely gentle, and therefore easily missed. This can be because the fish are educated and are wary of our bait, our tackle or our approach, but sometimes fish are merely curious and not particularly hungry, and they simply pick up a bait to sample it rather than wanting to eat it. Sometimes fish are feeding ravenously on tiny, plentiful food items, and if your bait is one of these they will simply sip it in and carry on eating without giving any real indication of a bite whatsoever.

It's at times like this when the fish are bubbling madly around your sensitively set float that you know a bite is very close indeed. Get ready my friend!

Missed takes

The long and the short of it is that if you're not catching fish, perhaps you're getting the bites and not knowing about them. Years ago, a friend of mine ran a large, crystal-clear commercial trout fishery. He spent all day watching the anglers on his water and he came to form many considered opinions about their abilities. One of the most certain of these was that 99 per cent of takes from those trout were missed and generally not even registered!

Eye witness

The best and simplest way of knowing if you have a bite or not is to actually see the fish take your offering. If the water you're fishing is clear, reasonably shallow and you're not fishing at too vast a distance, then devote a great deal of care and time to engineering a situation where you can actually see what is going on. If you're fly fishing or lure fishing, you might decide to target a single fish or a group of fish and try them with offering after offering until you get them to accept. You might have to try several different patterns and as many different types of retrieve, but the chances are that in the end a fish will make a mistake – and you'll see it! If you're bait fishing, then you might consider putting out some free offerings in a zone of water where visibility is good. Wait until fish move in and start feeding, and then carefully introduce your hook bait. Watch it closely because as fish begin to feed heavily they can stir up the bottom and cloud that visibility. Watching fish at close quarters take bait, fly or lure is infinitely thrilling, so be careful not to strike prematurely. It's all too easy to pull a bait from a fish's mouth in the excitement of the situation when the adrenalin is really pumping.

Circumstantial evidence

Of course, actually seeing the fish take your offering is not always as simple as you'd think. In an ideal world you would see the fish approach, open its mouth, take the bait and whoosh, you're playing it, but it's not always like that. Say you're fishing a tiny fly 5ft down in quickly moving water for a big grayling.

The thrill of the chase – In the photograph above, a large carp is on the point of taking a surface bait. Now is the time to still your beating heart!

You can just about make out the fish and you just about know where your fly is, but you're never going to watch it disappear. Instead, you have to gauge where your fly is and watch the body language of the fish. For example, if the grayling suddenly moves 6in right, left, up or down, then it's a safe assumption it is intercepting something in the current – and that something might be your fly.

If you're trout fishing in a similar situation, you will often see just a gleam of white as the trout opens its mouth. Again, something is being sipped from the current and it could be your fly. Sometimes the mere flash of a fish turning in the current to take a bait can be enough, or you might see a fish suddenly drop backwards as it reaches for something sweeping past it. So, you see, a real skill is emerging here. You've got to learn how to see the fish and also how to interpret its body language.

Distant clues

If you can't actually see the fish or the bait, then you've got to learn to identify the take itself, and by that I mean the moment a bait, a lure or a fly has been consumed. Again, in theory, this should be easy: a float should dive under, a rod tip should wrench round or line should fly off the spool. In the

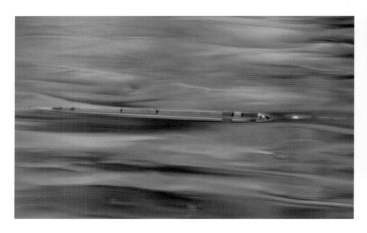

When you're float fishing, don't always expect the float to just bury. Sometimes, like this, it will actually rise in the water.

Alternatively, instead of rising or disappearing, sometimes the float simply rises so far and then lies flat. This is when a fish has picked up the bait and taken the weight of all the shot, too. It's best to strike at once.

real world, takes can frequently be infinitesimal. A line may merely tighten, or fall momentarily slack, or merely hesitate for a millisecond in the current. A float can just tremble and then remain still again. Even when you're lure fishing, don't always expect huge crash-bang-wallop takes. Sometimes you might just feel the smallest peck on the lure or a slight drag, as though it is pulling through weed. The important thing is to learn to use your eyes and recognize anything, any clue at all, that indicates something out of the ordinary is happening at the business end of your line.

Staying connected

If you need to work on what your eyes are telling you, so too must you improve your sense of touch. You'll soon be reading about touch legering (see pgs. 286–289), which is all about tactile fishing, but there's more to it. Let's suppose you are nymph fishing on a large reservoir, inching an artificial fly back close to the bottom. A trout can suck in that fly and blow it out again in a fraction of a second, and all you'll feel is the most delicate of touches – and probably not even that if there is any bow or slack in the line between you and the fish.

Ian shows fantastic touch legering technique. He's smiting down comfortably with the rod cradled under his shoulder and resting on his knee.

He's holding the line gently yet sensitively, with a loop round his first finger. He's feeling for any pull or tug, obviously, but also for the rasping that will signify a line bite and tell him there are fish in the swim.

His rod tip is pointed as directly towards the bait as possible. Obviously, there is going to be a loop in the line but he tries to keep this to a minimum.

After a series of frustrating taps and flicks, he gets a proper pull and he's into a fish.

Large but subtle

One of the most exciting examples of this in my fishing life is out in India, hunting the mighty mahseer. These fish can easily grow to over 100lb in weight, and they live in the most volcanic of churning waters, and yet, despite their size, they can still pick up a piece of paste or a dead fish so gently you can barely believe it is happening. You simply feel the line tighten for perhaps two seconds and then drop back slack again. There's no pull really, certainly not a tug, but just a gentle feeling that something is alive out there. So, just as you must learn to use your eyes, you must begin to trust your fingers and develop your understanding of the messages that they are sending to your brain.

The humble dough bobbin – Fishing doesn't get more low-tech than this! You will find that a piece of bread just squeezed onto the line between the reel and the butt ring acts as a superb bite indicator. Watch for it twitching and moving either up to the rod or dropping back to the ground itself.

Fighting the Fish

Make no mistake, fighting a big fish, especially in a current, is a true skill in itself, and consistent success is largely a matter of experience. A successful outcome to the battle is essential both for your sake and for the fish's. The chances are that you've put time, effort, thought and money into this hook-up and you don't want to mess things up now. As for the fish, you owe it big-time to land it, remove the hook and release it with the minimum of fuss and trauma. For these reasons, take the fight seriously, in fact more seriously than any other aspect of your fishing. Here are some basic considerations.

It doesn't get more exciting than this. Simon is holding onto a cracking pike, but it's at moments like this that your clutch has to be set perfectly so it can give line if there is any real danger.

Check your tackle

Make sure your tackle and knots are all up to the job in hand. Don't be tempted to fish too light in any situation. You might hoodwink a fish more easily with light line, but what's the point if you're not going to land it? Check and recheck all knots. Double check your hook for sharpness, and be particularly wary of a curled-over hook point. Check your line frequently for any signs of wear or abrasion. If you hook a big fish and the fight is a tough one, then it pays to change your line altogether. Make sure your spool has enough line on it or, if you are fly fishing, that you have adequate backing.

Side strain – Side strain is a fabulous technique. Using it, and being brave about using it, you can turn a fish's head and hustle it away from danger. I'm really concentrating on this big barbel and moving it away from some reeds.

Keeping the rod tip up – A very big wild brown trout powers away from the bankside. It's important that Richard gets that rod tip up quickly to cushion the shock and avoid putting extra strain on the light leader that he needs to use in clear water.

Think ahead

Always have a plan of action if you're about to strike into a big fish in challenging circumstances. Think what the fish might do when it's first hooked and think of a strategy to counter this. Make a strong mental note of any potentially lethal snags and have a clear idea in your mind of where you're eventually going to land your fish.

Consider your fighting technique. Don't let a fish work up pace, because it will be far more difficult to stop. The key is to be bold in the first stages of a fight and impose your will quickly on the situation. Try to pull the fish off balance. Once hooked, swing it away from weed and submerged branches.

Keeping up the pressure – This shot shows a fantastic reel hard at work. Notice the big drag adjuster knob on the right-hand side of the reel that's sensitive and very easy to use. Also, see how large the arbor (or spool) of the reel is. This loads the line in large coils so that it has less memory as it is cast through the rings of the rod. You can also load line back on it more easily during a fight as a fish begins to tire.

Make sure the clutch on your reel is set at exactly the right tension. Ideally, it should yield line under a pressure that is just beneath the breaking strain of the line. You don't want to give line too easily, because you want to wear the fish out quickly, but be wary of a screwed-down clutch that won't yield line at all and causes it to break. Ensure the balance is right before the hook-up.

Steer the fish

Side strain is an important technique in fighting fish. The concept involves moving the rod either right or left, parallel to the water's surface, to pull a fish off a potentially dangerous course leading it into snags. Go on. Pile on the pressure. You'll be amazed how tough your gear is and it's far better to take control now than it is to let a fish get into a snag.

Pumping is one of the essential arts of playing a very big fish. Start with the rod tip close to the water's surface and then gently and steadily lift the rod almost to the vertical, pulling the fish up towards you through the water. Then lower the rod tip once again towards the water's surface: the tension on the line is released and you can reel in quickly and rhythmically before repeating the process again and again. Of

When a big fish is moving over gravel bars, it often pays to keep the rod as high as possible to lift the line high in the water column.

course, there will be times when you have to pause because the fish powers away, but a steady pumping motion is by far the quickest way to land a big fish. Big fish can frequently be walked away from a potential hazard, providing they are not alarmed. In the very early stages of a fight, a fish may not even realize it is hooked. Keep the rod high, maintain a gentle pressure and physically walk the fish away from a waterfall, rocks, sunken trees or any other potential snag. It's often possible to lead a fish many metres like this – even for a couple of minutes – until you've manoeuvred it into open, trouble-free water.

Handlining

If a big fish buries itself in weed, then try handlining. Point the rod directly down the line towards the fish and tighten up as much as you can. Then grasp the line between the reel and the butt ring and pull backwards and forwards in a sawing motion. This can gradually work the fish loose and back into open water.

Braid or monofilament?

There's no doubt that modern braids offer huge advantages in terms of strength, limpness and load diameter. This makes them very useful alternatives in many fishing situations. However, if you are pursuing fish that fight deep and the water is full of rocks and snags, then treat braid with great caution. The problem is that if braid gets round a rock, severe pressure quickly frays it, leading to an inevitable break-off. Modern monofilament, by contrast, is much more abrasion resistant and should, therefore, be the choice in snaggy conditions.

Landing and unhooking

The fish is tiring and it's time to think about landing it. This is another crucial moment, with the possibility of a potentially damaging last run when the fish sees the net or you, the angler. Make sure your rod is held high and your clutch is properly set for this moment in the fight. If you are using a landing net, make sure it's a large one and that it's already in the water waiting for the fish to be drawn over it. Bring the fish

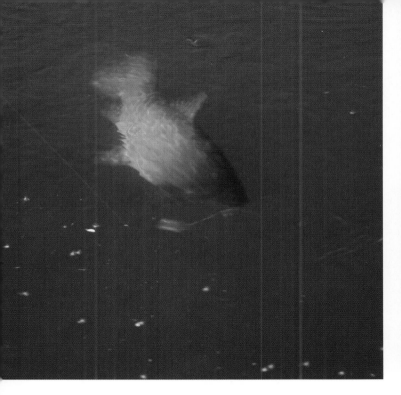

Last ditch attempt – *This is always a worrying moment. A big tench looked to be coming in comparatively easily but now it's twisting and that massive tail is powering it down towards the bottom again. Be ready to give line as soon as this happens.*

Caring for the catch – *If at all possible, net your fish and unhook it in the water so you never need to bring it into the air at all.*

to the net: if you chase a fish with the net you will only panic it into another run. If the fish is big, once it is in the net, put down the rod and take hold of the net's frame with both hands. Then simply lift the fish into the shallow margins or onto an unhooking mat.

Ask yourself whether you always need a net, which can in extreme circumstances dislodge scales or even tear fins. If you are wading, for example, it's comparatively easy to draw a fish to you, hold it in the water and slip the hook out. It can be held for a second above the water's surface if a fellow angler wants to take your photograph.

Always ensure that you have adequate unhooking tools. Forceps will usually be enough, but if you're fishing for predators and using treble hooks, you might need pliers for a more secure grip. Always have your forceps to hand, and make sure they are long-nosed in case the hook is deep. Consider using either a barbless or a micro-barbed hook: these may not be adequate for all situations, but they are much easier to slip from the fish's mouth and, consequently, they inflict less damage.

Put the net in the water and guide the fish to it. Don't chase the fish around with a net or you'll only disturb it further.

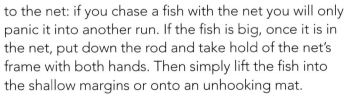

Expeditions at Home and Abroad

The majority of fishing sessions are probably only a few hours in length, but the highlight of anyone's fishing life is either the weekend expedition or, even more thrilling, a long trip abroad. Both call for specialized preparations.

On trips to far-flung Mongolia, you don't expect your tackle to arrive in a taxi. As long as it arrives, that's the key.

A weekend by the water

Even though you may be only a few miles from home, it still makes good sense to check everything out thoroughly before you set off, because the waterside can be a lonely place in the middle of the night if things are going against you. Weather forecasts are essential. You're planning to fish fairly close to home and you can go anytime, so it makes sense to choose favourable weather conditions. Even in summer, nights can be cold when it's pouring with rain or there's a strong wind. Thunderstorms can be particularly disruptive. Delay the trip if the weather is going to spoil things.

Ensure you have adequate shelter, bedding and clothing – that invariably cold period before dawn will catch you out otherwise. Don't allow yourself to become hungry or, worse, dehydrated. If you're not comfortable, you won't fish to your maximum ability and you'll probably cut the whole trip short. Creature comforts are more than just a luxury – they're essential.

Check and double-check all your tackle and bait. There is nothing more annoying than setting up for a two-day session only to find you've forgotten something crucial. That doesn't just mean the big stuff – crucial things can include less obvious necessities such as sun block, insect lotion and torches. Ensure your mobile phone is fully charged in case you need to make an emergency call.

Tackle and bait – Make sure you have all the tackle and bait you'll need before you set off on your expedition. Replacements can be elusive and expensive.

You don't get thrills like this in the UK. Here, angler and guide hook a big fish and set off down the rapids.

The mahseer, the big fish of these Indian waters, stops for a while behind a rock. At last there's a chance.

The big foreign trip

If you're going abroad – with all the investment of time, effort and funds that that involves – this may be the angling experience of your life, so get it right. Do your research meticulously. Make sure that you're going at absolutely the right time of the year for your chosen water and quarry. Getting this wrong can prove disastrous.

For your first serious expeditions, I would definitely recommend going with a professional outfitter who will provide the transport, guides, accommodation, permissions, boats and everything that the inexperienced person is likely to overlook. However, there are good and bad outfitters, so don't rush to the first one that pops up on the Internet. Phone as many as you like, ask them all the same questions and compare their replies. Remember that the cheapest isn't necessarily the worst and nor is the most expensive always the best. Ask to be put in touch with people who have been on the trip in the past, and see what they have to say.

Now the angler digs in. The fish has made it to a deep, fast pool and there it is sticking. But at last, the angler begins to make headway on the fish, bringing it back upstream yard by yard.

Finally the fish is close. This is a great moment.

Guide, fish and angler in complete harmony. This is what these big trips are all about.

Fishing tackle

Ensure you know the exact methods and gear that the trip will demand. To go with inadequate tackle makes no sense whatsoever. You're forking out a lot of money for the expedition in the first place, so don't ruin your chances by cutting corners. Remember that most of these trips will be way into the wilderness where there's little chance of stocking up on gear. Take more than you think you're going to need, especially line, hooks and flies, all of which can easily become trashed.

It's never more important to get your clothing right than on big trips abroad. If you're too hot, cold or wet for days on end, your pleasure will be completely ruined. The ultra-modern, lightweight materials are a breeze to wash, so you only need two sets of kit along with some socks and a supply of underwear. If the weather is going to be cold, pack a couple of sets of thermals to wear underneath. Make sure you've got a totally waterproof shell as well, and also something warm and snug for your head, from which most of your body heat escapes. If you're going somewhere really cold and need a sleeping bag, be sure to buy the best.

Be prepared

It may be stating the obvious, but ensure your passport is well in date, that you have a visa if it's needed and that you receive all the necessary injections. Don't get neurotic about the latter, however: stick to what your doctor recommends and don't come out looking like a colander. Ensure your cards have plenty of credit available: you can never be absolutely sure what lies in store. Check that your travel insurance is up to date,

On big trips into the wilderness, you've got to be a bit of a woodsman. It's often important that you catch your fish and you cook it simply to keep yourself fed. This lenok trout of 3-4lb is going to provide a worthy lunch.

Garnished with a few berries, it looks a feast fit for a king.

FISHING EXPEDITION CHECKLIST

• Loo paper – many airports in the developing world run precariously short!

• You can always do with strong tape to wrap round rod tubes or luggage, or to coil round a small torch so that you can hold it between your teeth.

• A small pair of sharp scissors can often cut through things a knife can't, but make sure you pack any scissors in your checked-in bag that goes in the hold and not your carry-on bag!

• A good, piercing whistle is a real boon in a tight spot when you need help.

• It's a good idea to have a dental check-up before leaving, but a small phial of clove oil could save you from many a sleepless night.

• Don't forget pens for children if you're visiting a less developed country – much better than sweets and probably more appreciated.

• It's not a bad idea to know at least a few words of the local language. Even just 'please' and 'thank you' said with a smile will put you in pole position!

• Never forget Deet or a similar insect repellent, a head net and perhaps even mosquito coils. Take your malaria tablets as instructed if you're going to an infected area. I've had malaria and it ain't funny!

covers the area you are travelling to and extends beyond your expected return date. Take more money with you than you think you're going to need and hide it carefully in various pockets about your person. A good strong money belt strapped to the chest is a sensible investment if you're visiting any of the more dangerous parts of Africa, Asia or South America. And be sure to take plenty of small bills, because change isn't always readily given.

Hints and tips for the big trip

Take care of yourself physically. Any accident or ill health can ruin things for others as well as yourself. Drink several pints of water every day. Always go for mineral water – fizzy is best because you can tell if the top has been tampered with. In camp, make sure that the water is boiled, and add some flavoured, vitamin-enriched powders to make the taste more acceptable. In most countries you should avoid ice in drinks like the plague (which it may be!). The same goes for ice cream. Don't let your guard down when you get back to a city and a hotel: camp food is often plainer, simpler and more hygienically prepared than it is in the kitchens of a big city restaurant.

In tropical climes, make it a habit to shake your boots out each morning in case any creatures have

set up shop, and don't go near scorpions, snakes or other nasties. If you do get ill or stung, don't panic, and be prepared to take local medication and advice.

Allow yourself plenty of time for transfers to airports: if it can go wrong, it probably will. Because of this potential annoyance, work on your patience levels. You may find your patience tested at airports, hotel check-ins and camps with guides who come from different cultures and have looser schedules and unfathomable – or so it may seem – timetables.

Try not to moan, however tough conditions become. You will only demoralize yourself and those around you. Look on the bright side and you will soon see the beauty around you.

If you're homesick, don't be. You will be home soon enough, and by the time the bills are opened, the chores are sorted and your work has begun again, you'll no doubt be wondering why you ever longed for a return to your old humdrum routine.

When you come home, give your body some time to readjust. Your sleep patterns will be disrupted, so don't worry if you wake up at 4 a.m. every morning for a week – your body will recalibrate. Take care with food, though, and give your stomach a chance. Don't gorge on your favourite, rich meals for a while if all you've been used to for weeks is plain rice.

Night Fishing

To be a true, all-round angler you simply have to take on board the concept of night fishing. There are certain species that feed predominantly at night, most notably, perhaps, sea trout. Many other species are likewise more confident once dusk pulls in, especially on pressured waters.

You will find that the very biggest roach often feed best as darkness seeps in. This battled old hero weighed 2lb 11oz.

Time of the season

The time of year also plays a big part in fishing. In the warm months, particularly, daytime temperatures can be too high for fish to feed comfortably, and it's often only as temperatures begin to drop after nightfall that they begin to look for food. Even in winter, night fishing can be the most productive time for species such as roach, barbel or chub.

On the sea, too, the night is an important time, and there can be good winter fishing off the beach for cod and whiting or, in the summer, for bass and sea trout in the surf.

Be prepared

Remember that, even in summer, temperatures at night can fall quickly, and it can become very cold, especially just before dawn. Make sure your clothing is adequate: you can always take clothes off but you can't put them on if you've left them at home.

Ensure that you have enough food with you, and especially a flask of soup or coffee. This can be comforting in the wee hours, and gives you a much needed energy boost.

You must also ensure you have an adequate light source. My preference is for a large, powerful torch for emergencies and a smaller, dimmer light for tying on hooks, baiting up and other chores that demand complete vision. But be disciplined with the use of

An angler waits quietly for the carp to begin their night feeding.

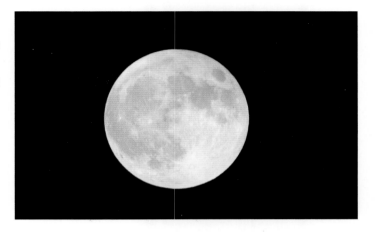

Nights of the full moon can, at times, be very successful for some species.

torches. Use them as little as you can and learn to depend on your night vision.

Plan ahead

For your first night trips, it's best to stick with waters that are familiar to you so that you have a good overall mental plan of the banks and the water features. Waters are very different at night, so any familiarity is a benefit. It's also a great help if your first trips are with a friend, especially one with night fishing experience. You'll find both the experience and the company reassuring. Furthermore, it's a good idea to choose nights for which good weather is forecast for your first trips. It also makes sense to begin your night fishing career when there will be a decent moon.

Visit the venue during the day and make mental notes of where you will be fishing after darkness. Check out the banks, steep drop-offs, fences, trees, snags – anything that could prove dangerous or hamper your fishing.

Bait fishing

One of the major considerations with bait fishing is ensuring your bait is cast into the area in which you want it. Line up features on the opposite bank to get angles right. Trees or tall buildings stand out against the darkest night sky, and give you a target at which to aim.

The trees in this landscape will stand out against the night sky and serve as helpful landmarks.

Now that you've got your angles right, you need to get the correct distance, so cast to your chosen area in the daylight. Once you've positioned the bait exactly, either tape the spool or clip the line so that the required distance is guaranteed for every cast.

Make your life simpler by strapping white or reflective tape on items such as the landing net handle and the unhooking mat. In the heat of night action you don't want to be fumbling around, and turning on a torch can scare that big fish when it's close to the bank. Also, keep everything in its right place so you can find it fast when things get hectic.

Don't neglect the margins

In modern-day bait fishing there is an obsession with casting to the horizon. It's true that many big fish are caught at the 100yd-plus range, but carp and tench also love to feed around the margins, especially at night, when they are often looking for leftovers deposited by daytime anglers. It's a good idea to take an unsliced, white loaf with you and, once darkness has fallen, scatter 20 to 30 small pieces around the margins.

Have a rod ready. Reel, rod, line and an unweighted large hook are all you need. Flick out a piece of crust into the general area of the disturbance and wait for the line to run out. Don't be in too much of a hurry to strike and, when you do, use a slow, controlled, steady lift. Anything wild or panicky can result in a break-off on a big fish close in.

Fly fishing

Begin your nocturnal fly-fishing adventures on open water: trees will often ruin the cast. They also block out the light from the night sky and make everything darker still.

It's always worth staying on into the darkness for many species, pike especially.

If you're wading, be very careful – for your safety's sake and for the good of your fishing. Wild fish are particularly sensitive to disturbances at night.

Don't be too ambitious to begin with – make your casts short and precise. Learn to use your ears, and this way you'll hear any rises and be able to pinpoint them. You'll also begin to gauge where your line and fly are lying in the water.

If you have the choice, cast towards the west for the first part of the night, especially if you're out on a boat. You'll find the afterglow of the sunset helps to silhouette the rise of a taking fish. If you're out very late, end the night by fishing towards the east to benefit from the first of the dawn light.

Sea trout almost always move once true darkness has fallen.

Sea trout

Don't start too early on a sea-trout pool; wait until darkness has firmly settled. This way, you won't spook any jittery fish and you'll be casting to trout that are confident. Equally, don't give up too early in the night. There can be a dead period after midnight until around 1.30 or 2 o'clock in the morning. Things can be brisk again from then until dawn, when often the biggest fish come out. Sunrise also gives you a third bite of the cherry – the period that the great sea-trout fisherman Hugh Falkus used to call 'extra time'. You also stand the chance of an early morning salmon if you're prepared to delay your breakfast.

On a well-stocked sea-trout river, try to stick to a single pool all night long. There'll be fish coming in as the night progresses, and the less you move around the river, the fewer disturbances you create. Also, the more you fish a pool, the more you get to know it.

Geiri knows the benefits of night fishing only too well, and is making the best use of the short Arctic night.

Caring for the Fish

Good anglers love their fish and always want to do their best by them, and this is an important part of the sport. Angling is now very much in the public eye, and we are always being judged by how we behave and by how we treat our catch. Looking after our fish is a real skill in itself and is absolutely central to what we do. Think very carefully indeed about every aspect of fish welfare and you'll be well on your way to becoming a better and more compassionate angler.

Sarah shows exactly how a fish should be photographed. This 20lb-plus mahseer is cradled in the water and kept constantly moist, imperative in the strong heat of India. You can't do this, of course, on a winter pike session!

Be fair

Before you even put a bait in the water, just remind yourself that every element of your tackle must be up to the job in hand. A weak knot, frayed line or inadequate reel could result in a breakage and a hook left in a fish. Equally, are you absolutely sure that you stand a good chance of extracting a fish from the water where you are actually placing your fly, bait or lure? If the snags and potential hazards look just too serious, then give the fish a break and move on to an easier area. There's no point in hooking a fish that is bound to break you in seconds, and a hooked and tangled fish can easily remain tethered to a large underwater obstruction and literally starve to death.

Fish for the table

During your angling career, at times you're very likely to want to eat your catch. After all, this is the most fundamental reason for fishing. The act of taking a fish as food for your family is a noble one – and an ethical one when compared with the abuses that are so common in the production of poultry and cattle. A quick, decisive blow to the back of a fish's head with a properly weighted and balanced priest means that death is absolutely instant and painless. Again, this compares well to the poor fishy souls dredged up by trawlers, left to virtually suffocate and then thrown into freezers, sometimes still alive.

A jewel of the seas – Notice how carefully Juan is holding this juvenile sea bass. Bass can take up to 12 years to reach 5lb in weight. It is essential that any bass, particularly undersized specimens, be returned as quickly and carefully as possible.

Obviously you should not take rare fish, threatened fish or immature fish, and don't take more fish than you need at any particular moment. There's no sadder sight than a freezer jammed full with the frosted remnants of last season's catch.

1 Always try to unhook a pike in the water if you possibly can.
2 When removing the hook, ensure that you have long, strong pliers, so that your fingers stay away from any sharp teeth.
3 If possible, fish for pike using single hooks, as they're much more easily extracted than trebles.

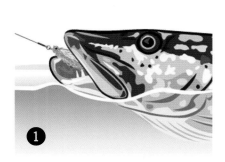
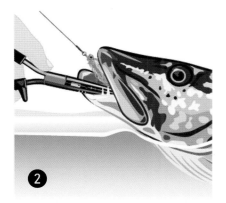

If you don't lay a fish on an unhooking mat, put it in the shallows where it remains moist.

Handling the fish

So, let's say that the catch is to be returned. Whenever possible, unhook a fish in the water without taking it onto the bank. You will have a pair of forceps and you will be using a barbless or semi-barbed hook so that removal is instant and easy. This way the fish doesn't have to be touched or lifted out of its own environment – it is that emergence into the air that fish really don't like.

Unhooking fish in the water like this is easy if you are wading or if the banks are safe and the margins are shallow, but this is not always the case. If a fish needs to be netted, ensure that the net is large, that the mesh is soft and that the design of the mesh is modern and won't catch the sensitive rays of the fish's fins. Once a fish is lifted from the water, place it on something soft and damp – thick moist grass, a bed of waterweeds or a purpose-built unhooking mat.

Don't let a fish flap around – sometimes a wet cloth over the eyes is a good way to calm it down. Handle the fish as little as possible, and always make sure that your hands are thoroughly wet, especially in hot conditions.

Weighing – if you must

It is imperative that you get the fish back into the water as soon as you can do so. There are occasions, however, when you might want to weigh a fish. Perhaps it is a personal best, a fish that means something special to you. Perhaps it could be

The moment of truth – A big fish is hoisted onto the scales. The fish is safely cradled in a big sack so that it can't fall out. It is wet and dark inside the sack, keeping trauma to a minimum.

a record, either for the water or even nationally. Perhaps you are part of a scientific survey. All are acceptable reasons to weigh a fish, but make sure that you do it in a correct and caring fashion. Always weigh a fish in a wetted, soft sling that is big and strong enough for the fish in question. There is nothing more damaging than a large fish falling out of an undersized sling. Preset the scales before putting the fish into the sling so time out of the water is reduced. Try to do the job with close friends. More hands make for quicker work, and it's not a bad idea to rehearse the routine with a log or a stone so the operation with a fish will go as smoothly as possible.

A photographic record

Many of the same comments are applicable to photographing a fish. Have all your equipment ready to take a photo. Don't mess with flashguns and apertures with the fish out of the water – make sure all that is done beforehand. If you must hold the fish for a trophy shot, support it as completely as possible. Make sure that its stomach isn't distended or straining unnaturally. Put as little pressure as possible on the fish's bone structure. Bear in mind that all the fish's natural life is spent supported by water, and once it is out of its environment it loses this cushioning effect.

My own favourite photographs are not trophy shots at all. I much prefer to lay fish in shallow water or on weeds and water flowers in the margins. The advantages of this approach are enormous: most obviously, the fish suffers much less harm this way and that's the important thing, but also the fish takes centre stage and it's the beauty of the catch that attracts the eye. There will also be other important 'props' in the picture that are all part of the story – the type of waterweed or flowers, the fly or lure and general tackle used. What this creates is an overall picture of the day, and a photograph like this doesn't require my ugly mug in it to be truly complete!

Careful release

Once a fish is ready to be returned, support it against the current in shallow water where the pace isn't too quick. Hold the fish there for as long as it takes for it to recover. In warm conditions, when a fish has fought hard, and especially if it's been weighed and photographed, this may take many minutes. Don't lose patience. You have inflicted this discomfort on the fish and it's up to you now to look after it to the best of your ability. Too many fish appear to have revived, only to turn over once they are out of sight, often in deep, powerful water that they're not yet equipped to combat. Wait until you are absolutely sure the fish is ready before letting it swim away.

Fish photographed like this just above the water's surface make the perfect portrait.

Fair to the fish *– Held just above the weeds, only inches from its natural environment, this barbel poses for a quick photograph before being released.*

The broader picture

Care of fish is more than simply looking after something that's taken the offering on your hook. As anglers, it is up to us to watch the aquatic environment and protect it from pressure. On a simple level, removing litter, watching out for pollution and reporting any suspicious incidents to the relevant authorities are things we should all do. On a wider level, it's part of our duty to attend work parties, if we can, that replace gravel riffles, plant willows and generally benefit the whole of the aquatic environment. Remember that improving the water like this doesn't just help our own fishing, but it also helps all waterside wildlife. In the UK,

Insisting on upright behaviour – Before you let a fish go in the current, make absolutely sure that it is strong enough to remain upright and cope with the flow. If it falls on its side, then it will be very vulnerable. If necessary, you will have to wade out, recapture it and hold it again until its strength returns.

Gaining strength – Big Indian mahseer fight until they're exhausted. By putting them on a stringer, they can be tethered for an hour or so until their strength returns completely. Only then is it safe to slip them free.

for example, members of the Salmon and Trout Association, the Wild Trout Trust and the Anglers' Conservation Association all show concern and commitment for healthier watercourses. Our care for fish shouldn't just stop with a day on the bankside.

Tackle choices

Let's end this section with a few questions that we can ask ourselves. First of all, do we really need to use treble hooks when often singles will do? As we have seen, singles are much easier to remove from a predator's jaw and cause much less damage.

Secondly, are we waiting too long to strike, just to be sure of hooking the fish? Always strike as quickly as possible when using a bait, for the longer you

delay, the more deeply a fish is likely to take it and the more potential damage will be involved in the unhooking process.

Thirdly, is our bait-fishing rig totally safe for the fish? This is especially important when carp fishing with modern techniques. If the line breaks, is the hooked fish going to be left towing a large lead weight around the lake, or have we made sure that the weakest link is as close to the hook as possible?

Notice how I haven't even mentioned the use of keep nets in this particular section. While I accept they have a place in the match scene, for general angling I find them almost impossible to justify. I'll leave that one with you for now.

Easy does it – Grayling are very difficult to unhook. They writhe when held, so, if possible, slip a barbless hook from their lips while they lie in the shallows.

■ CHAPTER 2

THE TACKLE

Many anglers place too much confidence in their tackle, thinking that all they have to do is buy the right rod and success will be guaranteed. Far from it. The skill is in choosing the right tackle for the job in hand. The focus of your attention should be the fish and your strategy, but the tackle is there to help you in your approach, and should be as effective as possible. So choose the best tackle you can afford, and then concentrate on applying your angling skills.

Introduction to Tackle

Tens of thousands of years ago, our hunter-gatherer ancestors regarded fish simply as an aid to their survival. I don't know if you could call what they used then tackle: methods were crude but effective – rocks aimed at the skulls of salmon lying in ankle-deep water, spears, bows and arrows, primitive poisons, harpoons, dams to drain off water – any way would do. Around 15,000 years ago, the first crudely fashioned fish hooks began to appear, made from bone or flint. Then, a mere 2,000 years ago, rods and reels started to be used in areas of China and Macedonia. They were, however, a far cry from the light, beautiful and efficient gear that we demand today.

A lure angler's selection – There's a bit of everything here: a couple of plugs, a jerk bait, a mouse pattern and a few rubber fish. They're all exciting to use, and demand different techniques. The skill is knowing exactly what every lure in your box will do – how deep it will work, the violence of its action and the best way to work it on the retrieve.

Pleasure above efficiency

We, in the developed world, are fortunate. Few if any of us need to catch our fish to survive in an age when there is a supermarket on every corner. We fish for fun, as a sport only, and this is how tackle comes to play its part. We demand more than simple efficiency. Today, the right tackle does not just do a satisfactory job, it makes the job satisfying. If you use nice gear that is perfect for the fishing situation in hand, the pleasure of the experience is greatly enhanced. If you are always struggling with your tackle, then concentration is broken and there is no time to immerse yourself in the more important aspects of the sport. You know your tackle is right when it is so much a part of you that you are using it subconsciously, almost totally oblivious to its existence, treating it just like an extra limb.

Decisions, decisions

How do you know how to choose the right gear? A first trip to a tackle shop can be a totally confusing experience. Today there are so many companies making so many different items of tackle that even an expert often has difficulty coming to the right decision.

Generally, there are three key questions that you need to consider. What types of water will you be fishing? What species of fish will you be pursuing? And what methods will you want to use to catch them? Ideally, you need a tackle dealer that is welcoming, takes time with you and is generous with advice. It's also good to go to large tackle dealers as they tend to deal with many different companies, won't be biased and won't push you towards a brand or product that is not necessarily the right one for you.

Do some research

It pays to do your homework. Ask advice from fellow anglers on the bank. Look at each item of tackle and ask their views on it. While people might be coy about giving away their fishing secrets, most of them will want to brag about the gear that they are using.

Buy fishing magazines. All of them contain reviews on the best gear to buy. These tend to be relatively unbiased and will point you in the right direction.

Give yourself options – Whether you're float fishing or fly fishing, don't restrict yourself to a limited selection. To a degree, the more flies or floats you have in your box, the more likely you are to find the killing pattern on any given day.

Go to tackle shows and country fairs. Here you will find many of the major companies on show. It's a perfect opportunity to talk with their representatives and gather their views. Gradually, you will become totally clear in your mind about what you need, and you won't get talked into buying what you don't want.

Quality and choice

In the case of fishing tackle, as with many things in life, you tend to get what you pay for. Don't cut too many corners or you will find yourself with tackle that is unpleasant to use and that could let you down at the crucial moment.

Yet nowadays, fishing tackle is almost always of a standard we could not have believed even 20 years ago. Rods are lighter and more positive than ever. Reels are smoother and have clutches that actually work. Line is thinner, stronger, more abrasion-resistant and with less memory. Fly lines float better, cast better and sink faster. Hooks are lighter and stronger. The choice of lures is infinitely broader and there's always something new to try. All in all, it's a great time to become an angler.

Fly Fishing Tackle

Of all the different types of fishing tackle, it's most important to get your fly gear correct. You have no doubt realized that there is no such thing as an outfit for all fly-fishing situations. The right rod and reel for a tiny moorland stream certainly won't be enough to pursue Atlantic or Pacific salmon on a mighty river. That much is obvious, but how do you decide what kind of set-up you actually need? Above all, you're looking for balance. Your rod and reel should complement each other, and the line weight should make both work to perfection. Don't rush into making a decision when purchasing gear. Seek out advice and read product reviews.

Richard puts out a lovely line. It's poetry in motion, testament to skill and well-balanced gear.

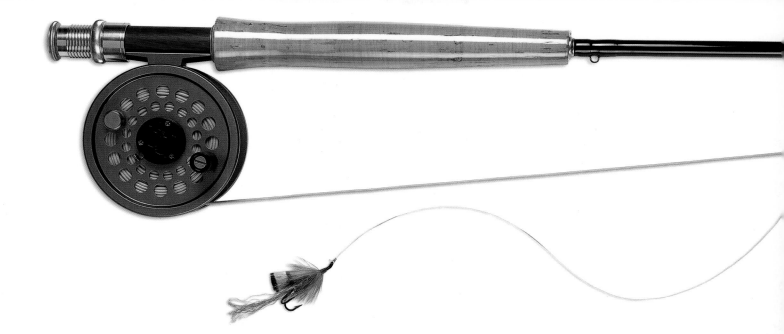

Fly tackle – A brand new fly rod and reel almost ready to go. I say almost, because the shiny cellophane wrapping has yet to be taken of the cork handle or it will sweat and distort once it is in use and gets damp. The rod should be well-balanced and the handle fit very snugly into your grasp. Note the screw fitting for the reel. This is to grip it tightly to the rod during the exertions of casting.

Choosing a fly rod

An old wag of a fishing writer once said that choosing a fly rod was much like choosing a wife – you hoped to stick with both for life. Although times have changed – both socially and piscatorially – a good fly rod is still a big investment and you should choose carefully.

The obvious starting point is to consider the type of fishing you'll be most often engaged in and buy the gear to suit that. Thereafter, during the course of your fishing career, you can add outfits as you travel and build up fresh experiences. Before moving on to greater detail, though, I will say this, albeit in hushed tones, I have a particular 9-foot rod rated 5/6-weight, which is allied to a 6-weight floating line, and this combination suits me for at least 80 per cent of the fishing that I personally enjoy, be it on streams, rivers or stillwaters. I can enjoy the fight of a 12oz trout and still have the confidence to land an 8lb salmon. It's certainly not the ideal rod for everything, but in many, many cases it will just about do. I realize the tackle trade won't be very keen on this particular admission, so I'll hurry on to more conventional comments.

Choose a reputable make, preferably from a company that offers a lifetime guarantee, because rods do have a habit of breaking, either in action or in a car door! Choose, also, a rod that is cosmetically pleasing: you'll be spending a long time together. Consider how the rod feels. Are you happy holding it? Does it seem light enough? Is it responsive enough? If at all possible, try the rod in action or on a casting pool if one is available, and do make sure the rod is the right length and weight for the job that you have in mind for it. There's no point in buying a light 3-weight outfit if you're going to spend your time fishing for sea trout!

The four major rod actions

Most rods, especially for trout fishing, come in four major actions:

• An ultra tip is an extremely fast action rod. By fast action, we mean that it will return very quickly to its original position. Rods like this are ideal for the more experienced caster and are excellent for distance casting, but they require power and precision timing and they are not the best bet for the relatively inexperienced.

• A tip action rod is still fast, still good for long distances, but just a little more forgiving of mistakes.

• A middle- to tip-action rod is more forgiving still and, while it can cope with distance casting, it's

Tackle galore – Lovely fishing tackle is a joy to behold and to use. You won't need a battery of rods like this, but remember that different rods play different roles. Similarly, certain rod actions can make a huge difference in the distance you cast, and different lines on different reels will allow you to fish at a variety of depths.

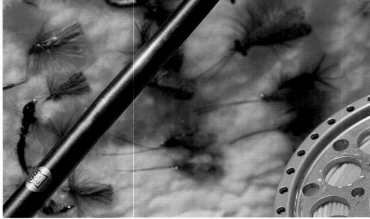

If you're fishing smaller rivers and streams, a lighter rod – perhaps a three- or four-weight – is going to be more applicable to the job.

also happy at short- to medium-range. This rod is the ideal all-rounder, perfect also for the beginner.

• A middle- to butt-action rod is a slower action rod that recovers less quickly after it's been bent. The rod flexes closer to the butt rather than to the tip. Rods like this are ideal for delicate presentation at shorter distances. This type of rod also encourages slower casting of a short line when you are targeting a rising fish… in other words, it's a really good river rod.

A weighty subject

Before we proceed, you need to know about the weight rating system. All rods, whatever their length, are classified by the weight of line they ideally cast. There's some latitude in this, but it's comparatively narrow. The line weight is based on the long-held

AFTM system formulated by the American Fishing Tackle Manufacturers association many years ago. This means that an 8-foot rod designated 7-weight is more powerful than an 8-foot rod rated 4-weight. The higher the number, the heavier the line the rod can cast.

The question of length

So, having dealt with this essential complication, we can move onto more interesting subjects. Let's begin with length. At 7ft, a rod is really only suitable for brooks, streams and smaller rivers. Your casting range is necessarily limited, and you'll probably be looking to harness the rod with a 3- or 4-weight line. However, there are tremendous bonuses. A short rod is easier to work in undergrowth. It's also as light as thistledown and can lay a thin line down with hardly any disturbance. Also, a short rod is supremely accurate when throwing a line out in tight loops to place a fly absolutely on the nose of a rising fish. You've also got to think of the aesthetics of what you're doing. No longer are we expected to feed a family with our catches – we go fishing to enjoy ourselves, and 7-footers are all about fun, feel and intimacy. An 8oz trout wouldn't seem much on a salmon rod, but on a 7-footer you can expect the scrap of your life!

At 8ft, plus a few inches, perhaps, you are stepping up significantly. With a rod of this length, probably married to a 5- or 6-weight line, you can be reasonably confident of fishing small to medium-sized rivers and even small stillwaters. The rod will probably have a fair bit of punch to it, and you'll be able to hammer out a line into a brisk wind. There'll be more spine to the rod, too, when it comes to playing a fish, and larger trout or even small summer salmon aren't totally beyond you with gear like this. Of course, an 8-footer is still light, still a joy to fish with and still casts with supreme accuracy.

Moving up

Once you reach 9ft, you're really moving the goal posts. As I've already guiltily confessed, a 9-foot rod teamed with a 6-weight line does me for most fly-fishing situations. For example, I'm happy fishing for grayling with it, trout in any sort of river, smaller stillwaters, and even Arctic char in Greenland. A 9-footer is a perfect river rod, and there's very little moving water that will be beyond it. You'll also be able to fish many of the smaller stillwaters with confidence, although you'll probably be out-gunned on the lochs, loughs or largest reservoirs. A heavy sinking line would also be taxing it to the limit, but for a floating or intermediate line, the 9-footer is incredibly versatile.

In the modern age, probably more people fish with 10-foot rods than any other, and that's largely because of the huge amount of reservoir work being done. A rod of this length will almost certainly have power and will probably be linked with a 7- or

A 9ft, 7-weight rod is a really good tool to start off with.

8-weight line. It will be able to cast a dry fly or a buzzer with accuracy and delicacy. It will also be able to haul back lures with beefy power. It can handle floating lines with ease and sinking lines without sweat. It will have the power to sink a hook into the bony maw of the oldest brown trout. You'll also be able to consider it for lighter salmon or perhaps pike on the fly. Why not try bass from the seashore with it?

Some companies make 10-foot rods to marry with a 4- or 5-weight line, which is perfect for the Czech nymph technique, of which you will read more about later (see pgs. 222–225). This method demands pinpoint control, and that is what those extra 2ft give you. Whether from boat or bank, the 10-footer can open up a huge amount of fishing to you and is only really out of place on the smaller waters with the lightest of lines for comparatively modest fish.

An 11-footer simply takes the 10-footer up the range in terms of power: you can fish further and heavier. You have added control in foul weather conditions. You have a bit more guts to deal with a larger salmon or perhaps a steelhead. Above 11ft and you are really moving into the designated salmon rod. These generally begin at 13ft but go right through to 15ft or even 16ft. You'll find them coupled with 8- to 11-weight lines, and they are generally designed for double-handed casting, often the spey cast. Once upon a time, rods of this length were astoundingly heavy, being made of bamboo or greenheart. Today, thanks to carbon, even a rod that seems to go on forever can still be light, crisp and a joy to use.

Choosing a double-handed rod

Coming fresh to the world of double-handed rods, there's probably a whole array of questions in your head. Which length? Which model? Do you even need to go double-handed at all? First, let's have a look at the question of length.

A 12-foot double-hander is ideal for smaller spate rivers. It will take an 8-weight line – exactly what you should be using for grilse, steelhead and heavier sea trout. A rod like this will give you good casting distance in tight, enclosed stretches of water and much more line control than a standard, single-handed 10-foot rod. You will find that you are mending the line better and you're fishing through deep pools much more efficiently. A 12-footer is also perfect for spey casting, so this makes the rod ideal for heavily wooded banksides.

A 13-foot rod is the perfect light rod for larger rivers. For example, a 13-footer is ideal for summer salmon fishing. This is the rod for floating or intermediate lines in the 8- to 9-weight category, and you will find that you are able to turn over much larger flies with a 13-footer than you can on any single-handed rod. This is the perfect length for most Scandinavian and Icelandic rivers.

Rods of 14ft are for larger rivers still. They are excellent for throwing out even larger patterns of fly. Many people find the 14-footer the perfect all-rounder because it's a great compromise rod. It will tackle the largest of rivers, but is still light enough to use all day long. You can also handle both floating and sinking lines with ease.

The 15-foot, double-handed rod is the ultimate big-river weapon. A 15-footer gives you great advantages when you are wading deep, because the longer leverage can lift a far greater length of line. The 15ft rod is an excellent all-season companion. It's perfect in spring and autumn when big flies are in use, generally on sinking lines. You'll find a 15-foot gives you superb line control at distances.

Salmon rods

So let's say you're fishing for salmon – which length do you want for your salmon rod? Well, a great deal depends on your own physique, on the type of river you're fishing and, to some degree, the time of the year. If you're fishing the summer on smaller rivers, then probably a 13-footer allied with a floating 9-weight line will be adequate. If, however, you're fishing a raging winter river, when you've got to get flies down really deep, then it's probably wise to go for a 15-footer and a sinking 10-weight. Think it out carefully: don't rush into the wrong choice.

There are also many specialized rods around: there have even been rods designed to take a 0-weight

Aslam's delight – Aslam is an Indian boy who was hired originally to scare monkeys from the camp, but he took to fly fishing magnificently. The gear he is holding is traditional salmon tackle, which on this occasion was pressed into service for the mighty mahseer of the Southern Indian rivers. It worked well at first, but then finally collapsed under the power of what was probably a 70–80lb fish.

line… you wonder whether it might defy gravity and never actually land on the water!

Saltwater rods

If the saltwater scene attracts you, you can easily find 8-foot or 9-foot rods capable of shooting out 9- or 10-weight lines. These offer the powerful action needed to cast into high winds, and also have the power to fight a big permit as it heads down into

The perfect pike kit – Remember, whatever you're fishing for, always make sure that your spool is filled to the correct depth. This will almost always mean quite a considerable length of backing goes onto the drum before the fly line. This is important for two main reasons: you need your fly line to be stored in the largest loops possible so that it does not kink. Secondly, if a big fish, such as an enraged 20lb pike, runs, you've just got to be able to give line, and that means backing. A bonefish, for example, will commonly take 100yd of backing off the reel.

The travelling fly angler – Destination fishing now is a major part of the fly-fishing scene. Multi-piece rods help enormously if you're considering air travel. Make sure your reels are well packed and protected against possible damage in the hold.

deep water. You might also consider gear like this for a jaunt after pike.

In short, whatever your desires, there will be a rod out there to suit you. Just take the time to make sure you locate the right beast for your purpose.

Other rod criteria

There are other considerations, too. Do you like the feel of the rod? Looks shouldn't be important but, inevitably, they are, so does it really turn you on? After all, if choosing a fishing rod is like taking a partner, you hope it will be for life. Ensure that the handle feels comfortable in your grasp. Are the corks top-quality? If not, they'll break down under repeated use. Is the reel seat a really secure screw fitting? Are the rod rings light but strong – double-legged if necessary?

The matter of how many pieces the rod breaks down into is of vital importance if you're a traveller. For example, you can take a 4-piece, 10ft rod onto a plane with you and eliminate those heart-stopping moments at the carousel. Does the rod come with a strong tube to protect it from knocks? Is there

a lifetime guarantee? That's something you really should be demanding these days. Read reviews, talk to anglers on the bank and don't just take the word of a tackle dealer who might be trying to get rid of last year's unwanted stock.

Choosing a fly reel

Once upon a time, fly reels were nothing but reservoirs for the backing and the fly line itself, and they would clatter like a bag of spanners if put under any pressure from the fish. Their drag systems were atrocious and, in short, they were pretty undesirable objects. Even today, there are a lot of suspect reels on the market. A simple test is to pick up any prospective purchase, hold it by the spool and shake it. If there's any wobble, however slight, you can bet it will quickly get worse.

But generally, the angling world has moved on. For example, far more of the fish species that are targeted in the 21st century really pull and can shred line off reels, so if the reel's clutch mechanism isn't up to the job, you're in deep trouble. There are many brands and models of reel on the market today, the vast majority of them of superb standard. They're not cheap, so it certainly pays to do your homework and buy the one, or ones, that are perfect for the tasks you have in mind.

Modern reels are supremely well engineered, so look after them. Make sure grit doesn't get into the workings.

Always make sure your reels are filled to the rim. This makes the retrieve a lot faster.

A reel for the light rod

Firstly, you have to choose a reel that matches your rod and is suited to the job in hand. If you're fishing small streams with a 3-, 4- or 5-weight rod, then you obviously need a reel of similar rating. It will be small and light, and it needn't have huge line capacity because you will probably be fishing for small fish that are only going to run a few yards. However, its clutch must be highly adjustable and smooth as silk. It's probable that you will be using lightweight tippets in these situations and they must be protected. When line is taken off your reel, there must be none of the jolts or jerks that can wreck the finest of points. There's no tolerance whatsoever when you use such light lines.

Capacity and drag

You'll come across the word 'arbor' used frequently in reel terminology. This word basically refers to the depth and width of the reel's spool. The deeper and broader the spool, the greater the amount of backing that can be loaded up. The larger the spool, also, the less tightly the fly line is coiled. This tends to make for smoother casting, as kinking is less pronounced. Generally, the large arbor reels, with their wide-looped storage, make for incredibly low line memory and all but eradicate those irritating coils. They also make retrieving line that much faster.

If you're fishing bigger waters with a heavier rod for bigger fish – say from 7- to 11-weight – the line capacity of your reel is going to be more important.

So, too, will be the drag system. If a big fish is running fast, you will need to adjust the tension of your clutch quickly, easily and effectively. Is the drag system, therefore, easy to operate, and will it operate successfully over and over, no matter how hard and frequently it is pushed?

Drag systems are also much improved these days. Look for one that is easily adjustable and offers 'low start-up inertia', meaning that it doesn't need an enormous tug to get the spool moving – perfect if you're fishing light leaders. Look for a reel that is suited to the line you'll be using, that is light, that fits your prospective rod like a glove and has a really strong, integrated reel seat. Most reels are made of graphite or top-quality aluminium. If you're choosing aluminium, make sure it is anodized if you intend to do any sea fishing, otherwise it will corrode.

When you're choosing, bear in mind that better quality reels tend to be more adaptable. For example, in its Gem reels, Hardy use Avcarb – a carbonfibre material used in the braking systems of Stealth Bombers and Formula One racing cars. Avcarb disperses heat very quickly indeed, and it hardly expands or contracts in either ferocious heat or freezing cold, so it doesn't matter whether you've hooked a monster at the Pole or the Equator.

Personal preferences

There are other considerations, too. You might want a reel that is not caged but has an exposed rim so

A good strong reel from a reputable maker will last you a lifetime through all kinds of challenges and conditions.

that you can control a running fish with the palm of your hand. If you are going to share your reel with a partner or friends, you might want a system that is easily changed from right- to left-hand wind. If you are fishing big stillwaters, where your approach can

Well-done, John, on a superb barbel picked up on a dry fly and light gear. What a fight and what an experience! Notice how John is using a reel with an exposed rim that is not caged so he has more control over the line with his hands.

change many times during the course of a day, you might want a reel system that features a series of spare spools so you can kit yourself out with a variety of floating, intermediate and sinking lines.

The fly line

As we have seen in the discussion of rods, there are different types of fly line as well as different weights. Some fly lines are meant to float, others to hang just under the surface film and others to sink at differing rates. For example, if you're trying to get a fly down as deep and as quickly as possible, then you'll go for a fast sinker. If you want to slowly explore the depths, then you'll go for a slow sinker. Most stillwater fly anglers, especially these days, have a whole armoury of different lines stored away on separate spools that are interchangeable. This can be important: you could arrive at the reservoir early in the morning and find a flat calm with fish taking from the surface. You'd obviously rig up a floating line and either a dry fly or perhaps something fished in the film.

The day clouds over, a wind begins to rise. There's nothing showing on the surface and you've got to get down deeper. This is where a sinking line is important. Or let's say the day continues bright. The heat increases as the sun rises, and the fish drop ever closer to the bottom. Now you've got to pursue them in the depths and a fast sinker is called for. The sun sinks. The wind dies. Once again, as evening approaches, the fish are on the surface. Now you need that floater again.

It's a good rule to choose the best fly lines that you can afford. Rods and reels are obviously important, but a top-quality fly line can make fly casting

Compact – Here you see an angler out in mid-river fishing intently, happy in the knowledge that all the tackle he's ever going to need for the situation is safely stowed in his vest. He's fishing a small, clear, comparatively heavily pressured chalk stream and it's on waters like this that presentation has to be absolutely perfect. If the fly is going to float, then it needs to do so beautifully. If it's going to sink, then you've got to get it down fast.

so much easier. Don't ever forget to look after that fly line. Wash it regularly in warm, soapy water to clear grit and sand, which make casting difficult and can ruin your precious rod rings.

Line profile

The decision isn't just about weight and where the line fishes in the water; there are also different line profiles. The most traditional is a double taper, which has a significant belly and is thinner towards each end. This means it casts well and the line closest to the fish lands gently. The weight-forward lines are intended for medium- to long-distance casting, and once the tip and belly of the line have gone through, the thin running line passes easily through the rod rings. Shooting heads consist of short lengths of fly line backed by fine braid, which produces little resistance when flying through the rod rings. These are more advanced and designed for very long-distance casting.

There are all sorts of very specialized lines. For example, Greys now produce the Wake Saver line. This is a full floating line with a short, clear, intermediate sink tip section merging into it. The sinking line eliminates leader wake on the slowest of retrieves and reduces the angle that the tippet makes with the fly. The high-visibility floating section helps detect subtle takes and the taper allows for good long-range presentation. The Wake Saver is suitable for a whole variety of techniques, such as static nymphs, wet hoppers, loch-style drifting and fishing suspended buzzers.

Salmon fly lines

Be aware that many lines are far too long-bellied to be cast in normal situations. Lines are made for angling, for the fly fisher out there wading the river, and not for the tournament caster on a platform.

When you are wading and spey casting, do bear in mind that the length of line belly you require is dependent on the conditions in which you are fishing. If you are fishing a small, tree-lined river, then a short-bellied line is needed to keep the 'D' of the cast relatively small and precise. However, when fishing on more open water, you can choose a mid-bellied line that throws a larger 'D', creating longer, unimpeded casts.

Master of the cast – The light is fading as Hardy and Greys' Andy Sowerby punches out his salmon line. As the dusk settles, Andy knows fish will be running up his native River Tyne. He is focused, easy in his movements and totally prepared for the take when it comes.

Similar considerations should be observed when you are wading. The deeper you go, the less line you can lift. Deep wading, therefore, calls for a short-bellied line. If you are wading shallow, a mid-bellied line can be fully utilized.

When fishing for salmon, the choice between floating and sinking lines is made with regard to water temperature and how deep the fish are lying. In running water, the current has an important bearing. If it is quick, fish will come up to a fly presented on a floating line, but they might find the line is going round so fast that the fly is skating. If this happens, a sink-tip line or a full sinker can help prevent the line skating across a quick current.

Line colour

The colour of fly lines has been a point of controversy for endless years. We will probably never know how fish actually see colour on the fly lines. It's perhaps best to take a logical approach. Choose fly lines that are designed to mirror nature – soft blues and greens tend to merge with the aquatic environment. However, the colour should be easy to pick out and watch without effort, because not all takes, even from large salmon, are overly dramatic.

With sinking lines, if you're fishing in the top layers of the river, choose clear lines to merge with water that is light and bright. If you're moving down between 2–6ft, go for green-coloured lines to reflect the waterweeds that begin to appear at these depths. Drop between 6–10ft, however, and it's a good idea to choose lines that are brown to merge in with the lack of light and increased sediment.

Backing

Your fly line will need to be attached to a long length of backing, both to fill the spool of the reel and also for safety if you have a big, fast-running fish. Ideally, you're looking for backing that offers low stretch, fine diameter and excellent strength. Look for a high-visibility colour such as pink, which allows you to keep track of a big fish in the water. Many modern backings are made from Gel Spun, which

Does colour count? – The question of fly line colour has exercised anglers' minds for many years. There is the feeling that a very bright colour can be picked up more easily by the fish, but generally a floating line is simply seen in silhouette at best. Perhaps when it comes to sinking lines, colour is more of an issue. Of course, a highly visible floating line does have advantages for the angler. It's possible to see even the slightest take much more easily.

This rod is set up for tackling large fish. Notice the reams of bright pink backing on the reel.

has an incredibly low diameter, giving you loads more backing on your spool.

The leader

The only other major consideration, apart from the flies (which deserve a chapter to themselves), is the leader that ties the fly to the fly line. Your leader is very important, because this is the length of nylon that is attached to your fly that dictates how your fly works and what the trout sees.

Once upon a time, everyone used standard monofilament, but there are many different materials available now. One of the modern materials used is copolymer, and a copolymer-tapered leader guarantees one of the best possible presentation methods. If the taper is finely tuned, you will achieve a perfect turnover of your flies, even under the most taxing of conditions. A high-diameter butt section will give an efficient power transfer, allowing the fly to be put down with precision and accuracy. Many copolymer leaders are also memory-free, so they lie on the water perfectly and they are transparent for maximum stealth in clear water and bright conditions.

Fluorocarbon leaders offer low visibility, enhanced by a clear finish that makes the line almost invisible. They have a high strength-to-diameter ratio, so you can fish fine with confidence; also excellent knotting strength, with high abrasion resistance.

Both copolymer and fluorocarbon alternatives offer enhanced strengths at very low diameter, and are often a favourite choice. Do be careful, though: these modern lines can be abraded quickly by a big fish in a snaggy situation. My advice is to stick with standard nylon if you know you're going to be pulling a specimen from the snags. Leaders, by and large, should be tapered, getting thinner towards the fly. This means they turn over more easily in the air and land with minimal disturbance.

You might also consider buying braided leaders: these are expensive, but they give ideal presentation. Choose a braided leader that is right for the job in hand. Some of them sink extremely quickly, whereas others will sit beautifully in the surface film. Most give an exceptionally good cast turnover.

Accessories

What else do you need? Well, sometimes you want to make a leader float or, alternatively, sink quickly. You can buy various sprays, pastes and liquids to achieve these effects. You can also invest in one of the proprietary substances that help to make dry flies float more perkily and more bushy-tailed than your own hot breath can ever achieve!

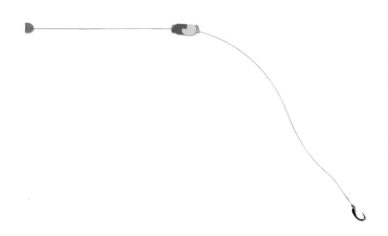

The strike indicator – Grayling will accept a nymph drifting with the current, but they take at lightning speed and it's all too easy to miss the event altogether. This is where the strike indicator comes in – a small piece of plastic, polystyrene or whatever is placed up the line so that the nymph floats beneath it at the required depth. Once a grayling sucks it up, the mini-float dives, you strike, and the battle is on.

Strike indicators can also be a useful acquisition. These are pieces of plastic that stick on the leader, show up brightly and act in the same way as a fisherman's float. Choose ones that are light, highly visible and stick to the leader during casting. You will find these very useful if you are fishing for grayling in the winter, for example, or using nymphs for trout deep down. (Do check local rules, however – they are frowned upon on some waters.)

A pair of sharp scissors is always a good idea, too, for snipping off unwanted ends. And of course you need forceps or haemostats to slip the hook from a beaten fish's jaw.

You'll almost certainly need a landing net, but in every situation you should ask yourself whether you really need to use it. You can often simply draw the fish to you, kneel by it and flick the hook out without a net at all. This is much kinder on the fish, as by keeping it in the water at all times, the stress is hugely reduced.

We'll come across various other items of tackle as we progress through the book, but the one essential is polarizing glasses. These are one of your most important purchases for two reasons: the first, and paramount one, is safety. You simply cannot take the risk of fly fishing, especially in a wind, with your eyes unprotected. One momentary lapse of concentration,

Nymphs

So what flies must you have? A vast percentage of what fish eat lives down deep amid the security of stone and weed on the bed of the river or stillwater. These creatures include freshwater shrimps, beetles, water fleas, tadpoles, water boatmen, snails of all sorts and a huge number of nymphs (see pg. 166). These latter will eventually ascend to the surface, shed their skins and transform into fully mature flies. All fish species love to feed on them as they're rising and hatching, as well as the flies into which they transform. It makes sense, therefore, to have a good selection of flies that imitate these small, generally dark-coloured foodstuffs. Don't be too confused by the welter of nymph patterns available because there are simply hundreds. The key is to choose flies that blend in with the surroundings – hence brown, green and black are generally successful – and retrieve them in a slow and lifelike way.

My favourite nymphs include pheasant tails, Montanas, mayfly nymphs, various olives and black spiders. I'd fish one or two of these patterns hard before giving up on them. Experiment with various depths if necessary, putting on an intermediate or sinking line if you suspect that the fish are down

Will it or won't it? – A big rainbow comes to inspect a nymph. This is the moment of truth – what you do next with your retrieve will decide whether the trout takes it or not.

deep because of cold or extreme heat. There's no magic fly, but there are expert ways of working it. Think how you can impart life and realistic movement. If you can, buy yourself an aquarium and install in it all manner of aquatic life. Spend time just watching how nymphs and underwater insects move – carefully, cautiously and in short erratic bursts. It's these movements that you are trying to imitate when you retrieve your fly through the water.

Bugs, shrimps and beetles

If your nymph patterns really don't work, you can try imitating the other food sources already mentioned. For example, a chomper fly imitates a *Corixa* or water boatman. Again, fish it in short, quick movements, generally not more than about a metre (3ft) beneath the surface. Try various shrimp patterns in pink or green, or even a hog louse imitation, best used on a floating line with a long leader. In summer, trout might well be preoccupied with feeding on water fleas often called daphnia, especially on large stillwaters. Huge banks of these tiny creatures drift round close to the surface in duller conditions but remain down deep when it is sunny. Small brown flies flecked with red can prove very effective in this situation.

The nymph patterns on the right, with the double beads, sink like a stone and are perfect for deep-water work in fast currents.

Fish fry

On many occasions, you will see large fish chasing smaller ones, because most fish species tend to be predatory at one time or another. This is especially the case late in the season when the urge to spawn is getting close. This is the time to use a fish or fry imitation, often rather inaccurately called a lure. The concept is to strip a fish imitation back quickly, and takes will generally be aggressive and hard-hitting. This is an effective way of exploring large areas of water on bigger lakes where location is a problem. Try flies such as Muddler Minnow, the White Fry, the Black Fry, the Minky, the Appetizer and the Baby Doll. Streamer fly patterns are also increasingly popular. Streamers don't look like much out of the water, but below the surface their movements are reminiscent of small, fleeing fish.

We haven't even mentioned the traditional wet flies that are usually fished in quick, broken water. These flies are not meant to imitate any one food form exactly but to give the impression of something

Big and small – *Remember, a fly can imitate the tiniest gnat or, seen here, a sand eel or small fish like a smelt.*

small and edible. They are generally fished down and across the current, and takes can be lightning fast. Top patterns include Butchers, Connemara, Blacks, March Browns and Peter Rosses.

Buzzers

In the evening, especially, you will probably see head and tail rises as the fish move through the surface film. You will see the head followed by the curve of

Quite a mix of flies – an imitation ladybird, would you believe! Even a wasp/bee pattern can have its uses.

the back, and the dorsal fin will frequently be held clear and sometimes the tip of the tail fin, too, before the fish goes down. Almost certainly, these fish are taking buzzers, and buzzer fishing is as exciting as it gets. Buzzers are small chironomid larvae that begin as bloodworms in the silt and mud of the bed (see pg. 168). These eventually turn into pupae, often red in colour, which rise to the surface and here they hatch out into the adult nymph. As the pupa – the buzzer – struggles in the surface film to slough its skin, it's incredibly tempting to most species of fish. Hatches are often prolific and it can seem that every fish in the water is feeding in the surface film.

Standard patterns have been around for years, but new, shiny epoxy buzzers are proving dramatically effective. Fish all buzzer patterns on floating lines so you can work them either in the surface film or an inch or two beneath. Other flies make easy targets in or around the surface film as they emerge, so if your buzzer patterns aren't working, or if you see larger flies in the air, try other patterns. Hoppers, Floating Snails, Hare's Ears and suspender patterns are all productive.

The dry fly

Now, we've got to think about dry flies, and the most obvious of all are mayflies, seen on both rivers and lakes from the late spring onwards. These are large, beautiful, up-winged flies, which mean that their wings stand proud and look like mini-sails (see pg. 170). There are endless mayfly patterns: the Green

A magician at work – *Fly tying can look like a magical occupation, fit only for wizards, but it's an art form that we can all learn. Tying your own flies is cheaper than buying shop-bought patterns and immensely satisfying. In fact, many people like tying flies more than they do fishing them!*

A fish's eye view – A mayfly pattern hangs in the surface layer. Does it look like the real thing to the trout? And what about that hook? Is the fly copying the natural perfectly, or just giving an impression of something edible?

Drake and the Grey Wulff are favourites. Take a variety of sizes and colours with you and try to match your artificial with the insects you see in the air or on the surface.

Throughout the summer and into the autumn, you will frequently see flies looking like the mayfly but only a half or a third as large. These belong to the olive family (see pg. 169–170). Olive duns are favourites, along with iron-blue duns and large dark olives. Make sure you have Greenwell's Glory and blue-winged olives with you.

A FLY-FISHER'S SELECTION

1 Streamer fly
A large streamer fly is useful for big trout, steelhead or pike – anything that wants a large meal.

2 Reservoir lure
A reservoir lure such as this is excellent for rainbow trout.

3 Wet flies
Traditional wet flies are best fished on quick rivers for trout and grayling.

4 Salmon fly
This is a good example of a fly that will attract salmon.

5 Dry flies
These are perfect for the summer and autumn trout river.

6 Nymphs
Nymphs are the standard patterns for deeper-feeding trout and grayling, and for many coarse fish.

CHOOSING THE RIGHT FLY

1. It's always advisable to buy the very best flies available – after all, they are the most crucial part of the trout fisher's armoury.

2. It's hard to tell a good fly simply by looking, so in the first instance, go for a proven brand or tier.

3. Make sure the tying of each fly looks neat, with no loose ends. Durability is very important, and you don't want something coming apart after two or three casts.

4. If you are buying a nymph, make sure that it looks slim and streamlined. It is very important how a fly behaves in the water – you need it to act as much like the insect it is imitating as possible.

5. It's also important to consider the hook type. Buy flies that are tied to hooks that have a good reputation. The last thing you want is a hook gape to straighten out when your first or best brown trout is sliding towards the net.

6. It's always a good idea to buy at least two flies of each pattern you choose. There's nothing more annoying than losing the 'taking' fly of the day in a tree, and finding that you have no replacement in the box.

Perhaps the flies in the air are sedges (see pg. 171). Their larvae, commonly called caddis grubs, build protective cocoons from gravel, sticks, sand or shells in which they shelter on the bed of the river or lake. You will find most sedges hatching out in the afternoons and evenings and you will recognize them by their large, roof-like wings, as well as by two large forward-pointing antennae. Artificials such as the Goddard, the Caperer and the Grouse-wing all imitate sedges.

You certainly won't miss a hatch of damselflies – those beautiful creatures with their distinctive, electric-blue bodies and wide wingspan. Damselfly nymphs are often more popular with the fish, but the dry damsel pattern is always worth a go. Don't strike too soon at a rise because trout will often drown large flies before eventually taking them in. Once you've seen the rise, count slowly to three or four before tightening.

Terrestrials

You should also have imitations of what are known as terrestrials – flies that are blown onto the water from the surrounding bankside. These include hawthorns – so called after the bush and flower that these flies really seem to relish. They have black bodies, long trailing black legs and white-coloured wings. Many will be blown into the water on a breeze and feeding can be frenetic. As the summer progresses, you will find more and more craneflies, or daddy-long-legs (see pg. 65), blown onto the surface of both rivers and lakes.

Of course, there are all manner of specialized flies for specialized types of fishing and species. Steelhead flies, pike flies, bass flies… the list is a long one and your fly collection will build up according to the variety of challenges that you experience. Remember, virtually every fish that swims can be caught on the fly, so the scope is endless.

Winter Fly Tackle Care

You won't want to spend half the winter fussing over your tackle, but it still makes good sense to devote a little time to its care in this slow period of the year. After all, tackle these days is astonishingly well made but doesn't come cheap, so it's worthwhile looking after your investment. Possibly even more important than monetary considerations are those of efficiency: come March or April, or a winter outing, you don't want your lines sticky or coiled, your flies rusted up or your reels sounding like bags of spanners. To fish well, you must have gear performing to its maximum.

I'm a great believer in mouse fly patterns like this one for all manner of fish. You will find that they take salmonid species if they're twitched furiously back across the surface. They are cracking for really big river chub and, with a wire trace, for pike, too. Keep them in a dry place in winter, though.

Rods

Clean them thoroughly with warm water and clean, scratch-free cloths. Check the rod rings for grooves, and replace any that are nicked badly. Make sure you get any grit or sand out of spigots or ferules and screw reel fittings. It's crucial to wash these if you've been using gear in saltwater. It's also a good time to wash out those rod bags, which could well be going musty. A drop of oil on the zips of your Cordura rod tubes could save frustration in the months to come.

Moving parts – Your reel and your rod's reel seat will take a real battering through the course of a season. They spend a lot of time in the water, and are frequently dropped on sandy banks. Grit can get into the mechanism and foul up clutch systems and screw threads. Winter is thus a time for washing and oiling and making these items as good as new.

Reels

Clean these in warm water and leave to dry completely. A gentle re-greasing can also be a good idea. Store your reels in a warm, dry environment throughout the winter months.

Lines

Take all lines off the spools and give them a really good clean in warm, soapy water. This is also the time for a little bit of fly-line treatment. Rather than putting your lines back on the reels, it's a good idea to store them on an old bicycle rim with the rubber tyre removed. You can get 15 to 20 lines on one rim and you'll find that this irons out any tight loops that tend to form when the line stays on the spools. Treat your lines carefully: come spring, they'll cast like new and they won't groove those rod rings.

Flies

Again, keep these in a warm, dry place, well away from moisture and dampness, which could lead to rusting. Check all your flies and make sure they are stored in a warm, dry cupboard and there's no leftover water in the boxes. It's a good time to check the hook points for sharpness and discard any flies whose whippings are beginning to look dodgy. We hardly need to add that winter is a great time to get down to tying your own flies ready for the next season.

Bags and nets

Again, give these a good wash – you'll be amazed how much dirt the average fishing bag attracts during the course of a year. Don't store bags and nets in an outside shed or garage unless you are absolutely sure these are totally rodent-free. A nest of mice over-wintering in a tackle bag causes absolute mayhem.

Chest waders

Store these correctly, preferably indoors in a stable temperature. Hang them from a wader rack rather than leaving them crumpled up on a shelf. It's a good time to check and mend any leaks. Now, too, is the time to give them a wash. Don't use normal detergent but try Nickwax Tech Wash. Once the waders are dry, spray them with Grangers XT, a water-repellent spray for all synthetic and breathable fabrics. Treating your chesties well during the winter can give them a whole new lease of life come spring.

Wading boots

Pay particular attention to these: are the laces frayed and in need of replacement? Look carefully at the soles. Perhaps it's time to replace them or to restick a sole that is coming loose. Give them a good wash to get out ingrained dirt and grit, and then store them in a warm, dry environment.

Bait Fishing Tackle

Don't get carried away too much with the business of tackle. At its most basic, tackle is designed purely to put out a bait, register a bite, play a fish and land it. There are lots of buffs in the bait-fishing world who have a very technical approach to tackle. Good luck to them. Listen and indulge them if you wish, but it's often far simpler to stick with the basics.

Box of secrets – A look into the tackle boxes of carp fishing experts can be mind-blowing. Carp learn very quickly, so rigs must always be one step ahead, and their intricacy is astounding (see pgs. 296–298).

Choosing carefully

The important thing is to choose your tackle with care, look after it and make sure that it's always in tiptop condition. If you treat your tackle badly, the chances are it's going to let you down, often at a critical moment. Also bear in mind that the tackle world never stays still. Companies are constantly forging ahead with new developments so, through the magazines and tackle dealers, try to keep in touch with what is happening.

Bait-fishing rods

Don't rush into a purchase. Take your time and, if possible, test a rod out. It's always best to have used a rod on the bankside before deciding to buy it. Friends, fellow anglers, dealers, fishing magazines and, to some extent, company brochures can all help you to come to a decision.

Make sure that you're absolutely clear in your mind about what you want your new rod to do. Sometimes, you will be forced to compromise, but don't sacrifice your ideas entirely. How does the rod feel? Does it balance nicely with your reels? Don't just waggle the rod or let its tip be pulled down by the salesman (a trick as old as the Ark). Put line

through the rings and see how it copes. Find out what guarantee is being offered on the rod – some companies now offer a no-quibble lifetime guarantee – a real bonus. Does the rod come with a travelling tube, always a nice accessory? Do you think you need one of the four- or five-piece models that can be broken down and stowed away in an aircraft locker?

Carp rods

With carp rods, the choice is particularly mind-blowing. Let's look at the most common lengths and ratings. A 12-foot, 2.5lb test curve rod offers plenty of power, is comparatively light to hold and, therefore, will probably bring added pleasure to the fishing experience. However, don't expect it to cast vast distances or haul really big fish from dangerous areas. If you want to cast that much further or you expect to contact very big fish indeed, then a 2.75lb or 3lb test curve will give added power. A 12-foot, 3lb test curve rod will cope with short- to long-range fishing, along with method feeders and PVA bags. It's a rod for most situations. However, you can go heavier still: a 12.5-foot or 13-foot rod with a 3.5lb test curve rating will offer maximum casting distance and really good line pick-up when you are striking and playing a big

Ready for action – Two fixed spool reels straddle a centre pin. Now I can fit a float on the centre pin and a feeder and a straight lead with the fixed spools.

Attention to detail – A thoroughly modern set-up with every option covered. Two of the rods are for fishing at long range, one halfway and the fourth in the margins.

CASTING WITH A CARP ROD

Pre-launch
Peter has baited up at the 100yd range and lots of carp are out there feeding. Now is the time to get the bait out. A powerful 12-foot or 13-foot rod, a big reel loaded to the rim and a heavy enough weight are all necessary. The line must be flawless, as a big cast like this piles on the pressure. Pete is gauging where he wants to put his bait and preparing himself for the cast.

The launch
Peter sweeps the rod forward, bringing his forearms in front of his face, his hands in the direction he wants to cast. Gathering speed, the rod will propel the bait to the baited area. This is a powerful cast, but Peter is in control. The terminal tackle, just visible in the top right-hand corner of the photo, is about 4ft from the rod tip: the perfect distance for maximum control.

Re-entry
Notice how Peter's hands and the rod are still in the same true line to the feeding area. The bait is about to land, and he is feathering its fall by controlling the line off the spool with his fingertip. By slowing the line, the cast force is diluted and enters with minimal splash. Once the bait hits the surface, he will keep the bait arm open to give line as the lead falls through the water.

fish. Rods like this are often the choice of anglers fishing for the biggest carp and even catfish.

Marker and spod rods

If you're serious about carp fishing, you will probably also want a marker rod. In the modern carping age, a marker rod is considered essential kit. Using a marker rod will give you a better understanding of the lakebed and enable you to find features such as depression, gravel bars, weed beds and silt gulleys. Most marker rods are around 12ft long and will allow you to throw the big float and lead required for the job vast distances.

Spod rods are now a common part of every carp angler's armoury and enable the angler to bait up well beyond catapult range. Choose a blank that is progressively compressed by the spod in order for the rod to work properly and propel the spod into the distance. Choose a rod that is happy working with small, medium and large spods, so you can cope easily with different situations.

Of course, not all carping work involves casting at the horizon and it's a good idea to have a stalker-type rod – something shorter, lighter and better adapted for mobile fishing to carp that you can actually see. Look for an anti-flash, matt grey finish so that the carp aren't alarmed. A rod between 8ft and 9ft in length is good, so you can use it in the tightest of situations. However, the rod must have power. Make sure it will be able to hold a big fish in snaggy conditions without danger.

Leger and float rods
Beyond this, you will probably want a general legering rod between 11ft and 12ft in length. Look for a test curve of around 1.5lb, which will make it suitable for most types of fish, including small carp.

A good touch-legering rod is all about comfort.

The rod should also have a screw-in tip attachment for a selection of quiver tips. You will probably want a float rod, too. For most situations, a 13-foot rod suffices, both on rivers and stillwaters, for trotting work and for fishing at distances on lakes. If, however, you're trotting a really big river, then a 15-foot may be a preferable length, because it will give more line control and better line pick-up. It's very important to decide how you will be using your rod. For most float fishing situations, a rod with a test curve of around 1lb is acceptable. However, if you're thinking about big carp, barbel or massive tench, then it's wise to go heavier.

Choosing a reel
The vast majority of reels used in the bait fishing world are fixed-spool reels of one type or another. For carp fishing, big pit reels now rule the roost, with huge line capacities and a bait runner facility. There is, however, a tendency to use reels for every type of work that is on the large side. A heavy reel only increases the general weight of what you have to hold and frequently makes the rod unbalanced. Nearly all fixed-spool reels these days have sensitive, smooth clutches. Most have rear drag adjustments, which are fine, but my own personal favourite is a front adjustment mechanism. For me, it makes everything just a little bit smoother. Do try any potential reel out on the rods that you own to make sure that the complete package feels right in the hand.

The centre-pin reel
Centre-pin reels are an absolute joy. You don't have to own a centre-pin to relish your river fishing or close-in carp and tench work, but you are missing a fantastic way of fishing if you never try it out. Centre-pins give you a measure of control that you could never previously imagine, and the thrill of playing a big fish on a pin is something you will never forget. Perhaps, however, it's for river work that the centre-pin really comes into its own. You won't be able to cast huge distances – nobody can with a pin – but that's not the point. When it comes to trotting, control is absolute, and while a centre-pin is not as easy to master as a fixed-spool reel, the benefits are immense.

Reel control – It doesn't matter if you're using a centre pin (left) or a fixed-spool reel (right), you want the reel to balance the rod comfortably, and to fit your hand.

The multiplier reel

For really heavy work, a multiplier reel is the tool you'll need. Perhaps you're trolling for pike on vast waters or fishing for huge catfish. These are situations where the reel will be subjected to immense pressures and must hold vast lengths of high-diameter line. This is where the multiplier comes into its own. Of course, in addition to this we have lightweight multipliers designed to flick plugs, spinners, spoons and rubber jigs with highly focused accuracy.

Fishing line

There have been huge advances in the design of lines in just the last few years. Diameters have come down and strength has risen. A lot of the ultra-thin lines are of copolymer construction, which gives amazing strength to diameter possibilities. Some of the older copolymer lines were susceptible to abrasion and could break unexpectedly, but these problems are increasingly a thing of the past.

For some situations, braid is a good option, having many advantages. It is limp and easy to cast, and it's also very fine considering its incredible strength.

Camouflage line – Look how well this blue fishing line blends into the water around it.

However, like copolymer line, braid can snap very quickly and most unexpectedly, especially in rocky situations. Indeed, if the swim that you are fishing is very snaggy, particularly with hidden boulders, it's probably best to stick with the old-fashioned but very reliable monofilament for most purposes.

Lines also now come in a bewildering array of colours. After many years of fishing in India, I've grown to think that the more closely the line merges with the water colour the better. In India, green lines that blend in with the turquoise-coloured waters of the river seem to do far better than white lines. It may be mere coincidence, but why take chances?

Never be tempted to use too fine a line for any fishing situation in the hope that you will buy more bites that way. There's no point in getting bites if you lose the fish. Check your line carefully after any major battle, especially the last few metres, which take a lot of strain. If you are in any doubt, take the line off and re-spool. Store line away from sunlight and make sure knots are always secure.

Hooks and other terminal tackle

There is a bewildering variety of hooks on display at any good tackle shop, but make sure that the hooks you choose are exactly suited for the purpose in

A near run thing – Look carefully at this photograph. You will see the line is frayed almost to breaking point, and the hook is bent totally out of shape. This is what a big Spanish barbel did to me a few years back. Another couple of minutes and it would have been gone. Nothing highlights more clearly the need for tackle that can stand up to the job.

Squeeze those barbs – A barbed treble hook is always tricky and potentially dangerous to extricate from a fish's mouth. Lose the barbs and you won't lose any more fish.

mind. Supply yourself with a wide range of hook sizes, because you don't know what the successful bait of the day is going to be. It could be a small maggot or a great lump of sausage meat, and it's stupid to be caught short. There are all manner of different hook designs on the market, but the over-riding concerns are strength and sharpness. Don't pursue any fish in a situation where the hook you are using could bend and straighten.

As for sharpness, many hooks these days are chemically etched and keep a point very well. To check that the hook is sharp, just run the point over your nail to see if it makes a slight impression. A bigger issue is whether to go barbless: there's little doubt that a barbless hook is best for the fish, so for that reason I would recommend barbless. Alternatively, go for a micro-barbed hook or simply flatten the barb down on a normal hook with a pair of forceps or small pliers.

Weights and floats

When considering leads and feeders, think carefully about what a swim needs and what will be your best approach. Sound travels extraordinarily clearly through water, and a heavier lead or feeder than is necessary will be heard and felt by fish many metres away. Some leads are silvery coloured and flash in sunlight, and I'd say, as a diver, that it's best to avoid the more garishly coloured swim feeders. Choose both subtle leads and feeders that merge as much into the background as possible.

Choose your floats with equal care. It's a common mistake to use such a light float that you can't control your tackle properly. However, bear in mind that a heavier float automatically creates a heavier disturbance. Think about the size of your float in shallow, clear water. You don't want too much of it under the surface, especially if the fish are wary, and don't make the mistake of thinking a transparent-bodied, plastic float can't be seen.

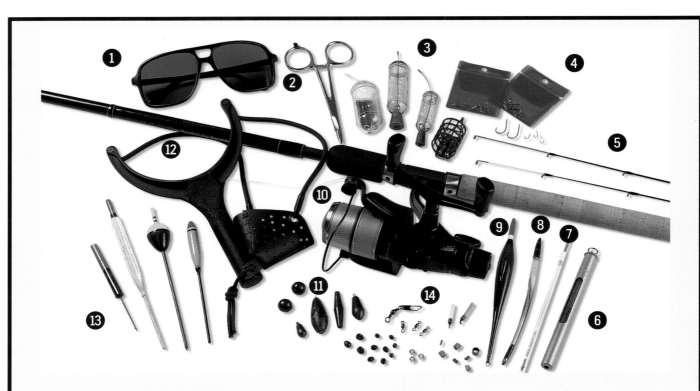

BAIT FISHING EQUIPMENT

1 **Polaroid glasses:** These allow you to see beneath the surface glare.
2 **Forceps:** Use forceps for easy hook removal and flattening hook barbs.
3 **Swim feeders:** A selection of these will suit different waters and conditions.
4 **Hooks**: Always take a selection of hook sizes for different types of bait.
5 **Quiver tips:** These offer good bite indication.
6 **Thermometer:** It's always useful to know the water temperature, and many experts take a thermometer.
7 **Waggler float:** A transparent waggler float for still or slow waters.
8 **Quill float:** This is perfect for close-in fishing on a lake.
9 **Avon type float:** This type of float is for fast water and big baits.
10 **Fixed spool reel:** A modern fixed spool reel – the best of buys.
11 **Leger weights:** A selection of these, including bombs and bullets.
12 **Bait catapult:** This allows you to fire small bait (eg. maggots) far from the bank
13 **River floats:** A selection of river floats, together with a baiting needle.
14 **Terminal tackle:** Shot to weight the line, swivels to prevent the lure twisting, beads and float rubbers are part of the kit.

Long-stay gear

I'm afraid it's beyond me to get into the confusing world of long-stay session accessories. If you look at some brochures, there is a totally staggering array of bivvies, umbrellas, bed-chairs, sleeping bags, cooking equipment, tackle barrows and even bivvy slippers for sale. Once again, my advice is to buy the best you can afford after due consideration. Aim to stick with tried and trusted brands.

TACKLE TIPS

1. Make sure that you always have a white quiver tip with you: it is very much easier to see than a red one, especially in poor light.

2. If you're not getting bites, look very carefully at your hook length. Sometimes, if you have a long hook length and the current is fast, the bait will lift from the bottom and revolve slowly in the flow of water, looking very unnatural. If this is the case, shorten your hook length to just a few inches.

3. Touch legering is the most exciting and efficient way to detect bites. Simply point the rod as directly at the bait as you can, pull the line away from the bottom ring and hold it between your thumb and forefinger. You will find it's easy to hold the rod in one hand and feel for the bites in the other. Strike as soon as you feel a sharp tug or a slow draw on the line. It's almost impossible to put into words the sort of sensation I'm trying to describe, but practice will very soon make you perfect. It sounds almost like magic at first, but it's a method I now use whenever I can.

Ready for the river – A selection of typical and traditional river floats. There is plenty of buoyancy in the bodies, which helps them ride the current and not get pushed under when it's rough.

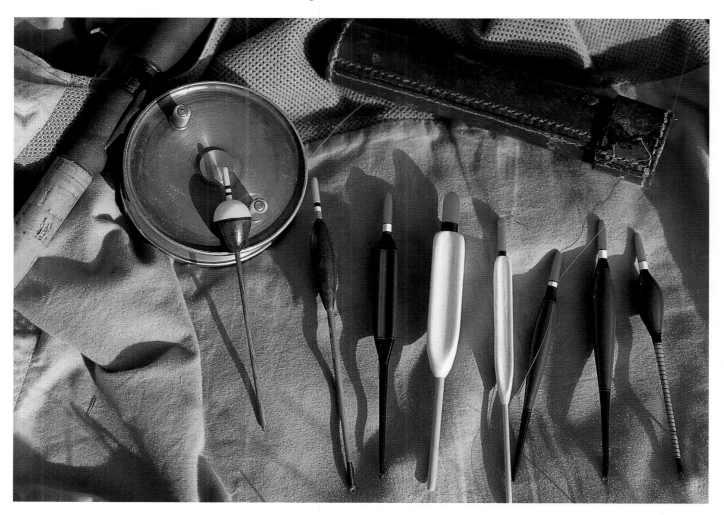

Lure Fishing Tackle

Many people start their lure fishing with an outfit that's adapted from their float-fishing set-up, which is a fine way to begin, but you'll get more pleasure if you use something that is designed for the job. With lure fishing, you will be casting and retrieving all day long, so you don't want a rod that is too heavy, or a reel that is bigger than you really need. The rod and reel need to be matched, and they need to be right for the lures you'll be casting and the fish you're targeting.

Hooked! – No doubt what item the pike fell for! This plug lure was worked close in around an island.

The lure-fishing rod

For really taxing work, say salmon fishing in big, swollen rivers, by all means go for a rod perhaps 11ft in length and capable of casting anything up to 4oz in weight. However, a rod this size takes its toll on the arm muscles, and it makes sense to go much lighter for a lot of spinning. For bass, sea trout, medium-sized pike, most steelhead and perch, rods of 7–8ft are more than adequate, and often a 6-foot rod can give you the thrill of your life. Indeed, I've had some of my best ever fishing with a 5.5ft wand with a casting rating of $\frac{1}{10}$ – $\frac{1}{3}$ oz. Small summer salmon, pike to 15lb, a 4lb sea trout, a black bass just under 5lb – all tremendous, unforgettable stuff.

The North American and Japanese angling markets excel in light, technically advanced rods that are designed for single-handed multiplier use. They're quick, precise and responsive but with real power in the butt. In cramped, overhung conditions, casting accuracy is massively increased with a shorter rod.

Casting reels

As for your reel, most fixed-spool reels will do, providing they are not too heavy. A relatively small fixed-spool reel – one you would probably use for float fishing on stillwaters or swim-feeder fishing on rivers (see pgs 268–269) – will be ideal, providing it can take a 100yd of 8–10lb line. If you are using a

Scottish majesty *– Sarah is lure fishing on a mighty Scottish loch with a very suitable lure-fishing rod. Lure fishing does not come more inspirational.*

light rod, you don't want to use too heavy a reel with it. The whole outfit will feel cumbersome.

If you really want to get into the lure-fishing game – and you certainly should – you will want to check out bait-casting reels. These are simply small, delicate multipliers, but they're ideal for accurate casting and careful retrieve. Most modern bait-casters are cut from one-piece aluminium bar stock and are incredibly strong and light. They retrieve very quickly, perfect for the lure angler who wants to give his or her surface plug a quick spurt. The modern

The lure-fisher's gear *– A light, responsive reel with a delicate clutch mechanism is vital. Note that the rod below has a screw reel attachment for added security during constant casting.*

braking systems mean that over-runs when casting are now almost always a thing of the past. Drag systems are very precise on bait casters, and they can be loosened or tightened with lightning speed – very useful in a battle with a big fish in and around snaggy areas. They also have the ability to work efficiently with both nylon and braid, an important advantage for any lure angler who will probably want to use both lines in different situations. Many modern bait-casters also feature a quick-release thumb bar that disengages the spool and makes for very rapid casting. This is vital when you're fishing shallow, clear water and you see a quickly moving predator.

Always look after your bait casters and keep them well oiled. Take care of them on the bankside, too: never put them down on a sandy beach, for example, lest particles get behind the spool and into the mechanism.

Suitable lines

Braid is very much the line to use with a bait-casting reel. It's very thin for its strength, extraordinarily limp, and it therefore casts like a dream. It seems to have absolutely no disadvantages and will probably be the answer for 90 per cent of your lure fishing. However, under extremely rocky conditions when a fish is expected to fight long and deep, braid can be exposed. Modern braid is tougher than the material on sale just five or ten years ago, yet it still cuts quickly and unexpectedly if rubbed under pressure against a sharp rock edge. Under these sorts of conditions, nylon monofilament can be the material of choice. Modern nylon is much less springy and more durable than it used to be. The strength to diameter ratio is also much improved.

Knots and traces

Whether you are using monofilament or braid, take care with your knots. You will nearly always have a wire trace at the end of your line. Of course, in certain circumstances, the need for a trace is obviated – if you're spinning for salmon, steelhead, trout or black bass, for example, and you are absolutely sure there are no other toothy predators

in the water, wire is not necessary. However, in any water where there may be pike, zander, dorado, tiger fish – anything with teeth capable of cutting braid or monofilament – then, for the fish's sake, you should use a wire trace.

Many shop-bought wire traces tend to be too short. A big pike, for example, can easily engulf a small lure right down to the back of its throat in an instant. A wire trace that is just 15cm (6in) or so in length is absolutely useless in this case. My advice, in nearly all circumstances, is that a wire trace should never be less than 30–38cm (12–15in) long. Also, as with your knots, make sure that all swivels and snap links are 100 per cent up to the job in hand – far too many fish are lost by links, especially, opening out under pressure.

Spinners and spoons

Both of these artificial baits provoke a response from predators, either because the fish are hungry and they mistake the lures for small fish or because they are territorial and are angrily protecting their patch. On a spinner, a vane or a blade always rotates around a central bar as you are retrieving the lure. Some patterns have lifelike plastic worms made of soft rubber attached. This makes the spinners more attractive and also encourages the fish to hang onto

This pikelet has seized a spinner all but its own size. Never underestimate the ferocity of the predator.

Spinners – *The spinning, spoon-shaped blades on these spinner lures create flashes and vibration in the water, which attract predators in from a good distance.*

the lure longer once it has been engulfed. Buzz baits have plastic skirts over their hooks, which imitate swimming crayfish. Spinner baits can go through the most weeded of waters and they are best for searching out fish holed up under lilies or deep down in undergrowth. Flying condoms have taken the world of the salmon angler apart. These lures produce a heavy throbbing action and have proved effective for all manner of species.

Spoons wobble through the water with a slow, erratic motion, making them look like a wounded fish. Spoons can be trolled behind boats, as well as being cast and retrieved, and their weight takes them down to great depths. The action of a spoon in the water often depends on the style of retrieve and, if you vary this, it can give the impression of a wounded or sick fish in distress. It's also possible, if the water isn't too

Spoons – *Spoons have been around for ages, but this traditional lure often works a treat. Notice that these lures are fished with a wire trace.*

snag-ridden, to fish spoons very slowly indeed. Cast them out, let them sink and hit bottom, then twitch the spoons back a metre at a time, letting them grub along the bottom and lie static for anything up to 30 seconds before pulling them on their way again. Working a spoon this way creates a dramatic impact. The bottom suddenly erupts with puffs of silt and the predators see a crippled, silvery shape scuttling along the bottom, looking for cover, seemingly terrified.

Plugs

A plug is simply a wooden or hard plastic lure designed to look and move exactly like a small prey fish. The advantage of plugs is that you can choose one for whichever depth of water you want to explore. There are all sorts of plug designs and

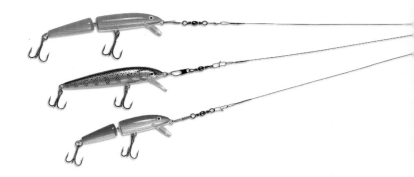

Plugs come in endless sizes, shapes and colours. Some are jointed, some work on the surface, some in mid-water and others, in deep water.

you may find them bewildering at first. However, as a rough guide, it pays to buy a selection along the following lines.

Start with a few shallow divers that work from just under the surface down to 1.8m (6ft) or so – ideal in weedy, summer waters.

Buy a few top-water plugs that work exactly where their name implies, right in the surface film, where they splutter and splash and really cause a commotion.

You will also need a few deep divers that work at depths greater than 6ft and can go down as far as 30ft. These tend to be bigger lures and they're mostly used in deep lakes throughout the northern

This shot of a plug was taken on an autumnal day, when one has to work hard to interest any fish.

actions. It's just like fly fishing: one day only one type of plug will catch anything and the rest of your box will provoke no response whatsoever.

Jerk baits

Jerk baits are the beasts of the lure jungle, and these baits have built up quite a reputation for catching big fish. Most of them float.

If you are going to jerk bait successfully, go for a stiff rod designed for the purpose and a solid leader that will avoid tangles. A braid line helps to ensure that the action you impart through your rod tip is transmitted all the way down to the lure and isn't softened by the stretch of monofilament. Really work the rod tip. Crank down fast to rip the jerk bait deep. Occasionally let everything go still, so that it rises with an enticing wobble.

Your main consideration is the depth of water you will be fishing and the level at which you think the fish are feeding. For this reason, it's important to know the sink rate of every jerk bait in your box. If it's cold and you know the pike are down deep, go for a jerk bait that sinks perhaps a metre per second and can get you down to where you think the fish are lying.

Here we've got an imitation black rubber lizard that is about to be hooked up ready for a bass session. Notice, too, the lead above the hook, which will slide down to the lizard's head and take it right down to the bottom rocks in deep water.

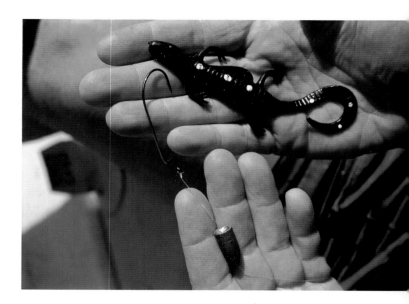

hemisphere. They are especially useful in winter or in very hot weather when the fish go down deep to escape the sun.

Floating plugs that dive when retrieved are very useful, too, because the speed of the retrieve determines how deep they dive and this means that you can explore a wide variety of depths. These are particularly good when fishing close to any sort of structure. The diving action is produced by the angled vane – or lip – that is at the head of the plug.

It's essential to build up a collection of plugs with different colourings, different sizes and different

Notice the heavy lead head on this rubber lure. This will enable you to cast far, to fish deep water and to work heavy currents.

and flashy. When visibility is less than a couple of feet, go for fluorescent, white or the shiniest silver. Sometimes, in very clear water in bright conditions, black lures are the only successful ones.

Fishing the jig

The jig is a simple concept that uses a large, single hook with a lead head moulded around its eye. Then a soft, plastic body is impaled around the hook. The size of the lead head is important, because it determines how deep the jig will work. However, it's the plastic body that is vital. These come in endless combinations of shape, colour, size and action. Some are like snakes, others frogs, others small fish. It's a fantastic world of piscatorial imagination.

A jig is ideal for working along or near to the bottom, and is especially useful when conditions are difficult, perhaps in cold or coloured water when

Think about colours, not just with your jerk baits but with all your lures. If the water is murky, you need to use a plug or jerk bait that is brilliant

Jig-a-jig – A typical selection of plastic lures, often called jigs. They look and feel like natural prey. The weighted head on the hook takes the rubber jig down to the bottom in a fluttering motion and you can twitch it back to the surface. Red is an attractive trigger for most predators.

the fish are reluctant to stir far. Jigs are versatile and you can retrieve them in mid-water, vertically or even trolled behind a boat.

I love rubber crayfish for black bass… let it twitch its way down through the water to the bottom and then pull it back slowly in short, scuttling motions. I love all shad patterns for good-sized pike. Make sure the rubber bodies are tough enough to resist the attention of innumerable sharp teeth, and accept that many a tail is going to be completely nipped off.

Build up a wide selection of body colours. As a rough guide, in clear water, start out with natural patterns such as rainbow or brown trout. If the water is slightly more cloudy, look for patterns that have

stripes or bars. Fire Tiger is a good starter here. If the water is coloured, then contrasting patterns and colours often make an impact. If the water is really clouded, go for vibrant colours and jigs with a really powerful action that send out strong vibrations through the water for the fish to pick up on.

Bear in mind that the deeper the fish, the heavier the lead you will need to keep in contact. Think about currents, which can lessen your contact and make the jig work less effectively. Try jigging vertically if you're in a boat, letting it rise up and flutter back towards the bottom. If your jig is coming back constantly covered in weed, then you're fishing too deep, so use one with a lighter lead head.

HOW A PIKE LOCATES A LURE

A pike has sharp eyesight, especially in decent light and clear water, when it can probably see its prey up to 20yd away, but in low light or muddy water it resorts to vibration and smell for prey location. A moving lure – especially one that rattles – attracts predators by the vibrations that it sends out through the water. These are picked up by sensitive detectors along the fish's lateral line.

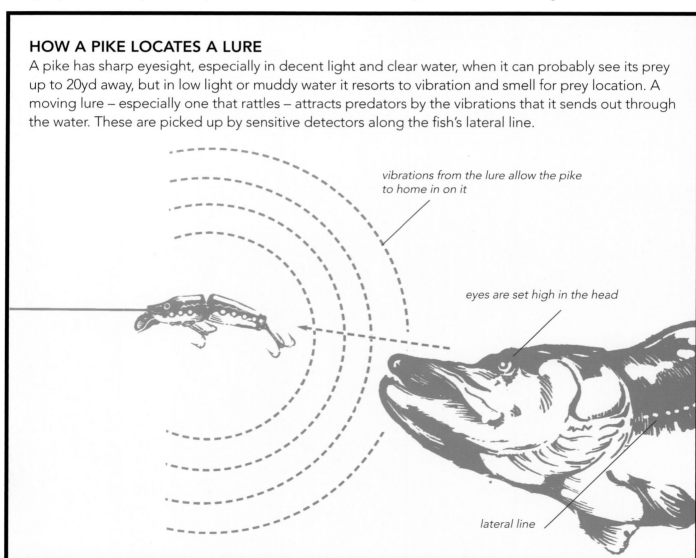

vibrations from the lure allow the pike to home in on it

eyes are set high in the head

lateral line

LURE FISHING EQUIPMENT

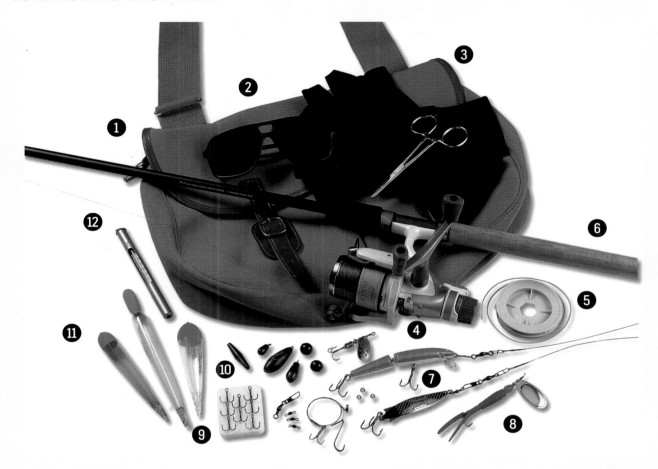

1 Shoulder bag: When you're travelling light, this will carry all your gear.

2 Polaroid glasses: These help you see the fish through the surface glare.

3 Forceps: Forceps are necessary for removing hooks safely and easily.

4 Fixed-spool reel: A fixed-spool reel is essential for trouble-free casting.

5 Trace wire: This is a must for all predators with sharp teeth.

6 Spinning rod: Light and not too long, a good spinning rod should be comfortable and not too tiring on the arm.

7 Plug: A jointed plug gives out good vibrations as it wiggles through the water.

8 Metal spoon: A metal spoon has a good action in the water and catches the light. Note the spoon and plug are attached to wire traces.

9 Treble hooks: A selection of treble hooks for dead baiting.

10 Weights: Useful for taking a lure down deeper in the water, and for anchoring a dead bait on the bottom.

11 Pike floats: A selection of pike floats in various sizes to suit different waters and dead baits.

12 Thermometer: The temperature of the water can be crucial. If it is very cold, then dead baiting is likely to be more successful than a spoon or a plug.

Sea Fishing Gear

Fishing the seas and oceans offers huge possibilities for different angling techniques. The fish themselves can be huge – perhaps a 1,000lb marlin – or they can be small and discriminating, yet still just as exciting to catch. A bonefish, for example, weighing just 3lb, can run off a 100yd of line with ease. A sea bass can pull like a small salmon, and a pollock never knows when it's beaten.

A lovely sea bass next to the plug that was its downfall. Bass like this one, around 5lb in weight, are great opportunistic feeders, combing the shoreline for worms, crabs and any small fish that they can come across. This is why plugs and spinners work so well.

Sea fishing rods

Any sea rod has to be of good quality – the saltwater will test any weakness in the finish or the materials – and must be able to withstand the rough treatment that it's likely to receive.

Boat rods

These are arguably the bruisers of the sea scene. Boat-fishing itself is all about blood, sweat and tears, particularly if you're after big fish deep down in bad weather. Any boat rod has to be tough, of high-quality material and finish, and has to be able to stand up to devastating punishment. However, a boat rod needs to have two subtler characteristics: it has to have power, but it also needs a measure of feel. All power and no give, and you might as well fish with a broomstick. Also, unless the rod has some flexibility, it will reach a point where it can go no further and will simply snap. More and more anglers are using the uptide rod now from a boat. This has a longer casting butt and a longer, softer tip, which helps in casting, bite detection and playing a fish.

Look for good quality rings, screw reel seats, comfortable handles, strong spigots, good quality whipping, top line guides and end rings incorporating large rollers.

Shore rods

Rod designers probably face the biggest number of challenges with shore rods. Today, there are endless

At home on the seas – *John Wolstenholme is an internationally renowned angler from South Africa. In the seas around his home, many dramatic fish species are there to be caught. He wouldn't have been able to catch this impressive marlin without a sturdy rod.*

materials, lengths, tapers, styles and blank designs from which to choose. Each individual shore caster will also have his or her own style of casting and own whims and fancies. Again, look for a rod with comfortable, well-spaced handles and the strongest rings. Make sure that you buy exactly the right shore rod to go with the style of fishing that you will be doing. Think how heavy a rod you need: are you fishing a storm-battered cod beach in the winter or casting for flatties on a gently sloping sand beach in the summer?

Sarah is enjoying this wild landscape of rugged rocks and frothing surf because she has the right rod for the occasion.

Punching it out – Fishing the surf for species like sea bass is a big thrill. An 8-weight outfit is ideal for most conditions.

If you're spinning, normal freshwater gear will generally suffice, but do hose it down after use lest the reel fittings and eyes begin to rust. Also, clean out the spigot joint very carefully to avoid sand and grit getting in there and spoiling the tight fit.

Saltwater fly rods

Increasingly, rod makers are designing purpose-built saltwater fly rods as the numbers of fly anglers hunting fish in saltwater is growing all the time. In general, saltwater fly rods have low-profile blanks to cut through the heavier winds with ease. However, the blanks also have to be strong because fishing in the sea will generally put them under more pressure than fishing in freshwater. Furthermore, it is a good idea to go for at least one large diameter butt ring, if not two. These allow rapid clearance of slack line, which is vital if a bonefish is making for the horizon. Some of the meatier saltwater fly rods offer an additional fighting grip handle with which to play big fish such as tarpon with greater ease. A saltwater-anodized reel fitting will completely eliminate any problems of corrosion.

Rods of 6-, 7- and 8-weights will be ideal for fish up to 20lb or so – bonefish, sea bass, pollock, wrasse, codling, permit and the

like. The 9-, 10- and 12-weight options are necessary for tarpon and the exotic big game species.

Sea fishing reels

As with rods, the emphasis here has to be on quality and strength, but careful cleaning and maintenance will go a long way towards increasing the life and efficiency of a reel that is expected to take the punishment of sea-fishing conditions.

Boat-fishing reels

Just like the rods that go with them, boat-fishing reels have to be tough and expect to have the guts ripped out of them. A boat reel will be expected to haul up heavy fish, often from massive depths and frequently in heavy swells. Virtually always, the reel for this type of work will be a multiplier, and it must be strong and well made, with a large spool capacity. Good gearing is also essential, and this has to be precise, strong and completely reliable.

Shore reels

Shore reels also have to work hard. Once again, the multiplier reel is the strongest option available and helps with really long casting. However, if you are contemplating lighter work, especially light bait-fishing from rocks, piers or groynes, fixed-spool reels will be up to the job. You can also use fixed-spool

Purpose-built saltwater gear like this can pay dividends. You can be confident that the rod fittings won't jam.

The fly and the sea – Saltwater fly-fishing is the most exciting development in fishing today. Rods and reels are being designed that are perfect for the challenges of the tide and the surf.

reels for practically all sea spinning work. Make sure sand and grit doesn't get into the works, and be sure to always wash them down after you use them in order to prevent corrosion.

Fly reels

There are now many saltwater-compatible fly reels on the market, anodized to prevent corrosion. They should also feature sensitive and robust drag systems, as the fighting power of sea fish is frequently extraordinary. Large arbor reels are particularly applicable to saltwater work, as they have the capacity to store at least 300yd of backing.

Lines and rigs

Choose your lines with great care. Make sure they are heavy enough for the job because they will take a severe pounding. Check lines frequently: the wear and tear of fishing over rocks, through heavy weed beds and over sharp sand and gravels takes its toll. Braid might well be an option, but remember, just as in freshwater fishing, it can be suspect in very snaggy conditions.

Choose your hooks and leads carefully, too. With hooks, especially, do make sure they do not corrode or lose their point.

Use your lead! – A selection of sea-fishing leads all designed to hold different types of ground. Some leads hold better on sand, whilst others are designed for shingle, mud or boulders.

Clothing

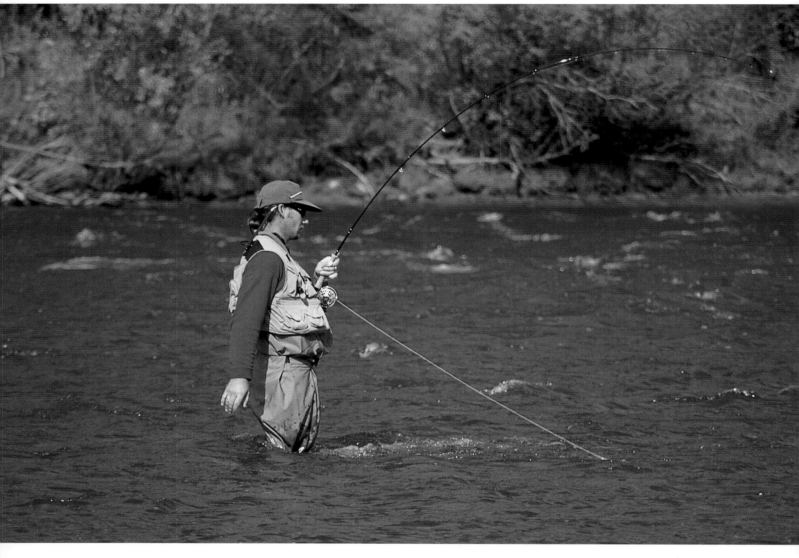

Modern-day angling clothing is light-years ahead of what was available even ten years ago. Modern fabrics and designs have revolutionized life for the angler, whatever his or her discipline. Now there is adequate protection against all weather conditions anywhere in the world. In the past, reliability and efficiency in breathable clothing has come at a high price, but modern technology has allowed great strides forward in efficiency, durability and, importantly, cost. Always buy the best you can afford. Look after it and you will fish through anything the world's weather systems can throw at you in complete comfort.

Equipped for the fight – This angler is dressed for battle with the fish with his chest waders, fishing vest, hat, polaroids and comfortable clothes.

Cold- and wet-weather gear

For the most atrocious weather conditions, you will need an outer shell that is tough, durable, fully breathable and totally waterproof. You will also need a hood system that is adjustable and comfortable to use. A lightweight mesh lining inside the hood makes for a great fit. The lining will also follow the movement of your head, allowing for clear, unobstructed vision.

Also, look out for well-designed pockets – and plenty of them. Reinforced elbows and shoulders are desirable, too, as are hand-warmer pockets and 'D' rings for attaching nets and wading staffs. Full length will be necessary, unless you're wearing chest waders, in which case a short or medium length will suffice.

Savage – John Gilman knows his clothing and laughs at the weather as a result. Notice how well-equipped he is, too, with proper wading gear, including his chest waders and a retractable wading staff.

The layer system

In foul conditions, it is important to wear a base layer system next to your skin. A fully breathable top and trousers provide a vital link between the skin and outer garments, which will keep you dry and comfortable in all temperatures. Look for garments that are thin, warm and lightweight. They should dry quickly and be fast-wicking for maximum transport of moisture away from the skin.

In between, you will need good-quality fleeces. These will double as a top layer in mild conditions and a middle layer in cold months. They should be lined, with interior pockets.

Gear for mild weather

In milder conditions, lighter jackets and trousers can be used. These should still be totally waterproof, windproof, durable and breathable, however. Always ensure that the zips are strong and of good quality

The fishing tailors – My tackle shed proves I have a coat and waders for all occasions!

Test the cuffs for adjustability and ease of movement. Always try clothing on to ensure complete comfort and effortless movement. Practise casting, too, so you know there's no tightness around the armpits or shoulders.

Hot weather gear
Pay special care to blocking out the sun's rays. Never be tempted to fish shirtless, and be careful about fishing for too long in shorts. Many modern, lightweight, quick-drying shirts offer technical sun protection.

Wading gear
Breathable waders are great. However hot the weather is, you can wade and walk long distances in comfort. Even in the cold, you can use them over base-layer thermal pants – just double them up if it's a few degrees below!

Wading staff
If you're going to do any serious wading, I would recommend a wading staff. These give an amazing amount of extra support in a heavy current or if you're moving over an unstable bottom. A wading staff retractor is also vital so that when you reach your fishing point, you can begin to cast unhampered.

Lifejackets
Automatic lifejackets that inflate within seconds of water immersion are also highly recommended.

They are compact, light and also they won't interfere with your freedom of movement.

Useful accessories

Never neglect headwear. Hats will keep you warm in cold conditions, dry in wet ones and will shade you from the sun in the tropics. A brim also cuts out reflected light and works in conjunction with your polarized shades to let you see the entire picture. In many situations around the world, you will need a midge-net hat for warm weather work.

Gloves can really save the day when it's cold and wet. Neoprene is a great material for gloves. Check that cuffs are elasticated for an easy fit. A flip-back forefinger and thumb will help with intricate work. Thermal socks are essential for cold weather work.

Fishing vest

A fly vest is useful for the angler on the move. Most fly vests have enough pockets to cope with the majority of fly-fishing situations. Check that your vest is light, breathable and pleasant to wear all day long. Stretchable, load-bearing shoulders add to the comfort. You will need retractors for tools, and pockets both inside and outside the garment.

Keeping cool on the flats – *Here, under blistering sun, you want clothing that's going to protect you from harmful rays and keep you cool. Nothing tight-fitting, everything quick-drying. Shirts and trousers so light you hardly know you're wearing them. And hats!*

■ CHAPTER 3

FLY FISHING

For hundreds, if not thousands, of years, anglers have been trying to imitate insects with their own creations made of fur, feather or hair. The idea is to convince trout, grayling and salmon – commonly called game fish – that the imitation is the real, living insect.

Introduction to Fly Fishing

I don't think that the fly angler has ever had it so good. There was a time, not long ago, when a salmon rod weighed the best part of 2lb, and even the lighter trout gear was a torment to use. This was not only physically crippling, but also spiritually damaging, for fly fishing is all about grace. It's a sport of whispering lines, of feather-light casts.

You can never spend too much time sussing out the river you are about to fly fish. An aerial position like this allows you to see the riffles, glides and pools with eagle-sharp eyes.

The finest of sports

To put it simply, fly fishing is beautiful: that's why at any game fair you'll find non-anglers watching fly-casting exhibitions with total joy and amazement. Fly fishing is lovely to watch and it's lovely to execute. Think of cricket and a perfectly timed cover drive. Think of the delicately curving free kick as the soccer ball hits the back of the net like an exploding shell, or the perfectly executed golf swing that sends a ball seemingly eternally down the fairway, an athlete rippling cheetah-like over the hurdles, the blur of the baseball bat, or a perfect half volley over the tennis net, down the sideline and away. Fly fishing is all of these things, and the acts of snaking out a 40yd spey cast or flicking a light, tight line under the grabbing fingers of an overhanging tree are real physical joys that you can savour. You don't even need to see a fish to have a wonderful day with a fly rod in your hand – but when you do…

Dreams and memories

As a child, fishing was the source of all my dreams, dreams that I've been privileged to live out as an adult. I can cast my mind back to countless moments of head-spinning delight – and soul-wrenching disappointment – that fly fishing has brought me…

It was in June 1963 that the neb of a great trout engulfed my little blue-winged olive the very instant it settled on the choppy waters of the lake. I'd never, ever known a fight like it. My knees, trembling between my boots and my short trousers, nearly gave out under me, and when the beaten fish went rigid over my pathetically inadequate landing net and finally broke free, I sobbed. The memory still brings tears to my eyes.

It's 1964, I'm beside a flooded Welsh river with salmon everywhere on the move, and a fish porpoises over my fly. Next cast, it takes and the fly line slides mysteriously off into the muddied water. My first salmon is suddenly cartwheeling, cascading out of the pool and down the rapids, with me in pell-mell pursuit, shouting – no, shrieking – for help. Finally, I have him cornered in a tiny rock pool and I cradle him out – I've caught my first salmon, at last.

Steelhead in the snow; bonefish in the baking heat; grayling on a Scottish river when the air is so cold your line freezes in the rings and the spent salmon are dropping back past you, struggling their desperate way to the sea; the mayfly hatch; a sea-trout river at night; the rivers of Kashmir; the lakes of New Zealand – the memories that this sport can bring us are endless.

Blessed guardians

Fly fishing is also, without doubt, the most riveting way to explore and understand the environment. Blending into the waterside, we experience scenes, sights and sounds that most people never will: the kingfishers piping up and down the river; the hunched-up heron in the margins; the cluck of the water hen; the stately white dagger throat of the grebe; the spiralling mayflies, gossamer wings illuminated by the gold of the sunset; the misty valley when the salmon are as steely as the dawn. We experience profound pleasures that other sports people can't even begin to imagine.

We are privileged and we know it, and with the privilege comes responsibility. I wouldn't even begin to preach about collecting litter or shutting gates, because I know such acts are instinctively part of us all, but let's just think about the fish for a moment, a creature so wild, so noble, so beautiful and so graceful and yet so often misunderstood or ignored by the public at large. Do let us bear in mind that although, for us, fishing is the best fun of our lives, it's not so for the fish. Let's ensure that we tread as lightly as possible along our riverbanks and bring compassion and understanding to all we do there.

This bass has just grabbed a deep-fished fly lure.

Food, Feeding and Flies

Around the middle of the 19th century began a great boom in the entomology of fly fishing – the study of the insect species that are of such great interest to the fly angler. There's been a growing focus on the imitative properties of new fly patterns ever since. Of course, to imitate the fish's food you've got to be able to identify it and recognize it first.

This big cock salmon fell to a fly moved very slowly across the current. The colder the water, the deeper big fish like this are likely to be hanging. Wait for a gentle but unmistakable pull before striking.

Real-life identification

To help in the complex task of identifying flies, there have been many scientific tomes published on the subject. These can make for heavy reading, so I'm going to miss out the Latin-quoting, professorial approach and try and get you down to the waterside where, really, everything begins and ends.

Beneath the surface

So, you're standing there, fly rod in hand, tackle in your bag or your vest, looking at a river or a stillwater – and nothing, simply nothing, is rising. What is going on? Surely the fish need to feed? Well, a vast percentage of what fish eat lives down deep amid the security of stones and weed on the bed. The creatures we're talking about include freshwater shrimps, beetles, water fleas, tadpoles, water boatmen, snails of all sorts and, of course, a huge number of nymphs. The nymphs will eventually ascend to the surface, shed their skins and transform into fully matured flies, and trout love to feed on them as they're rising and hatching, as well as on the flies into which they turn.

A lot of the trout's food under the surface comes to them along with the drift of the current. Trout position themselves so they can see clearly what the river is bringing to them. The best lies offer the best views and these are generally taken by the biggest, most aggressive fish. The drift of food isn't constant throughout the day: it increases, obviously, when fly life is particularly active. It also reaches its height during the hours of darkness when many aquatic creatures believe it's safe to move. Take time out to watch how natural foodstuffs behave in the current: it's vital that your own offerings copy these natural foodstuffs as accurately as possible.

Fish, trout especially, don't always rely just on the drift for their food. Sometimes they'll adopt a more workaday, hands-on approach and actually dig for nymphs in weed or among stones. Bass will hunt small crayfish and you'll find bonefish chasing crabs. So, whatever you're fishing for, it often pays to put an imitative pattern right down there on the bottom and work it slowly and tightly. Often takes will be powerful

and unmissable, but frequently you'll just notice a slight tightening or slackening of the line. Strike immediately the moment your suspicions are aroused.

If you adopt this careful, imitative approach then don't be in a hurry to move on. It's likely that you're fishing the nymph in a subtle, difficult-to-spot fashion, and you could make several casts and work an area thoroughly before your fly is spotted.

What a trout sees and what it makes of what it sees we'll never know exactly, but it is instructive to see how unlike the real insect our own artificials inevitably are. One of the major problems always, it seems to me, is the hook itself. A silver hook, so much the norm, frequently catches the light and reflects it in a most unnatural fashion, thereby giving off a warning to the trout.

Try a nymph

So, it doesn't matter that nothing is rising, because now you can try your first choice, which is to fish a nymph deep and retrieve it slowly and thoughtfully.

Don't be too confused by the welter of nymph patterns available – there are simply hundreds. The key is to choose flies that blend in with the surroundings – hence brown, green and black are generally successful – and move them back in a slow and lifelike way.

My favourite nymphs would probably include Pheasant Tails, Montanas, mayfly nymphs, various olives and black spiders. I'd fish one or two of these patterns hard before giving up on them.

Experiment with various depths if necessary, putting on an intermediate or sinking line if you suspect that the fish are down deep because of cold or extreme heat.

There's no magic fly, but there are expert ways of working them. Think how you can impart life and realistic movement. It's a good idea to buy yourself an aquarium – it needn't be very large – and install all manner of aquatic life in it. Spend time just watching how nymphs and underwater insects move – carefully, cautiously, in short erratic bursts. It's these movements that you're trying to imitate when you retrieve your fly through the water.

Imitative alternatives

If your nymph patterns resolutely refuse to work, then you can try imitating the other food sources that I've already mentioned. For example, a chomper fly imitates a *Corixa* (water boatman) accurately. Again, fish it in short quick movements, generally not more than about 3ft beneath the surface. Try various shrimp patterns in pink or green, or even a hog louse imitation, best used on a floating line with a long leader. In summer, trout might well be preoccupied with feeding on water fleas (daphnia), especially on large stillwaters. Huge banks of these tiny creatures drift around close to the surface in duller conditions, but down deep when it's sunny. Small brown flies flecked with red can prove very effective in this situation.

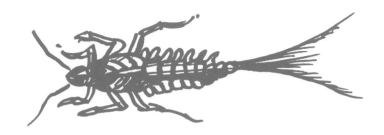

NYMPHS
If you take a sample of stones or weed from the gravel, the chances are that, if it's a fertile water, you'll find scores and scores of nymphs which will live there between six months and two years depending on the species. Eventually, they'll leave the water and hatch, and at this stage they become very active and particularly vulnerable to predators.

DUNS AND SPINNERS
The nymphs finally rise to the surface where they are trapped in the surface film until the wing case splits open and out climbs the winged fly. It's now called a dun and it remains on the surface of the water until its wings are dry. This dun stage can last for just a few minutes or up to several days in the case of mayflies. It will then be transformed again by shedding the skin to become a spinner. Now the fly is ready to mate.

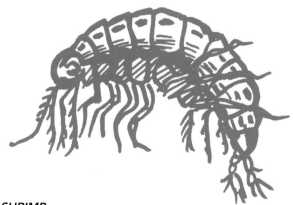

SHRIMP
Freshwater shrimps are found both in still and running water and they are heavily preyed upon. Look for them in shallow, stony, weedy areas. You'll find they're a particularly important food source during the colder months of the season when there's not much fly life about.

Not all flies are imitative, and Tinseltown like this does play its part. 'Flash' flies like this are particularly good for predatory fish or even for trout if they're feeding on fry and fingerlings.

Still nothing doing? Now is the time to use a fish or fry imitation, often rather inaccurately called a lure. The idea here is to strip a fish imitation back quickly, and takes now will be aggressive and hard-hitting. This is an effective way of exploring large areas of water on bigger lakes, where location is a problem. Try flies such as the Muddler Minnow, the White Fry, the Black Fry, the Minky, the Appetizer and the Baby Doll.

Let's suppose that you're beginning to see movements just beneath the surface, often resulting in a boil displacing water. If there's a ripple on, you might suddenly notice flat, calm spots amid the chop. These are caused by trout coming up towards the surface and intercepting nymphs as they rise from the bottom to hatch out. This is the time to make sure that you're fishing a floating line and letting your nymph patterns sink just a foot or so beneath the surface. Move them back slowly towards you. Don't rush, and be ready for subtle takes.

Quite a buzz

Better still, you are now seeing what we call head and tail rises, actually watching the fish move through the surface film. Sometimes you'll see the head followed by the curve of the back. The dorsal fin will frequently be held clear, and sometimes the tip of the tail fin, before the fish goes down. Almost certainly these fish are taking buzzers, and buzzer fishing is as exciting as it gets.

Buzzers are small chironomid larvae that begin life as bloodworms in the silt and mud of the bed. These eventually turn into pupae, often red in colour, which rise to the surface, and here they hatch out into the adult nymph. As the pupa – the buzzer – struggles in the surface film to slough its skin, it's incredibly tempting to the trout. The hatches are prolific, and it can seem that every fish in the lake is feeding in the surface film.

Standard patterns have worked well for years, but the new shiny epoxy buzzers are proving dramatically effective. Fish all buzzer patterns on a floating line so that you can work them either in the surface film or just an inch or two beneath. Let them hang

FLAT-WINGED FLIES

There are thousands of species of flat-winged flies, for example, houseflies, mosquitoes and crane flies. They're characterized by their six legs and their two flat, short wings. Many are land insects, but there are several hundred aquatic species as well. Buzzers or midges are among the most important for the angler. Buzzer fishing can be useful in almost any month of the year.

   The life cycle of the buzzer is egg to larva to pupa to adult. Remember that all these can take on a wide range of colours. For example, the larva can be red, grey or black with virtually any shade in between. Pupa can be orange or black and they can even change colour. The adults too can be many various shades. For this reason, it's a good idea to have different-coloured buzzers in your box. Red and black are the usual favourites, but don't neglect olives, yellows and different shades of green.

   It's probable that on many waters buzzers make up the principal food source of the trout population, so don't overlook them.

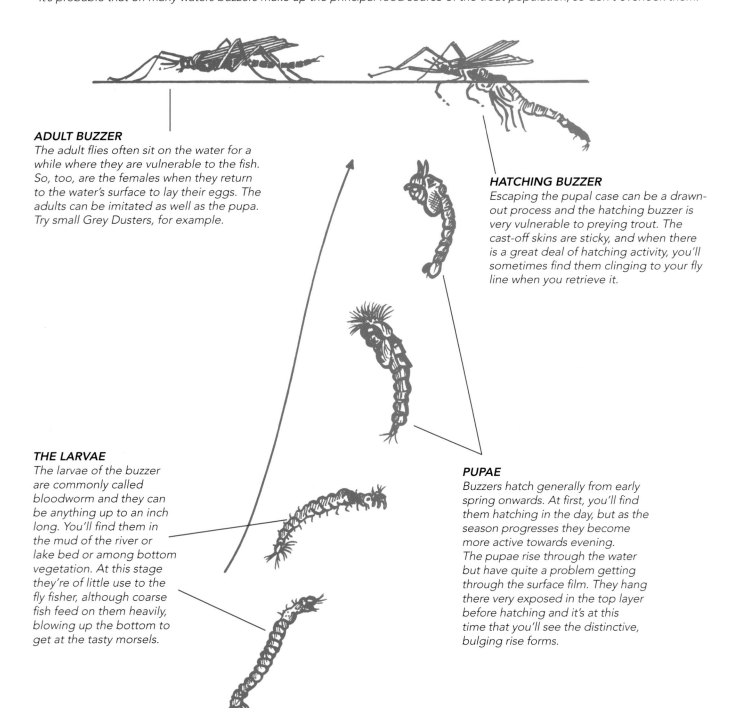

ADULT BUZZER

The adult flies often sit on the water for a while where they are vulnerable to the fish. So, too, are the females when they return to the water's surface to lay their eggs. The adults can be imitated as well as the pupa. Try small Grey Dusters, for example.

HATCHING BUZZER

Escaping the pupal case can be a drawn-out process and the hatching buzzer is very vulnerable to preying trout. The cast-off skins are sticky, and when there is a great deal of hatching activity, you'll sometimes find them clinging to your fly line when you retrieve it.

THE LARVAE

The larvae of the buzzer are commonly called bloodworm and they can be anything up to an inch long. You'll find them in the mud of the river or lake bed or among bottom vegetation. At this stage they're of little use to the fly fisher, although coarse fish feed on them heavily, blowing up the bottom to get at the tasty morsels.

PUPAE

Buzzers hatch generally from early spring onwards. At first, you'll find them hatching in the day, but as the season progresses they become more active towards evening. The pupae rise through the water but have quite a problem getting through the surface film. They hang there very exposed in the top layer before hatching and it's at this time that you'll see the distinctive, bulging rise forms.

Okay, this streamer doesn't look much out of the water, but below the surface its movements are mightily reminiscent of a small, fleeing fish out of its depth in the main flow of the river – an easy target for a hungry predator.

Larger flies, streamers, big lures and salmon flies might not imitate anything exactly but rather give an impression of movement, fluidity and of a ready meal. In short, anything that looks alive and is of edible size is frequently going to be investigated.

motionless, or twitch them slowly back towards you. Watch the path of individual feeding fish and place your buzzer where you predict it's about to arrive.

Other flies make easy targets in and around the surface film as they emerge, so if your buzzer patterns aren't working, or if you see larger flies in the air, try alternative patterns. The Hoppers are excellent, as are Floating Snails, Hares Ears and the various Suspender patterns that are often tied with a little polystyrene ball to keep them hanging in the crucial zone. Fishing the surface film is one of the most productive forms of fly fishing there is.

Moving to the dry fly

Let's say that you're now seeing something altogether more dramatic – a splashing, noisy rise with the trout sometimes leaping clear of the surface altogether. This means that fish are chasing flies that are about to move from the surface and escape. A major hatch is on the boil and this is real guzzle time. You can still fish your nymph, buzzer or other type of emerger with success, but it's now that you can move on to the most exciting kind of fly fishing of all – the dry fly. However, to pick the right one you've got to look carefully at the insects in the air around you.

The mayfly

Perhaps the most obvious of all dry flies are the mayflies that are seen on both rivers and lakes from late spring. These are large, beautiful, up-winged flies, which means that their wings stand proud and look like sails. Mayflies begin their lives down deep, as nymphs, and then ascend to the surface where they hatch into a dull, rather drab dun. These then dry, often in the margins of the river or lake, and transform once more into the fully formed spinner, which mates, lays eggs and then dies. You can't miss mayflies: they are so large, so iridescent and, frequently, so amazingly numerous. The air can seem full of them. The windscreen of your car can be literally coated in the bodies of the spinners as they die. There are endless mayfly patterns; the Green Drake and Grey Wulff are favourites. Take a variety of sizes and colours with you and try to match your artificial with the insects you see in the air or on the surface.

The olive

Throughout the summer and into the autumn you'll frequently see flies looking like the mayfly but only a half or a third as large. These belong to the prolific olive family. Once again, try to match your imitation with the hatch and copy closely the size and colour of the natural. Olive duns are favourite, along with iron-blue duns and large dark olives. Make sure you have Greenwell's Glory and blue-winged olives with you.

UP-WINGED FLIES

Up-winged flies belong to the family Ephemeroptera. There are many different types of insect in the group, but, big or small, they all have sail-like wings and either two or three long tails. Olives and mayflies are the two most important members of the family as far as anglers are concerned and the mayfly is particularly dramatic. These truly are beautiful insects when mature and illuminate rivers and lakes generally from around mid-May to early June. The mayfly season is very short and the adult insects live for only a few hours or days, during which time mating and egg laying are its sole functions.

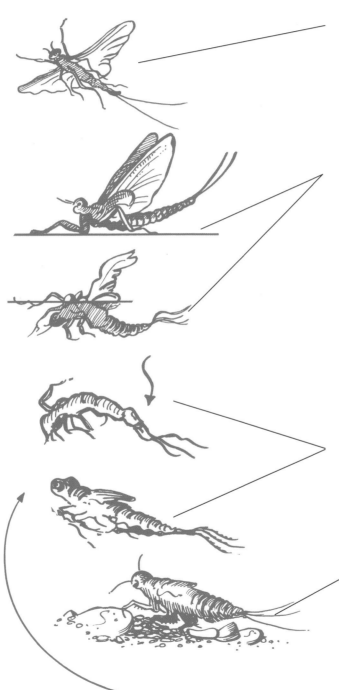

THE SPINNER

The dun then moults again and becomes the shining adult, known to scientists as the imago but to anglers as the spinner. Spinners swarm over the water during May and June, unable to feed because their mouths have degenerated. Mating takes place in flight and the male dies, falls to the surface and is eaten by birds or fish. The female lays her eggs on the water's surface and is now 'spent'. Once again, the body presents a tasty meal for a fish.

THE DUN

At the surface the wing case of the nymph splits open and the winged fly emerges. It's now called a dun and it is forced to remain on the surface film until its wings are dry enough for it to fly. This can take minutes or up to 30 hours, depending on the species of the fly and the weather. Again, the dun is now very vulnerable to trout attack!

THE HATCHING NYMPH

When the nymphs are preparing to hatch they become very restless and often make test runs to the surface and back to the bottom again, an activity that leaves them very vulnerable. Eventually, however, they will rise to the surface for the final time and there they will begin to shed their skin.

THE NYMPH

The nymph of the up-winged fly lives among stones and bottom weed. There are many different sorts of nymph – for example, there are 40 species of mayfly alone. Nymphs vary in size, but they're all eagerly taken by trout, especially when they move around looking for hiding places.

The sedge

Perhaps the flies in the air are sedges. Their larvae (commonly called caddis grubs) build protective cocoons from gravel, sticks, sand or shells, in which they shelter on the bed of the river or lake. The caddis nymphs eventually come to the surface and hatch out looking like reddish-brown moths with two large, forward-pointing antennae. You'll find most sedge hatching out in the afternoons and evenings, and you'll recognize them by their large, roof-like wings, as well as by those antennae. Artificials such as the Goddard, the Caperer, the Cinnamon and the Grouse Wing all imitate sedges.

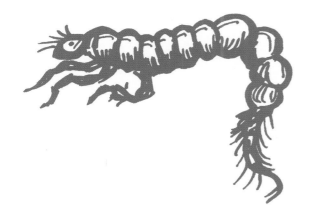

CADDIS LARVA
Virtually all fish species, not just trout and grayling, feed heavily on caddis. These little grubs, which will eventually hatch out into glorious flies, generally form protective cases round themselves of either grains of sand, flakes of gravel or pieces of weed.

ADULT SEDGE
Caddis will then change into the pupa form, which ascends quickly to the surface and hatches out into the adult fly. Here we have the glorious sedge. There are all manner of sedges and they form an important part of the fish's diet through the warmer months of the year. You'll see sedges causing a disturbance on the surface of the water as they scuttle for cover.

The damsel and others

You certainly won't miss a hatch of damselflies, those beautiful creatures with their distinctive electric-blue bodies and wide wingspan. Damselfly nymphs are often more popular with the fish, but the dry damsel pattern is always worth a go. Don't strike too soon at a rise, because trout will often drown the fly before eventually taking it in. Once you've seen the rise, count slowly to three or four before tightening.

Also be aware of what are known as terrestrials – flies that are blown onto the water from the surrounding bankside. These include hawthorns, so called after the bush and flower that these flies really seem to relish. They have black bodies, long trailing black legs and white-coloured wings. Many will be blown into the water on a breeze and feeding can be frenetic. Try a hawthorn pattern on a size 12 hook.

As the summer progresses, you will find more and more crane flies – or daddy-long-legs – blown onto the surface of both rivers and lakes. These are incredibly popular with fish. They are big, prolific and relatively easy for the fish to catch. In the UK, especially, there appear to be fewer and fewer hatching sedges and olives, and daddy-long-legs are increasingly targeted. Don't worry if you don't see any fish feeding on the surface. The crane fly is so big and so desirable that your imitation will often pull them up from many feet down.

In a nutshell

So what are the keys to all this? Firstly, you've got to look at the water carefully. If there's no movement, fish deep. If there is movement just beneath the surface or in the surface film, that's where you've got to fish. If you actually see the full-blooded rise, then is the time to get your dry flies out. Observe what is lifting off the water, decide what manner of fly it is and do your best to imitate it as closely as possible.

This is a rough guide, but its aim is to convince you to use your eyes, have patience and begin to build up a knowledge that will be both satisfying and highly productive.

Fly Casting Techniques

Smooth, accurate and consistent casting is clearly one of the prime skills needed in fly fishing. Beginners often tend to look on fly casting as some sort of secret, hidden art, but it's not like that at all. The basic cast is easy to learn in just an hour or two. Although I've written about fly casting on many occasions and I've taught hundreds of anglers to put out a reasonably decent line, I'm indebted in this chapter to Michael Evans, a great friend and a full-time professional fly-fishing instructor, for his advice.

I love this shot of Misty Dhillon putting out a long line on a Himalayan stream at dawn. What is particularly impressive is how Misty gets his line to turn over so well even though he is using flies the weight of a small bird! Perfect timing and perfect technique in action.

A master fly-caster

Watching Michael perform is a revelation. It's hard to put into words exactly what makes Michael so superior, so poised and so supremely good to watch. Part of the mixture is certainly athleticism – his footing and how he shapes his body. There is a certain amount of power involved, true, but most of the energy comes not from brute force but from timing and technique. Michael can make a line arrow out like few others, and he obviously takes a very physical pleasure in putting out a perfect cast. In Michael's hands, casting becomes a goal and an objective in itself. Fishing, or at least the catching of fish, is a secondary consideration altogether. It's almost like clay-pigeon shooting in a way: there doesn't have to be a flesh and blood product at the end of the day to make a field sport well worthwhile.

Basic fly-casting

The first principle to take on board is that the rod must do the work, not you! Hold the rod and pretend that you want to flick a piece of mud off the tip. The flex of the rod is the action you want, not a gradual pushing movement. The line has to follow the path the rod top takes and the top of your rod follows the path of your thumb. The rod merely amplifies the movement of your hand, so always watch your thumb when correcting faults.

The first hurdle, and the hardest thing you will ever do, is to learn to get the line out. As your experience builds up, you will learn to false cast and shoot line but, for now, if you're starting on water, you must make do with first pulling 2 or 3 yards of line, plus your leader, out of the tip ring of the rod and dropping it onto the water in front of you. Then, by wiggling the rod tip from side to side, you can drag more out through the rod tip as you pull it off the reel. You need about 10 yards of free line in all, which by now will look like a plate of spaghetti on the water in front of you. Don't panic. This is what you want.

The roll cast

Now you need to learn the basic roll cast before any other, because however strong the urge may be to go

Michael Evans is pictured here demonstrating his mastery of the spey cast. If you ask Michael what the secret is to his casting success it would probably boil down to the two 'T's – Timing and Technique. Everything Michael does looks totally unhurried, unflustered and completely controlled. This is partly innate ability but, like any champion caster, Michael practises extensively.

straight to the overhead cast, which is the main one in the trout-fisher's armoury, you must not attempt to overhead cast a badly crooked line off the water.

The roll cast, therefore, is the first essential, as you can use it to straighten an untidy line before moving to an overhead cast. It also has other uses. You can use it as a cast in its own right when you have no room for a back cast, you can use it for safety when casting from a boat in a high wind and you can use it to get a sunk line out of the water.

The basic movements of the roll cast are lift, sweep and hit (see diagram on pg. 77). The lift starts with the rod tip touching the water. You then lift it slowly but smoothly up to the 11 o'clock position (12 o'clock would be vertical) and pause. This should bring the line nearest the rod top off the water with the rest feathering along the surface towards you.

Now we move to the sweep. Presuming you're casting with the right hand, swing the rod tip out to the right of you and sweep smoothly back in a wide arc round and up until your thumb is level with your right ear and the rod is pointing back to 2 o'clock. Pause again. At this point your wrist should have cocked back and the position of the rod should allow a loop of line to form behind your shoulder, curving down to the water beside you and looking much like the letter 'D'.

Now for the hit. Remember the flicking movement we discussed at the beginning. Drive your thumb forwards in a flicking movement as if you were swatting a fly on the wall just in front of you. Aim straight at the target, if you are using the roll cast to reach a fish, and stop sharply again at 10 o'clock in front of you. This should literally flick the line off the water and roll it through the air towards the target. The line should land in a straight line out in front.

Fishing is about poise and grace, but there are times when you've really got to make your body work. Here, Charles Jardine is really straining to hit into a fish that has sipped in a nymph at some range. It's imperative that he tightens as quickly and as strongly as he can or the opportunity will be missed. It's a lightning quick, almost balletic movement, and he is rewarded with the solid thump of a hooked fish. Calm and cool a good fly angler should be… but not always!

The overhead cast

As I have said, this is the main cast in the trout-fisher's armoury, and you must learn it before going fishing. The roll cast will get about 10 yards of line out straight in front of you, and this means that you've got enough line to play with to learn the overhead cast properly.

The overhead cast is essentially made up of three basic movements – a lift, a back cast and a forward cast (see pg. 77). Every cast you make depends upon the success of all three stages, and the key positions you should look for at each stage can be best summarized in three words. Tip. Top. Ten. Let's run through them.

Additional tips

Once you've learnt the overhead cast, you can consider elaborations such as the single and double hauls (see pg. 78). These are primarily to get distance

or to increase line speed to combat wind. Hauling is a technique where the non-casting hand tugs at the spare line being held between the butt ring and reel to increase the momentum and therefore the loading of the rod spring on the forward and/or back cast.

When casting, always grip the rod handle very gently with the thumb on top of the cork as if you were shaking hands with it.

If you are right-handed, you will make fewer mistakes if you start casting with the right foot slightly forwards.

If you're having trouble with your overhead casting, the cause may very well be what instructors call breaking the wrist, that is allowing your wrist to cock back at the top of your cast. To correct this fault, try tucking the butt of the rod inside your coat cuff. Although it feels awkward, this prevents the rod breaking too far back and will improve your casting.

Curved and slack line casts are designed to create 'mends' or to put slack into the line on the water to overcome drag, and they're normally only necessary when using a dry fly on rivers. The secret is to make sure you don't make any of the additional movements until after the power has been put into the line on the forward cast and the rod has reached the 10 o'clock forward position.

This is a photograph of a fly-casting demonstration by expert angler Bob Glynn. Notice the straightness and rigidity of the wrist. Notice how the handle is held and how the rod is pointed at the exact target where Bob wants to land his fly. Most casting instructors would agree that it's important to keep the wrist rigid on the cast and not to let it break, especially when the back cast is taking place.

The spey cast

Let's now look at salmon fishing and the spey cast. There's no magic about a spey cast, and in simple terms it's merely a speeded up roll cast, which you can now already do. Spey casts have several advantages over the overhead cast. They are more efficient for wide-angle direction changes. They can be carried out in places with little or no room for a back cast. They are also a lot safer because the fly never goes behind the caster. You only need to be clouted in the back of the head once by a 2-inch brass tube travelling at full speed to understand the benefits. Although it is almost impossible to learn the spey cast from a book, let me attempt to explain the principles. Let's concentrate on the single spey and the double spey. The choice of which to use depends solely upon the wind direction.

With an upstream wind, the single spey (see pg. 78) is used because the fly and loop are swept

Ken Whelan, that doyenne of Irish fly fisherman, has put out a light line on a small river for summer grilse. Notice now how he's flicking the rod tip in a left-to-right circular movement so that the line is lifted and looped back across the current. This will give him valuable seconds during which time the line will not be affected by the current and the fly will not, therefore, be pulled unnaturally off its course. Successful fly fishing is as much a matter of mental effort as physical prowess.

upstream before hitting out to the target. If it's a downstream wind, you'll need the double spey cast (see pg. 79) where the fly and loop are kept downstream prior to hitting out to the target.

Which bank you are on will dictate which hand is uppermost on the rod. You will need to be able to cast either way round and it's no more difficult to cast from either shoulder as long as you remember to use equal force from both hands.

The single spey

If you're fishing from the left bank, your right hand is up. If you're on the right bank, your left hand is up.

Stand facing square onto the target. Leave the rod pointing downstream at the fished-out line with the tip of the rod at the waterline. To do this, your hands will be rather awkwardly crossed with the rod across your stomach.

Now, to waltz time, LIFT. Raise the rod by bending your upper forearm at the elbow slightly towards the near bank. Aim for about 10 o'clock on your rod clock. Pause for the count of three and now move into the SWEEP. Turn right with your upper hand and sweep away out and round an imaginary plate sitting on your right shoulder until your right thumb comes round to the side of your right shoulder and up to a position level with your right ear. Pause again for the count of three. This movement should have swept the line and fly upstream so that at least 3yd of line and the leader splash down approximately a rod-and-a-half's length away from you upstream. The 'D' loop formed behind the rod is facing the target.

Now for the HIT. Punch the rod smartly forward, stopping sharply at 10 o'clock in front of you, flicking the loop of line out, across and above the water. This is a wrist and forearm flick with both hands to flex the rod – it is not a shoulder heave.

The double spey

Now for the single spey's big brother. On the left bank, your left hand is up; on the right bank, your right hand. The double spey has just one extra movement to the single spey, but the double spey with a short line is easier than the single spey because the timing is less critical.

If you are standing on the right bank with a good downstream wind you must again face the target, but leave the rod pointing at the fished-out line downstream. With the rod across your stomach and your right hand uppermost, your hands will not be crossed.

Tow some line upstream. Lift just slightly and tow the rod top upstream until your hands are crossed over as they were for the single spey. This will bring enough line upstream to form the loop, but will leave the fly still downstream of you. That's vital.

Now LIFT. As with the single spey, lift up to the 10 o'clock position and slightly in towards the nearside bank upstream. Again, pause for the count of two and three.

Now SWEEP. As with the single spey, sweep out, around (that is, back downstream) and lift back up to level with your right ear. As you do this, the line will peel back down and round before forming the 'D' loop behind the rod just off your downstream shoulder. The foot of the loop and the fly and leader will be anchored in the water. Pause again for the count of three. Now HIT. Drive the loop out with the movement you learned with the single spey.

After you've learned these two basic casts you'll be ready for the snake roll, which is probably best taught by an instructor. Only use a snake roll if there's a downstream wind, or it can be dangerous.

Additional physical skills

Casting sounds difficult, and it can look difficult, but it's not a magician's art. Try it on your own at first, but do get professional advice after a while to iron out any faults that you may be building into your action.

Casting, however, isn't the only physical skill to be used in fly fishing. General physical fitness can be very useful if you're fishing wild streams and you want to walk a fair way. Acute eyesight is really important, too. You should be able to recognize hatching insects, and it's essential that you're able to see your small, floating dry fly in low light conditions, so if your naked eye isn't up to it, get spectacles!

Hand-to-eye coordination is also an important part of the fly-fishing game. You need to time so many things in fly fishing – all aspects of the cast, as well as actually striking the fish when you have a take. Playing a big fish is also a skill that you will gradually learn. There's a good halfway house between bullying a fish and being too weak with it, and if you know the strength of your tackle and you're confident with it you can put a surprising amount of pressure on any fish. Don't let the fish dictate what goes on.

A question of attitude

When it comes to mental attitudes perhaps from the outset I should emphasize enjoyment. Don't be afraid of the seeming complexities of casting. Although there are over 30 casts to master, these shouldn't be regarded as intimidating but as pleasing challenges to meet head on. The same applies to fly recognition – you don't need a degree in natural history, just eyes, a textbook and some common sense. Fishing is fun, so keep it that way…

… which leads me immediately on to the philosophy of acceptance. Sometimes you'll succeed and sometimes you'll fail. If you fail, try calmly to work out why and accept blanks as part of the overall fun of the sport. Don't set yourself impossible targets and make a rod for your own back. Don't demand to be king of the river each and every day, because you'll be setting yourself up for endless disappointments. Learn to enjoy the successes of others around you just as much as your own. That way, every single fish that's caught will be a bonus, and your companions will rejoice for you, genuinely, when you have your great times.

None of us is fishing for survival, so you needn't be greedy for fish. Catch a fish or two by all means, but don't terrorize the water. If the fishery you are on is totally wild, then tread even more lightly along it. Wild fisheries are always lightly stocked, and they can be destroyed if anglers show a grasping attitude.

Ian Miller is seen here fishing a Canadian river in autumn for big salmon. What is interesting is the fact that he is using a traditional single-handed eight-weight fly rod rather than the more common double-hander that you'd find in the UK. This lighter approach is particularly applicable if you're wading deep and if the salmon are very spooky.

Take in everything that's happening around you on a fishing trip. This isn't pious nonsense, it's the true to way to stay in the game for the rest of your life. Observe and appreciate wildlife: it can be absolutely spectacular, especially on our wilder waters. Speak to your guides. Listen to the murmur of the water over the shallows. Enjoy the freedom of the riverbank away from the office. Marvel at the beauty of the fish lying in the water beneath you.

Be bold and imaginative. Think of new techniques and new fly patterns… fly tying is a skill that I can't even begin to go into here, but it's an art form all of it's own, and one you might care to take up as your passion develops. Read widely, and I don't just mean the instructional stuff. There is an enormously rich literature of fly fishing that goes back decades, and

it can be so rewarding if you delve deeply into it. Relish the passion of those who have gone before, and aspire to become not just a more successful angler but, in all ways, truly a better one.

Winning the battle

You've done all your homework, the fish has taken your fly and it's a good one. In fact, it's so big and so powerful that your heart is in your mouth, the blood is pounding through your temples, your knees are beginning to shake and your mouth is going dry. How do you ensure that you're triumphant and that your hopes don't melt like snowflakes in the sea?

- First, try to avoid being seen by the fish. Very many big fish of all species will not immediately realize there is danger on first being hooked. Once they see the angler, or the angler's boat, then the fireworks really begin.

- It's particularly important to remain as inconspicuous as possible when it comes to the final landing stage of the battle. It's surprising how many fish can summon up energy for a last charge. A tired hook hold or a frayed line might just give at this last moment.

PROBLEM SOLVING

Despite everything, your casting is not really progressing as you'd like. Let's have a look at some possible solutions.

1. Are you sure your rod and line are matched? It's no good using a heavy rod with a light line, or vice versa.

2. Is your back cast working properly? Are you letting it open out nicely behind you so that it's straight and level before you begin your forward cast? If you're letting that back cast droop and fall toward the ground then you're in trouble.

3. Is the line travelling with enough speed? Don't be frightened of the whole process – attack the job with vim and vigour! Of course it is possible to overdo this, but it's better to err on the positive side than the negative.

4. It could be that your fly is simply too heavy to cast successfully. Very big lures do demand special casting techniques. It's far better to start off with a small nymph tied on a size 14 or 16 hook.

5. Are you trying to push your fly into too strong a wind? If there is much wind, it's easier to have the wind behind you. If it's blowing straight into your face, then even an expert will have problems. It is best to go out the first few times in conditions that are as calm as possible.

6. Is your leader too long? In certain specialized conditions, it's a good idea to have a long leader, but when you're beginning, don't tie one up that is longer than your rod. For example, if you're using a 9-foot rod, then an 8- or 9-foot leader is about right.

7. Are you being too ambitious, making too many false casts and trying to get out just a few too many yards of line? At first, style and technique are more important than distance. Providing your casting is tight and neat, it doesn't really matter if you are getting out 7 or 17 yards of line. It's better to concentrate on good short casting to start with rather than going for wild, long casts that are probably landing noisily and scaring fish away. You will find that your distance builds up gradually the more times you go out.

8. It could be that your fly line is sticky for some reason. Strip it off the reel and give it a good wash in warm, slightly soapy water. You'll be surprised at how much dirt and grit comes off. Once clean, you will find that your line slides much more easily through the rings.

- Always keep calm and don't panic. If you lose your head you will lose your fish.
- If a big fish is close to danger, say rapids or a weir pool, try 'walking' the fish. To do this, you simply hold the rod at right angles to the river and walk smoothly, slowly and steadily upriver. The chances are that the fish, puzzled, will follow and you will be able to lead it out of danger.
- With a running fish, if it's a big one, you simply have to let it go – though hopefully not over the tail of a pool into rough water where there's always a chance of the line getting caught round rocks.
- Make a fish work for every yard of line that it takes from you by putting on the maximum pressure that your tackle will stand. Exert this pressure by tightening down the clutch of your reel or simply slowing the revolving drum with the palm of your hand. In extreme cases, a glove will avoid burning.
- It's vital to know when and how to put the pressure on a fish. During a run you will begin to sense that the fish is slowing down and tiring. At this point begin to increase the pressure noticeably. Hopefully the fish will come to a dead stop. It might rise in the water and even splash on the surface – a dangerous moment this and one to be avoided by keeping the rod low, perhaps even parallel to the water.
- You must know pretty accurately what your tackle will withstand in terms of pressure and you mustn't be afraid to go to the limits. It's usual to see timid anglers playing fish with rods only half bent. The length of the battle will be increased enormously to the detriment of the fish's health. A weak hook hold is also much more likely to give. Be confident in your tackle and really go for it in the fight. Never let a fish dominate you.
- A serious problem is a big fish that settles out in mid-stream where the water is quick and deep. It can settle and clamp itself so firmly that you might think that the fish has gone and you are hooked to the bottom. This is very probably not the case, and once you feel the dullest kick you will know that you are still hooked in. Now you must begin to pump. Take hold of the rod, up from the butt round the first eye. Pull gently but firmly upwards. As soon as your rod is vertical, or even a little over your shoulder, wind in quickly as you lower the tip towards the water. Repeat this process as often as you can and you will find that the fish gently moves towards you, hardly aware of what's going on. Pumping is one of the most vital arts in landing a big fish, so learn it and practise it with confidence.
- Always be aware. Keep your eyes wide open during the fight and don't develop tunnel vision. Keep looking around, looking for potential snags that could prove dangerous in the later stages of the fight. Be aware of patches of slack water where you might position a boat or try to lead a fish into. Be aware of any possible sandy, shelving landing areas that you can make for when the fight looks to be coming to an end.
- Let's suppose a fish is hooked and you've got line hanging loose round your feet. Let the flowing line run through your fingers, but remember to exert pressure on the fish as it does so. Always make sure that line hanging loose during the retrieve doesn't snag round bankside vegetation or your own clothing. If this happens a quick-running fish will pull the line tight and you won't be able to give it any extra.
- Keeping your line free is particularly important on a boat, when fishing for bonefish for example. Keep your decks clean of clutter so there's nothing to foul the line.
- If a fish becomes seemingly irretrievably weeded, hand lining can often work. Reel in until everything is tight and point the rod as directly as possible to where the fish is snagged. Now get hold of the line between the reel and the first rod ring and pull it backwards and forwards in a sawing motion. You will find this exerts far more pressure on the snagged fish than the rod itself can muster. What you'll often find is that the fish in a big blanket of weed begins to come towards you slowly.

- If a river fish is snagged in weed don't try to pull it upstream. Instead, get downstream of the fish and pull in the direction of the current.
- When you are landing a fish, never net it and remove it from the water if it's going to be released. Instead, draw it into the shallowest of margins and kneel down beside it. Slip the hook free with forceps and guide it back to deeper water once it has recovered its strength. If a fish is to be killed, then do the job neatly and cleanly and precisely with the right tool and don't rummage around for a rock!
- Finally, always make sure that you are using the right strength tackle for the job. There's no point putting hooks into fish that you know you're never going to be able to land. Also, if you have any doubts about your leaders, your hooks or your knots, then replace or retie immediately. It's essential that you have absolute confidence in your tackle.

Remaining vigilant to the end – It's at moments like these, when you think the battle is almost done, that you've got to be particularly careful, especially in crystal clear water. Many game fish will discover a last burst of frenetic energy when they see the angler and his guide towering above them. The trick is to keep the rod high and make sure the fingers or the reel can give line in an instant. My good friend Ian Miller proves that his English fly fishing techniques work just as well on the mighty mahseer that grace the rivers of the Himalaya.

Dry Fly Tactics

It's late afternoon. The stream is placid and a big trout is rising steadily on the fringes of a willow tree. A dry fly is tied on the tippet, and the current takes it down towards the surface-skimming branches. A wagtail hovers dangerously close, but then the big, black neb of the trout breaks the water. The line is tight, the rod hoops and the reel screams.

Howard Croston has walked a long way into a mountainous area to fish this clear-water stream. He's working his nymph close to the aquatic vegetation, confident that big, shy fish are lurking nearby.

❶ Run of fast white water
Better for nymph or wet-fly fishing, or for using small dry flies fished close in.

❷ Deeper, slower pools
These will often need a bigger fly pattern to draw fish up from 10–15 ft down. Fish these slowly and let the fly drift in the eddies and surface film.

❸ Steady runs
Three- to five-feet deep over gravel and sand. This is perfect dry-fly water.

Visual excitement

No wonder the dry fly is the world's favourite tactic. Dry-fly fishing is the most visual of all river fishing, and provides a mixture of both efficiency and excitement. There are several variations on the dry-fly theme and most are based on a single fly cast upstream or, on occasion, if rules allow, downstream.

Choosing a pattern

Whereas fish can be fairly relaxed over patterns of nymph, they are frequently much more picky when it comes to the taking of a dry fly. 'Match the hatch' is an adage as old as fly fishing itself, but that doesn't mean it's lost its relevance. When choosing a pattern, you just have to look at the naturals that the fish are feeding on. It's important to match your artificial to the natural in three important areas: shape, size and shade.

Many patterns of fly are broadly generic and can suggest many things to a feeding trout. Quite what

the fish sees and why they reject one fly but accept another will always remain something of a mystery. Moreover, it's not just the choice of your fly that is so vital – presentation is at least as important. As a general guide, always carry a selection of Adams, in both standard and parachute dressings in a range of sizes, along with CDCs, olives, sedge patterns and, in the months of May and June, mayflies.

Using floatant

Floatant will keep the fly perky on the surface. Rather than smearing floatant on the whole fly, put it on your fingers first and then apply to the part of the fly that you wish to float. This will improve presentation immensely, and also helps to degrease the leader. A floating tippet can drastically reduce the number of takes you'll get when fishing the dry fly. Degreasing ensures that the leader tip sinks, making it much less obvious. Talking of leaders, it's worth the extra expense to buy one that is tapered. This ensures the accurate casting and good turnover of the fly that are both so important when fishing dries. Get everything right, and you'll substantially improve your catch rate.

The upstream dry fly

Upstream dry-fly fishing is considered the standard approach to rising fish and, on many rivers, is the absolute rule. Always approach from behind the fish, to ensure that you remain concealed in the fish's blind spot. Its cone of vision does not extend directly behind the head, so, providing you move your feet quietly, you can approach undetected. On crystal streams, this is even more important because you need to get into casting range before the fish is aware of your presence.

When fishing the upstream dry, you can achieve a realistic, drag-free drift quite easily as the fly line will drift towards you with the current. What's vital, however, is to retrieve the slack line at the same speed as the drift of the fly.

The first rule is to make your cast so that the line lands 3–4ft upstream of the target. When rising, a fish will often drift back on the current to intercept the fly and then return upstream to its habitual lie. Casting too short will meant the fly lands behind the fish's chosen position.

As the fly drifts downriver, track its drift with the rod tip while retrieving slack line and slightly lifting the rod tip. You can mend the line again if you need, to extend the drift further. All this makes the fly look unattached to the line – an essential factor in this method.

When the fly is past the fish's position, make a roll pick-up and quietly lift the fly off the water. Don't bother letting the fly drift for more than a few feet past the fish as it's a waste of fishing time. Recast gently, and try the fish at least a few times more.

The downstream dry fly

This is a somewhat underused tactic, but you must check the rules of the water being fished first. If allowed, the downstream dry can be one of the few

Early summer in the northern hemisphere sees the mayfly hatch, a thrilling phenomenon. Mayflies are big and beautiful, and trout just adore them. Yet despite their size they can be hard to imitate, and there are many patterns to choose from. Perhaps the most important consideration is the presentation.

ways of approaching that hard-to-reach fish. With this method, the fish sees the fly first but can't see the tippet until it is too late. Downstream dry-fly fishing also allows you to drift the fly in the dead centre of any fish's feeding lane without lining or scaring the fish. On very heavily pressured water this can be the only method that will produce results – even though you rarely get more than a single chance.

Preparation

Stand well back from the water when fishing downstream. The vision of the fish is much better in front than behind, and you'll be spotted much sooner. Carefully check the length of the cast needed. If you are going to wade, before you enter the water and cast to the fish, mark its position in relation to a prominent object such as a rock or a bush.

Now you're in the water and know where the fish is lying. Make your first false cast off to one side of the fish while you judge the cast length and the angle. False casting over the fish itself will cause it to spook. What you're doing is preparing that perfect first cast, which is by far the most likely to be taken. Next, make your presentation cast high over the target and then stall it to create lots of slack in the line. This gives you the drag-free drift that you're want. To perfect this, practise as often as possible. The first cast must count.

The fly and line are now in the water and you have to ensure that the fly reaches the fish first. Control of slack line is the key to downstream dry fly fishing. If you give too little line, the fly never reaches the target. Too much line leads to disturbance on the water and so much slack that setting the hook is difficult. If you've judged the cast accurately, the line should just be starting to straighten as the fly arrives at the target. You will only get this one window of opportunity, so make the absolute best use of it.

Highland magic – *It's late afternoon in the highlands. There's a good wind blowing insects off the moorland. This is the time to try a floating line blowing along with a large imitation bouncing on the surface – something like a daddy-long-legs pattern is ideal. Keep moving after every two or three casts until you find a different fish.*

IMPORTANT POINTS TO REMEMBER

- With all dry fly tactics, keen observation of the fish and insect life is essential. Don't rush to tie on any fly, but consider each and every rising fish carefully. What is it feeding on? Where is its preferred lie? Where is it taking food? Where are you going to position yourself for the cast? Where should the line and the fly land? What bankside cover can you use? How close do you need to get to the fish? Once the fish is hooked, are there any dangerous snags that could spell ruin?

- When you are upstreaming, try to land your cast 1–1.2m (3–4ft) from the target. Allow the fly to travel slightly to either side of the head of the fish. Aim for no more distance than 6in from its head. If your line goes over the fish, you will simply scare it.

- As with every fishing method, there are variations on the technique. Sometimes, it's good to use a pair of dries. One is tied directly by a short length of nylon – 30cm (12in) or so – from the bend of another, generally larger, fly. This technique helps you spot rises to a tiny dry that may otherwise be almost impossible to see, especially in low light. You can even hang a small nymph off a big dry using the dry as a perfect sight indicator that can often attract a fish itself.

- Absolute accuracy is one of the major keys to successful dry-fly fishing. A few hours spent casting at targets on the lawn at home will lead to many more hooked fish on the river. You are never so expert that practice won't make a difference.

Dry Fly Fishing in Action

There's a river anything between a couple of metres and 18m (20yd) across. It's clear, with deep pools and shallow ripples, and the day is sunny with patchy cloud. Brown trout are the quarry. They're probably wild, but even if some have been stocked, they're still very alert and not easy to fool. So, before anything, watch your approach. Once you're close to the river, stop, look and listen. Alarmed fish don't always flee. They might just sink to the bottom and stay quiet for half an hour. Just because you can see fish doesn't mean to say that you haven't spooked them.

This angler is tackling a stretch of quick water, which can often pose problems. Look at how he holds his rod high, and how he maintains contact with his fly.

Look for clues

Before you start, stand and watch from a spot where you can observe a lot of the river, such as a bridge or a bend. Look for cobwebs on that bridge and see what the spiders have been catching over the last 24 hours. You'll probably find sedges, midges and a host of other flies. See if you can find similar in your fly box. Look in the fields around you. If the pasture is dominated by sheep, the dung flies will be black. If cows abound, those same dung flies will be coloured brown. That gives you a clue to the sort of colouring your imitations should follow.

Watch the insects hatch around you. Look for the duns emerging into the spinners with their long tails. Try to catch them in your hands or in a net for a closer look and a comparison, again, with what you've got in your box. Different styles of egg-laying can help in fly recognition. For example, blue-winged olives migrate upstream in clouds at walking speed. They're heading for specific areas that attract a huge proportion of the flies in any given area. Mossy areas are particularly attractive to olives. The fish will follow flies a good half a mile upstream to egg-laying spots such as this. Wild browns, especially, seem to know instinctively where to find them. Mayflies, on the other hand, are more like bombers when it comes to laying their eggs. Their nymphs can burrow into almost any riverbed material and thrive there, making the adults much less specific when choosing egg-laying territory. All these signs give you a clue as to what the trout will be feeding on.

Watch the trout

Non-feeding fish will show an almost total lack of movement, lying doggo on the bottom. You might have scared them, as I've said before, but more likely they're just not interested. Heavily feeding fish will take up to 10 insects a minute, feeding at all levels from top to bottom. That's why, if you haven't frightened wild browns, they can be one of the easier fish to catch. You'll also see random jumpers and flashers splashing out here and there. These are generally just knocking off parasites, or sometimes taking bigger flies well above the water's surface.

Watch them carefully. If you see trout with their heads down and their fins splayed out, then these are probably fish asserting their territorial rights and they might not be easy to tempt.

Study the rises fish make. The water displacement indicates the size of the trout responsible. It's true that the biggest fish may sip in a fly with hardly any fuss, but they generally have trouble disguising themselves all the time. Listen for big splashes – the biggest fish don't survive solely on insect life but mice, frogs, shrews and crayfish, too.

This is what a day dry-fly fishing the river is about: taking your time, watching everything going on around you and reading the signs nature is giving off.

Avoid being seen

On smaller streams, don't wade unless it's really necessary. In the majority of cases, you can reach fish easily from the bank, especially if you use a 10-foot rod. The trend is often for 8–9ft lengths, but a 10-foot can get a line round corners, trees and reeds that defeat smaller rods. A matt finish to your rod is a great idea because the flash of varnish in the sunlight is a killer giveaway.

So you've found your fish and you know what it's feeding on, you've got your imitation and now it's time for you to make a move. Approach low down, Apache-style. Don't go closer than a rod's length from the water. False cast as little as possible and remember that a dark fly line flashes less than a bright white or yellow one. Now cast a foot above the water so the line, leader and fly all settle like thistledown. When you recast, be careful of spray landing over your targeted fish. It's good to throw your line to the side to get rid of the water droplets before dropping the line back in the fishing position.

A good fight – *A rather beautifully spotted and well-proportioned brown trout is held for a second to the camera. It sipped in a nymph and fought well at close range.*

Wet Fly Fishing

When you're nymph fishing, you are trying to imitate a real-life food item as accurately as possible. Traditional wet-fly fishing, however, is different. A traditional wet fly is more an impression of a life form than an exact replication. This isn't true of all wet flies – the Connemara Black, for example, does look somewhat like an insect being pushed by the current – but most traditional patterns, such as the Dunkeld or the Silver Invicta, fall into the category of attractors. They look a little like food items, but it is the flash in the water that catches the fish's eye and teases it into an attack. With these flies, it is all about exciting a fish's curiosity.

Working the fast water – Al knows that the wet fly works best where the water quickens and falls away, often with crests of white and nearly always working around rocks.

Fast-water fishing

These flies work well because they are generally fished in shallow, rough, quick water where the fish don't have much time to make up their minds. The light, too, is being refracted and the current is whirling food around here, there and everywhere. The fish see your flies, find them interesting and make a grab.

In general, wet fly fishing is carried out on wilder, untamed rivers, usually over stony or rocky bottoms. This isn't the correct method for placid, weedy chalk streams. You're looking for quick, riffly water between 1–5ft deep. You'll often be wading, getting yourself into positions that you couldn't hope to reach from the bank. To some degree, you're fishing blind, covering as much water as possible and keeping very mobile. However, as with all forms of fishing, there are various skills involved. For example, you'll need to read the water to look for little pots and holes behind larger rocks or the creases between fast and slower water. Fish in quick water will always be trying to conserve their energy by hanging out in places where they can find some sanctuary from the current. They still need to be able to see what is happening around them, though, and they need to keep a beady eye on what's trundling past.

The wet-fly method

Wet flies are fished across and down rather than upstream, which is more typical of a nymph or dry fly. The cast is made at about 45° downstream, doing so is allowing the fly, or your team of two or three flies, to follow the current down, gradually moving across it to end up on your side of the river. The major skill here is to avoid the current catching the fly line and pushing at it, making the flies work unnaturally quickly across the current or even causing them to skate across the surface. You must slow your fly line down to give the wets time to fish at the right depths and at the right speed. To accomplish this, mend your line to prevent the current dragging it. Mending is an essential technique in most forms of river fishing, but never more so than when fishing the wet fly.

You won't miss takes when they come, because your flies will be moving quickly, forcing the trout into fast, decisive action. You'll either feel a take with your fingers or you'll see the line tighten quickly and positively across the stream. The fish is generally self-hooked, and almost the first thing that you'll know is that your rod is bent and the line is ripping steadily through the water. This is undoubtedly an exciting, dramatic and effective method.

Wet-fly fishing may not have all the sophistication of the dry fly or the nymph – after all, you're not imitating food forms precisely and you're not targeting specific, sighted fish – but wet-fly fishing does demand a good reading of the water and that all-important skill of constant line mending. And fishing the wet fly keeps you physically fit. Good wet-fly rivers are often in wild, hilly terrain, and this method will keep you constantly on the move, forcing you to walk, wade and stretch yourself physically.

Juan is oblivious to everything except for how his wet fly is pulling across the current towards the fish that he can see moving.

Fly Fishing Stillwaters

All stillwaters offer different challenges. The fish might be obvious in a small pool, but they can be difficult to tempt if there's a lot of fishing pressure. Alternatively, on huge lakes location is the key and you need to have a real awareness of where the fish are. This variety is what keeps fly fishers going back to stillwaters season after season.

Lough Melvin is one of Europe's most spectacular waters, with many species of fish to be caught: salmon ferox trout, brown trout, sonaghan trout and the famous gillaroos.

Approaching a stillwater

On a small stillwater the best time of the year is almost certainly late spring through to early summer and then early autumn. Ideally, you're looking for a mild, overcast day with a light breeze. If you can, avoid weekends and holidays because on small fisheries the fishing pressure can have decidedly negative consequences. In fact, when phoning to book a ticket, it's not a bad idea to ask just how many people are likely to be out on any particular day.

Don't be in a rush to speed to the nearest fishable point. Take your time. Walk round the water. Above all, watch for fish and look for areas that are less pressured. Perhaps these areas are difficult to cast into because of trees or reeds, but you can bet that's where older, wilier fish will have taken up residence.

Small waters can be intense and the fish can be clued-up, so don't do anything to alarm them further. Some might snigger at your ultra-cautious approach, but let them. Who cares, providing you have the last laugh? So, put your tackle together well away from the waterside and if you get any tangles, or even when you change your fly, slowly creep out of sight to deal with the problem.

Always start with good, proven, standard patterns and begin with short casts covering the water in a radial, clock-face pattern. Don't be in too much of a hurry. Let the fly sink well down before starting a retrieve, and always keep that retrieve as perky and lifelike as you possibly can. If your concentration sags, your chances, too, will droop.

Keep your rod slightly off to one side, with the tip close to the water and the line straight to the fly. This way, you'll move the fly in a more lifelike fashion, and you'll hook more fish on the take as well. In all stillwater fishing, a major reason for failure is not detecting the takes in the first place.

The depth that you're fishing and the speed of your retrieve are always much more important than the pattern of fly you're using. Have confidence in your fly, then forget it and concentrate on exactly how you're working it.

Keep your eyes wide open, and if you see a rise or a cruising fish, immediately cast to it. Don't land the fly right on top of the fish, but just in front of it so that it will come across the sinking fly as naturally as possible.

Enjoy your day. OK, you've bought your ticket, but don't bust a gut to get a limit – if a catch limit is still in force on the water. The more you relax, chill out and let the character of the water seep into you, the more you'll form a connection, the more you'll understand and the more successful you'll become.

The year on large waters

Whether you're on a lake, a lough, a loch or a reservoir, there are certain guiding principles that hold true and can be taken from one to the other.

The early season can be cold and dour, but you'll want to get out and make a start. Preferably you're looking for an overcast, comparatively mild day

STAY OR MOVE?

Let's say that you have a water pretty much to yourself. Well, should you fish specific areas intently or should you keep on the move?

- A lot depends on what the fish are doing. If you see plenty of fish rising in front of you then it's worth staying to work out a strategy.
- If the water appears absolutely dead, then, if it's rainbows you're after, it's probably wise to keep on the move, looking for a group of fish willing to make a mistake.
- Browns, however, are a slightly different kettle of fish, pardon the pun. With them, on smaller commercial waters, it's often better to settle down in an area that you know is likely to produce fish and concentrate on it intently. Work an imitative pattern very carefully, very close to the bottom, in slow, short retrieves. In fact, the whole cast can often take 10 or even 15 minutes to fish out. Look for the slightest possible signs of a take. Often the line just lifts a fraction but it's enough to put a hook into a big fish.
- Learn from your mistakes.

191

when fish are more likely to be moving and you're less likely to freeze your hands off. It's important to keep mobile during the early season because the fish could be anywhere. They won't yet have settled into predictable patrol patterns, and you'll come across groups of fish all over the place. In general, aim for water around 10 feet deep that is reachable from the bank.

In all probability, you will be using heavier, sinking lines, possibly with larger flies. Remember to roll cast a sinking line out of the water before trying to lift it to the overhead cast. Otherwise, a tangle and a potentially dangerous situation could result. Remember to cast slowly, too, because it takes time for heavy lines and flies to get up to speed. If you are using a sinking line at this time of the year, be sure you know its sink rate so that you're sure at what level you are fishing. When the line lands, count it down in seconds in order to search out different depths. Make a mental note of how far down you are when you connect with the fish, for future reference. If you're fishing a lure, retrieve with long, steady pulls and keep retrieving until an ideal casting length of line comes back to the rod. Have confidence in your fly. When you're certain that you've explored a range of depths without success it's better to change the colour rather than the pattern.

Mayfly madness – It doesn't matter what stillwater you are fishing, the two weeks or so of the mayfly hatch probably represent the very cream of the sport, the highlight of your year. It's when these big, succulent flies are hatching that the very largest of trout are likely to come up and take an imitation. The obvious lesson here is never to fish with too light a leader.

If you're really going to fish any stillwater, however large, to its absolute limits, it's important to know what the lakebed is composed of. Large rocks, for example, can often be the hiding place for very big trout. Gravel and small stones are frequently favoured by salmon if they can gain access. Larger stones are very likely to attract snails and, therefore, bottom-feeding fish. Muddy holes are frequently the homes of bloodworm. Of course, in very deep waters it is difficult to be absolutely sure what's happening 100, or even 40, feet beneath your boat. That's why, on the really big lakes, a guide is such a valuable companion.

BUZZER TACTICS

There's no more exciting way of taking fish in stillwaters than off the surface or immediately beneath it, and this is where buzzer fishing is such a central technique. You can expect to pick up trout, especially, all the way through the season, and even in winter if you're prepared to go deep.

1. Late in the day sees the most vigorous action to buzzers. Look for areas where the day's breeze has blown a covering of scum until there's a thick surface film. The buzzers will have trouble hatching out into midges here and the trout know it. Look for swirls, heads, backs, dorsals and tails, and listen for that distinctive smacking sound.

2. Start with either one or two buzzers on your leader. Begin with a hook size of 10 to 14. Black and red are traditional. The new epoxy-tied buzzers are particularly deadly, with their flash and natural look. If you don't get any action, then make the effort to change colour, size and materials.

3. Begin with a leader strength of 3–4lb breaking strain, but if you're fishing a water with big fish then scale up, and if you decide to fish on at night, when the biggest fish of all are likely to feed, then 7lb or even 8lb isn't too much.

4. You can grease the leader to within a few inches of the top fly. This is important to prevent the buzzers from sinking too deep, and you can also watch the floating leader for any signs of a take. Alternatively, use a large dry fly, both as a sight indicator and as a controller, so the flies don't sink too deep. A Muddler is a good one, or even a crane fly.

5. Take your time and try to identify the route individual fish are taking. Once you do this, you can place a buzzer a yard or so in front of it and twitch it back across its nose while it's on its natural patrol route.

6. Keep everything as tight as you can. Watch your leader or top fly like a hawk. You'll need to do this in failing light conditions especially. If you can, cast westwards, towards the setting sun. You'll find this gives you just a little bit more light on the water.

7. Either leave the buzzers stationary in the surface film or give them slight twitches. If feeding activity is really frenzied, a slow, continual retrieve can produce smash takes.

8. Don't be in too much of a hurry to leave at the end of the evening. If the rules allow it, continue fishing into darkness. This has proved particularly effective on some of the big western loughs in Ireland, where some of the guys stay out until 2 o'clock in the morning.

What will the fish actually be feeding on in the early part of the season? The answer can be varied. In Lough Corrib in Ireland, for example, early season floods often scour out the feeder streams and wash minnows into the lough. The trout go mad on them and minnow patterns work well at this time. Otherwise, trout are probably down deep, feeding among the stones and dead weed looking for beetles, shrimps and any nymphs, and that's where you've got to use imitations.

In early spring things are likely to change as the first hatches, most notably of buzzers, take place. The trout will now be settling into steadier feeding patterns and fishing can become somewhat more delicate. The fish are gaining condition during this period, often gorging on the vast numbers of buzzers hatching. Look for them over deeper areas, probably where there's weed or silt on the bottom beneath.

As we move into late spring–early summer we're still not done with the buzzers, but olives begin to appear in numbers and the fish will often switch to them. You can take many fish from the surface on dry olive patterns, but it still doesn't do to neglect the sinking line for most of any successful day.

The olives stagger on, but some time towards the very end of spring, depending on the weather and geography, the mayflies begin to appear. In Ireland, for example, this is the start of festival fishing. These gloriously beautiful and highly succulent flies take over and fishing on the dap, especially, is the vital form of presentation. Everything eats the mayfly: salmon if they're in the water and even pike! If there's ever a glut period, this is it.

After the mayfly, there's often a lull in fishing through mid-summer. In Ireland, many fishermen will move off to fish for salmon and sea trout. Late summer can see some tremendous sedge hatches. It's also in August that many fish are down deep, feeding energetically on the banks of daphnia. Locating the fish now can be difficult, and in many conditions you will need a sinking line.

Perhaps the best daphnia support anywhere is provided by the sonaghan trout of Lough Mevin, which straddles the border between Northern Ireland and the Republic of Ireland. Sonaghan are rather like sea trout, averaging 12oz to 1lb, and they fight frenetically. They are obsessive daphnia feeders. If the weather is right, the daphnia will be down and they will stay there, too, during heavy rain. You'll need intermediate lines with sink tips. Choose black flies with a bit of flash on the tail. The Bibio is good and the Clan Chief is a real Irish favourite. Don't cast long, because the sonaghan hit fast and you can miss at least 40 takes before you land a single fish unless you're really tight and in touch.

These sonaghan highlight one of the biggest problems for the fly fisher – detecting and striking takes. At least with the sonaghan you generally know when one has nipped at the fly, even if converting a take into a securely hooked fish is a different matter altogether. The major problem on so many waters is simply detecting the take in the first place. This can be especially difficult on stillwaters when there is little

Changing levels – Large waters, and reservoirs especially, are very prone to changes in water level and a rise or fall of 6m (20ft) or so in just a few days is not unusual. This really has the effect of pushing the fish about: for example, if heavy rain falls and the lake rises rapidly, expect to find fish flocking into the margins where all manner of terrestrial insects will be trapped. Fish can become quite preoccupied at times like this and refuse the imitative offerings we are used to fishing. When a lake is low, it's also a good idea to make a note of any obvious features so that you can fish to them when the level rises again.

or no current and it's harder to keep a direct line to the fly. It's quite possible to have a take and know nothing about it at all, so concentrate with all your senses and really focus on the line.

From late summer and into autumn, you'll find that many of the trout are beginning to feed on fry, and fish patterns worked quite quickly really come into their own. Watch for small fish sheering out of the water as trout attack them.

This is also the time of the year when crane flies proliferate and many big fish come to take them from the surface. Fishing the daddy-long-legs is hugely exciting: one minute your fly is just hanging there and the next second there's an explosion and you're playing a fish that's seemingly come out of nowhere.

In Ireland, a lot of crane-fly fishing is done on the dap with live insects, but large artificials work very well. Learn to twitch them from time to time to impart life, and don't worry too much if they begin to sink into the surface film looking like a crippled, dying insect. You can leave the daddy static on the water, simply keeping in touch with it as your boat, if you're afloat, approaches the fly. Alternatively, you can twitch it slowly back towards you in a faltering retrieve. Keep an open mind and try both tactics.

High-altitude waters

Wherever in the world there is high-altitude, barren moorland you are likely to come across splashes of water anything between half an acre to 30 acres (12ha) or more in extent that hold trout. Frequently, partly because of the altitude and partly because of the poorness of the soil, the trout are small, but this isn't always the case and there are some amazing discoveries to be made.

Of course, making the best use of these gems calls for a certain amount of independence. These are waters that are frequently totally unfished or barely fished. They are usually miles from the nearest road and often they can only be reached over hostile terrain. You have no way of knowing what the water holds, and there's little or no local knowledge. The weather can be unpredictable. These are barren, desolate places that demand a brave approach.

Safety is a major consideration. Don't go out if there's any doubt about bad weather coming in, and be particularly wary of fog and mist. Have a very detailed map with you and a compass that you're able to use. Take warm clothing, even in mid-summer: the weather can change dramatically very quickly. Take plenty of water, especially if you're walking distances with kit in hot weather. Don't carry more than you need and don't encumber yourself with unwanted fish as you leave: put them back and make the walk home easier. Always tell somebody at base camp where you're going and when you expect to be back. Don't fish for longer than you've told them: you could endanger people in an unnecessary rescue attempt.

So much for the cautions. What do you actually do when you get to that water that was, just a couple of hours ago, a splash of blue somewhere above the 3,000ft contour line on the map? Well, keep your eyes open for any sign of moving or feeding fish and watch out for fish-eating birds giving you a clue to location. Look for weed beds, lilies (yes, even at that altitude!), sandbars, in-flowing streams and obvious drop-offs – anything that gives you a clue where to begin.

You will probably not see many fish rise, because the waters are likely to be comparatively poor. Try, to start with, fishing as deep as you can with anything small and black. Move it slowly, trying to represent any one of a score of insect forms that the trout might recognize. Work the shoreline diligently. Cover all the water in front of you in a rhythmic, methodical way, and then move 30yd or so along the bank. Keep going until you find fish. Don't be panicked into changing flies all the time: it's more important to work them intelligently than it is to worry about what's on the end. After all, these probably aren't educated fish and they aren't likely to be too wary of your tackle. However, they will be wary of you. Humans will not be part of their daily life, so move and cast with care. If you're wading, don't splash about.

Still no joy? Try a fish-pattern fly worked back quickly in mid-water or nearer the surface. Or try a large terrestrial pattern fished dry – a daddy-long-legs is the obvious one to go for here. Let it drift on the wave and twitch it back to you in a very slow retrieve.

Keep going. Fish in waters like this are notoriously unpredictable and can suddenly come on the feed out of nowhere. If you're not endangering yourself or others, try to stay on until the last of the light. This is often the prime period on these waters.

Don't risk going too light. I can't begin to tell you what to expect, but you could be in for a surprise. Many of the fish might only be a hand's span, but it's quite possible you will hit into something that takes your breath away. People do, all over the place, more often than you think.

Now this may sound selfish, but if you do hit lucky with some unexpected fish, keep quiet about it. Tell very close friends, perhaps, but don't broadcast the news, because stocks of wild fish can frequently be much less dense than you'd think and they can be quickly and disastrously thinned out.

Big lakes

You can fly fish in waters the size of the Caspian Sea, but most lakes and reservoirs aren't quite that big! By big stillwaters I'm thinking primarily of places probably a mile or more in length, and though they may look daunting to beginners, they still have their features.

Always bear safety firmly in mind. Most large waters are best fished from boats, which can be dangerous if the weather is unkind or there's a flaw in your boating technique or equipment. Be particularly careful of waters that possess a great number of rocks just under the surface of the water – these can be very difficult to spot, especially in poor conditions.

The weather is crucial on these large waters and a big wind can make certain areas unfishable. What you're really looking for is a breeze of between 2 and 4 in strength, which makes drifting long lanes of water possible. It always helps if you have a boatman to keep you on course, but two anglers ought to be able to operate quite successfully if they use teamwork. The great advantage of drifting is that large areas of the water are opened up and explored with the minimum of physical effort.

Cast with the wind behind you to the front and side of the boat. You will have to retrieve, of course, faster than the boat is moving. Drifting works very well with the dapping method. On large waters some drifts can take virtually all morning and you can often cover several miles of water and hundreds of feeding fish.

Local knowledge can be important for many reasons. Most vitally, locals will know which areas of the lake are particularly prolific at specific times.

However, there are still age-old rules that the visiting angler or beginner can follow that should catch him or her some fish. For example, if it's a hot, bright day, then from mid-morning to late afternoon many fish are likely to be found in the deepest part of the water where there is an element of cool and protection from the sun. Fast-sinking lines can get down to the fish and produce results under the most unpromising conditions. Alternatively, look for shallow, sheltered bays where there's good cover and plenty of natural food. If there is aquatic vegetation, you'll often find trout close in, feeding hard, even in bright conditions. Look out, too, for a bottom of gravel or large stones. These are particularly useful

A big, crystal-clear lake on a baking hot day produces some of the most difficult conditions you will ever come across. Leo is standing near the shore, but you'll notice from the angle of his line that he's casting not far out into the lake but a long way down the margins. This is because fish will often come into marginal weed even when the weather is hot and the water shallow. They are looking for the food that margins attract, and if they're not frightened by a footstep or a falling line, they can be easy to tempt. The other, more obvious approach is to fish way out in much deeper water, probably with a sinking line.

A BIG LAKE

spawning streams
Not all inflowing streams attract spawning fish, but local knowledge will direct you to those that do. You'll often find fish amassing near the mouth of spawning streams near to the end of the season. They're very catchable then.

contours
Try and build up an impression of important contours on the lake's bottom. You'll often find fish feeding along the ledge where the shallows drop off to the deeps.

rocky outcrops
Always investigate rocky outcrops. They harbour extensive food supplies and fish will hang close to them.

shallow bays
Always investigate shallow bays carefully, especially early and late. If you can be the first on the water you'll often find that fish come in during the night to feed in the margins and they can still be there at dawn.

the deeps
Search out the very deep holes in very warm or, alternatively, very cold conditions.

rocks
Look out for rocks, weeds, fallen trees, sunken boats – anything that breaks up the contour of the lake bed. Find a feature and you're sure to find a fish – especially if it's black bass that you're after.

feeder streams
Feeder streams are often favourite places because they can bring extra food stocks into the water. In very hot conditions the incoming water might also be cooler and contain more oxygen.

in the spring before major fly hatches because they harbour colonies of water shrimps and snails.

You'll often find that bays fish well very early in the morning or late at night, especially if they haven't been pressured during the course of the day and the fish driven from the shallow water. Above all, keep your eyes open. Look for rises and even the activity of waterfowl. For this reason, it's a good idea to take a pair of binoculars with you when afloat and investigate anything that looks promising.

Trout may have well-defined feeding routes in smaller bays on larger waters, but out in the main body of the lake they tend to be very mobile, constantly on the fin looking for food. It's the same with salmon in a lake: they'll have well-defined travelling zones and places where they like to rest up. Local knowledge plays a huge part in pinpointing these places. If you're new to a big water it makes sense to go out with a guide for the first day or two. They'll fill you with ideas and, above all, confidence.

A SMALL STILLWATER

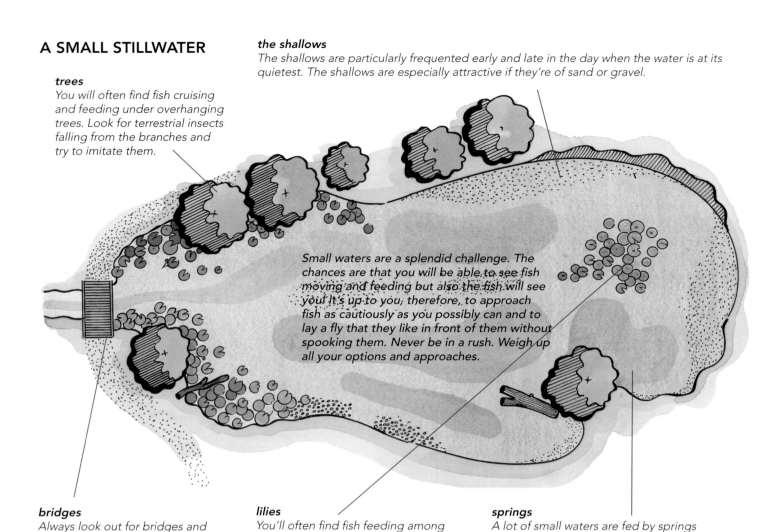

trees
You will often find fish cruising and feeding under overhanging trees. Look for terrestrial insects falling from the branches and try to imitate them.

the shallows
The shallows are particularly frequented early and late in the day when the water is at its quietest. The shallows are especially attractive if they're of sand or gravel.

Small waters are a splendid challenge. The chances are that you will be able to see fish moving and feeding but also the fish will see you! It's up to you, therefore, to approach fish as cautiously as you possibly can and to lay a fly that they like in front of them without spooking them. Never be in a rush. Weigh up all your options and approaches.

bridges
Always look out for bridges and other man-made obstructions as fish will congregate close to these.

lilies
You'll often find fish feeding among lily pads. They scrape the snails and tiny insects from the underneath of the pads and from the stems.

springs
A lot of small waters are fed by springs as well as by feeder streams. The water is frequently well-oxygenated and cold and so attracts fish in warm conditions.

Small stillwaters

Some of the very best stillwaters in the world are slightly enlarged puddles, but their lack of size doesn't mean that they can't be rich in food life, and they often produce huge fish.

Many of these small waters are commercially run and stocked, but not all. In wilderness areas, you'll often come across small, wild fisheries. Above all, treat small waters with great respect and think tremendously carefully about your approach. Be careful of marshy banks, for example: a heavy footfall will send out tremors that the fish will feel easily. Make use of trees

and bushes around the banks and use them as ambush points.

On small waters, it's frequently possible to stalk individual fish, and if you see one that takes your fancy spend as much time as it takes to build up a picture of its patrol route. You can then place a fly in front of it before it actually arrives.

Observe small water etiquette. Don't, for example, remain on your favourite point all day. Others might wish to fish there. Don't move in too close to an angler already fishing – he might be stalking a fish that's very special to him. Keep your voice down because that could spook somebody else's fish.

BOAT ANGLING TIPS

• If you are on a large, unknown water with possibly dangerous rocks, go out with a local boatman, at least on the first few occasions.

• Some larger lakes are like small seas and bad weather can spell real danger, so avoid it. Don't go out in a boat unless you are confident, and always wear a buoyancy device, even if you can swim (and I strongly recommend that you should be able to).

• Even if your engine is the most reliable in the world, ensure you have oars. On very large waters, a map and a compass can be useful.

• If you're on your own, an electric outboard is very helpful, especially if you're fishing buzzers. It's hard to row and cast to feeding fish at the same time.

• Think carefully about your drifts. Consider the direction and speed of the wind and the ground you want to fish over.

• Generally, you can dap or fish most wet and dry flies on an unrestricted drift. If you want to fish nymphs or buzzers you might well want to slow your boat down using a drogue. When you are fishing normal wet flies on the drift you have to retrieve just fast enough to keep in touch with them but not so fast that you're pulling them at an unnatural speed through the water.

• Don't forget to lift your rod tip and let the flies dibble close to the surface before removing them to re-cast. Trout will very often follow right to the boat itself.

• Boat etiquette is important. If you get a feeling that you're harming the sport of others in any way then stop immediately. For example, don't drop anchor if you're on a drift with others behind you. Never motor through a drift that either you or others are working. Instead, go back upwind in a wide arc before

settling back to fish in line. Never go close to a bank angler, especially with your engine on. If you're approaching a quiet bay at sunset where others are fishing, cut your engine speed right down to avoid noise and wake. If your boat is hired, leave it as tidy (or tidier, come to that) than when you picked it up. Remove all rubbish, even if it doesn't belong to you.

• Always switch off your engine and lift it up before gliding in to a rocky, shallow landing place, and always leave your boat in a safe position. Make sure it is properly tied up to something immovable on the bank. Don't leave a boat washing around if there's a swell or if a rising wind is forecast. Try to pull the boat as far as possible out of the water where you know it will be safe.

• Sitting on hard wooden seats all day long can be uncomfortable. Think about taking a cushion, or even your own fishing chair if the boat is big enough.

• It's never a bad idea to have your own set of rowlocks in the car in case they're missing on the hire boat.

• Keep a spare set of dry clothes in your car. You never know when you might get a soaking and it may be a long journey home.

Dapping

The art of dapping is traditionally associated with large waters, generally in the late spring or early summer when the mayflies are in the air. This method was pioneered on the great loughs of Ireland, where it is still practised with fierce enthusiasm. However, anglers worldwide have realized that dapping is effective and exciting, often catches the biggest fish in the water and is a real skill to be mastered. Dapping is really a boat-fishing method, although it can occasionally be done from the bank.

The perfect conditions for dapping will probably include a little more breeze than we see in this photograph. If conditions are particularly calm, then it pays to check out wind lanes and anywhere the water is ruffled.

Dancing on the water

In essence, dapping consists of drifting with the wind in a boat across comparatively shallow, rocky ground where the mayflies proliferate, and dancing your own mayfly on the surface of the water. Long rods are used, together with silk or floss lines that catch the breeze. In Ireland, at the end of the leader, live mayflies – anything between one and six of them – are commonly attached to a hook size 8 to 12. Collecting mayflies has become something of an Irish tradition. At times during the mayfly hatch, the trees and bushes around the shores of lakes such as Corrib literally heave with the insects. For generations, boys have set out to catch the living mayfly to sell to anglers. However, perhaps thankfully, imitation mayflies serve just as well.

THE LIFE CYCLE OF THE MAYFLY

Mayflies are magnificent creatures, one of the world's largest up-winged fly species, and when they hatch they create a stunning picture on the water. The life of the mayfly begins as the egg hatches and the nymph appears (1). The nymphs live among stones and vegetation and are hunted by trout. As their time to emerge approaches, they become more active and increasingly vulnerable. They will even come to the surface a few times immaturely and can be intercepted by the trout as they rise or fall (2). The critical time comes as they wait in the surface film for their wing-cases to split open (3). Once they have emerged as winged flies or duns, they have to wait on the surface for their wings to dry sufficiently to allow them to fly to the bank (4).

The dun sheds its thick skin again, sometimes after several days, to become the spinner – the shining, spiralling, iridescent pinnacle of mayfly life. This is when mating takes place and the females return to the water's surface to lay their eggs, which sink to the bottom and eventually hatch out as nymphs (5). Soon after the egg-laying process, the spinners die, and the dead and dying insects yet again make attractive prey.

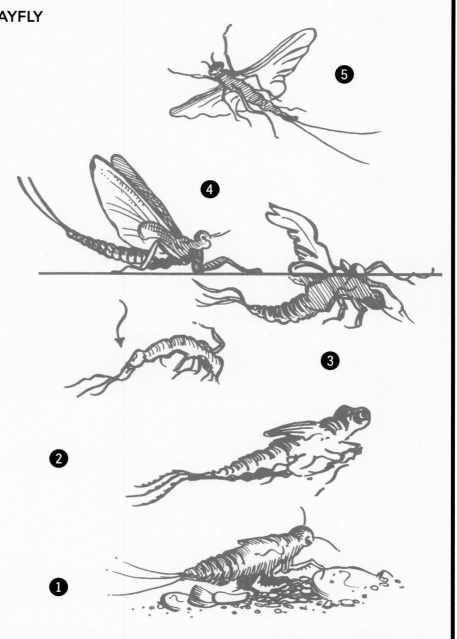

Dancing the fly – Dapping is generally carried out from boats but if there's a decent breeze it's possible to dap from the shore if you keep your rod high.

The dapping method

Let the boat drift, sometimes for miles on larger waters, holding the rod vertically, paying out the dapping line until it clears the tip ring, then lower the rod so the mayflies are skipping on the surface of the water. Don't drag them about unnaturally. The aim – and the skill – is to make them appear as lively and natural as possible, and that's particularly important with the artificial. Twitch the rod tip from time to time, so that the flies skit from one side to the other. Make

use of the wind, to keep telltale line off the water and to impart as much life as possible to your flies.

When you get a take, don't be in too much of a hurry to strike. Sometimes a trout will submerge the flies before sipping them in, sometimes it will merely splash at the mayflies – real or artificial – in an attempt to drown them before taking them. In this case, do nothing, as the trout will probably return. Delay your strike until you see the line going out and tightening, then merely lift in to the hooked fish.

This isn't simply a method for the mayfly season. You can dap with any large naturals such as grasshoppers, sedges and daddy-long-legs. Equally, try the same method with imitations.

A decent breeze is generally considered important for dapping, as you do need a bit of a wave. I've dapped in terrifyingly strong wind conditions when my guide has only just been able to keep control of the boat. The fishing has been fantastic during these conditions, but do bear in mind that no trout, however magnificent, is worth risking your life for.

The tackle box

Traditionally, rods are 14–16ft long. Telescopic models are favoured as they can be extended or shortened according to conditions. However, a long trout rod or light salmon rod can also be used if you don't want to make a special investment.

Centre-pin reels are generally used in Ireland, with 100yd or so of 15lb nylon backing in readiness for a really big fish taking off. To this is attached a length of special dapping floss, designed to catch the wind. The length of the dapping floss varies according to the state of the wind and length of the rod, but 10ft to 12ft is generally considered about right. To this is attached the leader – 4–8ft of 6lb nylon monofilament. It is unwise to go lighter than this because you're likely to catch some very big fish. All these measurements can be changed according to the weather conditions. In a very stiff wind, you probably won't need the floss at all, as it's only there to help catch the breeze when there isn't much of it about. Equally, use a heavier leader if you see some really big fish moving, as very little of it ever touches the water at all.

Neill shows all the concentration needed for a successful dapping drift. Ian holds the boat up perfectly so the fly is skipping on the waves. Notice the broad-brimmed hats and Polaroid glasses. These are essential items for fishing in days of sun and wind.

Fishing the Popper

Poppers are flies constructed to float on the surface and make splashy, noisy movements on the retrieve. They are designed to look and behave like a small creature that has fallen into the water and is struggling for its life. The aim is to trigger the predatory instincts of a variety of species into making an attack. Poppers can emulate frogs, newts, small snakes, lizards, water rats, mice, even fledglings. Just imagine the number of baby birds that must fall from the security of their nest and perish in the water and you'll understand why many bass, trout and pike make a living that way.

Ian Miller makes a splash with his popper, simulating a fallen creature struggling in the water, to attract a pike as the sun slides down behind the trees.

Popper-fishing tackle

Poppers are generally made from a variety of materials. The tails are usually fluffy and wildly coloured, while the bodies are made out of wood, plastic, cork – anything that floats. Vitally, the head is scooped out so the face is saucer-shaped. It's this concave front that makes the popper 'pop' along the surface so efficiently on the retrieve.

If you're fishing a popper, and it's definitely one of the most exciting of all fly-fishing techniques, then a 7- to 8-weight rod is probably going to be ideal in most circumstances. If you are popper fishing for pike with really big flies, you might want to go heavier. Poppers are not very aerodynamic, and large ones are particularly hard to cast, especially when they get wet, so you need a powerful rod if you're going to achieve distance and accuracy consistently. Most popper-caught fish aren't going to scream off line, so huge amounts of backing aren't necessary, but you will need a sensitive clutch. You will be using floating lines almost exclusively with poppers, so a 7- or 8-weight line will match your most commonly used rods. Don't go too light with your leader – takes on poppers can frequently be true smash-and-grab affairs.

When and what

Poppers are best fished in warm, calm conditions, especially at dawn and dusk. For black bass, for example, poppers are not effective when water temperatures fall below 15°C (60°F), especially if the surface is rough. Poppers work well at night for many species, when there is a big moon and little cloud cover, and they can be the only way to put a fly to fish hidden under mats of weed or lilies. Black bass, particularly, will come out for a well-placed popper.

Don't be afraid to go large – black bass will consume flies half their own length – but big isn't always best. Sometimes a species will go for a popper so small you'd think it would be overlooked.

Popper control

Think about how to work your popper. On landing, let it settle and don't move it for 30 seconds or more. Straighten up any slack line until you're tight to the

fly, give it a sharp 15cm (6in) tug and leave it again for up to 30 seconds before repeating the process. Many fish will be lying deep and need time to sense that your popper is there, to focus on it and make their minds up to attack. If you 'pop' back too quickly, a lot of fish won't even know you're there.

Poppers always fish best around any sunken structure, whether it be vegetation, masonry or old ironwork. Keep your rod tip low to the water, or even sub-surface, when you make that pull. This way the popper pops enthusiastically but you pull it less far across the surface, leaving it closer to the structural zone you are fishing towards.

Watch the popper carefully for signs of emerging fish. When one is close, only pop the fly if the fish is undecided or turns away – many species prefer to take it stationary.

If a few of you are fishing together on the bank or from a boat, try a popper race: cast them side by side and retrieve them close in tandem. This multiple disturbance is a great fish attractor.

Coaxing difficult fish

If fish, black bass especially, are cautious, make the retrieval tug just a twitch so that the commotion is reduced. All fish species can be scared by a loud pop.

Hard-bodied poppers are durable and stand casting against structure, so you can get in really close to fish afraid of open water. However, if fish are taking gingerly, a hair or fur-bodied popper feels more like real food and will be held onto fractionally longer.

If the fish are still spooky, keep changing size and colour, or change shape to a frog, lizard or mouse. A fish will often be angered into attack if you keep popping him in his own stronghold. Although he might not be hungry, territorial instinct will take over and he'll just have to do something about the intruder.

A beautiful Spanish bass, taken off the top with a popper.

Fly Fishing Rivers

There's a whole range of joys to river fishing, not least the bubbling, singing environment itself. Some anglers like to get close-up and intimate on small, crystal rivers, while others prefer long casting and big takes at distance. Whether you're into the majestic river or the gurgling stream, the approach and the skills are basically the same.

Fly fishing in the winter when conditions are harsh and the icicles tell you that temperatures are way below freezing can be particularly dramatic. It is also when big grayling are probably at their best.

A wild world

Above all, in the vast majority of cases, you are pursuing wild fish, and that's one of the real joys of it all. However, wild fish nearly always mean fish stocks under pressure, so return almost everything in a caring, humane fashion and create as little stress on the river as you possibly can.

Approaching a creek

My definition of a creek is something no more than 3–4yd across and frequently less. You'll find them curling through meadows or woodland, often with many sharp bends and a continuing succession of small pools and fast riffles. The water will generally be clear and the fish are almost certainly wild. Primarily you'll be expecting trout.

The first thing to bear in mind is your gear: travel light – a 7-foot rod should be enough, with perhaps a 3- or 4-weight line. A few nymphs, a selection of dries, your glasses, drab clothing, chest waders and you're off.

Little fish – Any fish should be judged in the light of the water it comes from, so if you are fishing little more than a meandering brook, catching a tiny but mature and perfectly formed brown trout like this should be enough for you. Unhook small fish very carefully and remember what the pressure of your fingers can do to such a fragile specimen.

From there on, it's all about true creepy-crawly stuff. Make good use of every bit of bankside cover that you can. Learn to cast on your knees, on your stomach or even on your back. Watch carefully for rising fish. In the deeper pools, shuffle to the bankside and spend 10 or 15 minutes looking through the water until you see fish. Watch to see how they are lying and upon what they're feeding. Then work out your strategy.

There are few, if any, rules of etiquette when it comes to creek fishing. You can fish up, down or across – whatever you think will best serve your purposes. Try jigging a fly directly beneath your rod tip in deep water under some fallen branches. Don't ignore the quick white water… there can be a lot of food here and trout can be attracted in numbers. Try letting your line and fly just float down with the current to an appealing spot that you can't reach with a direct cast. Once it's there, don't let out any more line, but retrieve with short, tiny tugs.

Look out for places that anglers will never have fished before because of the difficulty, such as long, heavily wooded stretches that you can probably get to with chest waders, and make your way slowly upstream. Don't be afraid of walking all the way to the limits of the fishery where the footsteps have died away. Wild fish are wary fish, and the less education they've had the better it is for you.

Above all, take your time and don't rush. Look at the water, watch the fish, consider your approach and set about your task with patience and delicacy. One wrong move and you may well blow the whole plot.

Approaching larger rivers

Here I'm talking about waters from 5yd wide to 100yd or more! Obviously, in many cases you're not quite as eyeball-to-eyeball with the fish as you would be on a smaller river, but that doesn't mean to say that you can let your commando skills slip. Larger rivers call for wading or for longer casting, and you are going to need a bigger rod. Rods of 8ft and 9ft will do for the medium-sized river, but for the really monstrous spates you'll need anything between 12–15ft if you're going to put out blinds of 30yd or more. Of course,

Battle plans – *I really like this photograph. The angler is about to fish the pool, but before he does, he takes time out to study it as carefully as he can through polarizing glasses. He's not just looking for fish, although that will help him plan an attack, he's taking mental note of the river's depth, drop-offs, the current speed and direction and any large boulders that might offer sanctuary to fish. Only when he's quite sure that he has the geography of the pool committed to memory will he begin to fish – a good lesson for anyone new to a river.*

it's worth checking first of all whether such long casts are really necessary. Is there no way of getting closer to your target fish? Long casting can be fun in itself, but the heavier gear will necessarily land less softly and could scare fish.

Big rivers have a whole array of features, and it's really good to start by walking your entire beat – even if that means several miles. Leave your rod and just walk, taking mental notes or, even better, sketching a plan of the bankside itself. Look out for islands and the slack water they create. Look for deep, slow eddies close into the bank. Has a fallen tree created a big, deep, slow pool behind it? Are

there any feeder streams entering? These are nearly always top places: small fish gather to take the insects washed to them, while larger predators mill around in the slightly deeper water. Look for pools beneath waterfalls where the water is deep, strong and well-oxygenated. Hunt out long, steady glides with a gravel or sand bottom. All your target fish will love to hang here.

The big river can be an awesome proposition, but don't be intimidated. Get to know it, work out its character and soon it will all begin to make sense. It's the ultimate test of your watercraft, so don't shirk it.

Fishing cold waters

Cold-water salmon are probably the most difficult of the lot, but they will take a fly if it can be seen and if it is presented perfectly. When the temperatures are low, salmon live in a near torpor, unwilling to leave their secure lies, and certainly not willing to chase a fly moving quickly over their heads. It's vital, therefore, to get a visible fly right down among the fish and to move it slowly and methodically as close to their noses as possible. A boat can be useful in these circumstances, as it puts the angler in the very best position to present a fly with precision in a known taking area.

Generally speaking, a medium-sink, double-taper fly line is the perfect starter for cold conditions, although a fast-sink line can play its part in very deep, dark pools when the fish are stubbornly remaining on the bottom. It's tempting to go for big rods and heavy lines, but the angler mustn't over-rod himself and lose control of his tackle, especially if there's a strong wind about. A 14-foot or 15-foot rod is about right, even for a larger river, but it's sensible to go shorter if the pools are more intimate.

Fly choice is all-important in cold water early in the season, and it's vital that whatever is used makes a strong impression. If the fish are lying half frozen in deep water, their reactions will be much slower than those of summer fish, and they will not be willing to come to the surface to chase flies across a pool. A 5–8cm (2–3in) tube fly is about right for a medium to large river, and preferably a fly with bright, attention-grabbing colours such as hot orange, red, yellow and black.

It's really important to visualize what the fly's movements are in the pool, to work it, to instil life into it, and yet to make sure that it is searching every possible salmon-holding lie as thoroughly as possible. In icy conditions, when the water itself is dead and dour, the fly has to practically tap a salmon on the nose before a take is induced. Even then, after a slow, gentle draw on the line as the fish rises slightly from the bottom, the salmon may well sink back down to sanctuary behind a boulder once again, refusing to take.

Get in line – The River Moy at Ballina in Ireland can be crazy at times, especially when the tide is right and the salmon are running up through the town in flotillas. This is when, quite suddenly, the bars empty and everyone heads for the river, either to fish or to watch. It's not fishing in the pastoral sense, but it's exciting and it's productive.

Summer fishing

Conditions can be easier in the summer when the water is warmer, lower and clearer and the fish are more actively on the move. Then you can generally fish shorter rods – anything between 10–12ft – and almost always with a floating line. This is the cream of the sport.

It's probably best to go for a double-tapered line, but match the leader with the fly, the size of the fish and the power of the water. A small fly on a heavy leader does not fish well, and breaking strains of

209

Low water *– Low conditions in summer almost always make for difficult fishing. The salmon will be holed up, often in deep pools under snags and overhanging trees, totally disinclined to feed. They may travel at night. If they're going to be caught, then it's frequently either down deep or in areas of running water like this that give a bit of life and vigour to the fly. Dawn and dusk are probably the best time to be out in the hope of waylaying a moving fish. Alternatively, wait for heavy summer rainstorms, coloured, rising water and fish on the move once more.*

about 8lb or 10lb are about right. It's important that the fly doesn't skate across the river, but actually sinks about 15cm (6in) below the surface. A multi-hooked fly is more difficult to sink than a single-hooked fly, as its extra bulk causes more drag in the water. Equally, a sparsely dressed single-hooked fly may sink faster and truer than one that is over elaborate. Moving to a slightly larger hook, say from an 8 to a 6, might also give a bit of extra weight. It's also worthwhile sinking the leader if you think it's necessary.

Even in the best conditions and when the river is full of salmon, the fly must be fished intelligently. If the water is very still, then a cast across the river can be made and the fly can be worked back by hand. If there's a brisk current, however, then it's important to cast well downstream and let the fly hang over the most likely water. It's also a good idea to hold the rod at right angles to the flow of the river, so that the slowest possible fly speed across the current is achieved. Lastly, it can be vital in a fast current to mend the line and prevent a large loop being formed, which would allow the current to pull the fly quickly off course.

The hotter the weather becomes and the longer the fish have been in the river, the more 'stale' they become and the more difficult they are to tempt.

They've probably seen several anglers by now, too, and they're getting used to fly lines and flies. Seek out new pools and fish that haven't been repeatedly covered, and that you fish after rain, when oxygen is pumped into the water and there might be a tinge of colour. An extra flow will also make the fly work in a more sprightly fashion.

Indeed, if conditions are really hard and the water is really low and bright, then a tiny fly might make all the difference – even a single-hooked black fly, no bigger than a size 12 or 14.

Work down the pools methodically with total control. Cast a couple of times from each stance, and then drop two paces downriver before casting again. Put the fly across the river and slightly downstream, and let it work across in a steady movement. Really concentrate as the fly swings round in the current because there are critical taking points. Don't expect big bangs… you'll probably get a gentle tightening of the line and nothing more. Don't strike frenziedly, but just lift into the fish. It's one of the wonders of fly fishing when you lift that rod, see the surface boil and hear your reel begin to shriek.

Spate rivers

One of the most exciting (and often cheapest) openings for salmon is on the small spate river. These are often wild waters, no more than 18–27m (20–30yd) across. They rise in uplands and have comparatively short, steep descents to the sea. Heavy rain makes them flood quickly, and salmon waiting to ascend will bolt up towards the spawning redds in great numbers. The key is to be in close contact with the weather and water conditions. You need to be on the river the instant it begins to drop and fine down. Timing is absolutely critical. Leave it a day too late, and the fish have already gone upstream and are uncatchable. Hit it exactly right and you can have the salmon fishing of your life.

Slightly stepped-up trout gear will often be fine for fishing on waters like this. A 9- or 10-foot rod, a floating line and a leader of 6lb or 8lb is often all you'll need. If the water is coloured, use orange or

black flies about an inch long. However, if you're not catching fish but you're pretty sure they are about, then change colour, change size and keep experimenting until you unlock that door.

This is very hands-on, active, close-up fishing. Travel light and be prepared to walk miles, often through very rough terrain. Look at all the little pools, gullies and holding areas, and make up your

Smoking river – The river at dawn, pewter, racing and full of promise. Often you will find fish of all species in the quick water at the very start of the day. They've pushed up into the rapids during the hours of darkness. Night has lent them security in the shallow water and they know that there are rich food stocks there.

mind exactly where the fish are likely to be lying and how best to approach them. As so often, it's all about patience and choosing the right strategy.

Chest waders will be essential so that you can get in the river and put your fly exactly where you want it, whether that be under fallen trees or behind a rock. Tightness of control is everything. You'll need to be able to make accurate, short casts in the most overhung of conditions. This is the place for the roll cast or the steeple cast. Sometimes you will simply let your line float with the current to the desired spot and then work the fly back. Don't hesitate to hang your fly in the current and let it dibble around a good area for a minute or more. Impart real life into the fly so that it looks like a darting fish, sufficiently realistic to arouse the salmon's anger or curiosity. Impart life by working your rod tip, moving it up and down and from side to side, especially in slow water where you just can't rely on the current to do the job for you.

You'll also have to master the 'mending' of the line, or your fly will constantly be pulled off course into the margins where the water is dead and useless.

Fish all these small pools and runs quickly, accurately and with supreme concentration. Don't spend over long in a place if you're not catching fish, or where you have no indication there are fish. Always be watching for salmon: you might well see them splash out of the water, but more often you will just see them glint, even in quite tainted water, if the sun is shining.

In these conditions, you're fishing for salmon that are always on the move, so you'll only get short, sharp openings of possibility before the fish leave the pool and are on their way again.

It's always very tempting to fish the quicker, more active water, but a good number of salmon will lie up in slow, seemingly dead stretches. Look for them lying inert in shade, particularly under overhanging

Waterfalls are cracking places to fish. In hot conditions the oxygen count rises dramatically. Perhaps even more importantly, the tumble of water cascading into a pool gives off a barrage of sound, sufficient to mask the approach of the angler and the lay of his line. Always remember that sound travels five times as far under water as it does above, so the noise of even a light nymph landing in a placid stream is instantly registered.

SALMON FISHING

Before you fish a salmon pool, take as long as it needs to work out exactly what's happening. Don't just begin to thrash the water, rather formulate a plan of attack. Consider the direction and speed of the current. Try to gauge how deep the pool is. Endeavour to find out whereabouts the salmon are lying and how deep you need to fish your fly. Look for salmon in mid-water or even coming to the surface. If you see this then a floating line is going to be all you need, otherwise you might have to go deep with a sinker. In particular, look for rocks and underwater obstructions that give the salmon a little protection from the main flow of the water. Start at the head of the pool and work your way slowly down, covering the water as thoroughly as you can manage. Concentrate all the time. Takes can be very gentle.

ROCKS
Rocks are a major part of the salmon's life in the river, and they shelter around them for large periods of time. Drift your flies as close to the rock as you can and always try to hold it for a short period in the dead water behind.

RAPIDS
Salmon will run up the rapids, often at night, into the next pool. They'll often rest for quite a while once they've done this so always concentrate hard on the tail of a pool. If the rapid isn't too deep and swift, it's often a good idea to fish from it. You will find that you're more directly in line with the fish beneath you and the line needs to be mended less.

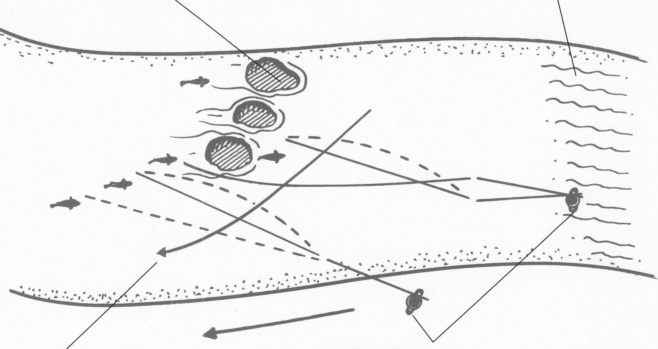

THE CURRENT
Watch the river and gauge the current speed both in the margin and in the middle. The water is going to be faster on the surface than down on the bottom.

FISHING POSITION
Choose your fishing positions very carefully. You want your position to give you the best possible opportunity of placing the fly close to the fish. If you see a number of fish, try to pick off the fish that is least likely to alarm the others. For example, in this diagram you could possibly hook the salmon that's lying furthest away and then let it run downstream, out of the vision of the others.

Notice the shadow line on the far bank of the river. The fast-sinking sun is the clue to this angler's position on the river. Fish that won't make a mistake when the light is on the water will frequently come to the fly in the increased gloom. If the sun is still up it pays to look for your fish under trees and bridges.

branches. They might be lying in the slacker water behind rocks. Wherever they are, it's up to you to find them, put a fly in front of their noses and work it back in an intriguing fashion.

Don't be too quick to strike, especially in slow water. Wait until the fly line begins to move off before lifting your rod. This is very important in all salmon fly fishing: a lot of salmon are missed simply by striking as soon as the take is registered. This works in really fast water where the fish virtually hooks itself, but where the water is slower always give it time.

The challenge of steelhead

Just like the salmon, the steelhead is a magnificent creature, and countless anglers have devoted their entire lives to its capture. So, what I have to say now is only the briefest run through the rules regarding this spellbinding creature. Steelhead fishing doesn't get better than in British Columbia, but you've got to time your visit accurately because the windows of

opportunity are fairly narrow. For example, on the Skeena/Babine system, September, October and early November are really favoured. In September the water is still warm and most of the fishing takes place on the surface with floating flies. October sees more fish moving upstream and you're still fishing comparatively shallow, but possibly now with a sink-tip line. October is a great month as the cool nights clear the water perfectly. In late October and early November you find the big, trophy fish on the move. The weather has cooled down appreciably, and sometimes you need to fish your fly more deeply in the water… although big, surface-skating flies can even be taken in snowstorms.

For steelhead, try a 10- or 11-foot reservoir rod, or a single-handed salmon rod. Keep with your floating line as long as possible and try large, surface-working flies, such as the Muddler Minnow. You can even add on extra bristles to make it skate more noticeably across the surface. This is especially exciting fishing, and you'll often see steelhead powering into the fly as it drags across the current. For general flies, the larger versions of European reservoir lures in various colours are excellent. Local anglers often tie flies that are made to look like the salmon eggs upon which the steelheads feed.

If you've taken this chapter in, you are unlikely to be out of your depth when it comes to steelhead fishing – until, that is, you hook one! Nothing, in my experience, fights better on a fly rod than a fresh-run steelhead. Those first 30 seconds often seem as though the fish is moving violently in every direction at once, and it's easy to lose your head totally, to panic, to let the reel overrun, to let tangles stack up and to lose the fish. Hang on, though. Keep a clear head, and wait for the initial ferocity of the fight to die down a little.

Fry feeders – *Look how these flies are tied to imitate small fish. They've even got tiny eyes for the predators to target in on. In the water these flies realistically twist and flutter in the current. Flies like this are taken by big trout, steelhead, taimen, pike, salmon…virtually anything big enough to consume them!*

As you can imagine, you need to be sure that your tackle is absolutely perfect for this job. This is raw, white-knuckle stuff. Check your leader for any abrasions, double-check all knots and make sure that the hook of the fly hasn't been blunted on rocks. Ensure, too, that the clutch of your reel is set at exactly the right tension – not too slack and not too stiff. Always fish comfortably, making sure that you are well balanced – in the event of a smashed take you don't want to go headlong into a freezing river.

Oh, and be careful of bears, both grizzlies and blacks. If they're on a pool before you it's good manners and good sense to move on. If they fancy fishing a pool that you're already on, then forget etiquette and clear off fast! I speak as one who had a juvenile grizzly gambol after him for a full 20 yards, and it's not an experience I'd care to repeat.

In quick, white water you often need a large fly that is instantly visible and makes a real statement to the fish. A big fly like this flowing past in the current won't be inspected minutely but grabbed because it resembles a living creature. Often colour can be important: for example, if fish have been feeding on prawns out at sea then a big orange fly can trigger an instant reaction.

Big rivers

Big rivers just steam along and, when they get to being a football pitch wide, can look hugely intimidating. Don't be frightened, however. Take time to work out their features and everything will slot into place. Wading a river is often a huge advantage to the fly fisher but be wary of fast currents or deep drop-offs. Don't wade unless the water is clear, you're wearing Polaroids and, preferably, you've got a wading stick. A flotation device is also important.

Big rivers can offer a wide range of fish species. You'll probably have resident fish like trout, grayling or even pike. But you can also expect to come across migratory fish like salmon, sea trout or even shad.

Look for the bigger fish, like running salmon, out in the main body of the water. However, you'll find smaller fish, perhaps modest trout or grayling, a little closer into the margins where the current is less pushy and where they feel safe from predators.

Big rivers the world over offer a wildly exciting challenge, and if you can catch them in good order you will enjoy the fishing experience of your life. Don't be too worried if conditions aren't kind to you, for example, if the river is in spate. You'll be surprised how many fish you can pick up in slower water close to the bank providing you use large, colourful, highly visible flies. Always fish in hope and you may surprise yourself.

ISLANDS
Islands are important because they check the flow of the river, and you'll find fish sheltering in the calm water downstream of them. Migratory fish, in particular, look for this type of slack water.

FEEDER STREAMS
Feeder streams will always hold a stock of resident fish that may be small but which are fun to catch. They're also frequently investigated by bigger fish either looking to spawn or looking for an easy meal.

THE RAPIDS
Investigate rapids very carefully indeed. You'll find resident fish feeding there on the abundant insect life. Migratory fish also have to push up rapids and will frequently rest behind boulders on their upstream journey.

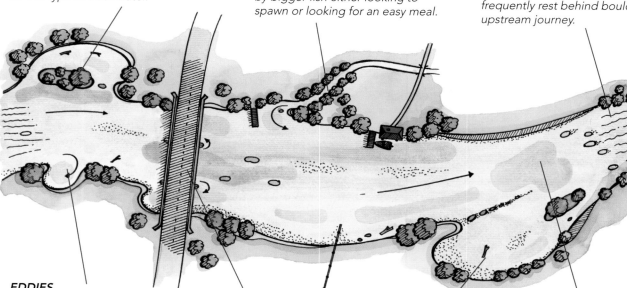

EDDIES
On any large river you'll find bits of water where the current just swirls round and round in an apparently aimless fashion. Eddies aren't generally very good during normal water conditions, but when the river is really up and flowing many fish will push into them looking for refuge. Try a large, colourful fly.

BRIDGES
No fisherman in his right mind can ever pass a bridge without stopping and looking over. Bridges give perfect vantage points and bridge pools are historically famous for holding fish. The currents created by the parapets generally deepen out the riverbed and form succulent pools.

LAGOONS
On large rivers you will find large, shallow lagoons where there is hardly any flow at all. These generally only harbour small fish, but come dusk big fish move in for the kill.

THE TAIL OF THE POOL
The tail of the pool is a critical area. Fish that are tired from the rapids enter the pool and rest up almost immediately. Also, the water is frequently comparatively shallow, so presenting the fly at the right depth isn't quite as critical as it is in the main body of the pool where the depth increases.

Small rivers

Fishing a small, clear river can be one of the most satisfying experiences in the fly-fisher's life. If the water is clear and prolific you will see a huge amount of fly life and, probably, different types of feeding activity. There's also something terribly intimate about the atmosphere of a small river and you can grow to love them in a way that you can't much larger waters.

Anglers will often fish their local small rivers a hundred times a year throughout a lifetime and never once get bored. They're always changing after every winter flood and big, resident, wild fish can present an individual challenge year upon year. On large rivers you don't always see the fish so you can't always tell if you are doing things right or wrong. On small rivers, however, the fish are nearly always clearly on view and if you're not catching, then you're making mistakes.

Some of the most difficult fly-fishing challenges take place on small, crystal-clear rivers that are immensely rich in fly life. Here, the fish are supremely sophisticated and, being well fed, need take no risks at all. Also, the chances are, they've seen every angling trick in the book and it will take something very special to wheedle them out.

ROCKY SHALLOWS
At dawn and dusk, trout and grayling will come onto rocky shallows knowing that there will be a feast of nymphs, shrimps and snails. Approach them carefully.

TREES
Terrestrial food items are very important in small rivers. You'll find smaller fish in particular always hovering under tree branches, safe from kingfishers and other predators.

LOGS
You'll often find the biggest fish in the river take up a lie where they feel supremely safe. Frequently a large trout or bass will base its territory around a large sunken tree trunk.

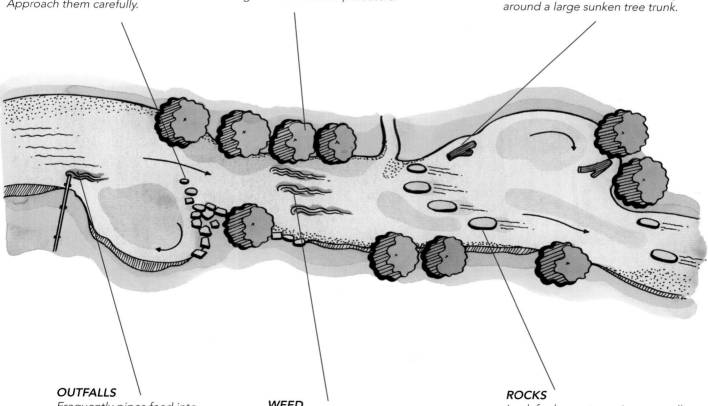

OUTFALLS
Frequently pipes feed into rivers and will attract fish, often because of the particles of food they introduce. Treated sewage is a favourite!

WEED
Weed is the very life tissue of rivers. It harbours huge amounts of aquatic insects and is, therefore, attractive to the fish.

ROCKS
Look for large stones in any small river and you're bound to find fish. This is especially so in those big, deep pools where you can only just see the bottom.

Nymph Fishing

Fishing the upstream nymph is a classic way to catch trout. It demands several different skills. Most importantly, you've got to find the fish, which involves spotting them individually, often deep down, or deducing where they will be lying in the river. For this, you need to think how the current is working, where food could be pushed and where the fish will be taking up vantage and ambush points. Recognizing all the factors that make up a trout's lie are of vital significance. As ever in the fly fishing world, don't rush when you are nymph fishing. Immerse yourself in the pace of the river and become one with its flow.

The angler is fishing for a winter grayling and might well choose the most minute patterns. In fact, he was successful with little black nymphs tied on size-20 hooks.

Reading trout

Once you've seen the trout, look at its body language. Is it moving from side to side? Do you see the white of its mouth as the lips part to sip in food? Is it rising and falling in the water column to intercept passing food items? If so, this is a feeding fish. If, on the other hand, it's lying doggo, close to or on the bottom, then probably it's not.

Let's say it's feeding. You now have to choose the right nymph and, more importantly, where to place it so it's at the right level in the water when it gets into the vision of the feeding fish. If you put on a heavy nymph and cast too far upstream, it will simply hit bottom and stay there, yards above your target. Equally, if you put on too light a nymph and don't cast far enough above your trout, then it will simply skate away downriver, unseen and untouched.

Nymph behaviour

One of the most important nymph-fishing skills is to know your flies. It pays to test them out in clear water, either at home or on the bankside, so that you can determine the sink rate of each item in your box.

The weight of the nymph is, of course, vital. The rest you can treat more casually. In most cases you don't need to worry too much about specific patterns. Providing the nymph is brown, green or black and of a reasonable size – generally between 10 and 14 – you're in with a chance. Most of the time, trout aren't targeting specific nymph types but are simply feeding off the food items drifting in the current, and drab colours represent a multitude of food types.

Spotting the take

So, you've found your fish, you've got into position without scaring it, you've made your cast, the nymph is in the feeding zone, but how do you know if it's been taken? This is the other great skill of nymph fishing, and it's probable that the majority of takes go undetected by most anglers. You think you know roughly where your nymph is but you're simply not sure. The deeper the water and the further away your nymph, the bigger the problem. Grease your

Summer days – A perfect stream scene. Water glistening in the background, thick weed growth, a pleasing rod and reel and a nymph all ready to go. This is precise, demanding fishing but also something very much to be enjoyed.

leader so that you can see it lying on the water as it drifts back towards you. If it stops or shoots forwards or moves from side to side, strike at once. The take will sometimes be so strong that your fly line will jab upstream.

If the rules of the water allow, you may want to use a strike indicator. This not only gives a supreme signal of a taking fish but, importantly, allows you to select exactly the depth you want the nymph to be. The deeper the water you're fishing, the more advantageous this becomes.

Signs of feeding

If you're fishing for a sighted fish, the game becomes even more exciting. When you think your nymph is in the zone, watch that trout for all you're worth. Note if it moves forwards, or from one side to the other. Does it suddenly rise up in the water or drop down towards the bottom? Any such deliberate movement suggests the trout is on the fin and moving quickly to intercept a food item, very possibly yours. If you're especially lucky, you might even see the mouth open. You'll see a gleam of white as the lips and inner mouth are revealed. That's sure proof that a food item has been sucked in and, if the leader moves at all, strike at once. Don't strike wildly with force. Simply lift the rod and tighten, and the fish will be on.

However, you need to be direct to your fly and herein lies another skill. It's vitally important to keep in touch with your nymph at all times as it moves back towards you with the current. This means well-practised hand-to-eye coordination. You've got to strip line back at the same rate that it is drifting along with the current. If you retrieve too slowly, you will end up with slack line. If you retrieve too quickly, you'll be pulling the nymph upwards through the water in a totally unnatural fashion.

Many skills are needed here, but the satisfaction is immense when you suspect your nymph is in the zone, feel it might have been taken, and tighten into an angry trout. It's a moment when everything conspires to create a piece of fishing magic.

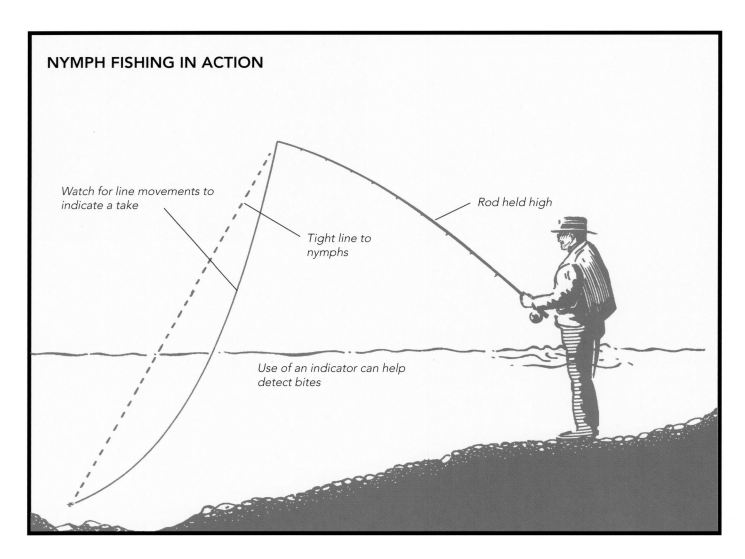

NYMPH FISHING IN ACTION

Watch for line movements to indicate a take

Tight line to nymphs

Rod held high

Use of an indicator can help detect bites

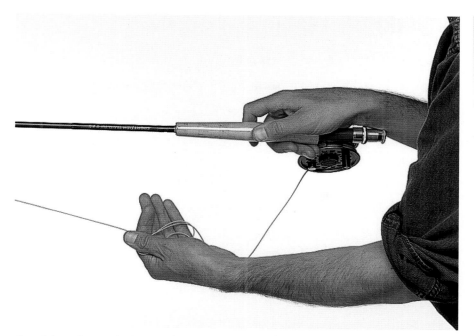

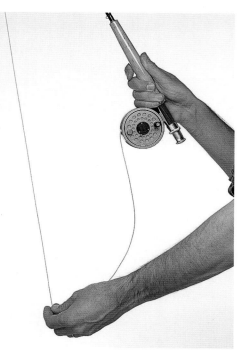

Careful retrieve – At times, when you want to inch your nymph imitation back through the water, it's vital not to have a lot of loose line dangling around. This is where folding it back into your palm can be useful.

The induced take – A trout is following your nymph. Pause, lift the rod and pull the fly line down with your left hand. The nymph will rise in the water as though it's about to escape. The trout just can't resist!

Fooled – A small, deep-fished nymph has accounted for this fine grayling. Although the nymph may look insignificant, it imitates very convincingly the small aquatic insects that grayling and trout both feed on. Grayling will often accept such an offering drifted down in the current.

Czech Nymphing

This close-in, intimate and intense form of fly fishing began in Central Europe in the Czech Republic, Slovakia and Poland. The method is exciting and extraordinarily efficient. In these countries, at least until the last ten years, catch and release was rarely practised and fish caught represented important additions to the family menu. Fishing might have been fun, but it also had a supremely practical nature.

In Central Europe anglers developed a very effective style of fishing nymphs. They wade very close to the fish, fish the nymphs deep along the bottom, and as soon as the line tightens, a strike is made.

The basic principles

In a nutshell, the angler is fishing a team of nymphs close to the bottom and attempting to imitate as closely as possible the natural insects upon which the fish feed. To make this imitation totally convincing, the angler has to get close to where his team of nymphs is fishing so that he can control it with absolute accuracy. The method, therefore, almost always demands that the angler wades. Long casting is not part of the skill, which depends almost entirely on working the nymphs with supreme mastery and reacting with lightning rapidity when a take occurs. Very often the fish will be seen, so it's important to move cautiously and dress in a drab fashion. And always watch how you wade: caution is a good thing.

The right gear

A 10-foot rod gives a greater measure of control than one of 8ft or 9ft. It has, however, to be light and delicate so that the angler can wield it all day long. A quick tip action helps an instant strike the moment the indicator slips under the surface. The reel is not too important, as there is not a great deal of casting to be done, but the line must be a floater and preferably 4-, 5- or 6-weight, with 5-weight being the favoured option in most circumstances.

Leaders are generally 10–12ft long with a heavy fly on the end and two imitations tied to droppers a foot or so apart. Leaders should be between 3lb and 5lb breaking strain, depending on the size of the fish being pursued.

A strike indicator is also a vital piece of kit. This must be large enough to support the weight of the flies, and it is set close to the depth of the water being fished so that it can hold the flies fractionally off the bottom. The strike indicator is also important for just that – indicating the minutest take. Frequently, bites are very fast indeed and the vast majority would be missed without this visual indication.

The necessary flies

Of supreme importance are the flies themselves. The technique depends on flies tied to imitate the tiny natural foodstuffs that trout and grayling eat in their natural habitat and are looking for in the general drift of the river. Caddis imitations are extremely important. So are nymph patterns, shrimp and any of the small foodstuffs that live close to the bottom amongst stones and gravel. The flies must look and act as naturally as possible and that is where one of the major skills of the method lies.

Absolute control – Czech nymphing is all about total control and knowing exactly where your fly is. If there's any suspicion of a take, the strike must be made at once.

The water and the fish

Czech nymphing is almost always a method for rivers. A perfect piece of water will be between 1m and 2m (3ft and 7ft) deep. It will be easily approachable by wading, and the main run of water to be attacked will be no more than two rod-lengths away from the angler. The current should be neither too fast nor too slow – a nice easy pace is ideal. It is important, too, that the nymphs can ride serenely down with the current without becoming frequently snagged around boulders, weed, fallen trees or other obstructions. For this reason, Czech nymphing is best practised over a gravel or sand bed that is comparatively level, with few sharp depth changes or contours.

The two main species targeted by the mid-Europeans themselves are the trout and the grayling. Both fish respond supremely well to the technique, and grayling in particular are very difficult to catch any other way, except when they come to the surface and take dry flies. However, the method is also extremely successful with members of the cyprinid family such as bream, roach, barbel and chub. In Greenland, it has proven a fantastic method with Arctic char, and in the States the few anglers who have tried it have found it to be a winner for black bass. In short, the method works with any type of fish looking for a small invertebrates such as snails, caddis, shrimps and beetles that live close to the bottom.

Different patterns – A well-stocked, Czech nympher's box. These patterns might look similar but they're not. They will all work in individual and quite different ways. Also, they will all be individually weighted so that they sink at different weights.

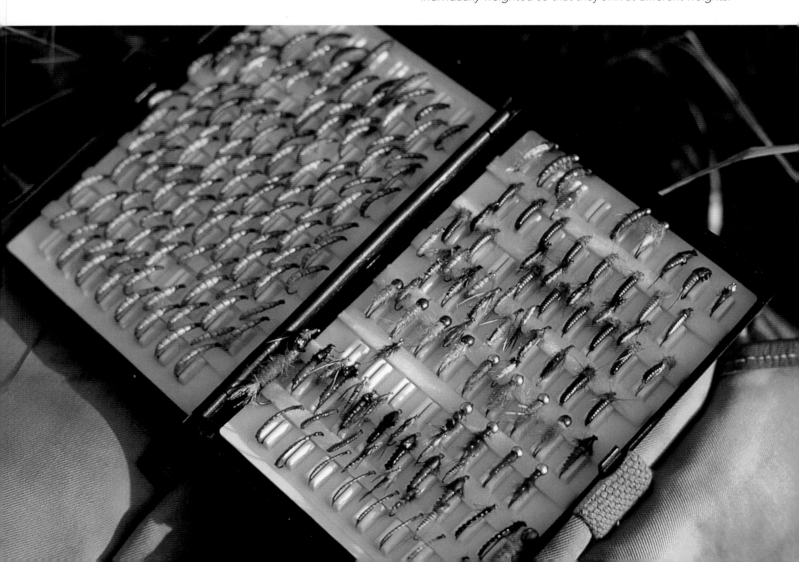

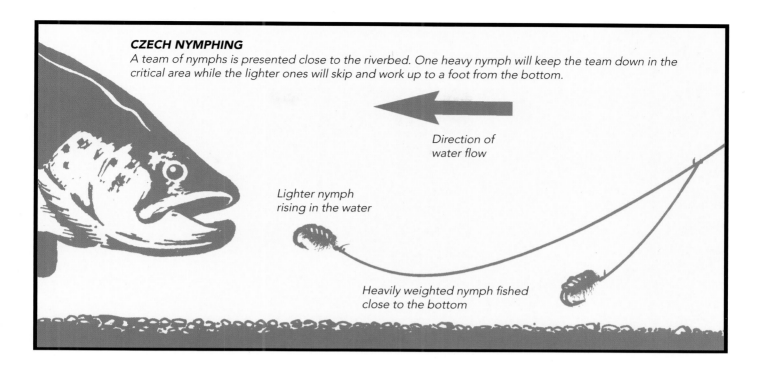

CZECH NYMPHING
A team of nymphs is presented close to the riverbed. One heavy nymph will keep the team down in the critical area while the lighter ones will skip and work up to a foot from the bottom.

Direction of
water flow

Lighter nymph
rising in the water

Heavily weighted nymph fished
close to the bottom

The Czech technique

So how do you do it? The angler gently wades out to where he suspects fish are going to be lying. Some 4–5yd of line are stripped from the reel, and the strike indicator and team of nymphs is flicked a little way upstream. The flies sink quickly and the angler must be immediately ready for a take. The rod is held high as the strike indicator floats down the current, past the angler and then away beneath him. This is so that he can keep a tight line and respond instantly to any movement on the strike indicator. As the strike indicator and nymphs move on some 4–5yd downriver from the angler, he lowers his rod until he can let them travel no further, then lifts them out and rolls the line back upstream to repeat the process.

If there is absolutely no action and no fish can be seen after five or six casts, the angler might well move down a few yards and begin the process all over again until he locates some fish.

Intense concentration

Because all the action is taking place so close at hand, the angler has got to move gently and remain unobtrusive. He has to watch his strike indicator like a hawk for any movement. All the time he is thinking how his flies are working deep down, very close to the bottom. The angler's job is to make them behave as naturally as is humanly possible. The action is tight and intense: it's literally eyeball to eyeball with the fish at a handful of paces. Polarizing glasses are essential in allowing the angler to see through the surface film and scan for any fish that might be present.

The all-important indicator

The strike indicator has a major role, both in holding the flies at the right depth from the surface and also indicating any take. If the strike indicator goes under, moves upstream or simply momentarily holds stationary, strike at once. Another of the big skills of the method is actually recognizing takes that can be very difficult to decipher.

The strike indicator has to be buoyant enough to carry the weight of the flies easily and must not be sucked down by the strength of any currents. It must also be very visible: it's a good idea to take different coloured strike indicators so they can be changed according to the reflections on the water. Red and yellow, and occasionally black and white, are favourite colours.

Knowing the Fish

Just by being a fly angler you are making a statement – you are in the business of becoming a fisher-naturalist. Your job is to present as close an imitation of a natural food source in the most perfect way possible to what is often a wild and suspicious fish. To do such a thing successfully in the hundreds of different situations you will face takes thought. Each and every challenge needs to be regarded calmly and rationally, and a whole host of considerations must be taken into account – what worked yesterday might not work today.

One of the world's mysteries – If people knew more about char and if char were more widely spread, then I have no doubt they would be among the top of the fly-fisher's quarries. They are beautiful, not easy to outwit and fight with heart-stopping tenacity.

Nature's changing world

The world of nature is never static. Everything about the water and the fish that live in it is volatile and constantly changing. Our lives are comparatively ordered because of the comforts that civilization brings to us. If it's cold, we switch on the heating. If it's too hot, we turn on the air conditioning. Whatever food we might fancy is almost always available to us. We are protected from the vagaries and uncertainties of the natural world. Bear in mind that this is not the case for the fish, which are constantly pulled hither and thither by changes in the environment around them.

Key elements

Food and security are just about the only considerations that enter a fish's mind when it is not spawning time. The multitude of considerations that cross our own minds is absolutely irrelevant. A fish wants to live – that's all – and that's where feeding plays such a vital part. Some fish that you pursue will be quite catholic in their tastes and take anything edible in a random manner, but fishing is rarely as easy as this. In most cases, you will find it vital to get close to what your target fish is eating. For example, if trout are on the mayfly, little else will tempt them; sea trout can become preoccupied with elvers and

refuse everything else; or you might find that bass want nothing but crabs.

You can find out what the fish you want to catch are feeding on by observation or by trial and error. What you've got to learn to do is use your eyes. You'll certainly need polarizing glasses to strip away the reflections on the surface of the water so that your gaze can penetrate right down to where the fish are feeding. You might find binoculars are useful, too, to bring everything into a sharper, clearer focus. You'll need time and you'll need patience. Don't rush into presenting the wrong fly in an impetuous way as you might find that you blow your chances completely.

Temperature

Bear in mind the water temperature and, if you care to, ascertain it with total accuracy by using a thermometer. There are some broad generalizations about water temperature that it's worth bearing in mind. If the water is warm most fish will be more active, as they are cold blooded and their body temperature changes with their surroundings. In warm water you might well find fish mobile and feeding hard, but be warned – the water only has to get a degree or two above the

Does life get much better? A glorious sunset, a calm evening, a plentiful hatch of fly and steadily rising trout. You have the whole world, seemingly, to yourself.

optimum temperature and the fish will feel discomfort and begin to drift off the feed. Perhaps you can keep them interested with smaller food items presented in a more sophisticated way.

Cold water, too, can suppress the fishes' appetite, and falling temperatures can make them all but comatose. Once again, small food items might be the answer, or perhaps something large and colourful to trigger an aggressive response. There's no simple answer. You've simply got to think the problem through and try different approaches until you find a solution. There's no point in fishing mechanically or thoughtlessly.

Water clarity

Take into consideration the colour of the water you are fishing, whether it be a river or a stillwater. Crystal-clear water can be good, because you can see the fish and what they're feeding upon with comparative ease, but, of course, the fish will be able to see you, too, and any clumsiness in your approach with extreme clarity. Your leader and fly line will also show up starkly. The situation is less demanding if there's a tinge of colour in the water: the deficiencies in your approach and methods will be masked to a degree. If the water is very murky, then the chances are the fish won't see you or your tackle, but they might not see the fly either. Opt for something colourful that grabs their attention.

Currents

Rivers obviously have currents, but so, too, do stillwaters, and these become more noticeable the larger the water. On really big lakes, especially after a wind, there can be real pushes and pulls of water beneath the surface. Currents are important to all fish: often they like to lie facing them so that they receive an ample supply of oxygen. The currents also bring them food, such as insects, drifting helplessly along and just waiting to be eaten. When fish decide to

The 'typical' fly-fisher's river just does not exist. Each and every one has its own individual character and, no matter how expert you are, you still need to take time to work out how a new water behaves. Spate rivers like this tend to be up and down like a fiddler's elbow according to weather conditions. Food stocks are comparatively unstable and the fish tend to move lies frequently, making spate rivers fascinating places to fish.

Distinguishing Features

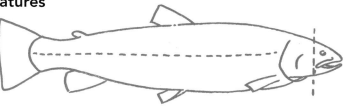

SEA TROUT

The sea trout's upper jaw reaches well past the hind edge of the eye. The salmon's upper jaw reaches only to the hind margin of the eye.

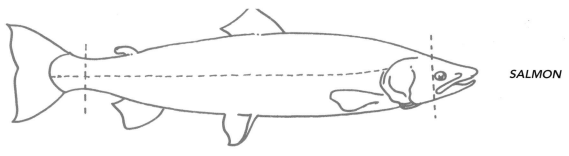

SALMON

It is often important for fishery management to be able to differentiate between trout and salmon parr. In brown trout parr, the tip of the adipose fin and the edge of the pectorals are red. In salmon parr, the adipose fin is slate-coloured. As in adult fish, the position of the eye relative to the end of the jaw is also important. It is also unusual in salmon parr for there to be any red spots below the lateral line.

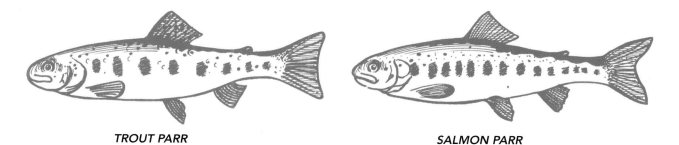

TROUT PARR   **SALMON PARR**

The tail in salmon and sea trout varies enormously. When relaxed, the tail of a big sea trout is straight but when stretched it becomes convex. The salmon's tail is more concave with two horns top and bottom. The base of a salmon's tail is also thinner with a pronounced wrist. The sea trout's broader-based tail has no wrist.

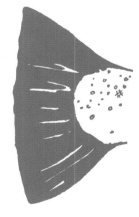

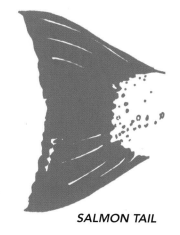

SEA TROUT TAIL   **SALMON TAIL**

move they'll often go with the current simply to save on energy. Think, too, how the current affects the way you present a fly. It can catch your line, form a bow and make your imitation behave unnaturally. Water is rarely a still, dead element – it's all about fluid movement, and we need to understand its many dimensions.

Light

Fish cannot control the light levels around them. Their lidless eyes are constantly at the mercy of whatever the weather sends, and they often find scorching bright light uncomfortable. Frequently, they'll go very deep or, if the water is shallow, they'll look for cover, perhaps in weed, under lilies or beneath an overhanging tree. In these conditions they may only begin to feed at dusk, or even well into the night – sea trout and Arctic char are perfect examples of this. However, if the light is more sombre, most fish will feed throughout the day, especially if there's consistent cloud cover and perhaps a freckling of rain. A wind can improve the

This stunning salmon is being admired and handled with tender loving care by an angler who has waded into the water to keep the fish as close to its natural habitat as possible.

fishing when conditions are dull, but on a bright day the ripples can refract the light and intensify it, putting the fish off.

Weather forecasts

You can see from all that I've mentioned previously just how important the weather is to the fish, and what an impact it has on the waters that they inhabit. It's important to keep an eye on the weather and to consider how changes might affect your sport. For example, the onset of a depression can be a bad thing, because fish generally enjoy stable weather and a well-ordered lifestyle. On the other hand, an extended period of high pressure can mean the weather becomes hotter and hotter, and this will cause the fish to become more and more lethargic. It's then that the approach of wind and rain can revitalize them, by pumping fresh oxygen into the water. Watch the weather and its changes, and observe how the fish respond. Build up your own picture of the waters that you fish, because each and every environment reacts in a different, unique fashion.

Territory

Most fish have their own territorial ranges. We talk about a trout having a lie, a place where it knows food will come to and where it feels secure. Often trout will stay in the same lie for months on end until a bigger fish, angling pressure or violent changes in weather conditions force it to move. Other fish have larger territories, especially coastal sea fish, which follow the tides, but you'll find that even these regularly come back to the same lie. It's important to watch your fish, to analyze its movements and to work out where best to put that cast so that your fly will be seen to greatest advantage.

Keep on learning

I know how tempting it is to simply buy your gear and a huge collection of flies, dash out and immediately start fishing, but don't. Always take the time to get to know the fish and attempt to work out what they will be doing on any given occasion. This isn't boring – it is fundamental to the sport of fly fishing. Fish are

A group of friends make their plans on a bridge in Slovenia. Bridges are magnets to anglers of all disciplines and to fish of all species. The height that a bridge gives allows perfect inspection of the fish beneath, their size and their position in the water.

not a commodity to be picked up effortlessly from a superstore shelf – they are living, vibrant creatures with distinct life patterns all of their own.

Every fish in the world can be caught on fly, and the chances are you will fish for different species in different waters, perhaps on different continents. You'll never stop learning: there are so many different factors that will influence whether a fish will take that fly or not. It's a fascinating quest that you are embarking upon. Sometimes the key information is well-known. For example, a lot of late summer trout feed on banks of tiny organisms called daphnia, and these rise and fall according to the light. On dull days they come nearer to the surface, but you'll need to fish deep in bright conditions.

Then again, you'll be told by everyone that salmon generally wait in the sea until high water swells the rivers, letting them pass up easily and unobserved, but there are exceptions. A couple of years ago, high winds pushed a school of dolphins into an English bay. The salmon were there waiting for a flood, but the big mammals so terrorized them that they fled up a river that was still low and clear. Pulse after pulse of fish flocked upriver, forced on by this most unusual of circumstances. As you can see, fly fishing brings you right to the core, the nerve centre of nature. A large part of the fun lies in catching a fish but, if you're wise, you'll discover that knowledge can be just as stimulating – and without knowledge, you'll never be a developing, successful fly fisher.

Wild Brown Trout

Wild really does make a difference. A fish that's been brought up in a hatchery and stocked into a water when mature will learn lessons quickly, but it's never going to be as perceptive and instinctively brilliant as the true, indigenous, wild fish. I don't know why; probably nobody does. Perhaps the redd-born egg that develops into a parr in the river and grows into a mature fish there has a oneness and a bond with the water that can never be replicated.

The old mill – The biggest wild browns on any river are often found close to mill ponds where there is depth of water and a large quantity of prey fish.

The wild brown's river

It's not just the wild brown trout themselves that are so special and so demanding; their habitat, too, can be exacting, and requires special skills if it is to be conquered. A wild brown trout river, in particular, is almost certain to be a devil to fish. It's likely to be crystal clear, it might not be very deep, and it's probably going to be made up of a series of diamond-bright pools and dashing, well-oxygenated rapids. There are likely to be overhanging trees, probably good weed growth, but almost certainly prolific insect life. All this adds up to clever fish in a crystal environment where competition for food isn't going to be too stiff. As any angler of experience knows, that's a combination to freeze your blood.

The subtle approach

Firstly, let's analyze the best approach to a wild brown trout river. It's dawn and you're at the riverbank. You need to be the first on a water such as this to stand any real chance of success. Every time you or anybody else casts over a wild brown trout, the odds of it being caught diminish significantly.

Sound is intensified by approximately a factor of five underwater. So, if you can, choose to fish from grass or mud rather than gravel. Above all, watch your footsteps. Women often have the advantage here, as they tend to have smaller feet and be lighter in weight. Moreover, they don't show that same self-defeating urge to hurry to the waterside and destroy their chances before they've even begun.

You'll obviously be walking upriver, simply because you're approaching fish from behind, but think how you walk. Become aware of your shadow, and be especially conscious that the shadow lengthens as the sun sinks. Even a quickly raised pointing finger can spook a fish. Avoid scaring small fish at the margins because they flee and trigger off a chain reaction of fear throughout the water. Most brown trout rivers are clear and shallow, so it's best to creep and crawl and make yourself as unobtrusive as a water vole.

Keep your voice down if you're fishing with a mate. In skinny water conditions, a wild brown can hear an excited voice or bragging tones metres away.

The colour and texture of your clothing are also important. Think drab and soft. A hat's good, if only to shield the flash thrown when the sun strikes your pale face. Put on a tackle vest rather than encumbering yourself with a bag. Wild brown trout rivers are all about mobility.

Casting for browns

Above all, on a wild trout stream, make every first cast count. Don't be impetuous. If you've got a guide, listen to him. Watch the lie, watch your fish and take your time until you've worked out a strategy. The more casts you put over any piece of water, the further your chances fall. Wild browns are expert at seeing you, so you need to learn to see them first. Obviously, you need polarizing glasses (although a horrifying percentage of anglers fail to use them).

The art of concealment – On crystal waters like this, the tricks are to make yourself as small as possible and cast a good distance to far-off fish.

On thin, clear water, you must learn to cast a long leader if you are to avoid putting the fly line itself over a fish. Put a fly line over a wild trout and it's goodbye. Practise casting lying down on your back, or at a crouch, or on your stomach. Learn to roll cast and spiral cast, so that trees are no problem. Cast slowly and methodically, not jerkily, and think about your silhouette all the time. You only have to strive for distance when you've spooked fish, and by striving you spook them more and more. Don't become that human windmill. Don't false cast on a wild trout stream more than you have to. If you can put out the line required in a single flick, do it. Try to cast a foot above the water, so that your fly and line fall lightly.

Natural cover
Use any natural disturbance to help mask your own unnatural intrusion upon the fish. For instance, fish close to a feeding swan – but not so close that you run the risk of hooking the poor bird. If you see drinking cattle, get close to them and flick a fly immediately downstream. You might even kick up a little silt yourself, to colour the water, if you're sure that you're not going to get shot by the bailiff or owner!

During the day, you're going to be spending a lot of time fishing in the surface zone with small olives or light Hare's Ears or similar small, nondescript offerings. Everything is light and tight, with short cast dead straight across the river. Let the fly swing downstream a rod length or two before arrowing them over the water again. Keep constantly on the move, seeking out new pieces of water and visible fish.

Paul Page – the England Fly Fishing team manager – fishes a deep run over large boulders. He's aiming to work the fly as close to the rocks as possible where he knows fish are lying.

A fish as fine as this just has to go back. It's only been out of the water for a second, and it will take a very short time indeed to recover. Stocks of wild brown trout need to be well preserved if a fishery is to retain its health.

On most wild brown trout waters, it will become easier later on in the day, and bigger fish come up around dusk, especially when sedges are out. Keep on the lookout for big, splashy rises.

Fishing deeper

If you want, you can go heavier. Goldheads and heavier nymphs fish deeper, so cast them upstream to get them down, bouncing the bottom. Fishing true wet fly is different; fish them down and across, very near the surface. Always fish on short lines, searching behind boulders, in amongst tree roots and snags. True wild brown trout fishing on streams is really inquisitive and searching. You need chest waders or thigh boots to get close to the fish – small, quick browns and long lines aren't a good combination at all.

Think quick, travel light

This is a demanding sort of fishing, and casting accuracy is essential. So, too, are quick reactions. Wild browns – smaller ones especially – take faster than almost any fish alive. Never let your eyes stray from your tippet. Strike at anything – a zip forward, a snatch in the current or a brief hold against the

stream. If a trout dimples where you think your olive might be riding, then strike and the fish will probably be on. Trust your instincts, and hone your eyesight.

There probably isn't a more physically or mentally demanding form of fishing. The wild brown trout and its dancing streams ask the utmost of you. You're always moving, watching, thinking and planning. Every piece of water is different and throws out a new challenge. You might decide to use some floating weed to break up the silhouette of your fly line. You might want to dull down your leader and rub it in the dirt if necessary. If you decide a strike indicator is necessary, then a piece of twig or a sliver of reed is less likely to alarm a wild brown than a shop-bought blob of polystyrene.

Don't fret about tackle. A couple of boxes of flies, some spare tippets (you're likely to lose a good few to the endless variety of snags) and you're really set for the day.

To get more fun than you'd ever believe possible and to lay down the lightest line that you've ever cast, think about fishing lightweight. It's for the flitting, wild brown trout streams that the 2-, 3- and 4-weight rods have been designed. Not only are these rods light; they can also cast with great accuracy.

Body language

All fish species speak strong body languages, but this is especially the case among the salmonids. Wild fish are invariably the quickest of all to react to changes, and they are more wary and more easily stressed when their carefully worked out lifestyles are challenged. Most experienced anglers recognize the most basic forms of body language – for example, when a trout is either hungry and actively finning the current looking for food or when it is much more relaxed, holding its position on the bottom and rarely bothering to intercept or investigate any passing food item. Other changes are more subtle and are often more difficult to read. All manner of occurrences can affect a trout's behaviour – bright sunlight, low water, rapid temperature change, the interference of man or the appearance of an otter or an osprey, for example.

Feeding with confidence – *If you see a wild trout working keenly in shallow water, then you can guess it feels secure in its world. In theory, if you don't make mistakes, this is an eminently catchable fish.*

Uncatchable – *These two trout pictured in clouded water seem quite oblivious to the angler. What's interesting is that they couldn't be bothered to get out of the way of something that should have alarmed them. We think of trout, rightly, as very wary creatures, perpetually looking for food opportunities or the threats of danger. However, there is another side to them – when conditions cause them to switch off they can be as comatose as any pike.*

Resting happily – *I saw this trout in high summer in a twinkling chalk stream among curling weed, and, despite his lack of movement, there was nothing at all wrong with him. He was simply happy doing nothing. A fellow angler drifted a couple of flies past him and he budged not an inch. Fin movement was at a minimum and the body was hardly flexing at all against the current… as close to asleep as it's possible to get.*

Sulking fish

Fish are very sensitive to their environment, and it doesn't take much to upset them, be it water temperature, currents or debris in the water. One thing that also plays a huge part in upsetting fish is, naturally, methods of catch and release. The arguments both for and against catch and release are massive. A general view is that special, large, wild fish should be released. When returning fish to the water there are certain vital rules to be followed to avoid producing a sulking fish that will be ever more aware of anglers. Barbless hooks make for quick, easy, painless unhooking. Try to keep the fish in the water while the unhooking process takes place. If you need to take a photograph, do it with the fish lifted just inches from the water and dunk it back in between each and every shot. When you release the fish, hold it gently against the current until it summons up the energy to move away. Ensure that your contact with the fish is minimal and is as gentle and unobtrusive as possible. Any fish bleeding from the gills is almost certain to die, so it's better to kill it and put it to good use in the kitchen.

Oddities – Here is a trout that you might think was frightened. It is holed up behind rocks with just its tail poking out to the world. Maybe it was my presence or perhaps it had been caught before. Strangely, I found it three or four times in exactly the same place over a period of about ten days when diving. Salmon frequently behave in exactly this way when they're running upstream. Perhaps it's a means of security for certain fish when they're not actively feeding.

Upon release – This is a small brown trout that was caught and released in a fairly uncaring sort of fashion. The photograph was taken between two and five minutes after capture. The fish is holding its own in the current but it is quite obviously distressed. The trout's skin is blotchy and its movements are erratic and jerky. The fish hasn't returned to its original lie and is drifting, looking for another area in which to settle.

Still recovering – This is the same fish half an hour after its release. The fish has now taken up physical sanctuary between an old brick and some waving water weed. It's wedged in uncomfortably, seeking out what current it can find and perhaps taking reassurance from the hiding-hole it's created for itself. In the event, it was two days before this particular trout returned to its original lie and began feeding again – a clear lesson that catch and release must be done properly.

Out in the storm – This trout is in some 3–4ft of water and seems disturbed by the leaves that are going past it. It refuses to hold anything like a permanent situation, but is constantly moving backwards and forwards across the current looking for relief. Remember your trout is a living, thinking creature that will go to great lengths to make its life as comfortable as possible.

The flood – Nor do trout like sudden floods of cold water. I stumbled across this one in a millpond that was only just beginning to fine down and where visibility was still only minimal. It looked miserable and was wedged in among boulders along the bottom where it had obviously found sanctuary. Silt and fine sand had collected on it and it obviously wasn't in the mood for feeding.

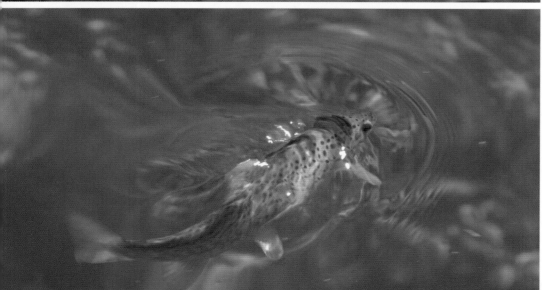

A happy contrast – This fin-perfect wild brown trout has just come to the surface, sipped in a small insect and is turning away with leisured confidence. If that trout had come to the fly, this is exactly the time that you would strike into the fish. Remember when you're dry fly fishing that most rises are missed by striking prematurely. It's far better to wait those extra two seconds till you see the fish going down with the fly between its lips.

Dave Lambert proudly cradles a nice brown trout caught right at the death of the river season. Notice the warm clothing to keep a smile on his face. Take note also of his position in the water, kneeling down so that the trout is even more easily released back into the stream. At this time of the year, with spawning on the horizon, extra vigilance must be taken.

UNHOOKING TROUT

Guide your fish – be it trout, salmon or sea trout – into shallow water where you can approach it without danger. Try not to use a net, and do not touch the fish any more than necessary, if at all. If the fly is not in the lips of the fish, use forceps to access a deep hook quickly and efficiently. Ensure that the fish is strong enough to cope before it moves out into the current – a fish washed away downriver on its back will drown.

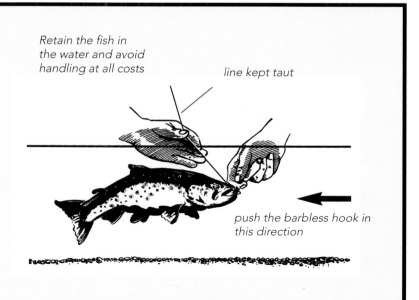

Retain the fish in the water and avoid handling at all costs

line kept taut

push the barbless hook in this direction

Summer Salmon

Summer salmon fishing on smaller spate rivers presents a great challenge. The fish tend to run during periods of heavy rain, when the river rises and colours. As it falls and fines down, the fishing can be excellent. However, the time window is brief and the fish soon wise up. An angler really has to strike when conditions are hot, but this doesn't mean to say that the usual rules of fishing go by the board. There's no room for the impetuous here. I was fortunate to meet up with the renowned Irish angler Ken Whelan on one of his favourite rivers, unfortunately when it was just a shade past its best. However, watching Ken was an object lesson in how anglers should approach these smaller, broken salmon rivers all over the world.

It's now on smaller, summer spate rivers, when the water is the colour of melted chocolate, that the salmon begin to flood up from the sea. The water is still too coloured to work a fly, but the salmon will be arriving – once the tinge falls out of the water you'll be in business. When you can see a bright orange or black fly a foot or so down, it's time to start fishing.

*▲ **Ready now** – The water now is in perfect shape falling, clearing with the fish steadying their run upstream and settling into pools (left). It's now that Ken (above) can target them. He moves quietly, confidently and continuously, fishing one good piece after the next, trying each place for 5–10 minutes before moving on.*

Setting out

'If only you'd been here yesterday', enthused Ken. 'I got here last evening and walked a mile or two of the river, just soaking it in, thinking how lovely it all was and looking out for fish. I helped a couple of lads land one, and we all enjoyed seeing it swim away again. There certainly were plenty of fish in the river just 15 or so hours ago, so we've got a chance, I guess.'

Ken's gear was heavy trout kit – a 9-foot rod, an 8-weight floating line, a 12ft, 10lb breaking strain leader, a sea trout fly on the dropper and a small shrimp on the tail. He would, he said, probably scale down the size of flies steadily throughout the day.

So, off we went, stopping first at a deep, slow piece of water that looked dead, dark and lifeless, the sort of place you usually associate with spinning.

'In places like this, you've really got to work the fly, because you can't get the current to do that for you. My advice would be to search out the tree line and to cast as far as possible under the branches on the far bank. Fish like to hang in the shade there. Look

really hard for your fish and you'll sometimes see them hanging in mid-water. Keep your nerve when they come after the fly – don't strike or pull it out in your excitement. Wait for them to catch it, turn and move the line before you lift into them. Water like this is frequently overlooked and it shouldn't be, because a lot of fish like to rest up out of the white water.'

Faster water

From there we moved down onto a perfect pool. The flow was channelled between the far bank and a rock outcrop on our side that served as a very tasty fishing platform. A line of alders and oaks hung over the main current, and Ken flicked his flies downstream under the branches. He fished the killing point as the flies swung round in the current and hung for an instant with devilish intensity. We both sensed the moment when a take was most likely and tensed. The sun was out, glistening off the dancing water, piercing the tree canopy with darts of light. Squadrons of damselflies crisscrossed the river. A perfect day.

Next we came upon a very quick little run, really nothing more than a thimbleful of water bubbling between two rapids. It was the size of a small sitting room, about 3ft deep and quite probably a holding pool for three or four fish. Ken decided on a single fly on the point for such a tiny little pot, coloured orange to suit the still peat-stained water. Then he fished it beautifully. You'd have to say he was flicking the line out rather than casting it, just bouncing the flies down with the flow and twitching them back, searching intently. The retrieve was all done with a neat figure-of-eight action – it's not good to have a lot of loose line out in a situation like this in case a hooked fish manages to make the downstream rapid and you've got to follow at a canter. I noticed, too, that he put a lot of rod top work into the retrieve, constantly jiggling the fly into life. He mended the line continuously, keeping in direct contact throughout the entire cast and then, right at the very end of the retrieve, he held the rod high and skated the fly hither and thither in the current. You just never know when an intrigued salmon might be following to your feet.

Testing the pools

On the next pool downstream, an alder craned helpfully over the river and I climbed it to watch. That orange fly certainly had a life of its own, flicking across the current like a small anguished fish looking for sanctuary. As my eyes grew accustomed to the water, I sensed the presence of salmon. Two of them. One was around 6lb and almost certainly not a taker. Its head was down and its body language was all dullness and sulkiness. The fly passed just a foot or so away from its head but its fins didn't even flicker. The other fish, however, seemed in half a mind to take. There's no doubt it could see the fly – whenever it got to within a few feet, the head would come up and the body would angle provocatively. The fins would work and you could almost sense the muscles flex. On one occasion, the fish even moved forwards in a short burst towards the fly, before easing off and dropping down in the water. There was obviously a third fish in the pool, too, because Ken had a strong, solid pull on the far side of the run where the tree shadow divided the water into light and dark. He was unlucky to miss it.

Anyway, another pool, slightly larger this time. 'There just has to be one at the tail there.' Ken waded more deeply, fishing the tightest possible line, determined not to miss another take, and just dibbling the fly back over where salmon had to be lying. 'I'll be flabbergasted if there's not, the water's just perfect…' Ken was a magician of action and movement, making his fly seemingly impossible to resist, but nothing.

Ken gave every one of these small pools around 15 minutes of very hard, concentrated fishing. Every nook was searched: these small river fish aren't big and they can literally melt into the tiniest pocket of water. You've got two chances: a new fish could enter the pool and be instantly vulnerable, or a resident fish could finally be needled into making a mistake. So, while it's tempting to keep on the move, don't sacrifice thoroughness on each and every pool.

The final pool

At last, we reached the end of the stretch and found a proper pool by normal salmon fishing standards. It lay around 80 yards long and Ken dibbled his flies over the neck and then worked the main body of the water, moving fast. He cast at 40 degrees or so downstream, the flies all but kissing the far bank, and then pulled them slowly a foot at a time across the flow. There was nothing mechanical about this. He varied the retrieve rate and action constantly. Watching his hands was a revelation: sometimes fast, sometimes slow, a pause, a twitch, a jab and then a long, steady heave. He worked quickly: a cast and then a good pace downriver. The process was repeated again and again with caution and concentration. It was a lovely pool – all moving water, no big slacks or back eddies, and not too deep. Once again I could see salmon whenever the sun broke through the cloud and glinted off their bodies.

He was done. Fishing like this is completely exhausting – you're not only working hard physically, but mentally too. Ken decided on a couple of hours' break and then he'd fish the dusk when salmon are always more active, stimulated by the coming night. We walked upriver towards the fishermen's hut, fishless but happy after a hugely satisfying day.

FLIES FOR SALMON

Salmon flies do not generally attempt to resemble food forms. They are frequently created on a whim or around a theory, often with no real natural pattern involved.

Size, colour and dressing

The first consideration is going to be size of fly and this is heavily dependent on the water temperature and the time of year. In general terms, the colder and murkier the water, the bigger the fly should be; the warmer and clearer the water, the smaller it should be. For this reason, for example, if you are fishing water that is below 8°C (45°F), then a fly of around 8cm (3in) in length is probably best. As the water temperature climbs, scale the fly down to 5cm or 6cm (2 or 2.5in). Once the water temperature is above about 10°C (50°F), things change dramatically and you might be looking at a fly tied on hook sizes 4 to 8. If the water becomes warmer still, let's say 13–16°C (55–60°F), you want flies between sizes 6 and 10.

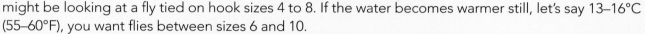

Next, I want to give you a rough guide as to colour. Actually, I'm far from convinced that salmon pay much heed to colour whatsoever, but whenever the water is clear I've always been recommended to use a fairly sombre fly that does not look too out of place. If the water, however, is murky, then a rather more colourful fly is needed to stand out from all the silt, sediment and floating rubbish.

The third consideration is the dressing of the salmon fly. Older patterns were generally dressed with feathers and, if you watch them work in the water, they somehow look stiff and unnatural. Modern flies tend to be tied more sparsely, often from fur, and they work much better in the water.

Temperature and depth

Temperature also affects the depth at which they will work. The colder the water, the deeper you want the fly to move and when temperatures are below 8°C (45°F), it's best to keep the fly as deep as possible, perhaps even touching bottom. Boddington tube flies are excellent for this type of work. You can move them along slowly, almost feeling them rub the bottom silt and debris.

As the water warms, you'll want to fish with a floating line and a lighter fly that swims somewhere in the surface layers. This means that for warmer water fishing you will be looking at flies that are lighter and will sink less quickly.

The size of hook on which the flies are tied is another factor. In all probability, the big flies of the spring and cold water are going to be tied on trebles or at least double hooks. As the water warms, single and double hooks begin to take over.

Always ask

A final consideration is the most important of all – local knowledge and advice. On any new water, the first job should be to ask the owner, the guide, a fellow angler or the local tackle dealer what flies they recommend and use. Local knowledge is not always accurate, but it would be arrogant to ignore it and it does give you some confidence when you're starting out.

Grayling Methods

Fortunately, the days of grayling being reviled are rapidly slipping into the past. Grayling are one of the most fascinating of all our fly-caught species. They're beautiful, hard-fighting and tremendously obliging – happy to feed in the heat of the summer and in the coldest depths of winter. They're also highly demanding: because they are shoal fish, their defences are multiplied many fold and it's much more difficult to creep up on a shoal of grayling than it is on a single, solitary trout.

Rob Olsen holds a magnificent grayling. Rob likes to be mobile and not stay at one piece of water for too long, which makes him the perfect grayling angler. Grayling tend to shoal up in small groups, so take three or four and then move on, constantly searching new pieces of water.

Getting to know grayling

Being a good trout fisherman doesn't automatically help when it comes to grayling: you'll find that grayling occupy different lengths of the river – another good reason for saying they don't compete with trout in most environments. Furthermore, grayling can be much more discriminating than trout when it comes to taking the artificial. A big grayling in clear water, especially, will refuse virtually every fly in the box, and if it does take the very last one, the take is likely to be so gentle that well over 90 per cent are missed. Grayling are never spread through a river like currants in a cake, and it's very important for the angler to remain mobile and search large areas of water to locate them. You will rarely see them rise, but look for them down deep in slower pools where they might just look like pieces of sunken branch.

The leveller

There are those trout anglers who think that a leveller, a strike indicator, a float, or whatever you like to call

Riding the surface – Choose your leveller carefully: it should be obvious to the eye, ride the stream elegantly, be buoyant enough to carry the nymph at the required depth and not be dragged under by every weed frond, and yet be forgiving enough to dip to the most tentative of grayling takes. Its shape can also be important – use a slim leveller for placid water and a more rounded design for rougher streams.

To strike or not? – The leveller has dipped fractionally under the surface. There's a bit of an obstruction on the bottom – ideally, you'll be working your nymph or nymphs quite close to the bottom – so it's an agonizing decision. Strike unnecessarily and the very action is likely to disturb the shoal; delay it too long and the take is missed.

Burying – You're in no doubt when the leveller goes down as deeply as this. However, be warned – it doesn't happen often. Watch out, too, for the leveller just holding up in the current for a second, no more – this, too, means that a grayling has sucked the nymph in. Very occasionally, if you're very lucky, the leveller will actually move upstream a fraction – a dead give-away as the grayling seizes a nymph and moves back to its position.

Autumn and winter grayling – *The great advantage of grayling is that you can fish for them during the cold months. However, there's often a severe leaf fall coating the river bottom. This is where a leveller really does come into its own – you can set it so that the nymph rides just clear of the offending vegetation. This leveller is set a fraction too deep, but a couple of trial runs and you'll soon be able to gauge the depth perfectly and run the nymph through just above bottom without catching the leaf stems.*

it, is unsporting. This could well be the case in trout-fishing circles but when it comes to grayling, believe me, you will catch 20 grayling on the leveller for every single one that you catch without. The reason? Quite simply, a grayling can sip in and
spit out an artificial in the blink of an eye, far more quickly than a trout can, so immediate observation of a take is essential. A second use of the leveller is implicit in its very name. Grayling generally feed at very specific depths and what the leveller does is keep your suspended nymph in line with the fish. Without a leveller, your nymph will simply plummet past the fish and hit bottom; some fish might stoop to take it, but you'd be missing the prime of the shoal. Experiment with setting the leveller at different depths until you find the critical taking point.

Crystal streams

Grayling fishing and crystal-clear water go hand in hand – the species just isn't happy in waters that are warm, murky or not sufficiently well oxygenated. Grayling, for these reasons, flourish from Alaska to Mongolia to the chalk streams of southern England. One of my happiest memories of this most visible form of fishing is in England's Derbyshire Dales, on the River Dove; I remember a particular pool that was so clear the grayling could be seen clearly at a depth of some 14–15ft. It was hugely difficult to gauge exactly how deep the fish were lying and at what level they were feeding. Getting the fly a couple of feet over or under depth would ruin all chances of success. The fish were literally at my rod tip but, over the years, proved more frustratingly difficult to catch than almost any other fish that I can remember.

Wading – To get the very best out of your grayling fishing it pays to get as close to the grayling as possible, so that you can fish really tight and present the fly with maximum accuracy and delicacy. There's nothing about good grayling fishing that is sloppy or left to chance. The closer you can get to the fish without disturbing them and the shorter the line you're using the more immediate will be the strike to the most hesitant of takes.

Success – This grayling sipped in my friend's fly just as he was lifting it off the bottom and past its nose. The grayling thought the fly was about to escape, so it hit in a hurry and was well hooked; most grayling won't be. Often, you'll find them only attached by the merest sliver of skin, so go very lightly in the fight. Take your time, and if one should jump, lower your rod tip to decrease the pressure on the hook hold.

Pike on the Fly

John Horsey is a long-term consultant for the leading UK tackle company Hardy and Greys. He has a long list of competition honours behind him, and has represented England for many years on the international scene. He is also the acknowledged UK expert on fly-caught pike, and I feel very privileged to have him pass on his secrets to us in this fascinating piece.

One of our most experienced international fly fishermen, John Horsey's special expertise is on larger stillwaters and recently he has pioneered pike fishing on the fly at Chew Valley Reservoir.

A worthy quarry

Most of my pike fly fishing is carried out on the big stillwater trout fisheries. A lot of these places in the UK were stocked illegally by very naughty pike anglers wanting to further their sport. Pike, nowadays, are hugely well established, so there's no point complaining about it, especially as they are such mighty and worthwhile creatures in their own right, particularly in the autumn and winter months when the trout fishing tails away. Today, thankfully, there's a very enlightened attitude towards pike, even in big trout fisheries. It's generally accepted that, providing that the big fish of 12–15lb and above are released, there's very little chance of an explosion of jacks, which is the major concern.

Tackle for pike

Let's look at tackle first. I go for a 9-foot, 8- or 9-weight rod with enough backbone to put out large flies and deal with big fish. Don't worry too much about fly reels: an 8-weight can easily be pressed into service, or go for a 9-weight if your budget stretches that far. With a reel, the main thing is to look for a really efficient braking system.

You need three basic fly lines, so that you can search as much water as possible. You'll need a floating weight-forward line, a clear intermediate and a fast sinker. These three cover the basics, although, if you really take to your piking, you might very well find you want to branch out and explore a range of different line types.

Pike flies

The main difference between piking and trouting is in the bigger flies that you'll be using. Most of them will be between 3 and 9 inches long! Many manufacturers try to turn their saltwater patterns into freshwater pike ones, but that's simply not good enough. The important thing is that your flies are tied with EP fibres, because this very mobile synthetic material gives the fly masses of movement. The other major advantage is that the fibres don't hold water. As soon as you've lifted the fly out, it's all but dry, and that means even the biggest fly is light enough to cast with ease.

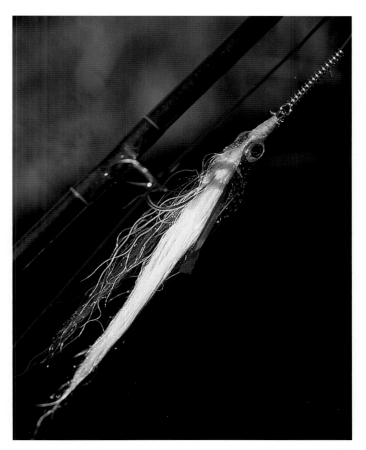

Endless patterns – Pike fly anglers will argue endlessly over patterns. True, some colours, sizes and materials work better than others, but all aim to achieve one objective: to imitate a small, struggling, vulnerable prey fish.

To some extent, the bigger the fly, the bigger the fish, but that's not a cast iron rule by any stretch of the imagination. What you do need, especially if you are tying your own flies, is really good quality hooks. I generally squeeze the barbs down on all my own flies. You just can't afford to take the risk of a big pike sucking a fly in and having a barbed hook go deep in an instant – pike of 15lb and above are too precious.

Special gear

The other major difference with pike fishing, as opposed to trout, is that you must use a wire trace of some sort. I like the Rio Toothy Critter. This is an all-in-one tapered leader with a wire trace connected. It's smooth, it works well and it's extremely convenient. Increasingly, I'm using Pro Leader, which

Wow! This is one of the most stunning pikes I personally have ever seen. It weighed over 30lb and fell for a surface-fished fly.

consists of an inner core of Dyneema covered with a stainless steel mesh coating. Unlike conventional wire, this can be knotted – a great advantage – and if it does kink after you've caught a fish, you can pull it through your fingers and it will straighten out at once. It comes in 10ft spools and is expensive, but it's worth it.

You'll need a long pair of forceps, an unhooking glove and a very large landing net. Scales and a camera are also useful. I should recommend unhooking mats – especially if you're fishing on a boat or hard stony banks – but I like to unhook my fish as often as possible in the net itself and let them go without lifting them from the water at all. However, if they are really large and you want records, then that's a little different.

You will also need polarized glasses, because a lot of success comes from spotting the fish and watching them take. On my favourite lakes, we chase

them in just 2 feet of water. It's almost like bone fishing, and you can get really, really close to them in the boat. Once the shadow of the boat goes over them, however, they're off in a flash. For this reason, concentrate on scanning the water close to you rather than looking too far afield.

Pike fly techniques

When it comes to methods, I've generally found that surface lures can be slow fishing, and I usually go subsurface. Pike fly fishing is all about location, and unless you can see the fish you just have to search as much water as possible. Often you'll need a sinker to get down really deep, but I tend to start close to the surface, work the middle zones and then, if all else fails, dredge close to the bottom. I like drifting on the drogue, too, as this allows me to cover even more water. So, you can see that searching the water really is the key. If you catch a pike, be immediately prepared for another, as you'll often find them clustered in specific areas.

You will find pike hotspots, but not in the conventional sense. Forget the usual recommended structures – tree roots, drop-offs, reed beds and water towers. Big reservoir pike aren't like other populations. Pike don't lie in wait, they don't mount ambushes, but they cover vast amounts of open water looking for prey. They're young, incredibly fast-growing fish and they learn – for example, you'll often find feeding fish around the usual stocking points.

The retrieve

The retrieve is important, and it pays to change styles all the time. I like a stuttered retrieve, a jerky figure-of-eight retrieve and a sink-and-draw type of action. These are my fail-safes, and I tend to switch from one to the other through the course of the day.

You'll very often get fish following. They simply ghost from the depths and follow the fly, keeping a few inches behind. If you stop retrieving, they stop. Start retrieving and they start up again. Infuriatingly, they won't make that last lunge. You can try taking the fly out of the water and flopping it down hard near the fish. This can trigger an instant take. Frequently, it's best to change fly, try a different colour and size, and retrieve it in the general area where you last saw the fish. Swapping flies is made easier if they're attached with links, but these have to be very strong indeed to withstand the continual punishment of casting.

The moment when a pike takes a fly is absolutely critical. Don't strike. I describe a pike take on the fly as a clunk-click type of action. At first, you have a pull and feel something like a metallic tug. That, I believe, is the clunk, the fly being sucked in and hitting the pike's teeth. Then, there will be a moment when the line goes slack. This is when the pike is actually following you and the tension decreases. The pike will then close its mouth – the click – and you'll feel a long, steady pull. How do you react? Well, keep pulling on the line, almost as though you are strip striking. It's nothing wild, but a calm, measured response. Don't forget, if you strike at the first pull,

Notice the wire trace – it's absolutely essential to use one, and not too short a one at that, when you're fly fishing for pike. Failure to do so will often mean a nylon leader being severed and a pike being condemned to a slow and lingering death.

you'll lose the fish every time by just pulling the fly out of the pike's open jaws.

I play my pike as hard as I can to get them in as quickly as possible. A long fight, especially in warmer water, simply tires them enormously, and a pike at the point of exhaustion is in a dangerous condition. I find that I can play a big pike with a 9-weight rod far harder than I can with a traditional 3lb test-curve dead-bait rod. I know that takes some believing, but it's absolutely true.

Fierce but fragile

Pike are at the head of the food chain in waters such as those described here, and the only creature they really and truly have to fear is man. For this reason, I recommend single hooks, crushed barbs, forceful playing techniques, long pliers and unhooking procedures that take place, as often as not, in the water. Pike grow big and can certainly look menacing, but in actual fact they are very susceptible indeed to bad handling, and a bleeding pike is inevitably a dying pike. I love my trout but I adore my pike, and the mothers of 15lb and over – sometimes way over – are a welcome addition to any fishery. Catching these beauties on the fly is efficient and exciting, and once you've become used to it, dead baits will be a thing of the past.

CHAPTER 4

BAIT FISHING

In essence, bait fishing is as simple as it gets. All you've got to do is put the right bait to the right fish, in the right place at the right time, in the right way – and bingo! But, of course, any one of these five considerations can cause problems. It's always best to think every part of your approach out in every circumstance. Don't rush. Consider all the options. Above all, make a plan and stick to it until it's quite obvious that it's not working. For this reason, try always to have plans B and C cooking away in your mind as possible fallbacks if necessary.

Introduction to Freshwater Bait Fishing

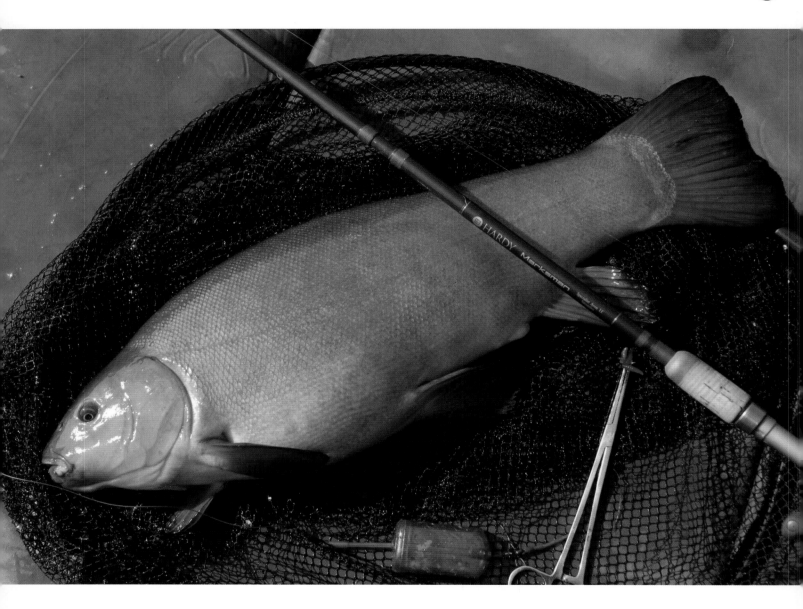

I used to live very close to a large day-ticket bait-fishing water. I walked around it virtually every day unless the weather was absolutely foul or it was physically frozen over with ice. I watched some anglers succeed there, but the majority, however, failed. Why? On the simplest possible level, most of those that failed were just fishing the wrong places. It sounds very basic, but the vast majority of anglers would leave their vehicles, walk a short distance and then settle down in the nearest available place.

This is one of the most gorgeous tench you will ever see. It is absolutely fin-perfect and slim prior to spawning. Everything involved in its capture is there – the unhooking mat, the feeder and the plastic maggots that succeeded in enticing the fish.

First find your fish

More times than I can count, if anglers I've seen failing to catch fish with bait on a piece of freshwater had merely moved another 10–100yd, they would have physically seen evidence of many feeding fish. Over and over, they were fishing where practically nothing was happening, and they were doomed to failure from the outset. My basic, most logical advice, therefore, is to leave the tackle safely locked up while you walk the water and look for the signs of where fish are present and where they are feeding. Location is the key, and though it's an oft stated and obvious fact, it is frequently overlooked.

Do it right

Of course, there were other factors, too. The anglers who succeeded were those who chose the best method for the particular swim on the particular day. If legering, swim feeding, float fishing or even free-lining was the best method, they'd choose it.

They were also the people who fished the best method in the best possible way – with calm control and consistent accuracy. Their feeding would be spot-on, their casting pinpoint and their bait presentation immaculate. They would concentrate like hawks and strike at bites, however slight. Nothing they did was slapdash, clumsy or left to chance. It was an education and a delight to watch them.

Have another look at the 'Detecting the Bite' section in Chapter One. When you are bait fishing, bites can be exceptionally sensitive and might merely nudge a quiver tip, dip a float or tremble the line between your fingers. There are some baits and methods that on some occasions might produce a bigger bite, but not always. Do not make the mistake of thinking a very slight bite is necessarily the result of a small fish taking interest. Frequently, the bigger the fish, the more warily they will actually pick up a bait.

Never be in too much of a hurry to leave the waterside at the end of the day. The increasing shadows and the darkening water almost always encourage non-predatory fish, especially, to move more and to feed more aggressively.

Some useful tips

Before we move on to look at all the many forms of freshwater bait fishing, let's just run through a few tips that could prove vitally important.

- Target shallower water in the early part of spring as the water begins to rise. Fish will often over-winter in deeper parts of the lake, but as their metabolism speeds up, they will come to feed on the fertile shallows.
- Target areas of the lake that get a lot of sunlight, especially in the colder months of the year. It's not just a question of temperature: the light itself stimulates many members of the cyprinid family in particular into greater feeding activity.
- Don't overlook the western bank of any stillwater in the dawn period. It will receive the first rays of the rising sun and the water will warm up more quickly there, encouraging serious feeding activity.
- Travel as light as you can. Watch the water and move on to any fish that are rolling or bubbling. A mobile approach is particularly important in understocked waters or when the fishing conditions are difficult.
- Never overfeed – it is best to put in less free offerings than more. Until you get to know a water particularly well and have been successful enough to start experimenting, use baits in which you have confidence.

Distance fishing – *Using a marker float like this can be a boon in telling you exactly where you have laid a carpet of bait.*

Bring on the Bait

In the bait-fishing world, new, wonder baits are always appearing, perhaps flourishing for a few years and then usually disappearing. In part, this is due to commercialism: companies are constantly looking to make a quick buck and the new bait that promises instant success is always going to win a gullible audience. The skill in choosing your bait lies in seeing through the hype and recognizing exactly what fish want at any given moment in their lives.

The guzzler – This shot of a carp shovelling in sweetcorn was taken in a large European lake. I have no doubt that the slight clouding of the water also encouraged the fish to feed hard.

Positive and negative

There are certain rules. Look at what fish are eating naturally. If they're consuming something with gusto and in real quantities, the chances are that they will mop it up if it's on a hook, too. So, if it's large enough to go on as bait and you can get your hands on it, by all means use it. I can think of loads of examples where I've been successful once I'd cottoned on to what the fish were eating naturally: fish eating the weed that was growing on the pilings of a bridge out in Spain; fish eating caddis grubs found in profusion under the stones in a Czech river; some North American small-mouthed bass that were thoroughly addicted to stonefly larva; Indian mahseer going pop-eyed for freshwater crabs.

If fish have become scared of a particular bait, there's no point in trying to use it. In many parts of the world, the popularity of angling has caused waters to become heavily pressured, and if fish have been caught or hooked on a certain bait, the chances are they won't be eating it again. If you want to hoodwink them a second time, you'll just have to move on to something different or more sophisticated.

Getting it right

This is where making your baits more appealing and more unusual becomes a real skill. Take a bait as humble as luncheon meat. Most people will use a piece about the size of a stock cube. The fish soon come to realize that these uniformly sized pieces of meat spell danger. The thinking angler will use a tiny piece of meat – just a shard, just enough to cover a small hook. If that doesn't work and the water is high and clouded, he'll use a huge piece of meat, perhaps half a tin, and he won't cut that piece with a knife so that it's all neat and uniform like everybody else's. He'll pull it apart with his fingers so that it's ragged, with bits falling off, making it much more attractive and much less suspicious.

A further skill is to get fish used to the baits that you will be using. Pre-baiting is an art. You don't want to pre-bait so much that you'll fill the fish up and find them totally unresponsive when it comes to casting out, but equally you don't want to pre-bait

The fertile river – Turn over any rock or stone in a fertile river and you will find clusters of natural food underneath. The caddis grub in particular is an excellent bait.

so stintingly that you never turn the fish on to what you're offering. In short, you've got to try to assess how many fish are out there and how hungry they are, and then give them enough of your bait samples to get them excited, to switch them on and to keep them looking for more.

The hair rig – The hooking of baits has progressed massively over the years. Putting a bait straight on a hook now is comparatively rare. This particular shot shows a pellet effectively hair-rigged (see pg. 257). Presenting a pellet like this keeps the hook point free and enables a clean strike.

Ring the changes – Too often, anglers use luncheon meat cut into perfectly regular shapes. The fish get suspicious of these, though, so it's best to tear off some meat, leaving it jagged so that pieces fall off in the stream.

Cubed meat – If you are going to use cubed meat, then vary how many pieces you use. If the water is coloured, three or four pieces won't go amiss. As the water clears, two is probably about right.

Ploughman's bait

Let's look at the main categories of bait and see how the skilful angler will take them, adapt them and improve them so that he's one step ahead of all the rest. Perhaps the most common baits for many years have been those you find in your kitchen. What we like to eat, as a general rule, the fish like to eat.

Probably more fish have been caught on bread over the centuries than on any other bait. Bread can be used in crust, flake or paste forms. The great advantage is that fish both like and recognize the taste and smell of bread. Bread is also easily seen, both in coloured water and at night. You can use bread big or small, floating or sinking, and have confidence in it. If the fish are spooked, change the form in which you use it. If you've been using paste, change to flake. If you've been using flake, try some crust. If you've been using white bread, change to brown. Perhaps you could try flavouring your bread with smears of cheese. Virtually all fish adore cheese, either on its own or made into a paste with bread. Today, in most countries, it is sadly overlooked. This is a great shame as there's a huge variety out there - soft cheese, hard cheese, cream cheese, processed cheese – and it has great smell, great texture, is easy to see, and you're always going to be able to offer a suspicious fish something new. Like meat, you can use a tiny piece or a huge piece. Apart from out-and-out predators, there's barely a fish that swims in freshwater that doesn't like cheese.

The magic of sweetcorn

One of the most popular baits worldwide over the past 30 or 40 years – especially for cyprinids – has been sweetcorn. The little yellow grains drive fish of scores of species absolutely crazy. They are visible, give off a great smell and their taste appears to be addictive. There's a lot you can do with sweetcorn: you can use grains singly or even chop them in half, or you can pack 10 grains on a big hook. You can use the juice to flavour groundbait or, if the fish become wary of the original yellow, you can colour it black or red or orange.

Short and sweet –- Sweetcorn was traditionally fished on the hook, but for many species, carp especially, it's often best now to fish it on a hair-rig (see pg. 257). A short hair like this will also fool the tench.

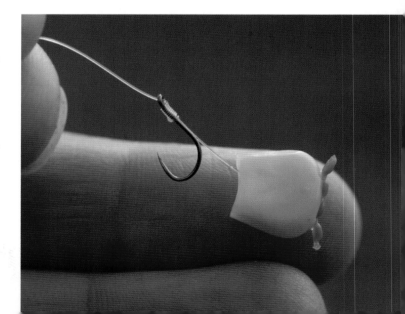

Particle baits

Perhaps the greatest appeal of sweetcorn is that it is a particle bait, a form of bait made up of numerous small items. Again, cyprinids adore particle baits. Baits such as maggot, hemp seed, nuts and pulses all preoccupy a fish, dominate its thinking processes and often drive it into a feeding frenzy. There are several problems with particle baits, however. Firstly, the fish become so preoccupied with them that often they won't look at larger hook baits used over a bed of these particles. You've therefore got to use the particle on the hook, and presentation can be difficult. Also, especially in summer, fry and fingerlings can be a problem with particle baits such as maggots, not to mention eels that sneak out as the dusk falls. So, while particles can turn your swim into a foaming pile of bubbles, they can also make a rod for your own back.

This is where slightly larger particle baits score heavily. They're small enough to preoccupy the fish, yet large enough to present comparatively easily. Peanuts (properly prepared) are as addictive as sweetcorn. Tiger nuts, tares, butter beans, Brazil nuts, broad beans, cashew nuts, kidney beans, soy beans, chickpeas and black-eyed beans also do well. I've had success with diced-up jelly babies and even some types of mints. All these baits work well, probably for comparatively short periods, but they are so numerous that you can keep chopping and changing and coming up with a winning formula. So, it does make sense to visit supermarkets frequently, scouring the shelves looking for those obscure tins and packets that other anglers have probably never even considered.

Natural baits

Earlier, I discussed weed, caddis grubs and the like, and the skilful bait angler will learn to make increasing use of natural baits. Naturals will always catch fish, simply because they are there in the wild, forming a part of the everyday menu. Worms are obvious, but caddis grubs, shrimps, slugs, wasp grubs and bloodworms are good, too.

You can buy worms commercially or pick them from the surface of any grassland on a warm, moist night. Look after your worms, keep them damp and throw away any dead or dying ones that will infect the healthy. Worms, like many of the best baits, are immensely adaptable. They can be chopped up to form a really enticing groundbait, used in halves, used singly or in bunches to attract any fish species from perch to salmon. Moreover, they're exactly what river fish expect to find after heavy rain.

This simple, straightforward, sugary sweet bought from the local supermarket smells good, tastes good and takes hours to break down in the water. A perfect bait for all fish.

Shrimps and prawns, both cooked and uncooked, have proved immensely popular with many species of fish over the last few years. Perch have been particularly susceptible.

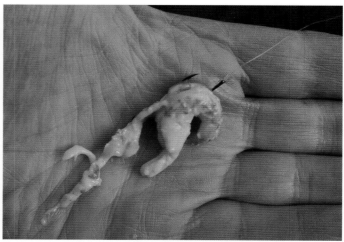

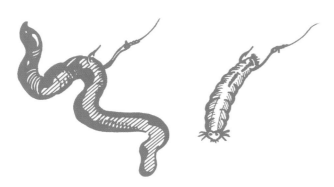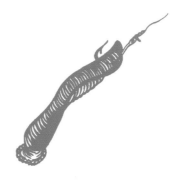

WRIGGLERS

Thousands of worms are washed to their deaths during floods along rivers each year, and fish have come to recognize them as safe, nutritious food. Caddis grubs are another great natural bait. They inhabit the bottom of the river, living in cases glued to stone and gravel. Prise them out of their cocoons for one of the least suspected of all baits.

CREEPY-CRAWLIES

Slugs are a good bait for many fish, especially chub. The size of hook depends on the type of slug used. If you can, try to use a slug without any weight at all – they're often heavy enough to counteract a slight current. Look out too for all manner of nymphs, leeches, crickets, grasshoppers, moths, snails, anything of hookable size on the natural menu.

I'm not sure where I stand any more on the question of using a small dead bait to catch a larger fish. It somehow seems mean to catch a perch and then kill it to catch a pike. Nevertheless, there are endless amounts of sea fish already dead and for sale in fishmongers, and while we tend to think of these primarily as baits for pike and the big predators, small silver sea fish, such as sprats, can be excellent for many members of the cyprinid family. Moreover, in tinned anchovies you've got one of the best, most instant and most overlooked baits in the entire fishing world.

Special baits

A far cry from the natural is the laboratory-produced special bait, perhaps a boiled bait (a boily as they've become known) or a paste consisting of endless amounts of carefully prepared, chemically based ingredients. All of them have a great smell and this makes them particularly effective in waters with low visibility. The boily has revolutionized fishing for carp in particular, but also for other members of the cyprinid family. It's a bait that usually consists of a dried powder added to eggs and flavouring, mixed into a paste, rolled into balls, boiled to give it a hard skin and then used on the hook or as free offerings. Most boilies are based on high-protein mixes with all manner of essences and additives to

make them taste, smell and look good. Boilies can be made buoyant to pop up from the bottom so that they hang enticingly above weed or silt. Mini-boilies are also on the market and are perfect for smaller members of the cyprinid family. You can make your own boilies or you can buy them.

The pop-up – The boily here is buoyant, so it can carry the weight of the hook and wave just off the bed. This makes it highly visible to a cruising fish and allows it to be sucked into the mouth with minimal effort.

MAKING BOILIES

I don't propose to go through the entire process of making boilies here, because the recipes can be picked up from the packets of the ingredients you will need to buy, but I will pass on a number of useful tips.

- Before starting to make boilies, always wash your hands carefully in unscented water.
- Make sure all the utensils that you use are really clean.
- If you're going to make boilies on a regular basis then it pays to invest in modern tools such as sausage guns and rolling tables.
- Never smoke when you're making bait.
- Always use boiling water at every stage of the game. Hot water isn't good enough.
- Always follow the instructions on the packets and don't cut corners.
- Ensure that you measure ingredients exactly and don't make haphazard guesses. You'll need proper measuring equipment for this.
- Don't exceed the recommended dosage – you'll kill the bait totally.
- Have everything in front of you before you begin. Baits will go off if you have to rush out for forgotten ingredients.
- Make sure everything you use is fresh – especially the eggs.
- Mix everything thoroughly.
- Tidy everything up and wash everything thoroughly once you've finished.
- Allow baits to cool and then store them carefully.
- Develop a smooth-running routine and you'll soon be turning baits out like a mini factory!

THE 'D' RIG

(1) Tie the hooklink to the hook. Place a piece of shrink tubing over the knotted hook. Slide a piece of stiff mono through the shrink tubing. Thread the stiff mono though a 2mm rig ring and then through the hook eye to form a 'D'.
(2) Heat the shrink tubing. Cut the stiff mono to length.
(3) Using a cigarette lighter, carefully burn the tag end to form a blob.

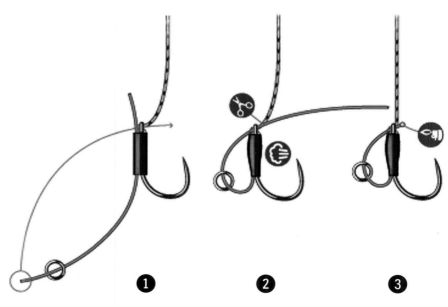

Groundbait

I've already talked about building up your swim and preparing your fish with free samples of your hook bait, and this is often quite sufficient. There are times, however, when you want something a little more noticeable, and that's where a groundbait that explodes in the water, with plenty of visual impact, comes into its own. The oldest and most commonly used form of groundbait is simply breadcrumbs, but in the modern world the new groundbaits have all manner of different additives to increase their scent and visual attractiveness. Consistency is important, too: light groundbait can be used for shallow stillwater, whereas heavier groundbait will be needed for quick, deep rivers. Mix your groundbait up, drop it into the water and see how it behaves.

Don't use groundbait – or any bait, come to that – slavishly. Think carefully whether the fish you are

A beguiling mix – The contents of a carp fisher's bucket can be intriguing. The boilies are cut in half to release more smell. One ingredient, hemp seed, is oily and terrifically aromatic. Other pulses and beans complete the mix.

Careful presentation – These floating dog biscuits have had a groove filed along their undersides. This fits the hook shank neatly, and then the biscuit is superglued into position. Now you know the biscuit won't come off for at least an hour or so in the water.

Breakdown – Think carefully about how your bait and the free offerings around it behave in the water. Pellets, for example, may gradually break down, especially in warm water, leaving piles of powdery food that fish love to eat.

hunting really need to be approached in this way. The more individual baits – especially heavy ones like boilies – that you throw in, the more the fish will be aware of your presence and your intentions. The same, too, obviously applies to balls of groundbait going in like mini hand grenades.

The skilful angler needs to think carefully about all this. Some years ago, one of my closest angling friends caught a massive barbel on one single cast. However, he'd prepared for that cast. For the previous two hours he'd thrown in tiny pieces of luncheon meat. He hadn't thrown these in all at once and alarmed the fish beneath, but he'd thrown a piece every five minutes. After two hours, he'd perhaps scattered 40 tiny bits of meat into the swim without alerting the barbel to any danger whatsoever. When his own tiny piece of meat appeared, it was the most natural thing in the world for his big fish to suck it in and be caught.

Opportunistic baits

Always keep your eyes open for clues along the bankside. Overhanging trees often drop ripe fruit into the water, which can attract and hold fish for long periods of time – mahseer in India, for example, love fallen oranges. Think of baby birds nesting under bridges and on water towers, and how bass, congregate around such places waiting for falling fledglings. If a wind gets up, watch to see if craneflies are blown from the grass into the water, and note which fish species come up to take them. It's the same with grasshoppers falling into a stream. Watch the cattle in the meadow. Eventually they will come to the lake or river to drink and stir up any mud that is there, and in that mud there will be many hiding insects. Fish know this, and they will come towards feeding cattle as though the dinner gong has been struck.

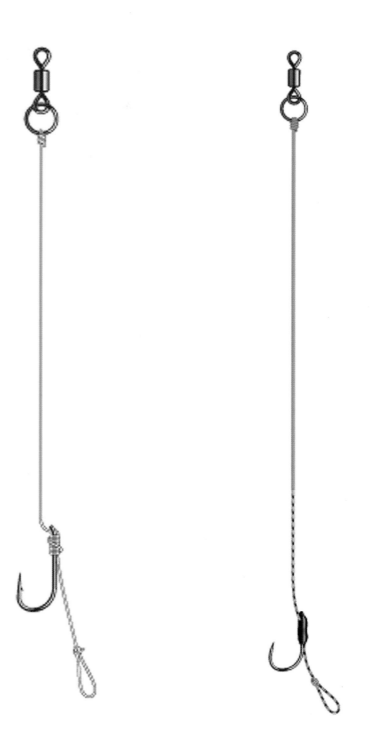

STIFF RIG
Made of stiff (25lb) fluorocarbon hooklink material, this rig has excellent anti-tangle properties, is virtually invisible underwater and is difficult for a fish to eject.

COMBI-RIG
The first few centimetres of coating is stripped from the coated braid hooklink in this rig, creating the combination of a flexible hooklink for good bait presentation and excellent anti-tangle properties.

Bait Fishing in Stillwaters

A large stillwater, whether it be an artificial or natural one, can be a very daunting proposition when you are still a relatively inexperienced angler and new to the water. There are no fish in sight, and there may be no obvious features – such as beds of reed, weed or lily pads – that might cause them to congregate. So where on earth do you begin?

Many stillwater bait fishers settle on one place for the whole day and draw fish into it by feeding in bait, gradually and persistently. They will set up several different rods so they can fish close in or far out, as conditions and the fishes' movements dictate.

Finding the right spot

A good way to find a fishing spot is to ask advice, perhaps from somebody who knows a water better than you do, probably from the bailiff. Bailiffs always want to see anglers succeed – their living depends on the sale of tickets and a successful angler is one who will return to a particular water.

Failing this, there are several major factors to consider. Firstly, where is the wind coming from? Many, if not most, types of freshwater species tend to follow the wind, gradually moving toward the bank that it's hitting. In Europe, we are generally faced with westerly winds, and this tends to mean that the easterly shores are a good place to start.

Equally important is the question of cover. Smaller prey fish will never stray far from the refuge of reed and weed beds. A lot of fish also like to escape from the hubbub, so if there's a large, busy car park, then consider taking a good long walk with your binoculars to see what the more remote areas of the lake can offer. Bream and tench in particular will often move as far away as possible from commotion,

and the angler who is prepared to use his legs starts off at a great advantage.

What other strategies can you follow? Look at lily pads, a very common feature on many stillwaters. These pads have magnetic qualities for carp and perch in particular. However, you will have to remember that stronger than average gear is needed when you're fishing around the pads because the lily stems can be very tough indeed. Don't compromise on this, it's not fair on the fish if you lose it, leaving a hook in the mouth. Dribble in a few pieces of floating bait – bread crust or dog mixer biscuits are both ideal – and sit back quietly to see what happens. Watch for subtle movements amidst the pads. Then, perhaps, you will see the lips of the fish as it gently pulls the bait down.

The winter lake – Winter fishing can be particularly difficult, as the cold weather makes the fish slow down and move less. This means location is crucially important. Try fishing close to dying reed beds or the remains of weeds that you can see just under the surface. If you can find them, also try deeper depressions in the lake's bed.

A hot spot – *There are certain clues every experienced bait fisher looks for. Fish love to harbour under lily pads. They also seek out areas where surface scum has built up during the course of the day. All sorts of insect and food are trapped here and the fish won't be far away.*

Carp are very likely to be responsible, but rudd and even crucian carp will also scan the surface film. Once you see activity like this, simply flick out a hooked bait and watch for the line slithering off.

Using subsurface bait
A subsurface bait can also work well, especially if it's a natural one. Remember that the fish are in the pads not just for protection, they are also looking for food – snails are particularly fond of lily pads and provide a good mouthful for a carp. Try using a small float and, perhaps, a couple of lively redworms fished about 45cm (18in) under the surface. Perch and carp often find this approach irresistible.

Whatever you hook in the pads, try to get them out into the open water as quickly as possible. Upon being hooked, many fish can be puzzled for just a few seconds and this gives you a chance to bully them clear. If a fish gets deep down amongst the roots of

the lilies then you are in real trouble – you've got to set about the fight with real confidence in your tackle.

Reed beds and tench
Let's now look at reed beds, and at tench, the species that really adores them. Probably the most sought after type of reed are bulrushes. This is because bulrushes like to grow on a hard, clean, gravely bed – exactly the sort of place that tench prefer to feed. Bait up carefully with a mixture of sweetcorn, hemp seed, casters and a few maggots. Try to put the groundbait and your own tackle as close into the bulrushes as you possibly can. This is because the tench will often be swimming and feeding deep in the watery jungle. Laying-on is a super method for tench, very traditional, but nonetheless effective. This involves applying sufficient split shot to the line to keep the bait on the bottom and the float "cocked," or upright. Tench will often pick the bait up, causing the float to rise or fall flat – so pay attention!

Look out for tench bubbles too, clusters of tiny, pinprick type bubbles that explode and fizz on the surface. Sometimes bits of bottom debris will also

Old red eye – The red eye of the tench is the trademark of this very careful fish. Look for it in reed beds, especially bulrushes, and on the bottom, where it feeds on bread, worms or maggots. Bites are hesitant, and can take half a minute to develop. Don't strike at the first indications.

float to the surface, a sign that a group of fish is really rooting around and feeding hard… hopefully on your groundbait.

Varying your bait

If you're not getting bites, then ring the changes with your hook baits. Try three grains of corn on a size 10

hook, or one grain on a size 16. Try two maggots and one caster on a size 12 hook, or two casters and a grain of corn on a size 10. Sooner or later you're more than likely to come across a winning combination.

Bream are a species that quite frequently likes to hang out a long way from the bank, and this means it's often necessary to approach them with long

Monster mash – A perfect mash, this, of wetted bread and pieces of sweetcorn. Kept very moist, this mix will hit the surface and explode into an enticing cloud.

A classic combination of casters and hemp seed, perfect for pretty well every species of coarse fish. Tench, carp, roach, barbel and chub are particularly susceptible to these flavours.

casting. First of all try, if at all possible, to locate your shoal. Look carefully at the water in front of you and see if you can spot any flat areas in patches of rippled water. This could well be a fish moving heavily just under the surface. Or, most excitingly, look for bream actually breaking the surface in a head and shoulders, slow, porpoise-like roll. Alternatively, you'll sometimes just see the tips of black fins, or perhaps a big area of coloured water, which means the bed is being disturbed by feeding fish.

Once you've found fish, you'll probably need to put out some light groundbait to get them feeding. Perhaps they're close enough for you to do this by catapult. If they are, mix your groundbait very stiffly and fire out small balls, just a little away from the fish. Whatever you do, don't put big balls on top of them as you will scare them. Mix maggots and casters into the groundbait.

Using a swim feeder

If the fish are too far away for this, then you could try using a swim feeder on line of about 4lb breaking strain.

Vary your hook length – start off at approximately 60cm (2ft), though sometimes it's wise to go much longer than this. Your hook length can also be very slightly lighter – try 3 or 4 pounds breaking strength perhaps. A small hook, say a 16, and a couple of maggots are a good starting-off point for average sized bream in the 4–6lb category. No luck? Then try a pinch of bread flake, a small brandling worm or any cocktail of maggots, worms and sweetcorn. Just as when you're tench fishing, keep an open mind and keep on experimenting.

For bite indication, you can either use a quiver tip or a butt indicator. Don't be in too great a hurry to strike – some expert bream handlers advocate sitting on your hands till the reel handle begins to turn! This

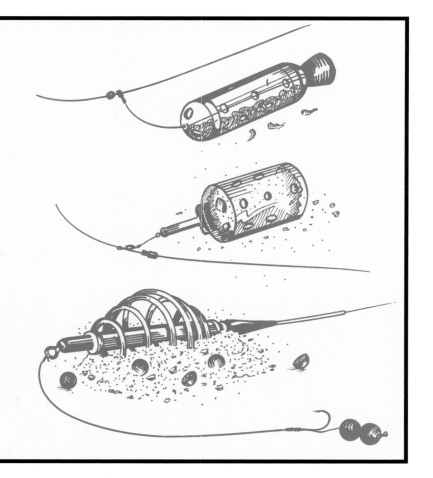

FISHING WITH A SWIM FEEDER

THE FEEDERS

Swim feeders come in all shapes and sizes, designed for use on both still and running waters. The block-end feeder (top) is perfect for maggots on any water. The other feeder (bottom) is open-ended and plugged with groundbait that explodes when the feeder hits the water. The feeder has the advantage of placing a carpet of bait very close to the hook.

THE METHOD

The method is very simple. The coiled feeder is packed tightly with stiff groundbait that is embedded with food items. The hook bait is pressed into the groundbait and the whole ball is cast out into the swim. Because of the weight, great distances can be achieved, especially on stillwaters. The idea is that the fish home in on the scent of the bait and a feeding frenzy begins.

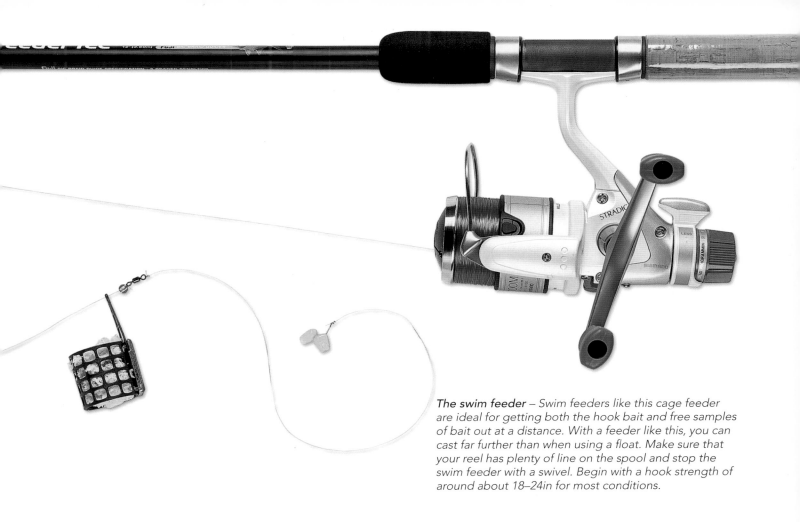

The swim feeder – Swim feeders like this cage feeder are ideal for getting both the hook bait and free samples of bait out at a distance. With a feeder like this, you can cast far further than when using a float. Make sure that your reel has plenty of line on the spool and stop the swim feeder with a swivel. Begin with a hook strength of around about 18–24in for most conditions.

is to prevent you pulling the bait out of the bream's mouth, and they often do take quite a time before they pass it beyond their lips. Try to bully a hooked bream away from its fellows as soon as you can, or the fish will plough through the shoal, causing great alarm as it does so.

Loading up a spod – Here we see good friend Andy Charlton loading a spod with a mix of groundbait. Spods are fired out long distances with heavy gear and the aim is to lay a carpet of bait anything up to a 100m or more from the bank. Don't fill the spod too full with groundbait that is too stodgy, in case it doesn't empty properly.

Bait Fishing in Rivers

In an ideal world, you'd want to start fishing on a clear and sparkling river where you can actually see decent fish of the sort you want to catch frolicking beneath the surface. However, let's presume this isn't the case, so where on earth do you begin?

This angler has waded way out into the river to fish a deep run under a tree on the far bank. He fishes with a float so he can move a bait very naturally, and he's expecting quick, decisive bites.

River hotspots

The major factors to consider when reading a river are the strength and direction of the current, the depth, the amount of cover and the make-up of the riverbed. Most species of fish like to hang where the current is neither too strong nor too slow, where there's a fair amount of water to cover their backs, where they can find shelter from predators, and where there is clean gravel or sand over which they can find food easily.

Once again, though, let's look at some typical river hotspots and discuss some of the best approaches to fish them. Above all, anglers – and fish, fortunately – are attracted to mill pools or weir pools where foaming, well-oxygenated water tumbles over the sill. There's no doubt that fish welcome this freshening of their environment, especially in summer. And when you have low, hot conditions, you will find big populations amassing.

But how do you fish a mill pool? There are various areas to concentrate on: try right in the quick, foaming, white water for roach, chub or barbel. Where the current steadies up a bit, but there is still a lot of depth, is an ideal haunt for bream. As the mill pool shallows and glides into its traditional riverbed, it produces streamy, gravely water, often with abundant weed – perfect once again for barbel and chub.

Foaming water conditions

Let's look in greater detail at the foaming water under the mill itself: it will be deep there, anything up to 3–5m (10–15ft), or even more on a large river. Try fishing tight under your rod tip with a float and a big lump of bread flake on the bottom. The current will move your tackle around every now and again, lifting the bait up and nudging it over the bottom stones and brickwork. This proves irresistible for both roach and chub, so expect bites to be quite ferocious. As for groundbait, dunk two or three slices of bread in the water and once they're thoroughly wet, mash them up and dribble them in around your float so you have a curtain of falling crumbs.

Top spots – A weir like this is a magnet to many fish species. The falling water oxygenates the river beneath, and the action of the quick water also tends to dislodge the aquatic insects that the fish are looking to feed upon.

Rafts are always magnetic for chub, and for barbel to only a slightly lesser degree. A raft is simply all the drifting weed, leaves and rubbish that builds up when it catches against the overhanging branches of a tree. Soon the rafts can have the surface area of a fair-sized rug and the fish love the shelter on offer. The strategy here is to sit a good 5 or 10 yards upstream and just flick in thumbnail-sized pieces of squeezed bread over a period of half an hour or so. Feed in perhaps 30 or even 40 pieces; a couple every minute is fine. The purpose behind this is to allay any suspicions the chub may have of the hook bait.

Now you're ready to fish: a size 4 hook with a big piece of bread squeezed around the shank is all you need. Place an SSG shot about 15cm (6in) up from it, 5cm (2in) if the current is quick. Simply flick the bread a yard (1m) or so upstream of the raft and let it sink down underneath. Prepare for an almost instant bite.

You can hold the line round your fingers and feel for that rat-tat tug. Strike and then bully the fish hard from the tree roots, return it upstream and then try again in half an hour or so and you will probably be rewarded with another fish or two.

Fishing the crease

Bends nearly always attract fish, especially on typical lowland rivers that have been dredged in the past and offer few features. They're also very attractive in the winter, especially when the river is in flood. Look for what anglers call the crease – that's where the current is separated from the slack water that

Reading the water – In this water, there are areas of shallow gravels with quick currents and other areas where the water deepens and slows. As a general rule, try the shallows both early and late in the day and go for the deeper water when the sun is up. There is also a bend in this river, where you will find that roach and chub in particular tend to congregate.

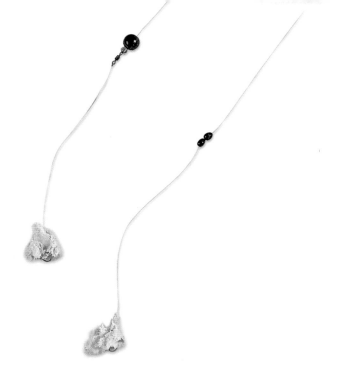

A floating bait can be legered. With this rig, the buoyant bread crust will hover a few inches above the bed of the river, held in position by the weight of the leger.

To catch a chub (see pgs. 318–321), the rig could hardly be simpler – a largeish hook (perhaps a size 4) baited with bread, and a single SSG shot, or even a couple of smaller shots if the water is slower moving and you have more time to sink the bait.

all bends produce. You'll actually see where the fast and slow water meet – there is a real dividing line. This is the crease where chub and roach especially love to hang. Here, they can move in and out of the current, sometimes intercepting food, sometimes deciding to rest. One of the best methods of fishing is a very light leger. Alternatively, and much more enjoyable, is to float fish using a decent-sized stick float that trundles a bait around the bottom, just a little bit slower than the river is moving. Once again, bread is a good bait, this time pinched on a smaller hook, say a size 10. A bunch of two or three maggots also works well. Dribble in loose feed – a few pieces of bread, say, every five minutes or so, or a dozen maggots every cast. Bites are very distinct.

Fishing with bread

It's often worth taking a large unsliced loaf to one of the long, featureless straights on your river. At first, this stretch of water may not look very promising. Start, however, pulling small pieces of crust from the loaf and throwing them out into mid-river. Watch

carefully as they float off downstream. If there's a chub population about, there is a good chance they will be attracted up in a few minutes after ten or so crusts have drifted over their heads. You will soon see action – bow waves, big splashes, loud sucks. It's exciting stuff, and all you need to do is put a matchbox-sized piece of crust on a size 4 hook, wet it just a little, and then flick it underarm out into the current. Let it float down naturally until you see it engulfed. Don't strike immediately or you'll pull the bait out of the chub's lips – wait for the line to draw tight.

Just an example of what you can do with your loaf! Bread is one of the most adaptable forms of bait you can possibly buy. Another brilliant advantage is that it is so accessible.

Float Fishing

Before we look at one of the most engaging skills in float fishing – long trotting – it's wise to look at the theory of floats in some detail. It's not at all uncommon to see anglers using totally the wrong float for the job in hand. The basic rule is to always use a float that is heavy enough to cast and to control in the water.

This evocative shot, taken at sunset on a winter river, uses the laying-on method. A roach has just taken the bait, lifting the shot from the bottom, and the float lies flat before sliding under the surface.

Size matters

Make sure that the float you choose is big enough for the job. There's nothing worse than scratching around with a float that is too small, either to be cast the required distance or to hold out in the current in a wind. A big float can always be over-cast and drawn back into the baited area so as not to cause too much disturbance. A big float also gives you far more control than one that is too light.

Shapes and styles

Floats are either basically long and thin or have a certain type of body. The long, thin ones are probably the most popular, and are generally made of peacock quill, reed or plastic. The bodies on floats are often made of polystyrene and these can be placed down towards the bottom of the float to give stability in rough water. Those floats with bodies near the top are generally meant for streamy, fast water where surface stability is required.

A lot of modern floats can be rearranged by using a variety of different tips that can be inserted into the top. These tips can be of different colours, which will help with visibility if you change swims or as the light alters. Also, if you're having trouble registering bites, a finer insert tip can often help. Many floats are now made with clear plastic bodies, often called crystals. The idea here is that timid fish in clear water cannot see them so easily, and are less likely to be alarmed.

The Avon float

Let's have a look at the most common types of floats, beginning with Avons. These are good trotting floats for long distances. Some Avons are made as crystals, for shallow water, and some are made with wire stems to give greater stability in turbulent water. Loafer floats are similar, and designed for longer distances and bigger, heavier baits such as meat or bread. Loafers are perfect on fast- or medium-paced rivers and swims where the surface boils.

All the floats you'll ever need – *These photographs show a selection of floats. The river floats with the fluted bodies (bottom left) can grip the current well, while the non-fluted floats are perfect with big baits and streamy conditions. The middle image shows a second selection of river floats. The one on the left, a stick float, is perfect for fine work for smaller fish in clear water conditions. The yellow-top float would be ideal for a worm bait, and the other two would work well in fast-flowing conditions. The image at right shows a selection of stillwater floats. The two floats on the left are wagglers, and the two on the right are designed for lighter, close-in work.*

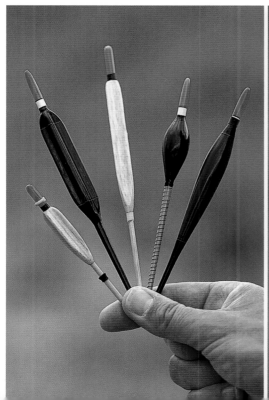

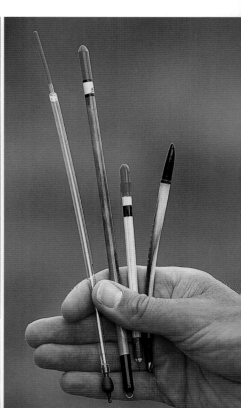

A nice shot of a river roach and the floats that are generally used to fish this environment. It's a shame there's just a little damage on the fish's flank, all too common in the age of the cormorant. The floats, of course, are made by that genius, Andrew Field.

Stick floats and wagglers

Most river fishing is done with the ordinary stick float. Fish these top and bottom – that is, attached to the line in two places – and string the shot down the line evenly, shirt-buttoned, as it's called. Smaller stick floats are designed for close-in fishing and delicate work. Large stick floats are designed to cope with faster, deeper water, and they can also take bigger baits, but don't use them a long way out, or your control over them will suffer.

Probably the most common floats are the ordinary peacock wagglers, which should be attached to the line by their bottom end only. These are ideal for all general approaches in rivers and lakes. Baits can be fished on the drop, as they fall through the water towards the bottom, by pushing the weight up towards the float. These floats are buoyant enough to allow a bait to be dragged through the swim without constantly registering false bites.

Crystal floats

A popular modern float is the loaded crystal. This is a clear-bodied, large waggler with a bomb incorporated into its base. The bomb allows the float to be cast long distances on a very straight trajectory. The clear body means that shy fish, in gin-clear waters, are less likely to be alarmed. However, the loaded base does drag the float deeper on entry into the water. This means that you have to be careful if the swim is shallow and the fish are feeding warily. It pays to over-cast and draw the float carefully back into the swim. Feathering the cast can also help reduce the speed of the float on impact.

Drift beater

Another outstanding float, especially for stillwaters, is the drift beater. Stillwaters are never, in fact, still. The wind sets up subsurface currents that can drag many floats out of position and make the bait behave

You can't beat float fishing in amongst lily pads, but make sure that the float gets right in there. I like the way a bait drops naturally through the water without any weight attached.

A dying art

Sadly, we are living in an age where the art of float fishing with a running line is being lost. This is partly because many match men use a pole with a fixed line, and partly because many specialist anglers are switching to legering and swim feeder fishing techniques. This is a pity, because fishing the float brings satisfaction and is an exquisite way of presenting a bait in the most natural of fashions.

This small controller float is set up to fish two well-soaked dog biscuits. In this particular case, there's a shot on the line to sink the biscuits just subsurface. This is a good method for carp fishing, but in this instance the biscuits were destined for a river chub!

unnaturally. The drift beater has a long antenna that keeps it stable in strong currents. It also has a visual sight bob that stands out at a distance. This is a perfect float for medium- to long-distance fishing on lakes in rough conditions.

There are many specialized floats, but these are the most important. Note, too, that most of these floats can be fitted with a nightlight insert. These are frequently of the Beta variety, which can give out a glow for many years. These come in ratings of 300 or 500 micro lamberts. The 300 version is generally visible for 5–10yd, whereas the 500 version can be seen for at least 25yd.

The speck of red – *Red is one of the most conspicuous of colours, and it shows up well even in dark water like this. Here the angler is holding the float back so that just the tip of it can be seen. The bait will be rising enticingly from the bottom.*

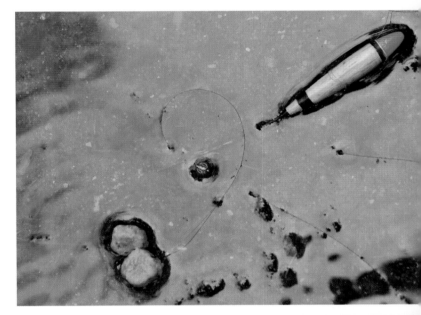

Long Trotting

There are many types of float fishing that require appreciable levels of skill, but perhaps the most demanding to master and the most artistic in action is long trotting. Long trotting is a term given to fishing the float downriver over long distances, certainly over 20yd, and often up to 100yd. It's one of the nicest ways to explore long stretches of river and get close to timid fish.

Phil simply flicks his float out into the middle of the river with a gentle, pendulum-like underarm action, exerting complete control so that the float falls onto the water with as little splash as possible, which is very important.

Benefits of the method

Long trotting is, first and foremost, efficient. It is an ideal way of finding fish in a featureless stretch of river. If there is no response after the first dozen trots, then move down 100yd or so if space permits and fish the next stretch of river. By travelling light and moving frequently, even a mile of river can be fished quite thoroughly within a morning.

The second major use of long trotting is to contact fish that are very shy and will not tolerate close human proximity, particularly in fast, clear and shallow rivers where wild species are easily spooked.

The long trotting technique

When long trotting, a longer rod is useful. Excellent reel control is necessary, whether this be centre-pin or fixed spool. The skills required in long trotting are many: the line must be mended continually so that control of the float is constant. If the current creates bows in the line, strikes will be missed and, just as bad, the float will be pulled off course and the bait will behave unnaturally.

It's also important to control the float, as it has to be guided towards promising areas and inched around snags. You can't simply let the float go with the flow and trust to luck. You've got to impose your own wishes on that small creation 80yd away from

Pin appeal – *You can, of course, trot a river using a traditional fixed-spool reel, but a centre-pin is the tool that is tailor-made for the job. A centre-pin gives you perfect control all the time and leaves you in constant contact with the float.*

you. You've also got to hold the float up occasionally so that the bait rises enticingly off the bottom, often prompting a fish into an induced take. Let the float travel out of control, even for a couple of yards, and you're risking calamity.

When the float does eventually go under at long distance, the strike needs to be instant and powerful, and must continue until the pull of a hooked

HOLDING BACK

Holding the float back is a trotting art form. Remember that the current is faster at the top of the water than at the bottom, so if the float is allowed to drift down uncontrolled it will pull the bait along at an unnatural speed. By slowing the float, you will make it move at the speed of the water deep down. It's a good idea to stop the float periodically. This will lift the bait off the bottom and make the line and lead less obvious, tempting the shy fish to bite.

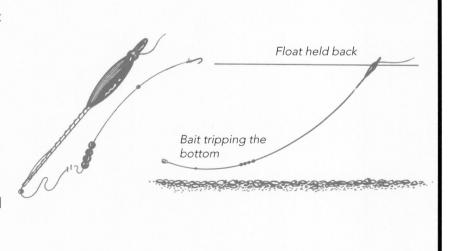

Float held back

Bait tripping the bottom

fish is felt. Everything has to be done gently, but confidently and with a smooth assurance. Hitting a fish, especially a large one, at nearly 100yd in a swift current can be quite a shock to tackle and angler alike. Take no chances with your line, hook or knots.

Playing the fish

After the fish is hooked, keep the rod low to avoid any splashing. Such activity will only alarm the rest of the shoal and make a hook slip more likely. Once the fish begins to come, keep it on the move with a steady, horizontal pumping action. Pull the fish several feet towards you, then reel line in as quickly as possible, repeating the process until you have the fish close. Now it's ready to be netted.

Trotting weather

Ideal conditions for long trotting are dull, overcast days when there is little wind to ruffle the surface. Bright sunlight leads to a lot of surface glare, which, in turn, makes seeing the float a long way off a headache-inducing job. Wind chop on the river is at least as bad, especially when combined with glinting sunlight. A wind of any strength, particularly across the stream, makes float control at long ranges even more difficult than it is normally. This does not mean to say that long trotting in breezy, bright conditions is impossible, but it does pay to build up experience on the calmer, duller days, when fish are more inclined to bite anyway.

1 THE POINT
A fishing position like this always works well because you are in line with the flow of the river, which helps your control immensely.

2 THE CREASE
There is a distinct line – the crease – between the slow water by the bank and the fast water in the main current. Fish love this area.

3 THE MIX
Water divisions always attract fish. They move into the cloudy water looking for food, then return to the clear water for extra oxygen.

Finding and feeding

If fish have been located at a considerable distance and you think it unlikely that you will scare them, by all means move down closer to them. Long trotting can simply be used as a way of finding fish and, once located, you can move in on them and fish in a more tight, delicate way.

Loose feeding is a problem at long range, and it is best to feed in dribbles of mashed bread, possibly flavoured and possibly containing maggots, casters or even pieces of chopped worm. This concoction will gradually drift down the river bringing fish on the feed or even pulling them close up towards the angler. If the hook bait is large enough to make a real statement – say a huge lump of meat, bread or a bunch of worms – then loose feed is less important. Remember, a big bait could need a heavier float than you have been using for maggots or casters.

Taken at range – This good chub succumbed to a lobworm fished under a float and trotted about 50yd downriver. The bite was dramatic and the fight protracted.

Trotting the stream – Note how these two anglers have put on chest waders so that they can enter the main current. This means that their floats are trotting directly downstream, making it easier to mend the line.

Legering

Legering is a term that means fishing the bottom of a body of water. When you're bait fishing, there are many times when you really do need to strive for distance in order to do this, as fishing close in under your rod tip isn't an option. Perhaps the water is very busy and the fish are pushed way out into the middle, or perhaps that's where the food sources lie and where the fish feed naturally. So, if you see activity at 27m (30yd) out or further, the most successful and straightforward method to use is the feeder/quiver tip combination.

Quiver tips and feeders – Above are quiver tip rods with a selection of quivers. Some of the rods are glass, some carbon, each with different test-curve weights.

Feeder fishing

Using a feeder is, essentially, a comparatively easy way to fish and I wouldn't rate its skill factor sky high. However, as in any form of fishing, feeders do have their own complexities. It's important when you are using a feeder to ensure that your casting is tight and accurate. It doesn't pay to cast a feeder into lots of different places, as you will simply break up a feeding shoal and have them scattered and wandering looking for your bait. The best way to make sure that your casting is spot on each time is to line up a feature on the far bank and cast to it repeatedly. You can even put a bit of tape on your spool once you've cast out so that you will be reaching exactly the same distance each time you cast.

For casting large distances, you can use either a block-end feeder with maggots or an open-end feeder with groundbait and samples of the hook bait inside (see pg. 268). In shallow, clear water especially, you don't want your feeder to enter the water with too much splash, so use as light a feeder weight as possible and, just as if you were float fishing, feather the feeder down at the end of your cast.

Bite detection

Detecting bites is a necessary skill when feeder fishing. Certainly, your quiver tip will sometimes be pulled right round, the rod nearly disappearing off the rests, and you will be in absolutely no doubt about striking. However, a word of caution – with a bite like this don't strike too wildly or you could have a break-off. On most occasions, however, the tip will merely flicker and nudge, and you won't be at all sure whether you are experiencing line bites or the real thing. Even the biggest fish can sometimes shake a quiver tip as though a gust of wind is blowing. It's up to you to experiment. If the tip quivers minutely, strike. If there's no hook-up, leave the next tremble and see if it develops. The more you strike unsuccessfully, the more you are pulling your feeder through a shoal of fish and unsettling it.

The next step is to experiment with your hook lengths. Go longer or shorter until you get a positive indication. Experiment with your hook baits. Try two

A maggot-packed feeder disgorges its contents.

maggots, or three maggots, or a maggot and caster combination until you find the answer. Perhaps the tip of a redworm will change everything around. Maybe your hook is too large, so drop a size. Perhaps it's even the wrong colour, so change that. There will nearly always be an answer. It's up to you to find it.

The method feeder has made a big impact on stillwaters all over the world. It certainly attracts fish

Feathering the cast – *Feathering the cast by slowing down the rate at which the line comes off the spool is the best way to consistently place a bait in exactly the same spot. Slowing the bait will also reduce its impact, lessening the splash.*

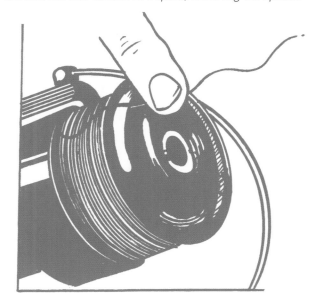

Ready for action – Notice how the quiver tip rod is held high so that as little line as possible falls on the water. This is the perfect day – little breeze, overcast conditions and the fish will be feeding well.

and, in heavily stocked waters, can prove irresistible. Bear in mind that you are casting out a comparatively heavy weight and you need to step up your line strength accordingly or you'll risk snapping off on the cast. Bites tend to be positive using the feeder method, so ignore flicks and nudges and wait for the tip to go right round. Another ploy is to leave the reel on backwind, and don't even think of picking up the rod until you see the reel handle beginning to revolve.

Simple legering

The feeder is a very useful tool, but it isn't the only way to leger at distance. I've already said that if the water is clear and shallow and the fish are spooky, the swim feeder itself can prove a major deterrent to the fish. In these circumstances, it's better to fish a simple lead weight and mix particles of the bait you're using with groundbait and then catapult the balls out to the

desired spot. On pressured waters, this can work well, because the lead is less obvious than the feeder and you can make the balls of groundbait so light that they don't enter the water with a huge splash.

The main problem with this method is that you've got to get your groundbait mix absolutely right. What you don't want is for the balls to break up in the air and scatter randomly over the water in front of you. Equally, you shouldn't mix the groundbait so that it becomes as hard as a stone and enters the water like a bomb. The ideal is for the balls to begin breaking up as they hit the surface and then carry on dissolving as they fall to the bottom. If you can manage this, you'll almost get a curtain effect as the bait streams down in a constant plume from surface to lake bed. Maggots and casters mixed in with the groundbait are perfect for this approach, casters particularly, because some will come free from the groundbait when it hits the bottom and will rise slowly towards the surface again, so that the visual attraction of what you're trying to achieve is even further enhanced.

The major skill with legering, then, is really to do with your groundbaiting. This is where many anglers fall down. The secret to intelligent groundbaiting lies in attracting the fish to the area and then holding them there. This is where the use of tiny particle baits comes in – grains of rice or hemp seed excite the fish, don't fill them up, are difficult to find and will keep them digging around your swim for hours to come.

However, be warned, the use of very small baits such as hemp can create a rod for your own back. The fish become preoccupied and stop looking for any bait that's larger than a pinhead. Present a large bait over a bed of hemp and you can wait a long time for fish to show any interest. This means you will be forced to fish lighter and lighter with ever-smaller hooks. A hair-rig often becomes necessary.

Hook bait alone

You don't always have to leger with either a feeder or with loose groundbait. Indeed, for big fish on clear, pressured water where they are ultra wary, either of these approaches can be detrimental. The more stereotyped your approach is in any situation, the less likely it is to fool the cleverest of fish. An alternative is to set up a rod with a leger weight and a big-impact natural bait alone. Lobworms do very well for most fish species. If the water isn't too crowded, simply walk round it and cast the lobworm towards any likely looking spot. Fallen trees, extensive reed beds, close-in weed and man-made structures such as bridges and boat jetties all shelter feeding fish. Pay particular

Two light leger rigs – *perfect for presenting small pieces of luncheon meat in a moderately flowing current.*

attention to your sighting techniques. Binoculars will help you pick out areas of clouded water or even the tips of tail fins as fish feed in shallow water.

If you find fish feeding like this, cast your weight and bait some 5 or 10 yards beyond them. Then slowly retrieve until you're pretty sure that the bait is nestling in close proximity to the feeding fish. Don't cast right onto their heads in these situations or the fish will simply bolt or, at best, they may stop feeding and sulk until they sense danger has passed.

Fast-water problems – *Fish can spot an unnatural-looking bait, and the movement of the food item in the water can be a crucial factor. In a strong current, a light bait is likely to be swung around and may even spin wildly at the end of the line. A single shot pinched onto the line close to the bait will keep it down and increase the chances of a fish treating it as part of its natural food supply.*

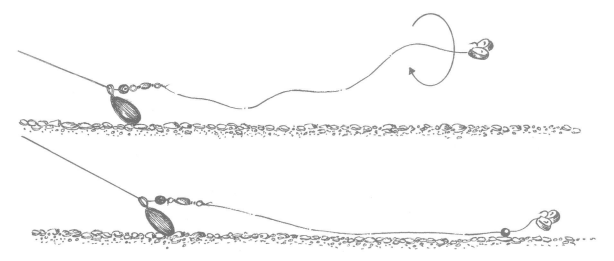

Touch Legering

On one level, touch legering can be seen as simply holding the rod in one hand, holding the line in the other and feeling for a fish to take the bait. It's that straightforward on a certain level but, as you'll see, there's a whole lot more to it. It's also probably one of my favourite three or four ways of fishing. Just why is it so magical? Touch legering is not only an extremely efficient method. Much more importantly, it is wonderfully thrilling and takes you right under the skin of the river and into the very living rooms of the fish that live there.

A shot of me on a very flooded River Wye touch legering for chub and, more specifically, for barbel. The rather worried look on my face is explained by the fact that I was actually filming an episode of Fishing in the Footsteps of Mr Crabtree. *Sadly, nothing was prepared to give that telltale tug!*

An electric connection

When you're touch legering, your line is like an umbilical cord connecting you with another life force. Through the line, the experienced touch legerer can tell you almost exactly what is happening in the swim before him or her. For example, the touch legerer will eventually begin to realize the difference between real and line bites. Soon, the line bites will tell him the number, the size and perhaps even the species of fish moving around in the swim. You will certainly begin to build up an almost completely accurate picture of what the swim contains and the make-up and contours of the riverbed. When you begin to get proper bites, touch legering will tell you exactly how the fish are regarding your bait and set-up, whether they are confident, wary or even downright petrified.

Travelling light

There's lots more. When you're touch legering, you don't need a rod rest. In fact, you shouldn't have one – belting the point of a rod rest into a gravel bank will alarm the fish even before you cast. Without one, you can also up sticks and move on in a fraction of the time most bank bait anglers need. Indeed, good touch legering is all about mobility and exploring the entire length of the river. Touch legering is rather like fly fishing in that you try here, there, everywhere, and in the process you find more new swims than you could ever imagine.

The method can tell you so much. If you're sharing a swim with a friend, and he casts in a swim feeder or a heavy lead and you immediately feel fish bolting into your line ('line bites' in the jargon of the

Legering the stream – *The anglers below are legering in quick water using worms as bait. They are holding the rod in one hand and the line lightly over the index finger of the other hand. Tucking the rod under the arm gives perfect balance.*

Reading the water – Lucy Bowden is working upstream, this time touch legering with a fly rod. However, using a nymph, just as Lucy is demonstrating, can also account for all species of coarse fish, especially roach, chub, grayling and even barbel.

touch legerer), you know that the fish are scared and scattering. It's just the same if your friend hooks a fish – you'll almost instantly get line bites as the shoal breaks up. You begin to realize just how spooky, how easily scared, the fish in front of you can be.

The real thing

It can be like that when you're getting actual bites. (Don't worry, you'll always know the difference between a line bite and a real one: it's impossible to explain, but you'll feel instinctively that there is something live down there, that the line is shrieking a message to you.) Decent bites from confident fish are quite unmistakable. These are slam-bang and you merely lift into the fish. One minute you're dozing, watching the kingfisher on the far bank, and the next your rod is hooped, your reel shrieking and you can't quite believe what a magical experience it is.

However, it's not always like that. Very frequently, you will feel bites that are merely a shake or a tremble. You can feel the fish pick a bait from the bottom, hold it between its lips and then place it back down again. This is not hocus-pocus. It actually happens a great many times, and it's fascinating. It's you and your fish at close quarters, both pairs of eyes bulging. It's showdown time at the OK Corral.

The fish knows you're there. You know he knows. It's a total battle of wits.

As the fish pose their problems, your brain is racing. Do you fish upstream? Do you lengthen or shorten the hook length that you're using? Do you use a bigger or smaller bait? How about hook size? A change of bait altogether? A cocktail of two or three baits, perhaps? Have you put in too much feed? Too little? Do you rest the swim and come back within an hour?.

Keeping you thinking

In these sorts of ways, touch legering teaches you as much about the fish as it is possible for a human to know. For example, your first cast is absolutely your most important one, because the more you cast, the more the fish become skittish about your presence in their world. Make the first cast as perfect as you can to stand the best chance of catching fish off guard. The design and size of your lead are both crucial.

Reading the water – You'll find that if you get out into the river like this, you're much more at one with the pace of aquatic life. You'll see more fish, and you'll also begin to really understand how the currents around you are working.

The heavier the splash and the shinier the leger, the more damage you're doing to your swim. You begin to realize that even throwing free offerings into your swim before making the first cast can prove disastrous. Heavy baits have a shotgun effect that can blast a semi-scared swim right apart. If you want to put in bait before fishing, why not do it the day before if possible? It should certainly go in a couple of hours before actually making that cast.

Touch legering demands that you approach every swim with the clearest possible plan of attack in mind. You've got to think exactly where to put your terminal tackle, where it's going to settle and from where you need to fish. Don't even think of casting out until you've got the best possible plan prepared. Your approach to even the same swim will differ session after session, depending on light conditions, water height, flow, visibility and weed growth.

The basics of touch legering

You don't want a rod that's too long and heavy if you're going to cradle it all day. Lighter, more sensitive rods make it easier to feel what's going on down the line. A good rod should be between 9ft and 10ft long and light enough to hold all day long. Match this with as light a reel as you can find that will still do the job adequately. In most situations, we tend to use reels that are far too large for the job in hand. It's very rare that you need a reel with 300yd of line on it!

Once your leger and bait are in position, hold the rod comfortably under your arm – that's where lightness comes in. Crook the line from between the reel and the butt ring around one or more of your fingers. I like to use the index finger, but I constantly vary this. Comfort is the over-riding issue.

Point your rod directly to where you think your bait is lying. You will have to consider the depth of the swim, the current and the weight of your lead to

At the seaside – *Touch legering is a very useful technique when fishing the coastline for species like bass.*

make these calculations. Try to eliminate as much slack line as possible between your fingers and your terminal tackle. This means mending the line busily until your terminal tackle holds bottom.

Wading is of great benefit when it's safe to do so. This cuts down the length of line between fingers and bait and, while touch legering doesn't have to be a close-in job, everything obviously becomes much more tight and intimate as distance decreases.

Find a relaxed position whether you are wading or standing, or sitting on the bank. Otherwise physical discomfort will soon become a nagging distraction and it's essential that you become as one with the river as possible.

You should feel so intimately in touch that one slight pull from your fingers will dislodge the bait and trundle it down in the flow. You should feel that if a fish even breathes on that bait you will know about it. If that sounds impossible, don't worry. You will very soon get to know the difference between a piece of floating weed on the line and a real bite. That proper bite is absolutely 100 per cent impossible to ignore. It's a life force that screams at your instincts even if it's comparatively gentle and doesn't wrench the line from your fingertips.

Free-lining

In many ways, free-lining is very similar to touch legering. The basic difference with free-lining is that the bait is kept on the move, so that it drifts downstream in a totally natural way. Many species of fish rely on the drift of the river to bring food to their doorsteps, and this technique exploits this method of feeding perfectly.

When you're free-lining, it always helps to be as far out into the river as is safely possible. This gives you more direct control and allows you to feel a bite with more immediacy.

The correct bait

Free-lining can only really be carried out effectively with a heavier bait. A lobworm is good, and multiple lobworms also work. I've used up to five on a single, large hook. Dead fish, sausage, luncheon meat and bread flake also work. You might also want to use a large split shot to increase the weight of smaller baits, or to add weight to a large bait in a very fast current. Above all, you must always know exactly where your bait is and be in direct touch with it. This means using a bait heavy enough not to get lost in the current.

Free-lining technique

To begin with, you need to be physically as directly in line with the current as possible. Unless you're on a very small stream, this will generally mean wading. If you're not in line with the current, you'll find that the push of the water creates big bows in the line and, once again, you will begin to lose the immediacy of contact that is so vital to this method.

Simply lower the bait into the water and then allow the current to take it away. Pay out line as it goes, but don't let line spill out too freely. Constantly check the line, lift the rod tip and ensure that you are always in direct contact with the bait. This might mean that you're constantly mending the line and ironing out any loops that the current is trying to create. The faster and deeper the water, the more often you will have to do this.

Why the emphasis on keeping in touch with the bait at all times? Simply because, if you're not tight to the bait, you won't know when you get a bite. Worse, if you do have a lot of slack line wafting in the current, it's easy for a fish to swallow the bait without you being aware of the fact, and the fish will come to harm. You should always make the welfare of the fish a priority.

In slower currents, you may need to lift the bait off the bottom and let it go again with the flow in a series of hops downriver. You might also decide to use a smaller bait in slow, shallow water and certainly remove any split shot.

When a bait finally comes to a natural stop, try and hold it there for a few minutes while always maintaining that direct contact. Why? Well, in any stretch of river, food travelling in the drift – such as your bait – tends to drop to the bottom in one of several specific spots. Perhaps this will be a depression or behind a stone, or even at the tail of some weeds. Whatever the cause may be, the fish

Use your loaf – Bread is a great bait for most cyprinids. Tear a bit from the centre of the slice, push the hook through and squeeze slightly around the shank for a fluffy yet secure bait.

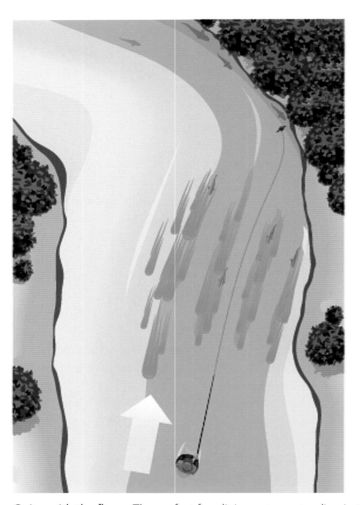

Making use of the current – *In this diagram, the angler has waded far out into the river so that he is fishing directly down the flow. This means he is in constant and direct contact with the bait and can feel any interest from the fish.*

become used to visiting these places on a regular basis because they know that they will always find a reliable supply of food.

When you decide to retrieve the bait, don't reel in wildly but twitch the bait back slowly and erratically. For many species, this can be just as effective as the drift downriver. Trout and perch, especially, will hammer into cleverly retrieved baits.

The free-lining bite

What exactly are bites like with free-lining? Bites, in fact, can vary widely. You can have plucks, tugs or full-blooded runs, so be aware. Read each and every situation and strike quickly once you are aware that a fish has taken. Better a missed fish – which will probably come again – than a deep-hooked one that you want to return.

Overall, this is a great method for river fishing. It's very effective, wildly exciting and allows you to be extremely mobile so that you can search out all manner of promising water. It's relevant for any species – trout, salmon, perch, barbel, chub, even carp.

Going with the flow – *The perfect free-lining set-up: standing in the current and letting the river peel line off a centre-pin.*

Fragrant food – It's amazing the sort of baits that will catch fish. Here we have an anchovy straight from the tin. The oil and the scent are absolutely perfect for chub and barbel, especially in a flooded river.

The surface bait – Chub, in particular, like to come up and intercept food either on or just beneath the surface.

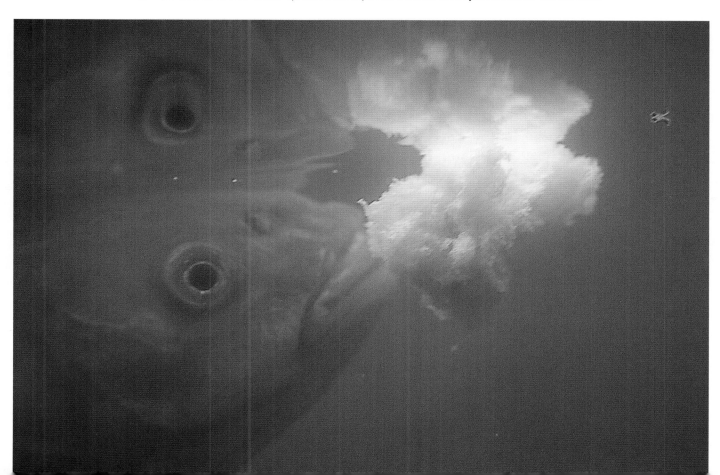

Carp Fishing

Throughout Europe, more people fish for carp than for any other species. Carp fishing is also becoming increasingly popular in the US. It's the size, power and undoubted beauty of the species that proves so attractive to the angler, and perhaps, above all, anglers like the challenge of carp because they are so very wary and cunning.

The author holds a very nicely proportioned common carp, though the slight scale damage indicates attack by otter or cormorant.

An intellectual challenge

Even in their wild state, in waters that are hardly fished, carp show the deepest suspicion of anything unusual. In lakes subjected to angling pressure, carp quickly become wise to the anglers' ploys and seem to have an uncanny ability to get the measure of any new tricks within a very short time. It is a constant battle of wits between fish and angler. When the anglers invent a new method or a new bait, it puts them at an advantage for a while. Then, however, the carp become wise and learn to recognize the new tricks that have been fooling them, and stalemate is reached again until the anglers have another brainwave.

A wise old fish

Carp can grow to a great age – certainly 60 years or more. This long lifespan helps reinforce their instincts and innate facility for learning. They don't learn in the intellectual way that humans learn, but they are capable of registering experience and acquiring a store of responses to these experiences.

If any fish can be described as intelligent, then big, old carp are the first contenders. These fish lead relatively ordered existences with only seasonal and climatic changes in their environment. Anything unusual will be noted, and even when the fish seem totally preoccupied with feeding, they are constantly alert. Moreover, like many other creatures, carp have the ability to communicate unease or fear. This needn't involve surging off in panic flight. Carp seem perfectly capable of transmitting signals to other carp by the subtlest body language, indiscernible to any but other carp, and certainly not to the angler.

The carp community

Watch carp in the warm sunshine of a late afternoon when they are resting and at their most infuriating to the angler. They may well have been basking for 12 hours, lying in the milk-warm water with their bellies caressed by beds of soft weed. They give every impression of contentment. You might see

This carp is simply wallowing in the weed, enjoying the sunshine that you can see reflecting off its back. Although it's sleepy and not feeding hard, a fish like this will sometimes be tempted by a bait. Try a piece of bread crust, a floating dog biscuit or even a worm cast just in front of its nose.

their eyes roll, and you can watch the languid movement of their fins. These are definitely not feeding fish, and they are almost impossible to catch in this condition. They are interested only in relaxing in the sunshine, perhaps even enjoying the company of their fellow shoal members. Occasionally, the sun will get too much for them and they will drift away into the shade of overhanging trees. It is there, in the cool, particularly as evening approaches, that the occasional fish will decide to begin feeding.

It might surprise a non-angler that carp exist as a real community. They really seem to know each other and the water they inhabit. Day after day, they will swim round in the same small groups, almost as if they were capable of forming particular friendships. Within

Over the masonry – Fallen masonry like this often attracts fish from bass to carp to pike. This big fish is intent on picking up bait that is well-positioned in one of its favourite sanctuaries.

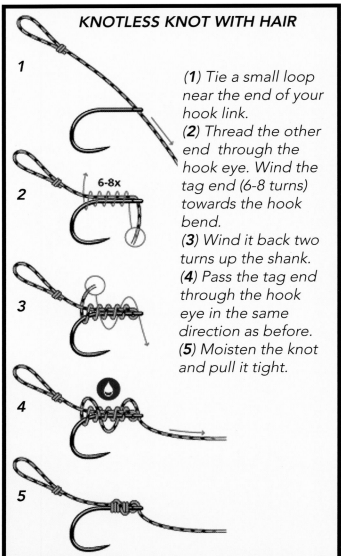

KNOTLESS KNOT WITH HAIR

1

2 6-8x

3

4

5

(1) Tie a small loop near the end of your hook link.
(2) Thread the other end through the hook eye. Wind the tag end (6-8 turns) towards the hook bend.
(3) Wind it back two turns up the shank.
(4) Pass the tag end through the hook eye in the same direction as before.
(5) Moisten the knot and pull it tight.

each group, there is a definite pecking order, with a leader who seems to decide the pattern for the day.

Feeding habits

In rich waters, the carp's diet consists almost entirely of small invertebrates – bloodworm, daphnia, shrimps, beetles and tiny snails. Their whole lake is a larder, heaving with juicy titbits. Unlike the fish in relatively barren, newly created lakes where there is real competition for food, these fish have no need for anglers' baits and are particularly difficult to catch.

Carp like these move slowly over the lake bed, grazing like cows. The fish are actually excavating

LINE ALIGNER

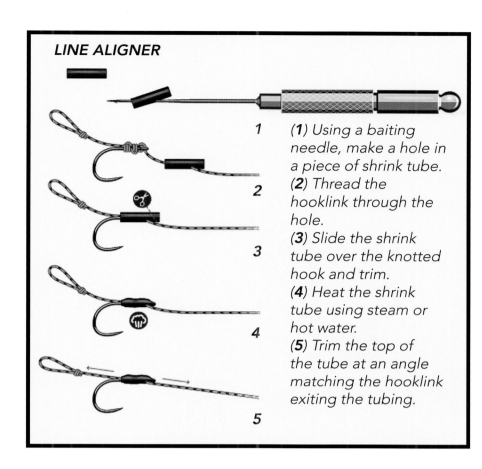

1

2

3

4

5

(**1**) *Using a baiting needle, make a hole in a piece of shrink tube.*
(**2**) *Thread the hooklink through the hole.*
(**3**) *Slide the shrink tube over the knotted hook and trim.*
(**4**) *Heat the shrink tube using steam or hot water.*
(**5**) *Trim the top of the tube at an angle matching the hooklink exiting the tubing.*

the silt, creating quite noticeable hollows around them as they suck in huge mouthfuls of mud, sifting it for food and expelling it through their gill flaps. Bubbles of gas billow from the gills as well and break in a froth on the surface. These fish are probably only going to be tempted by a completely natural bait such as lobworms, brandlings or a big, black slug.

The carp's senses

A carp's sight is surprisingly sharp, certainly in clear water. At a couple of metres or so, anything in the water stands out clearly. When a carp moves really close to a bait, details become pin sharp. The carp also has a good wide-angled view of the world above and gets a pretty useful impression of anything happening on the bank within a 100m or so.

Searching the swim – Here we see two carp moving slowly across a silty bottom, looking hard for food. This is the sort of area where they will expect to find bloodworm.

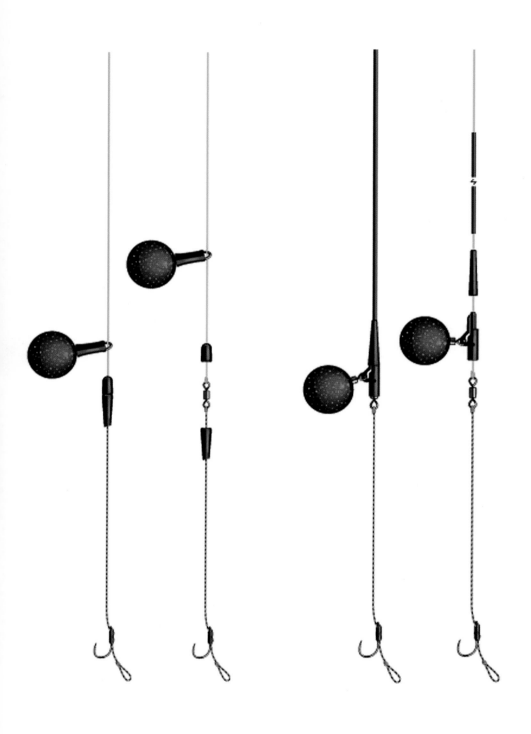

FREE-RUNNING RIG
This rig allows the fish to run with the minimal resistance.

SEMI-FIXED BOLT RIG
This rig holds the lead in place so the hook can prick the fish without causing it to bolt.

Shapes are blurred, but an angler moving without cover will alert a carp more than a football pitch away.

Carp also have a great sense of smell, necessary in the wild to detect bloodworms and swan mussels hidden under centimetres of silt. They also have a discriminating sense of taste. They can become really hooked on a particularly flavour of bait, for example, and then caution may be subjugated. However, they can also remember unpleasant associations, which is perhaps why baits fall from favour after a period of great success.

A carp depends a great deal on its powers of hearing, and every time a bait or a lead hits the water, it will register. I have seen carp shy away from a bait dropped 40–50yd away. Even a gun fired half a mile off can cause a carp to sink out of sight and hide amongst the lily pads for an hour or more.

The tactile senses of a carp are also highly developed. They will be able to feel lines dragging across their bellies or rubbing against their fins. Their mouths are also extremely touch sensitive and will often detect things that are wrong with a bait. Carp can learn to mouth baits gently, testing their feel before swallowing or rejecting them.

Digging hard – When carp get their heads down, the bottom can explode. This fish (left) has smelled the sweetness of sweetcorn and pellets, and is digging furiously. Watch carefully for bites – they can be surprisingly gentle as the fish simply sucks in the bait and doesn't move off.

Feeding frenzy – Wow! What you're seeing here below is almost the entire carp population of an 8-hectare (20-acre) lake gathered in one north-west corner. They are feeding frantically, stirring the water to a soup. I've witnessed this behaviour on half a dozen occasions over the last ten years or so, but I'm still not exactly sure of the cause. Perhaps a particularly rich bloodworm bed has been discovered and the feeding activity has drawn in group after group of carp.

Carp off the Top

Surface fishing for carp is the most thrilling type of fishing imaginable. You see the fish, you see their reaction to your bait and presentation and you see the take. Truly, you are a participant in the whole event. However, it's a challenging form of fishing: true, you see the fish but, conversely, they see you. You're fishing right on the surface, so the line, hook, knots and all the flaws in your set-up are more clearly seen. You're often fishing very close in, so camouflage, stealth and the most expert use of cover are all essential.

Wow! What a stunner! Great friend Neill Stephen is seen here with a magnificent 40lb 14oz common carp taken in the last minutes of a golden autumn afternoon. Does fishing conceivably get any more beautiful than this?

Slow and watchful

As with any style of fishing that demands consummate skill, don't rush carp off the top. Take all the time you need to walk your lake. Note any areas of scum where food will be trapped, making it easy for the carp to intercept. This includes scum lanes in open water, full of food pushed there by the breeze. Look out for cover, where the carp feel safe. Study areas of heavy weed, lily beds and thick reed margins. Never pass by thick, overhanging branches without first carefully studying the dark water beneath. Look for jungle areas where there are lots of fallen branches and tree trunks lying in the water.

You can also watch for specific fish. Often, you will be pleased if any fish comes along, but sometimes give yourself an added challenge by hand-picking your fish. Perhaps, it's special because of its size, beauty or a rarity of colouring or scale patterns.

Pre-feeding

A great deal of the skill in fishing from the top comes in your ability to feed the fish up to a state of readiness. Don't be in too much of a hurry to introduce your hook bait. Instead, take your time and gradually build up the carp's confidence with free offerings. Often, you can use the wind drift on the water to attract carp out of snaggy areas into open water. They will pick up the scent, begin to investigate and, hopefully, follow the moving food to where you can attack them more conveniently. Again, this takes time to achieve and you must exercise patience.

There are other considerations when it comes to the feeding process. Most vitally, don't overfeed. There are days when the fish appear ravenous enough to eat you out of house and home, but this isn't always the case. Sometimes you can push fish to a crescendo and then, quite suddenly, they'll begin to lose interest and drift back into cover and you've missed the opportunity. The key is to keep fish interested, looking and following the bait. If you get any impression the fish are tailing away and moving back to the weed beds, cut back on the feeding at once. Your aim is to build up competition and have them scrabbling for

Reading the signs – *You can tell a huge amount by the way a fish approaches a floating bait. In the photograph on the top, the fish is moving slowly and confidently, whereas the fish on the photograph below is obviously spooked.*

your bait. Fish in a hurry are less likely to take time looking for mistakes in your presentation.

Sometimes, when you have fish feeding really avidly, it's a good idea to cut off the bait supply altogether and starve them for 10 to 15 minutes. This achieves the effect of moving the fish around a great deal as they look for the last remnants of food. Then, when they see your hook bait, they'll often take it without their usual consideration.

Making use of the wind – *You can draw carp in from large distances by making use of the wind and drifting floater baits along long distances down stillwaters. Here, floating bait are catapulted out from the bank opposite the angler and pushed through weed beds by the wind. Carp are attracted and follow the stream of bait.*

Presentation is the key

When you are fishing on the top like this, take great care over your presentation. Line is the first problem. Thick line is very obvious when it lies on the surface, especially in bright light. Thin line, however, always runs the risk of being broken, and no caring angler wants that. Fortunately, modern lines are much thinner and more resilient than they were even ten years ago, and some of the fluorocarbons are now excellent. Another trick is to sink your line an inch or so under the surface where it immediately becomes less obvious. However, if it then rubs along the back of carp, it will immediately spook them, and any advantage is lost. As the light fades, the carp can lose sight of the line and begin to lose

caution, so don't be in too much of a hurry to go home early.

Alternatively, fish in areas of accumulated scum. Carp enjoy these places and the scum does obscure the profile of the line. The line can also be hidden in areas where weed brushes the surface. In the same way, you can often lay line over the pads of lilies, so it's not actually touching the water at all. This really is the thinking angler's game.

If you can, fish close in, so the only weight on your line is the bait and the hook. Sometimes, you can even dap a bait with no line on the water whatsoever, and fish almost under your rod tip. But if you must fish at a distance, you'll need a float to give some weight. A float also helps signal a take. If the fish are showing signs of caution around a shop-bought float, try taking a 23–30cm (9–12in) twig and threading this on the line so that it rests against the hook. You can achieve this by attaching it with bands or, if you can, drill a hole through the twig and thread the line through the hole afterwards. The concept behind this is that the carp will come to the bait and all it actually sees is a small, juicy offering resting against a dead twig.

Disguising the hook

Hooks, too, are a problem. Often the hook weighs more than the actual bait, which means that it lies under the water and is the first thing the carp sees. A heavy hook also pulls the bait down slightly compared with the natural, loose feed and, again, the carp are suspicious. A large bait, such as a piece of floating crust or floating paste, can be used to hide the hook and the problem isn't so great. The real headache begins when you are using small, floating particles. The hook can be hidden between several particles and this is a useful and long-lived method on many waters. Sometimes, the hook can be made more buoyant by gluing pieces of polystyrene to the shank or you can try hair-rigging a bait (see pg. 257). Keep working, keep experimenting and make the shallows your laboratory where you can see exactly how your line and hook behave.

Bait itself is an important consideration. Years ago, all you had and all you needed was a floating crust. Today, there are numerous recipes for floating, boily-type baits available (see pg. 261), but basically the use of baking powder and the oven can make virtually everything float. Floating boilies can be bought from most tackle shops, but most floater fishing these days is done with particles – especially any one of the many brands of dog and cat biscuits.

Time to strike

The question of the take must also be discussed. Often carp will rise to the bait, only to turn off at the last second, leaving a huge, splashy boil. Carp will also pick the bait up between their lips and test it, ejecting it as they surge away. It's tempting to strike at these occurrences, but all you'll do is pull the bait away from an already scared fish and spook it even further. All bait thereafter is treated with ever-growing suspicion.

The paramount rule, therefore, is to strike only when you're absolutely certain that the carp has taken the bait, and that has it has the bait properly in its mouth. Sometimes, if you're lucky, the line will stream off, but often it will just twitch and move a little way, very slowly, as the carp settles a few inches under the surface and begins to swallow it. If you're fishing close in, it is particularly important to keep your nerve when you see a fish come up and suck the

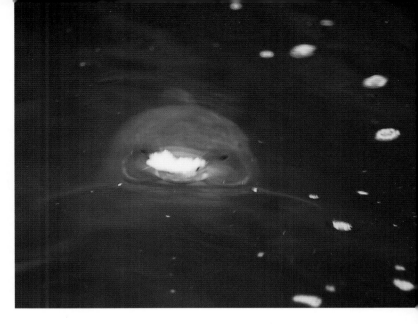

A very big fish this – *It's taken some time to build up the carp's confidence, but now it's definitely approaching the bait with food in mind.*

bait in between its lips. If you strike now, all is lost. Always wait until the bait is taken properly into the mouth, as only then can you strike with confidence.

The controller – *A controller float helps an angler cast added distances, and it's also very useful for signalling that the bait has been taken, especially if it's sitting amongst lots of similar ones. Be careful, though, as carp especially can become suspicious of controllers after awhile.*

Fishing for Barbel

Like all members of the carp family, barbel lead generally ordered lives, but they also reveal fascinating behavioural abnormalities, both as individuals and as shoals, in the face of crises or problematic situations. Many hours of barbel watching suggest that they are neither blinkered nor stupid but, indeed, are very aware of all the possibilities around them.

I love this shot of a fine barbel just netted and held in the flow for a second to be admired. The hook can be slipped from its mouth without the fish ever being taken from the water.

Observing barbel

The more I watch barbel from below the water-line, the more I realize that there is a very apparent sifting process going on as they garner all the information they can from their environment. They also have the ability to take fast, decisive action based on their observations.

For the angler, perfect barbel-watching water will be clear and relatively shallow, with good vantage points from islands or high banks. Good light is needed, and the barbel behave more naturally when the river is quiet.

Traditional feeding behaviour

Barbel like to feed in a leisurely fashion, generally in groups – companionship, I am convinced, is very important to the species, and they actually choose to touch when they can. They often concentrate on patches of open gravel and stones, where they look for all manner of insect life. Angling pressure tends to restrict daylight feeding, and during daylight hours they don't tend to move too far from the comfort zone of snags and overhangs. Barbel of a reasonable weight will happily nudge rocks the size of a house brick out of the way to get at the

You can see why barbel turn rocks over. This one reveals a wealth of caddis larva cases, some empty and abandoned, but several still inhabited and ready to eat. There are times of the year when these food items make up the bulk of the barbel's diet.

This barbel was photographed at a depth of 5ft in a moderately clear river at 9 a.m. on a September morning. It is feeding hard, in the company of five other fish, turning over small stones and dislodging quantities of silt that form obvious clouds behind it.

Barbel are quite happy to come into shallow water, where they find rich pickings under rocks and stones. Caddis are top of the list, but they also seek out snails, beetles, shrimps and small fish.

caddis hiding beneath. The fish I witnessed in one Bohemian river had very noticeable cuts and scabs on their snouts from feeding amongst the endless rough boulders.

When feeding fish chance on a bed of bait, such as assorted pellets, their feeding becomes much more concentrated and the barbel group closer together. Any small fish – especially minnows – that have been pecking at the pellets quickly move out of the way, dropping downstream to feed in the drifting silt.

Look for clouded water, the tips of fins in the shallows and, especially the coral pink of the pectorals. On a sunny day, look for a shadow rather than the fish itself. Take your time, and observe an area of water closely before moving on. Often, the shapes of fish take a while to emerge, but once you have a suspicion, focus intently on the prime spot. Polaroid glasses and binoculars also help the detection process. Above all, look out for 'flashing' barbel.

How and why barbel 'flash'

There cannot be a single barbel angler who hasn't watched that thrilling stab of silver in the water, the sign of a barbel 'flashing' – turning onto its flank and letting the light illuminate it for a give-away second. But what is in the mind of a flashing barbel as it declares its presence in this way?

Feeding strategy appears to be one of the explanations for some flashing patterns, but there are numerous times that barbel flash when they are apparently not at all interested in feeding. There are no definite answers to why barbel flash when they are not feeding, but suggested reasons include communication, hygiene and territorial instinct.

Unexpected feeding behaviour

Barbel will always amaze and excite us with the diversity of their behaviour. Part of their charm is that they are largely unknowable. Just when you think you

Diving for food – It is late summer, and this is the lead fish of a shoal. In 2m (6ft) of water, it repeatedly rises off the bottom, steadies itself in the current and then nosedives, wriggling – and flashing – along the riverbed for 3–4ft before righting itself and continuing normally. This action creates a silt channel close to the bed, and the followers hurry into it to feed on insects that have been disturbed.

understand them, they do something so bewildering that you feel you're back at square one, and just as amazed as you ever were.

Unthreatened, stable shoals, which can number over a hundred fish but are sadly becoming more

Parasites – Fish lice typically attach themselves at the base of the tail stock or close to the fins. When they drop off, the lice leave red, irritated sores, such as these behind the pectoral fin of a barbel from the River Wye in Herefordshire.

Serial flasher – In the course of a morning, this 7lb male barbel has moved rapidly around one area some dozen times, flashing 15 to 20 times on each circuit. It is now late May, just a few weeks before spawning, so is this the issue? Is he somehow marking his territory? Or is this simply a fishy example of joie de vivre? For certain, this is a flashing barbel that is not feeding.

In a scrape – It is late April, and the barbel are on the move after the lengthy winter period of inaction. This individual is grinding its body on stones. It's flashing, but it's not feeding and is alone. A closer inspection reveals that its flanks and fins are infected with Argulus fish lice, which may have been picked up during the winter when it barely moved from the bottom of the pool. So, is it now scraping itself free of its parasitic tormentors?

overhang. They are also tactical hunters, and barbel looking for a large feed are happy to wait until enough fry gather and then herd them to the surface, picking them off in the top few inches of the water. Sometimes, the force of their upward surge can carry them right out of the water, and they fall back with a characteristic splash.

Simple approach to a complex creature

I hope that the preceding photographs have made you think about the barbel as a complex creature.

I have already stressed that the barbel is normally a team player and operates best in groups – from two fish to several hundred. I have observed shoal members sticking together for many years; in the right circumstances they will probably live out their lives together, and there are obvious reasons for this. For one thing, a group of fish can detect potential danger more easily than a lone fish, but there are other mutual benefits. Feeding strategy is certainly one of them, and this may be one of the principal explanations for barbel 'flashing' (see pages 306–307).

All-day feeding *– The fish of the Wye shoal were happy to feed at any time of the day. Any emerging fly would be taken, and they enjoyed slurping in fallen moths and crane flies. These fish appeared totally in harmony with their environment, living and feeding both high and low in the water. Then anglers found them, and within two weeks the fish were no longer seen on the surface.*

and more rare, will feed at all hours of day and night, and both at the surface and down at the bottom. Such shoals are comfortable with their surroundings and will glean food from all locations rather than concentrating in corners and shadows, as angler-threatened barbel tend to do. The barbel will also use the strength of their size and their apparent companionship to exploit a food source – I have seen two, and even three, barbel physically join forces to cooperate in pushing over a particularly heavy stone to get at the food beneath. However, barbel are not alone in this technique, other fish species, such as sea lamprey, will also collaborate to hunt out well-hidden food.

Barbel can be phenomenally adaptable – I have even seen them feeding upside down in fast water so that they can hoover insects from the roof of an

It is easy to underestimate them, to think of them as 'mere' fish, but, by some means or another, they do learn from unpleasant experiences and become more wary and more difficult to catch. This really is where underwater observation comes in – you can see close up how tackle and bait behave. You can also gauge a barbel's reaction to anything new or suspicious in its orbit. In underwater life, nothing acts as it does in a diagram on the ordered page. You can sit back thinking you have the perfect rig but, believe me, it can look quite ridiculous down there on the riverbed. If there is any one golden rule, it is to make your terminal tackle as simple and straightforward as possible; the more complex, the greater the chance of a tangle; the more components, the greater risk of discovery.

Bait presentation

After watching hundreds of barbel baits in action, both in mid-water and on the bottom, I can safely say that many of them don't behave in a way that the angler expects them to. Diagrams in books and magazines may well show the bait and terminal rig lying together in nice, neat patterns, but what these diagrams overlook is the effect of currents, the push of water, the effect of flashes of sunlight and all those things that disrupt the best laid plans of barbel anglers.

If barbel have never been fished for before, it may take you a little while to wean them onto any bait. Barbel that have been pressured in the past are an even harder proposition. Remember that anything that reflects surface brightness, such as a shiny leger weight, will be treated with caution until dusk falls. Another tip is to use pellets for barbel, as these can make a good, clean alternative to particles such as sweetcorn or maggots that become 'blown' on some waters.

Fish close in when the water is dirty, preferably in slacker areas where there is less suspended matter in mid-water. Beware of weeds and leaves getting caught in your line and spoiling your presentation. Think hard about your bait, hooking technique, lead, hook length and exactly where you're going to put all this in any given swim. Barbel will quickly react when they feel a line in mid-water or see a rig that displays a bait in an unnatural fashion.

The isolated bait – This is another example of a bait sticking out like a sore thumb. I've now switched heavily onto pellets, but the pellet has to be positioned correctly. Look at it here. In this crystal-clear water the pellet stands out almost obscenely; even the minnows keep away from it.

Cover – This time the bait has rolled down the sand and is much closer to the relatively sparse vegetation. Here, the minnows feel much more confident pecking at it. It will be in an area similar to this that barbel, too, will accept a bait more readily.

The trough – *If you can get your bait into one of the mini troughs that many barbel swims are riddled with, then you'll be in business. With the help of the current, the bait will drift down until it catches in a particular, tight, attractive area. It's in these places that the barbel feed hard – you will see that even the minnows keep away from such areas out of fear of being sucked in along with the pellets.*

Wading

Whenever possible, it really does pay dividends to get into the water and wade as close to your fish as you can without spooking them. Wading gives all manner of advantages. Firstly, you can often see the fish much more distinctly and this helps when it comes to placing the bait. Secondly, the closer you are, the better you can control your presentation and your tackle. Thirdly, let's look at sheer enjoyment. When wading, you are part of the river and as close to being a barbel as you'll ever get! You'll also get a better idea of the current and feel of the river.

However, you must never take risks or wade any deeper than you feel comfortable with, and never wade into a current that makes you feel uneasy.

Make sure that your wading boots are good and stout, with a sure-grip sole. Always make sure that you have a good, safe, comfortable stance before fishing; don't balance on rocks or anywhere with a slippery surface.

The effect of light – *This picture was taken about 5½ ft beneath the surface of a clear barbel river. Some things about the presentation are good, especially the terminal gear lying on soft weed. But look at the effect of sunlight on the SSG shot and the parts of the exposed hook – to say they glint is an understatement. Think about using a less shiny weight and a smaller hook completely buried in the corn.*

Attracting fish – *Wading often helps stimulate a swim. Here you see a cloud of silt stirred up by the wading boot. That silt cloud may attract shoals of small fish, whose excitement, in turn, may send ripples of anticipation down the swim. Barbel definitely pick up on this whole feeding frenzy. Also, dribbles of bait from your pouch will move slowly down with the current sending out enticing flavours.*

The washing-line effect – Accurate, tight bait presentation is especially difficult after a flood or in the autumn months. Weed and leaves become dislodged and float downstream until they cling to your line. Weed attracts weed and soon the line is bowed and your bait is pulled out of position. The weed also highlights the presence of the line itself. If you're wading, you'll be more likely to notice if this is happening.

Barbel care and conservation

What I have to say about consideration for the welfare of barbel applies equally to every species. Through years of diving I have become convinced that fish are far less tough than anglers consider. For example, it's quite obvious that fish that have been caught and returned, but not kept in a net, have suffered trauma to some degree. You'd be surprised how long wounds inflicted during capture take to heal. Barbel are especially vulnerable to damage and danger; they fight valiantly, using up great reserves of energy. They are also frequently fighting against the current of the river as well as the strain of your tackle, and that greatly increases the exhaustion factor. Also, as barbel are often caught in the warmest weather, the lack of oxygen does nothing to aid a quick recovery. So, all in all, take the greatest care of your barbel.

To the bankside – Can there be a more lovely sight than a barbel caught in the sunlight? Be aware, however, that as soon as the fish leaves the water, those glistening scales dry out perilously quickly.

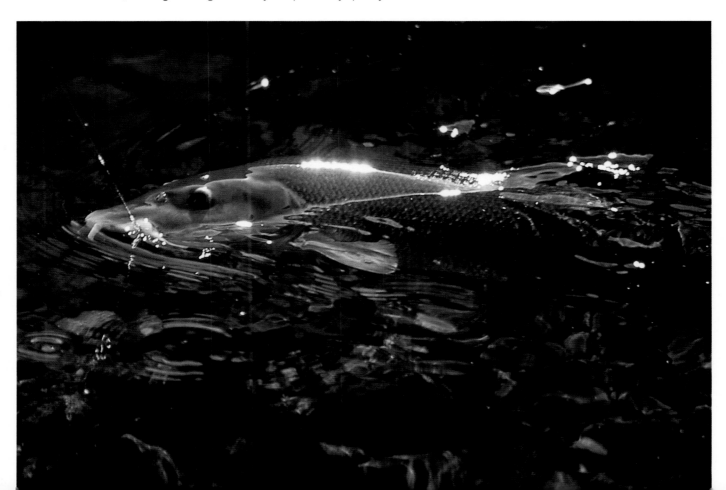

The barbel fight

Quite rightly the barbel is revered as one of the great fighters of freshwater, and newcomers to the barbel scene are often shell-shocked by the power and resilience a barbel will show. But what goes on unseen while you are fighting that barbel? Why is a barbel so special? Well, it may well be its perfect balance, large fins and muscular body, which combine to make it one amazing, rippling, fighting machine.

A reminder: many barbel are lost right at the end of the fight as the angler relaxes. To avoid this occurring, always ensure that the reel's clutch is set to give line to a last run and move the fish to the net slowly and gently so that it is not further alarmed.

Power – Here you can see a barbel of close on 9lb grudgingly prised from the bottom towards the surface. Not for long. Watch how the body arches and the fins flair. We are keen to talk about the size of the barbel's pectorals but look, too, at those pelvic fins and even the large anal fin. Within a split second of taking this shot, the barbel nose-dived and plunged irresistibly back to the riverbed.

The propeller – I love this shot I took of a barbel midway through a fight. Just look at the great sweep of that tail as it powers the fish away from danger. Note, too, how the whole body works in one sinuous whiplash movement.

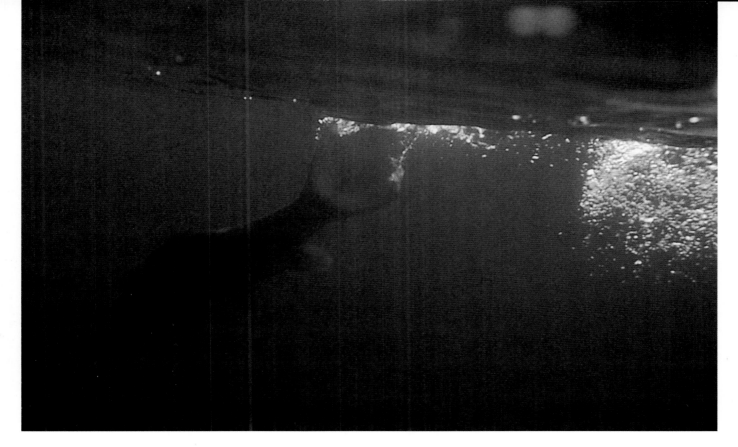

The last surge – *You know how it is… you've been playing a barbel for ten minutes – although it seems like more – and then you get the fish to the surface, where it eyes you cautiously. With most other fish the battle is now over, but not with the barbel. The view of the terrestrial world spurs it into a last-gasp effort and, with that mighty tail, it slaps the surface and powers off yet again. This is the moment when you don't want that clutch to be set too tight.*

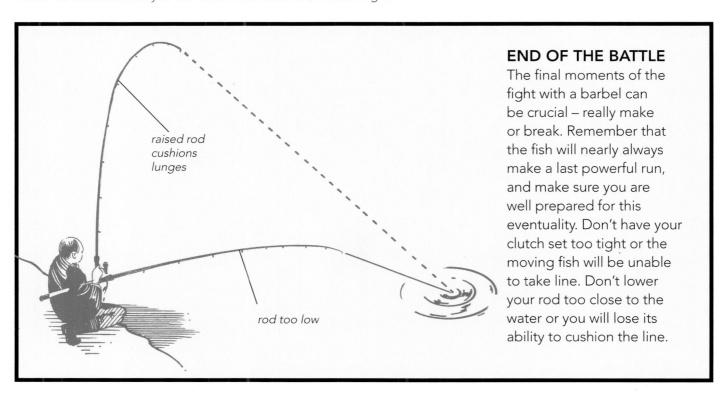

raised rod
cushions
lunges

rod too low

END OF THE BATTLE

The final moments of the fight with a barbel can be crucial – really make or break. Remember that the fish will nearly always make a last powerful run, and make sure you are well prepared for this eventuality. Don't have your clutch set too tight or the moving fish will be unable to take line. Don't lower your rod too close to the water or you will lose its ability to cushion the line.

Landing the barbel

There is no doubt that removing the fish bodily from the water onto the side of the bank is one of the most stressful elements of the whole catching process. The photographs that appear here show how I, ideally, like to treat any barbel that I catch… and that's by not removing them from the water at all, at any single stage. Believe me, fish recover much more quickly when they are kept in the water throughout the whole unhooking process.

The technique shown in the pictures below is the most fish-friendly method of dealing with fish after the fight. Obviously, however, it can only be carried out in those circumstances where you can wade or at least get right to the water-line in complete safety. Don't try it in swollen water or on steep, slippery banks. The fish is a very important creature, but the angler's safety is paramount.

A flash of light – This is what you see from below when the barbel is finally beaten and guided into the waiting net. It's interesting, too, that this is the moment that the light above the surface catches the scales of any fish most brightly… a key, perhaps, to those frequent, last-minute pike attacks on your catch.

Unhooking – Lift the barbel to the water-line so that the hook, often barbless, can be slipped from the lip with that pair of forceps that you should always carry clipped to your lapel. Even at this stage the fish is still largely in the water, with the river still coursing through its gills.

314

Releasing your catch – Kneel in the water and guide the fish from the net, still keeping hold of it with both hands. This is vitally important: if you don't keep control at this stage, the barbel can wriggle free only to find the current is too strong for it. At this point it could easily drift from sight and turn over in the current.

Taking in air – As you begin to feel power return to the barbel, and once you are sure it will not keel over in the water if it is left unsupported, then you can hold it with one hand back towards the tail. Note, too, that bubble of oxygen escaping from the gills; air was gulped just in those few seconds that the fish was held on the water-line. Imagine how much more air is taken on board if the fish is physically taken from the water for any length of time.

Complete return of power – This fish, a Spanish barbel in fact, is now working its body dynamically, totally ready to be let free. The fish has made its own mind up and off it goes, totally safe and not unduly stressed.

Barbel on ranunculus – This shows a barbel in its natural environment, resting on the weed that it lives amongst. The limpid nature of the fish is also emphasized as the water brushes its flanks.

Care at the bankside

There are times when you will want a quick photograph of a barbel out of its watery home. Or, perhaps, the fish is very large and you want to weigh it. There are numerous reasons for taking a barbel from the river, but do make sure the reason is a good one, and keep the period that the fish is actually out in the air to a very minimum. If you do require to get you and your friends' faces in a photo with your catch, remember it is up to you to go to the fish rather than vice versa, so that the time the fish is out of the water is reduced. I believe that it is especially important not to take the barbel any real distance from the water – get that fish back as soon as you can.

Be careful now – These are three special shots because they are a lasting record of a boy's first barbel, caught under the care and supervision of his father – a moment that all the family will be proud of forever. Note the concentration on Jack's face as his father, Tony, steadies the fish in preparation for the photograph.

Hold steady – Jack's brother, Christopher, is also standing by in case Jack or Tony lose their grip. All three made sure their hands were glistening wet before touching the fish. In an ideal world, I would like to have seen an unhooking mat brought into operation at this stage, but the grass was very thick, lush and damp. The barbel has been out of the water less than 30 seconds at this stage.

Speed is of the essence – Tony, Jack, Christopher and the barbel look up for two or three very quick photographs. I had already made sure that my camera was switched on, focused and ready to go, and the barbel was back in the water just 52 seconds after being taken from the water.

Fishing for Chub

I've never done chub justice. When I've wanted barbel… along comes a chub. When I've been obsessed with big roach… along comes a chub. Perhaps it's diving that's enlightened me. The more I've seen chub under water, the more I've come to realize why Izaak Walton called them 'the fearfulest of fishes'.

Chub are generally shoal fish, and their already keen senses work even more effectively with shared information. Look at those big eyes: no wonder they are hard to fool in clear water.

The fearfulest of fishes

Chub are fish of infinite variety. You'll find them feeding on just about every possible food source – digging up boulders to get at caddis, slurping fallen moths, chasing elvers. Underwater, you begin to realize just how keen their sight and hearing is, and they show endless cunning when faced with anglers' baits. Imagine the scene: I'm lying watching a group of chub some 10ft away; an angler plops in a float or a lead, ten or even 20 yards upriver. The chub immediately show unease. If the lead is increased in size or dropped closer, they will bolt. So, try to introduce your hook bait and loose feed as quietly as you can. If you're wading, introduce the feed by hand actually under the water level so there's no noise of its entry. Cast well upstream and let the bait move down towards the fish as silently as possible.

Chub and float

A float can be a really useful tool when chub fishing, though most anglers today prefer legering. The great advantage a float gives you is that you can move a bait up to a 100yd when searching for fish. Also, the bait will creep up to a chub silently without the dreaded splash of the descending leger.

The older and wiser chub become, the more they seek out surface cover and hang underneath it. To

If you let a float travel in open water, it will stick out like the proverbial sore thumb – the chub will see it coming at least 2–3yd off and either flee or make a big detour. If you are forced to use a float without any cover, try not cocking it but let it drift down flat on the surface; this is an unusual tactic, admittedly, but a far less obtrusive way of approaching a swim.

Now, even with the light on it, you'll see the float merge in with the debris. Also, if you hold it back slightly, the bait will rise up and the chub will see the bait before any line, shot or anything else disturbs them. Again, it's doing lots of small things right that makes the difference, especially with a difficult fish in clear water.

These particular fish are quite obviously on their guard, hanging close under a branch that's become festooned with passing weed and pieces of rush – any flotsam and jetsam the river pushes towards it. It's a good place for them to garner food as well as feel secure.

get a legered bait close to such fish would be very difficult. You'd have to cast it very close to the branch and that would mean the devastating chub-scaring plop. Far better to use a float to get the bait down past their noses. Running the float as close to the snag as you can. If possible, wade out into mid-river, a long way upstream, to give you a better angle and more control. Lengthen the distance between the float and the bait, so that the float is further off and less easily seen. Free-lining is an excellent tactic for really careful, spooked fish.

Chub and leger

Most anglers leger for chub because it's easier and, of course, it has done the job for years. However, never underestimate your chub. Richard Walker once said that they take about ten minutes to become unscared for every pound they possess in weight. I'm not so sure about this: I would say a 4lb chub doesn't become unscared after 40 minutes, but often as not vacates the area entirely!

Float free-lining – Letting a big bait waft free in the current is a good method for chub. A big lump of flake or a good-sized lobworm is often the bait to use. However, it is easy to lose contact with the bait, as the current manipulates the line into surprising contortions that you'd never guess at from above the water-line. Putting a small float some 7–8ft up the line can pay dividends. Put the shot to cock the float directly underneath it so that the rest of the line is unencumbered and the bait can rise and fall in the natural fashion that free-lining allows.

TAKING CARE

If the water is at all quick, it will pick even a medium-sized bait off the bottom to play around in the current in a totally unnatural way. Slow water often makes for easier presentation. The problem is that in a negligible flow the fish have all the time in the world to inspect a bait and reject it.

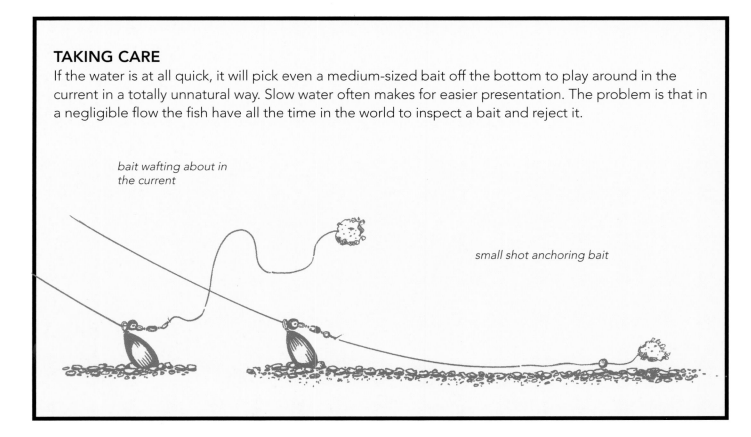

bait wafting about in the current

small shot anchoring bait

If you're legering, never use a lead heavier than you need to – the splash is more easily heard and more harmful. Feather your cast so that the lead lands as lightly as possible on the water; this really helps. It is traditional to quiver tip with the rod pointing to the clouds, but this is problematic here as it makes the line cut through the water at a steep angle, and in sunlight, the rays catch the line and highlight it sharply. Touch legering means the rod tip is down at water level, the line is closer to the river-bed in shallow water and is less likely to be marked out by the sunlight.

Once upon a time, the very best chub bait was a crayfish. Now, obviously, you can't use these highly protected creatures, but their legacy remains: present a chub with a bait they simply cannot resist and you may get a smash instant take. Big slugs work; lobworms, like this one above, can do the trick. Really use your imagination and try anything that excites the chub's interest and, especially, arouses its predatory instincts.

A dagger of light *– Shallow, clear water and bright sunlight paint the line from the lead to the rod tip with a banner that spells danger (see left-hand side of image below). Lower the rod tip so that the angle of the line through the water is less steep.*

Fishing for Rudd

Rudd are great grazers, especially when they weigh under 1lb, and they will feed for most of the daylight hours. This makes them particularly catchable and great sport for youngsters. A pair of binoculars is a good idea for picking out where the rudd shoals are roaming – you may well see either the flash of their scales or the exquisite red banner fins. Very frequently, you will just see the lily pads quiver as the fish rub against the stems.

This spectacular rudd was caught traditionally using a float and a slow-sinking piece of bread flake. The fish came from a small hole in the weed, exactly where you should always look for the species.

Undercover

Although crucian carp are primarily bottom feeders, they may also feed near the surface. What they do always require though, is cover. For that reason, lily beds are the ideal crucian haunt. Within them, crucians can feel confident enough to feed near the surface.

Rudd and lilies

If there are lilies on a water, then rudd will almost inevitably be among them, smaller ones especially. The reasons aren't that difficult to find: food, shade, protection from predators… they're even quite adept at skipping out of the water and lying for a few seconds on the top of a pad should a pike attack from beneath!

From looking at the many shots of rudd shoals that I've taken, it seems as if there are always one or two fish searching the water away from the direction in which the main body of rudd are moving. It's as though they are scanning 360°, presumably for pike or perch attack. This behavioural pattern is less marked when the shoal is moving fast, but then, generally, it has sensed trouble and is making its escape. You will often find rudd attacking a single food source if it's prevalent enough but, under most conditions, they will hang at all manner of depths sipping in food of every type – nymphs, water shrimps, bloodworm, buzzers.

Big rudd

Big rudd, in my diving experiences, appear to behave rather differently to their smaller brethren. The change in behaviour seems to take place when they reach a weight of between a pound and a pound and a half, probably when they feel less vulnerable to pike attacks. In short, they are more willing to leave cover and investigate what their whole environment can offer them.

Big rudd appear to be very mobile, and it's a good idea to put out a stream of baits if you're fishing with a floater on the surface. If you're trying to catch them from the lakebed, however, don't expect to hold a shoal of big rudd for long. Get a bed of

Protective behaviour – *There are a couple of interesting points here. There is one of the shoal apparently keeping guard from a possible attack from the rear. Also, note the gleam of light on the leading fish as they move between the pads. It's my belief that right now they are most vulnerable to a pike attack. It's as though the flash awakens even a dormant fish.*

particles down, as this gives you the best chance of maintaining their interest for as long as possible. Try putting par-boiled, white-grained rice into your feeder mix – they love it, and the tiny grains keep them hunting for long periods.

Cruising – *There is a large amount of insect life drifting on, or just beneath, the surface of any stillwater, and big rudd go with the currents, exploiting this food source. At night, their distinctive, splashing way of breaking surface is due partly to their technique of pulling down moths from the air itself. A large dry fly – a mayfly pattern – can be just as successful as a caster or a dog biscuit.*

Fishing for Tench

Observations above and below the water-line lead me to suggest that tench have well-defined patrol routes, and you will find the same fish in the same areas at the same times, day after day. They move in loose shoals, often predominantly male or female.

This particularly lovely tench was caught early in the year and holds next to no spawn. This fish is in peak condition and fought like a tiger.

Tench feeding

It is known that tench feed early in the day, but feeding spells frequently last longer than we think. As the light grows, they can simply see us, our tackle and any defects in our presentation more clearly, and they will make fewer mistakes. They are especially adept at picking up line falling from a float through mid-water; after sunrise a lead or a feeder with a small back lead can work more efficiently.

Big tench

The behaviour of big tench differs, in my experience, from that of smaller fish; they have larger territories and they frequently inhabit much bigger waters.

Below: This illustrates how tench like to behave in full light in smaller waters. You can see them searching the shade afforded by old, wooden sheathing, designed to keep the bank intact. Tench, rather like barbel, also like the comfort of friends and the feeling of fin against fin, body against body when they are in this semi-sleep mode. However, they can be enticed to take a big-impact bait, such as a lively lobworm, if it is positioned very close.

Above: When a tench is feeding, it swims slowly a little way above the bottom looking down intently for signs of food activity. In this mode it will also suck in free-swimming insects. When it decides on a patch to investigate, it moves down headfirst and feeds at virtually 90°. This habit gives quite a number of line bites when float fishing. I believe this is why laying-on has been so successful over the years; it simply means that a tench over the bait is well away from any line dropping down from the float.

Moving into the light – Big tench in large open waters seem to be remarkably unafraid of the light compared with smaller fish in heavily weeded ones. Admittedly, they do like the shade of lilies or bulrushes, but they are happy to feed out in bright, open sunlight, as you can see from this photograph.

Certainly, the new, large and comparatively barren pits seem to suit them very well. Food is plentiful in this environment and competition is frequently fairly minimal.

What to catch them with? Hook baits? Well, lobworms are a bit of a quandary for me – I've seen big tench catch sight of them, quiver with anticipation and move rapidly well over a yard to pick them up. Equally, I've watched a fish shy away from a lob

Just resting – Look carefully and you'll see the tench, a couple of pounds in weight, well hidden and seemingly in the land of nod. It certainly isn't objecting to my presence.

Patrolling – From what I've seen, one of the biggest problems catching fish in this type of water is actual location. The tench will often seem to patrol quite large areas – certainly several hundred yards is not uncommon. It is often important to lay down a carpet of bait and wait for the fish to come onto it. If you can prebait for several days, there is all the more chance of focusing the fish tightly.

when it's been virtually under its nose. When bites have been impossible to come by, I'd advise giving a lobworm a whirl if you're fairly sure that there are feeding tench in the area – it's always worth a try.

Getting its attention – However, as I present this piece of bread flake very close to the tench and swim back a yard or so, it begins to show evident interest. Its eye swivels until it makes contact with the bait. Its fins begin to work, and you can sense that it is weighing up a thorough investigation. Eventually, sadly, it moves slowly backwards and disappears totally into the weed growth.

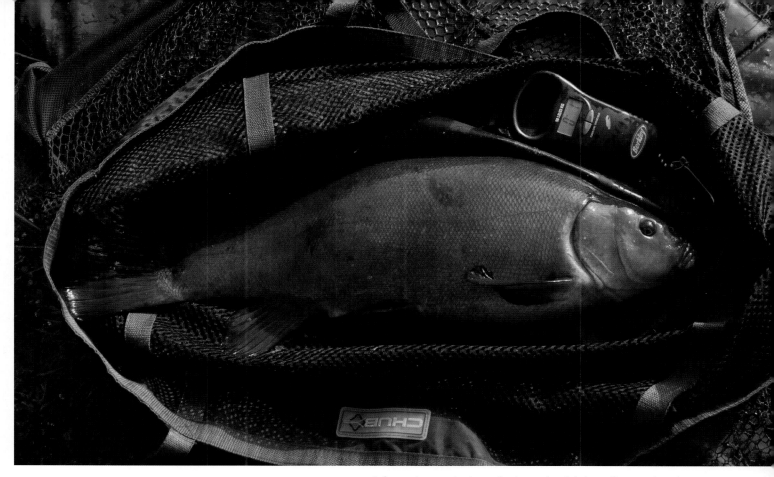

You can also try 'dragging' to attract the fish (see the diagram below).

Observations

It's obvious that the more time you spend looking at a water and getting to know it, either from above or below the water-line, the more you'll begin to understand. Equally, however, the more it can prove

A favourite tench shot of mine – the fish is well wetted and secure on the hooking mat, the scales were zeroed and the weigh sling was also kept wet so that the fish would come to no harm whatsoever. With practice, a big fish like this can be recorded by both scales and camera in well under 30 seconds and returned unharmed.

to be a puzzle! It is important for any angler to patrol the bankside, preferably with binoculars, and look for feeding fish before deciding on a pitch and putting out bait into an area that may be barren of fish.

raking up the bottom releases all kinds of food items

THE ART OF DRAGGING

A rake pronged on both sides, a decent length of rope, and you are in business. Simply throw it out, let it sink and drag it back through the silt. Scents and a host of tiny foodstuffs are released, drawing in tench, perch and bream. You are also clearing the swim of heavy weed growth and helping your presentation. Just check with other anglers around the lake first!

Fishing for Roach

It's high summer and the river is running warm and crystal clear; there is heavy weed growth – water cabbages in particular – but in between lie patches of clear sand and gravel where it is possible to watch large shoals of roach as they glide through the polished water. The fish are feeding almost constantly on the huge variety of insects that the river harbours during the warmer summer months.

Brrrrr! A freezing cold day when temperatures didn't get much above 2–3°C (36–37°F). Still, if you wrap up warmly, this photograph proves that fantastic roach still will make a mouth at a bait.

Centre-pin and boat

Alex and I are on the River Wensum, where a boat is absolutely essential to get us upstream to the place where most of the roach are feeding, among underwater cabbages alongside banks, metres deep in impenetrable reed beds. We see some roach rising to sip in struggling sedge flies and the whole impression is of a river teeming with life, well on the way to a full recovery. As for the centre-pin? Well, a better tool for trotting (see pgs. 278–281) has never been created. Control of the line and float is perfect and, without a bail arm, an instant strike can be made.

Life among the cabbages

Deep dredging as a tool of river management was initiated in the UK shortly after the Second World War. Unfortunately, it devastated not only the riverbed but also bankside vegetation. Fish, flora and fauna all suffered massively. Gradually, the Environment Agency, at least in south-east England, has phased out the practice, sending it back into the mists where it belongs. Happily, the River Wensum is already beginning to show the benefits.

The return of the roach has benefited the whole food chain. Pike are next on the ladder, and it's

River management – The mills are very important to the well-being of lowland rivers. Sensitive sluice gate management is vital to prevent over-rapid run-off, which can dislodge whole generations of small fish. This is the River Wensum, once by far the best river for roach in eastern England until it fell on hard times in the 1970s and '80s. The rumour is, however, that sensitive river management by the Environment Agency has seen huge improvements and the smaller fish have come back in droves.

The boat – A half-mile row sees the boys at the top of a fabulous glide. They've fed in half a bucket of loose mash and are putting up their gear. Soon, they'll anchor the boat out across the river so that they can trot the stream with perfect, direct control. The river here is about 2m (7ft) deep and the cabbage beds rise up to just over the mid-water mark.

Roach in sunlight – While Alex prepared to start running through his float, I was able to sink into the water and see just how many pristine, scale-perfect, young roach were swimming in the area. These fish, I guess, weigh between 4–12oz and are probably between two and four years of age. If the gods are kind to them, in three or four more years, many of them will be true specimens.

noticeable that the numbers and average sizes have risen over the past few years. Keep your eye out for riverbank wildlife, too.

The float and the cabbages

It is a fact that the underwater cabbages attract the roach with the shade and food they offer, but trotting through them isn't always easy. The cabbages are not a level playing field, but more like a green, underwater range of mountains.

You want your bait to travel as close to the top of the cabbages as possible, but, if you misjudge the depth, then you will consistently hang up. When you follow a bait downstream you realize that it rarely behaves as textbooks would have us believe. Bread flake, especially, seems to rise and fall of its own volition, and will frequently travel downstream actually above the bottom shot. If you modify your gear a little, by dropping the float down 8–10cm

The flat float – The bait and/or the shot is hung up on a cabbage leaf (above), and the float (below) is neither allowed to cock nor move off downriver. The mobile roach may chance upon the marooned piece of flake, but you can't really explore the river as you'd like to. The bread flake has wedged against a cabbage leaf above the bottom shot and further progress is impossible.

Another go – The modified rig has the bread flake just flicking the top of the cabbages (above) – ideal. The float is cocked (below), but the angler isn't adding shot to bury it deeper; if he did, every time the bread flake brushed a lip of cabbage, the float would drop, increasing the number of abortive strikes.

(3–4in), the bait should travel just over the head of the cabbages. Also, if you squeeze a little more air out of the flake before putting it on the hook, it will be less buoyant and will trundle downstream below the bottom shot. Floats are strange things when seen underwater, and fish see them very clearly. I remember catching a big, wild carp that had veered

A favourite fish – *A scale-perfect, fin-perfect and colour-perfect roach of one and a half pounds prepares for return to the river. The roach is a magnificent creature and perhaps the author's favourite species.*

away from a traditional float at a shallow local lake; it was only when I tied on a discarded goose feather as a bite indicator that the carp took the bait.

STRETPEGGING

This is an old and effective way of catching roach. Use a float attached top and bottom and set it well over-depth – in quick water, twice the depth is not too much. Let the float work its way down the swim, little by little, holding it back for a minute or two before letting it on its way again. This is a good way to search out water, but note the big loop of line that the fish will come to before the bait – often not the best method for clear water.

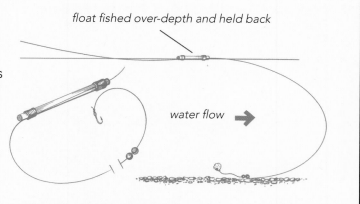

float fished over-depth and held back

water flow

Fishing a winter river

Underwater observations suggest to me that fish move around much more slowly in the winter river than the summer one. I suppose you'd expect that, as temperatures plummet and the whole life-cycle slows down. However, there is movement. Shoals of roach, especially, can be quite lively, particularly when there's a tinge of colour in the water – something you'd expect from your catch records. But this doesn't mean that location is not central to success on any winter session. Roach definitely hang close to cover. Look for dead cabbage beds, for example, sunken trees or anything that breaks up their outline and gives them a feeling of protection. Depth is also an issue. I generally find them in water over 5ft deep, but there are exceptions. In the river

Bright days – Roach are always unpredictable. Although they favour warm westerly winds and a coloured river, bright sunlight can spark them into unexpected movement.

Amidst the clutter – Mid-winter, a swim around 5ft deep and a shoal of roach is moving through comparatively gloomy water. It's a good roach swim – there's plenty of clutter around to break up their movement, and lots of food hidden in the bottom vegetation. Mind you, trotting a swim as dirty as this down on the bottom is pretty well impossible. Go for a light leger instead.

featured in this photograph, for example, they move into water just 2–3ft deep upstream of the mill. Don't make the mistake of going for the deadest water you can find – often you will find roach shoals deliberately seeking out water with some push to it. So my perfect winter roach swim? I'd look for water around 6–8ft deep but perhaps shelving up towards the end of the run. There will be some flow and definitely a number of snags.

The river and its roach

A big roach in winter is one of the craftiest creatures alive. If the water is clear and cold, then the roach's inherent wariness is magnified. You, therefore, must think very carefully about your bait and how best to present it. Light feeding – sprinkling in tiny amounts of bait until, one by one, fish begin to feed and eventually a whole spree is triggered – is often a good idea. Also, bites can be very gentle indeed, and your indication must be precise. Unless a river is heavily in flood, float fishing is a great form of attack, as it does search out greater amounts of water than the leger ever can. One tip though: try to retrieve your float close to the bank rather than through the

Making a move – At last a roach moves towards a falling caster. It gets to within a couple of inches or so, flares its gills, creates a vacuum and whips in that grub faster than the eye can see. One moment it's there – and a fraction of a second later, it's gone.

A lesson for the angler – The caster is in the mouth and soon the roach begins to chew. A sight like this makes you realize why match anglers catch so many fish in the winter, whereas bigger bait men, like me, struggle. An intricate shotting pattern helps to present a small bait like this with maximum delicacy, whereas a heavy shot close to the hook would never allow that unrestricted suck in.

swim itself, as winter roach are neurotically afraid of disturbance over their heads.

Roach perils

The life of a roach is not an easy one. Cormorants, pike, floods, disease, pollution and anglers – these are just a few of the threats to the roach's safety. The school of hard knocks has made a big river roach a very wary creature indeed. Public enemy number one is almost undoubtedly the pike, even though a roach knows full well how to interpret its body language. I'm not sure quite what triggers a pike into feeding mode, but I have a feeling that bright sunlight plays a part. I'm not saying that bright water conditions are necessarily best for pike fishing, but it is the light that kick-starts resting fish back into life. If you manage to get a catch, remember that keeping fish in nets is not a good idea. In matches, I accept they are necessary, but outside of matches we must phase them out if we really care about the good of our fish stocks.

A pearl of nature – This is how a roach should look – glistening silver, fins absolutely perfect and lips totally undamaged or torn. As the late, great Hugh Falkus said, 'It's a beauty such as this that makes getting up on a freezing dawn morning or staying on well after the sun has set and the frost is beginning to form worthwhile'. Falkus, a master of sea-trout rivers, was wise enough to appreciate the beauty of the apparently humble roach.

Wensum winner – David Lambert holds one of the most exciting river roach of modern times. Weighing 21lb 5oz and taken from the River Wensum, this is an almost miraculous fish in this day and age. The fact David took it trotting only increases its worth.

■ CHAPTER 5

LURE FISHING

Lure fishing is all about using artificial baits to fool predatory fish into accepting them as real. The more skilled you become, the more you will be able to deceive predators by imparting life into creations of wood, metal or plastic. This is the excitement of lure fishing. It's a real art form. It grips the imagination. A difficult fish? Well, you can try a different type of lure altogether, or a different model, a different size, a different colour or a different action. You can vary the retrieve. Perhaps a short burst. Perhaps a series of quick twitches. Then bang, wallop, the pike, perch or whatever is fooled.

Introduction to Lure Fishing

In the last 20 years or so, I have fished in approximately 50 countries. Before that, my angling activity was largely confined to the United Kingdom where, certainly until recently, the bulk of predator fishing was done with either live or dead baits of one sort or another. Lure fishing was generally only a last resort. If the live or dead baits had not produced any fish then, towards the end of the day, in desperation, a spinner or a spoon would be put on and cast around here and there with very little expectation of success. Not surprisingly, lure fishing was a long way down the league table of success for many, many years.

Small rubber fish like this are top lures for every species and perch love them. I personally like the fact of the single hook, which is much kinder on the fish and makes taking the hooks much easier. This is especially the case if you flatten down the barb with a forceps before fishing.

Opening our eyes

When I began to travel extensively, I was struck strongly by the difference in approach to lure fishing in other countries. Anglers in North America, Scandinavia and Central and Eastern Europe showed an imagination in their lure fishing that was almost impossible to find anywhere in the UK. Americans, Canadians, Swedes, Czechs and Germans took their lure fishing seriously, and it really showed. They had the tackle for the job, they had the knowledge, the enthusiasm and the techniques. Today, the UK is fast catching up with this technique. The Internet has vastly improved the ease with which anglers can buy the best lures from anywhere in the world, and information has been equally fast to spread. Moreover, attitudes have changed: 20 years ago, lure fishing was considered lightweight work by most serious British predator anglers. Today, that is not the case. The number of specialist lure anglers has rocketed and their results have laughed the prejudices of the bait men out of court.

A lesson from the Czechs

Of all the lure anglers that I have fished alongside, perhaps those from the Czech Republic have impressed me the most, and this is largely down to their determination. They will try and try again to find the right lure for any particular day and never stop trying. For example, they know that dark lures probably show up much better against a bright background on a particularly sunny day. On a day when there is no sun, predators will probably see the water as a veil of darkness, and this is when a bright, striking lure can come into its own. On overcast days, especially, lure fishing is all about trying all the colours and types that you have in your box until you get a take. If predators are not feeding hard, one particular colour or size or movement might just have a better triggering effect than another.

Lure visibility

Think about where your lure is working. If you are retrieving close to a dam wall, perhaps strewn with algae, a green lure is not going to be seen. Change

Missionary-style rods are the perfect tool for the travelling lure angler. They typically break down into five or six pieces so they can be stored out of sight in a car or packed into a suitcase. Buy one that comes with a secure travelling case and it will be safe in the hold of airplanes as well. My own preference is for a rod with a higher-end casting capability. This gives you greater scope with more species and a lighter rod.

it to a red one and you stand a far better chance of a predator spotting it.

In clear or cloudy water, you've got to appeal to the pike's vision as well as to its other senses. Shiny spoons, spinners and plugs can reflect light over a great distance underwater, especially when the sun is high. It's a good idea to use glitter on dull plugs to increase visibility. Make sure silver spoons and spinners are well polished to increase the flash factor.

In murky water, too, flashy and fluorescent colours can often do the job. Experiment with bigger or more violently active lures so that the fish can physically feel their presence. Try plugs with sound chambers, because a rattling ball-bearing can frequently attract a predator. In murky water, slow down the rate of your retrieve to give the predator more time to home in on what you're using. Keep working, keep changing, and always keep experimenting and on even the hardest day you will eventually find the key to success.

Fishing with Plugs

Plugs have been on the angling scene for generations. Traditionally they are fashioned out of wood or hard plastic, and their aim is to mimic a small-prey fish. A plug has an in-built swimming action, but the vital skill with this method is for the angler to impart life into the plug on its retrieve. The aim of every plug angler is to fool a predatory fish into thinking that what is only a semi-realistic imitation is, in fact, the real thing. A mechanical, unimaginative, monotonous retrieve is unlikely to produce results, especially in waters where fish have seen it all before.

Hitting rock bottom – In clear water, it can be a good idea to let your plug hit bottom once or twice. On a rock bottom, this will send out vibrations, and on a muddy riverbed it will send up a cloud of silt that can give the impression of an escaping crayfish.

How plugs behave

To get the best out of plug fishing, you need to know how a plug behaves under the water. Find some clear, shallow water with a hard bottom where you can wade, and then study the action of the plug you intend to use. How fast does the plug sink? If it's a buoyant plug, how quickly does it rise back towards the surface? How does the plug respond to a jerk-type retrieve? Try casting the plug as far as you can – does it tangle in flight? Do you need to feather the spool to prevent this?

Choosing the right plug

The choice of plug on any particular water on any particular day is also crucial. Many experts in the North American bass world talk about finding the right match or pattern. By this, they mean clicking with the right style of fishing at a particular period. For example, it would be madness to choose a surface-fishing plug in the middle of winter when the water is close to freezing and the pike are down deep. Equally, if the pike are lying in shallow, sun-warmed bays you wouldn't choose a great big, heavy trolling spoon or a deep-diving plug that works best at 12m (40ft). Of course, this is all basic stuff and mostly common sense, but the more experienced you become and the more you think about plug choice, the more you'll tweak the options and reap the fruits of your success.

Working the cracks – It helps considerably if you have an exact knowledge of the topography of your water. Working a plug in the nooks and crannies is a great way to find the fish.

Imitating nature – This fascinating creation, designed to look exactly like a lenok trout, was made by a master plug expert in the Czech Republic and possesses an excellent action in the water.

Fiery orange – In very murky water, an orange plug like this Shad Rap works particularly well. Fish can pick up the fiery orange at great distance.

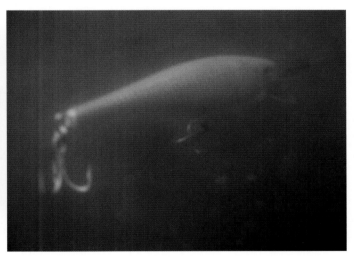

Black beauty – Black, like orange, works well in misty conditions. When the river was unexpectedly coloured, we found that all predators would hit much bigger lures than normal.

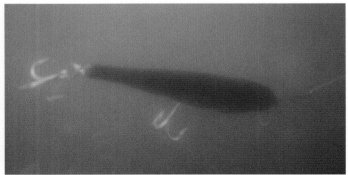

Lures in action – These shots were taken on an autumnal day, when one has to work hard to interest any fish. Constantly changing the size, colour and action of the plugs was the only way to arouse some occasional interest.

Fishing the right location

As in all fishing situations, you'll also need to think very carefully about where you are going to fish your plug. As we've seen before, predators aren't evenly scattered throughout the water, and you need to pinpoint exact locations. You need to be mobile so that you can work large expanses of water, and it pays to wear thigh boots or chest waders so that, if you can safely do so, you can wade out to tackle water that is impossible to approach from the bank. If you've got a boat, a canoe or a float tube, so much the better. The really successful plug angler will pop his plug where other pluggers fail to reach!

This, of course, is where accuracy counts. If you're aiming to work a plug alongside the fringes of a fallen tree, it's no good casting too far so that you get hung up, or too short so that you miss the killing zone. Work hard at your accuracy and be angry with yourself when you get it wrong. Don't tolerate slackness in your approach or your performance. Sweat blood over your plug fishing and success will come your way.

Fishing hard

'KN' was my Indian guide for a few years, and he is one of the best plug fishermen I have ever met. He worked incredibly hard at his plug fishing and left nothing to chance. He always replaced factory-

Precision – Neill chooses to lure fish with a short rod – 7ft – and a small multiplier coupled with braid line. The whole outfit is light, quick to use and devastatingly accurate.

fitted hooks with much stronger ones of his own, which were sharpened to perfection. He'd test every knot, and the reel's clutch would always be precisely correct for the fishing situation.

KN would scout the area to be fished with military precision. He'd spend 20 minutes investigating a pool, mapping out the approaches and looking carefully for any signs of feeding fish. He'd direct my approach completely. He'd go through exactly where I was going to cast, how many times I was going to cast to each place and how I was going to retrieve the plug. The plug would be replaced several times, even when fishing one single pool. Sometimes a deep diver would be put on if the central channel was to be worked. A popper might be tried over the shallows. If a fish followed and turned away, a different pattern or a different colour would be tried.

This latter point is an important one: KN, of course, wore my spare pair of polarizing glasses and he looked intently into the water wherever possible, following the journey of the plug back towards us. He was constantly watching for any following fish and its reaction to the plug.

Fishing with KN was both a totally exhausting and a totally exhilarating experience. Every cast was a deeply thought-out operation, and my success rate with him began to rocket as a result of his thorough and expert guidance.

Rubber lures come in all shapes, sizes and colours. Try different patters until you find what works on the day.

Fishing with Spoons and Spinners

Everything that I said about hard work and intense concentration referring to plugs applies to spoons and spinners. Once again, the skill is to make a piece of metal appear so realistic that it is engulfed by a predator. To do this regularly isn't always easy. You've got to consider the size, weight, pattern and colour of the spoon or spinner that you are going to use in any given situation. You've got to locate the fish with pinpoint accuracy. And you've got to work your lure with imagination in the hot zone. Fish slackly and you will be unsuccessful.

A silver spoon is still one of the best lures in any angler's basket. Fish spoons as deep as you can and as slowly as possible. It's a good idea to let the spoon actually hit bottom and then twitch it slowly across the lakebed. Pike are frequently attracted by the resulting puff of silt.

Sending out a message

Over the years, I've been fortunate in watching a great many expert spoon and spinner anglers, and here are some of the skills I've picked up from them.

Sunlight and clear water can spell real problems in many fishing situations, but when using spoons and spinners this isn't always the case. The sun glints off the blade in conditions like this, sending dramatic flashes through the water and attracting the attention of all predators.

It pays to polish spoons and spinners until they shine like new pins and reflect the sunlight even farther underwater. In these instances, choose big spoons and spinners – once again to increase the flash factor – and don't work the lures too fast, as a big, jinking spoon worked slowly gives out maximum flash.

Experimentation is what spoons and spinners are all about. While a flashing silver or bronze blade will generally work, there are equally times when a blade coloured black is the only one that fish will accept. You can also try putting a tail on a spinner – wool, tinsel, a strip of bacon rind, a small plastic grub, even a couple of maggots sometimes works. It often helps if a spinner has certain distinctive points of attraction: for example, a slash of red can imitate gills, and a couple of big, black spots can look very much like eyes, or perhaps they just give the fish a definite target to attack.

On any given session, it's a good idea to start with small lures that won't spook the fish, then step up in size until you begin to hit them. If the water is tinged with colour, you will probably end up using some of the biggest lures you have in your box to flash out

River success – This angler is fishing a clear river, and clear water is generally preferred for spinner and spoon work. Both types of lure send out good, strong vibrations through the water, and predators can home in on these even in dull conditions, but sunlight has an advantage as it strikes the bright blades and sends out flashes of light through the water, and this really pulls the predators in.

all the light available and to send a steady pulse through the water. If the water is coloured, don't work your lure too fast because the predators need time to home in on the bait and make a sure hit. When the water is coloured, copper or brass is probably the best choice for the blade. If the water is really murky, then a brightly painted blade is most likely the best – yellow, red or even fluorescent green. If the water is clear, then silver generally works best.

The all-Important retrieve

If you can see your quarry, think how to work the cast so that the lure is in its line of vision for the maximum possible time. The longer the fish has to watch the lure, the greater the amount of time it has to make up its mind to attack. However, if this approach isn't working, try exactly the opposite. Sometimes, if a predator only sees a lure for a short period of time, it will trigger an immediate, unthinking reaction. Each of these two wildly different approaches can be successful, depending entirely on the mood of the fish.

I mentioned KN watching for any follows. It's just the same with spoons and spinners. If a predator has followed, rejected and turned away, it's very unlikely to accept the same lure a second time round. It's much better, if you've seen a fish that you know is showing some interest, to change the offering. Go bigger or smaller, heavier or lighter. It often pays to rest the fish for 5 or 10 minutes before trying it a second time.

When you are working a spoon, you don't have to retrieve it so that it's constantly on the move. If the bed is comparatively weed- and snag-free, try stopping the retrieve altogether and letting the spoon flutter down and rest on the bottom. You can then twitch it a bit, kicking up silt and sand. Let it lie again. Jerk it back into life. After a minute, continue the retrieve before repeating the process. It seems strange that a predator such as a pike will pick up a piece of inanimate metal, but it's frequently a successful technique. However, watch very carefully for the take: this can be absolutely minute, so strike at any twitch on the line.

Spoon fishing for pike

Spoon fishing is as simple a way of catching pike as any and it goes back centuries. My view is that spoon fishing is particularly effective for pike in spring and autumn when they are very active and willing to attack fast-moving lures. It works well, too, for perch, zander and even chub.

When it comes to spoon choice, start with size: 4–6in is just about perfect. A single hook is also preferable to a treble, because unhooking becomes so much easier, especially if you're not very experienced. As for colour, opt for silver in clear water, copper or brass if there's a tinge to the water and brightly painted spoons when the water is really coloured. Also consider the weight of the spoon. Remember that getting the spoon to the correct depth is probably the real key to this style of fishing – even more important than the retrieve.

Sink and draw – In deep water, when the pike are hugging the bottom, you can use a heavy spoon like this rather as you would a dead bait, in the sink-and-draw style. Let the spoon go down and hit bottom, and then twitch it slowly back, lifting your rod tip so that it rises from time to time in the water. You'll often find that the pike hit it the moment it moves again or, very occasionally, will pick it from the bottom as it lies static.

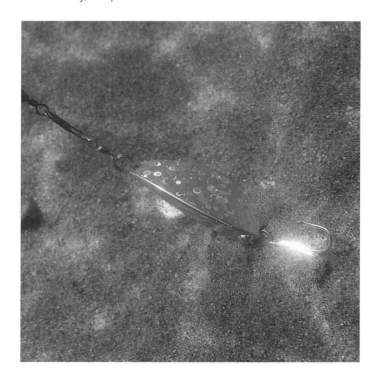

Spinning for pike

Pike love spinners and have been caught on them for decades. Begin with small spinners that won't spook the fish, and then step up in size until you begin to hit fish. If the water's tinged with colour you'll probably end up using the biggest spinner you have in your box to flash out all the light available and to send a steady pulse through the water; but don't work your spinner too fast – the pike need time to home in on the bait and make a hit. When you're tackling pike, especially big ones, check the quality and size of the hooks on the spinner. It pays to fit them with strong,

A team effort – Below, Tim has caught a super pike. Neill rowed and the team used a mix of spoons and spinners.

Spinner success – This is one of 15 fish (above) between 4–12lb taken in an afternoon's fishing. Don't make the mistake of thinking that spinners are only good for smaller pike. On British trout reservoirs in the past decade or so, they've accounted for fish of over 40lb. And it's not true that only big baits will catch the biggest fish. Some very big pike have fallen to lures only a couple of inches long.

Battle on – *Spinning for grayling calls for light tackle if you're going to get maximum enjoyment out of it. It's a good idea to cast the spinner slightly upriver and work it into the grayling's sight zone rather than out of it. This fish is being played on a modern spinning outfit – a light rod matched with a tiny reel, strong line and a box of small spinners.*

chemically sharpened hooks of the perfect size. I normally swear by barbless hooks, but for spinning I prefer a crushed-down barb to make more strikes stick. Don't skimp on the length of your wire trace: I personally never settle for one of less than 46cm (18in).

Spinning for grayling

Few people would think of spinning for grayling, but that's why I've included it here. Most fish species are more predatory than the average angler thinks and, at the right time of the year, virtually any type of fish will eat fish smaller than themselves. Bream can be predatory and so, amazingly, can roach, so it's not at all surprising that grayling will make a mouth at a small fish if they think the chances of success are high enough.

Of course, we're generally talking about larger grayling here. Fish of one and a half pounds and above will typically include fish in their diet on a

regular basis, particularly in colder, more barren environments where insect life is limited. Arctic grayling come regularly to lures and very big flies, but even in more temperate Europe, spinning – if allowed – can pick up some surprisingly big fish.

Spinning for bass

Spinners are a useful addition to the bass fisher's armoury, but they do get snagged in weed and it's hard to get them very close to features, where bass like to lie. The answer may be spinner baits, which are currently having huge success in the bass-fishing world. The elaborate spinner bait pulls bass out of the deepest cover with its combination of flash, action and colour, and its semi-snagless design makes it useful for fishing close to awkward features. It is, in essence, a combination of a spinner and a jig and, despite its amazing success rate, it resembles nothing that a bass would eat in the wild! Spinner baits also allow great freedom when it comes to

Sundance – At last, a decent bass has fallen for a spinner. It was hard work in clear water and blistering sunlight, but at least the shafts of sun really lit up the blade and made it dance. The bass were in a real following mood, often three or four fish patrolling the spinner out of their territory. It wasn't until Johnny began to work this particular spinner very, very close to the rocks indeed that we had any success at all.

choice of retrieve: a steady retrieve is possible, but you can also flip them across the surface or trawl them along the bottom.

Spinning for perch

Small perch can be quite suicidal on any design of spinner you pull out of your box, but bigger fish become much more thoughtful. As when fishing for bass, it's a good idea to customize your spinner – for example, try putting red wool, hair, real or plastic worms, rubber skirts, thin strips of bacon or mackerel

Striped beauty – There's a bit of a story behind this very pretty fish below. The setting was a very clear French river on a hot summer's day, so you could easily see the fish. I tried several different patterns of spinners before trying this particularly heavily spotted one. What had proved a blank day immediately picked up. In all, I had about a dozen perch, but not the ones I was after – in the hole I was fishing were at least three fish of 3lb or more. One looked about 4lb! Nothing I could do would tempt them, not even when I dug up some big, juicy lobs! A passing local suggested I catch one of the numerous lizards and let that trundle through the swim… I ask you!

flesh on the trebles. Keep changing the spinner design: if a big perch has refused a spinner once, it's unlikely to take it on a second sighting. Once you get under the surface, the spinner becomes, to me at least, something of a blur – an indistinct vision of light patterns and colours. It does help, I personally believe, if a spinner has certain distinctive points of attraction to it: for example, a slash of red can imitate gills and I like to see a couple of big, black spots that look very much like eyes. Or do they? Perhaps they just give the fish a target to attack.

Radial Casting

Spinning for perch is often the best way to locate shoals – you can work a lot of the water and move on if no result is forthcoming. You often find perch near to snags, lying in ambush just like any other predator, but groups of fish will frequently patrol in open water. This is where radial casting comes in. Working your way 'round the clock' means that all the water is being systematically searched.

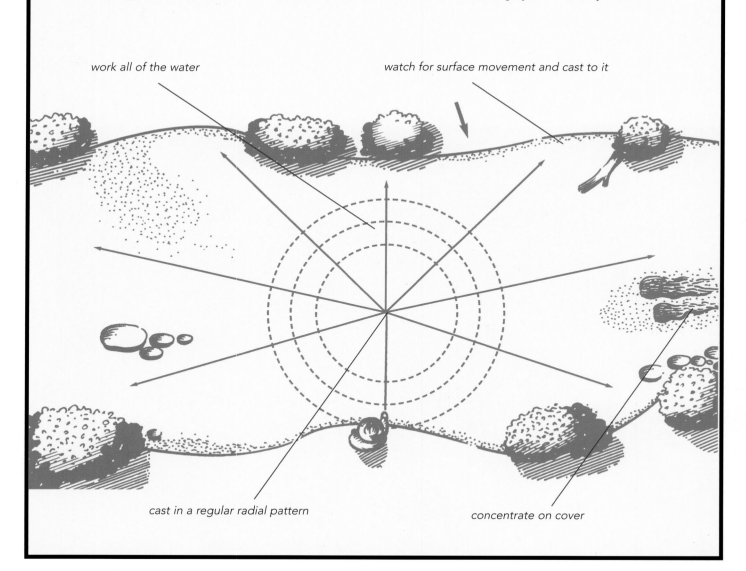

work all of the water

watch for surface movement and cast to it

cast in a regular radial pattern

concentrate on cover

Trolling – Trolled spoons are very effective on large waters. To get any depth, you'll need a downrigger or, more simply, perhaps a 2oz lead on the line. If water clarity isn't too good, choose a big spoon that rotates as much as possible to send out really strong vibrations. Lightweight spoons can be effective when the water is very clear and warm and the depths aren't too great. As you can see here, multiplier reels are used, and they are particularly good for trolling.

Trolling Spoons

The depth at which your lure is working is critical. You can make sure spoons are worked high in the water by retrieving them under a small float. You can bounce the lure along the bottom by taking it down with a lead attached to a weak link, but most lakebeds are too rocky for this approach. Think carefully about your trolling speed, too. Experiment until you find a speed that provokes most of the takes. Also vary your boat's course, as many predators strike as the lure changes direction in the water.

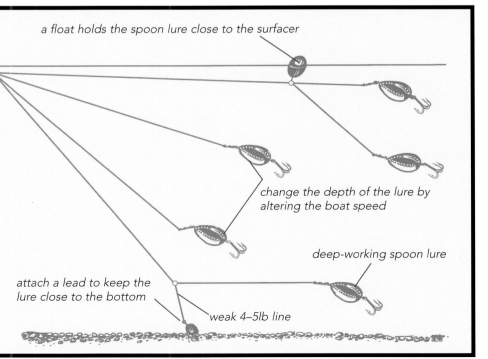

a float holds the spoon lure close to the surfacer

change the depth of the lure by altering the boat speed

deep-working spoon lure

attach a lead to keep the lure close to the bottom

weak 4–5lb line

Fishing with Rubber Lures

Of all forms of lure fishing, rubbers have to be the most exciting, demanding, thought-provoking and skilful way of catching a predator on an artificial bait. They are also extremely efficient. The method has been highly developed throughout the US, Scandinavia and Eastern and Central Europe. Rubber lures come in a bewildering variety of shapes, colours, sizes and actions. Look into the bag of an experienced rubber angler and you will find almost every living creature imitated – fish, worms, crabs, frogs, crayfish, crickets, sand eels, prawns, lizards, squid and any wiggly grub that you can imagine.

This rubber creation is an extraordinary imitation of the bullhead, a tiny fish found under stones on the riverbed. You would fish a lure like this very slow and very deep so it bounces bottom. Expect slow, strong pulls from taking predators.

Success in Scandinavia

The efficiency of rubber baits was brought home to me in a startling way. I was fishing for Baltic pike with my great Danish friend, Johnny Jensen, and two very talented Swedish guides. For a day and a half, I persevered with traditional plugs while Johnny and the two Swedes harvested fish on rubbers. I was wiped off the water and the message couldn't have been more stark. From that day on, I became a rubber addict, but you've still got to learn how to fish them.

What, then, were the lessons I learnt in those days on the Baltic, and have tried to build on since? The two guides, Pers and Hakken, spent an age on location – that's where reading features and structure is so vitally important. At that time we were mainly fishing bays, and much of their time was spent studying an echo sounder, looking for plateaus surrounded by deep drop-offs – a favourite area for hunting pike. Failing that, they would search out the thickest of reed beds. Once they had the right location, boy, did they know how to exploit it.

Casting was 100 per cent. They knew exactly where to put those rubbers. I wasn't fishing nearly as tight to features as they were and, as a result, failed to catch nearly as many fish.

Working the lure

There's no doubt accuracy of cast put them ahead of me, but they also had far more experience of how to work the lures once in the water. Watching Pers, I realized that what he was doing was very similar to fly fishing in that he spent every second analyzing the movement of his rubber, just as a nymph master is constantly aware of what the fly is doing as it nears a trout. Pers would watch, hawk-eyed, as the lure fell through the water, waiting for any twitch of the line that would signal the take on the drop. He would then leave the rubber on the bottom, totally alert to any sign that the motionless lure had been picked up. His retrieve would be immaculate – sometimes a twitch, sometimes just a stammer of the rod tip, then a bit of a spurt so that the rubber would rise and then flutter down again in an irresistible fashion.

Furious attack – Rising temperatures, clear water and hungry, aggressive pike… an ideal combination for using rubber jigs. However, they can still be adapted to working in colder, murkier water – but more of that later. This particular fish took very close to the boat, indeed, and you'll often find with rubbers that pike will stalk them for a long time before making a final decision. The answer is obviously to work the lure right to your very feet before removing it.

the line all the time with his left hand, waiting for a touch too slight to see.

A limitless range

One of the great boons of rubber fishing is the variety of lures. If one model, size, colour, action or whatever isn't working, it's easy to switch and try something new. With rubber lures, the idea is to appeal to the senses, so you're looking for a rubber that has the right colour, shape and feel, perhaps with a smell, and certainly appealing movement. In clear water, be careful about jig choice and experimentation. Colour is an interesting issue: what are the considerations? Perhaps you're looking to match the colour of the jig with the food type it is trying to represent. Maybe something visible in cloudy water. Shape is all-important, as is size.

Success at last – *It was a hot day and the glaring sun had sent the bass down deep. This small fish imitation, worked a good 20ft under the boat, finally did the business for Rafa.*

Finally subdued – *This same fish eventually glides towards the boat, but only after four or five powerful, snaking runs. Truly, those two days with Johnny, Pers and Hakken were an eye-opener. What did they teach me? Location, location, location. Also, their casting was just that little bit more specific than mine when I, too, took to the rubber. Perhaps I was afraid of over-casting and losing the lure, or maybe I wasn't quite used to the weight and flight through the air, but each and every cast of theirs was landing absolutely on the reed fringe, whereas mine generally fell a foot or two short. That difference appeared to be absolutely crucial.*

Just after my Baltic trip, I visited Spain, where I once again saw the importance of working the rubber intelligently. My Spanish friend, Rafa, was fishing for bass. Over and over, he made good, long casts, keeping the line tight and causing the lure to sink in an arc towards him. The lure's tail would have been working all the way to the bottom. He let it rest there for a while to allow the bass to move in and investigate. The odd twitch of the rod tip made the bass curious, then a short upward stroke kicked the rubber fish into life. Rafa worked it in a sink-and-draw fashion, keeping in constant contact. He was feeling

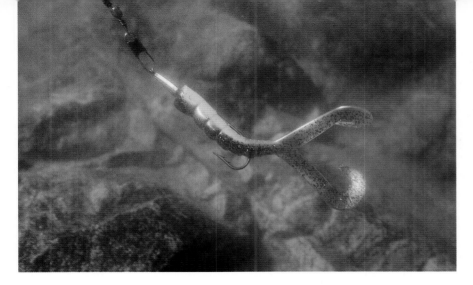

Movement – Motion gives the rubber that suggestion of life. Sometimes a single tail will be enough, but there are other occasions when a twin tail will make all the difference, as this exaggerates the movement. Twin tails catch the light more and glitter dramatically, and sometimes this extra dash is exactly what's needed.

Smell – Notice the large eye on this rubber – a great attack target for the predator to focus on. Make no mistake, many predators will follow rubbers very closely, get right up to them and deliberate long and hard before taking them. I believe that smell can be important in the final decision. Try dipping lures in a powdered flavour for added attraction. Failing that, keep them well-coated or injected with fish oil.

Feel-good factor – Rubber jigs score when it comes to texture, too, and this is where they triumph over plugs made of wood, plastic or metal. Many predators will actually suck the rubber and spit it out again once or twice before making a final decision. Large-mouthed bass are very prone to this, as are large perch. You can even let a rubber lie motionless on the bottom, like this, and curious predators will take.

Conservation – Catching fish is good fun, but their conservation must be top priority. Rubber baits are so attractive, they're often gulped right down, especially by large-mouthed species, such as pike, so to avoid harming the fish, follow a few simple rules. Use single hooks if you can, and if you can't, go for fine-wire trebles. Keep the tension on during the fight and you won't lose any fish. As for kit, always have long-nosed pliers with you, and a set of mini bolt-croppers to cut your trebles free if necessary. This rubber is fitted with a barbless single, so I will have no worries about unhooking.

Perhaps you want to imitate a known, desirable food item. There may be times when you want to introduce something to threaten or anger the fish so it will attack with hostility.

Know your rubbers

Just as a fly angler knows how the flies in his box act in the water, so a rubber lure angler must know how lures work in different conditions. Take a thermometer with you – rubbers behave differently when the water temperature changes and some go rigid and hardly work at all. Others achieve near meltdown when the water gets warmer. To test your

Be aware of temperature – This is one of my favourite rubber lures, with a great action in warm water.

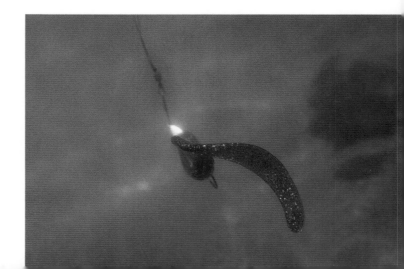

rubbers, use the humble, domestic bath. Try every temperature, test your lures and note the results.

Still at the bath side, classify your rubbers, from violent action to subdued motions. Pull each lure through the water to see how it responds. Try all sorts of hooking arrangements and hook sizes; changes will totally affect the way any rubber moves. Vary the weight of the lead head or go for a weighted hook. See how the rubber works when it is hooked up and in a current – your showerhead will come in handy here. Place it under the bath water, switch it on and, lo and behold, you're got a ready-made current to test your hooked-up rubber. The more you know about the action of your rubbers, the more successfully you'll be able to fish them.

Rubber action – *The tail of this rubber twitches in an irresistible fashion at a certain speed, and you, the angler, need to know this if you're going to make it behave like an escaping newt or worm.*

Heavy head – *This lure has a tail with a violent working action. What is also interesting is the heavy weight at the head of the lure. This makes it dive deep to search out those pockets of dark water. Work this lure slowly as close to the bed as possible.*

Fishing with Mini Lures

Lure fishing isn't all about using creations that are big and heavy. In fact, some lures can be little over half an inch in length and weigh no more than a heavy dry fly. The world of mini lures is a thrilling one – fishing in miniature is very tactile, very hands-on, with very little room for error.

It's a difficult day because it's calm and bright and the guys are fishing for pike with big streamer flies and the tiniest lures imaginable. In the end, a good fish fell for a crayfish imitation that was only about an inch long.

Pinpoint casting

Casting a mini lure – say a spinner or a plug of 1in in length and weighing a fraction of an ounce – is an art form in itself. Your rod might only be 6 or 7 feet in length. You will have an accompanying fixed-spool reel or a tiny multiplier that is light enough not to upset the balance. You'll probably be using braid or comparatively light nylon. The art of using mini lures is to flick your lure a short distance into a very tight area between weed beds, under overhanging branches, into a gap in the lilies or a hair's breadth from the reed margin. Accuracy has to be pinpoint. The underhand cast allows you to flick a lure into an opening between overhanging branches that would be impossible to reach from either side. It's a skill that has to be learnt. If you are right-handed, try a back cast for placing a lure between branches with an opening on the left-hand side. Again, you're flicking your tiny lure into an

area that no one else has considered. The fish know this: that's why they're lying there.

Try the forehand cast for flicking a lure under trees that show an opening on the right. You'll find that pinpoint accuracy is much more easily achieved with an underhand flick in this way than with a cast over your shoulder. All these casts sound difficult and complex but they're not. If you're worried, practise with a stone or a small lead weight tied on the end of your line. This way, should you get hung up, you can easily get your tackle free and you won't lose an expensive lure or risk waterfowl getting tangled up and injured. There are no exact rules – each mini-

Black bass are one of my favourite species. They demand total concentration from you and the more you experiment with different lures, the better your chances of success. Try every part of the water column and search diligently from the surface right to the lakebed. This mini lure was sipped in just subsurface.

lure situation demands its own approach and you will probably devise ones for yourself that I've never even imagined.

A versatile approach

Mini lures, whether they are spinners, plugs or poppers, can be used for all manner of fish, in all manner of situations. For example, take sea trout in a very low, clear river in high summer. You'll probably find them sheltering under bridges or under branches. They'll be seeking shade and respite from the sun and you'd think they wouldn't feed until night falls, but you could be wrong. Dig out that 6ft rod matched with 8lb line and put on a tiny silver Mepps spinner. Flick it with pinpoint accuracy above the shoal and it will land like a feather on the

On fly gear too! – *Don't forget that the biggest trout in the river grow large by feeding on mice, frogs and anything else that falls into the water. Sometimes a mini lure can be fished efficiently on a fly rod.*

Imitation can be about imagination! This lure was evidently meant to impersonate a small, striped mouse! Notice the ice on the ring of the rod. When temperatures are really low, work that lure as slowly as possible.

surface. Twitch it back so it glints and hesitates and rises and falls in front of the fish; chances are that soon enough one will make a mistake. Try a mini popper for a European chub or asp, or a black bass anywhere in the world. Rainbow trout will go for them, too, as will steelhead.

Mini rubbers

Perhaps the art of mini-lure fishing is never bettered than when using small rubber imitations for black bass. Bass can be the most critical of creatures, and to fool them with a rubber imitation is one of the most skilful of fishing forms. Your rubber will be an imitation nymph perhaps, or a small fish, or a tiny crayfish. Maybe it's a baby lizard or a newt, but the aim will be to fish it as naturally as possible. Hopefully, you will be fishing shallow, clear water and you'll be able to watch the bass's reaction to your lure. If you can see the fish and their reaction to what you are offering, you're halfway to success.

Generally, though, you will be fishing deeper, especially in bright, hot conditions when the bass won't emerge far from the bottom rocks. Once you lose sight of the fish and your lure, it's your line that tells you everything – when your lure hits bottom, how it's working and when a fish is showing interest. A bass can take your mini rubber at any stage during the cast. It might well intercept it as it's sinking through the water layers to the bottom. It might take it static on the bed or when it's twitched, even once it's been properly retrieved. Hold the line carefully throughout the cast from the moment it hits the water so you can feel if the bass are showing any reaction. Takes can be as gentle as a puff of wind on the back of your hand.

It's a good idea to let your lure lie a good while on the bottom and often bass will gather round it to investigate, looking for all the world like an aquatic parliament of owls. The odd twitch of the rod tip will be transmitted down the line and make your mini rubber skip a little bit. The bass will become curious. A sharp upwards stroke of the rod kicks the rubber into life and the bass might well move closer. Lift it from the bottom. Let it flutter back. Twitch it. Let it lie still. Chances are, eventually one of your actions will make one bass lunge in and make a terrible mistake!

This is what mini-lure fishing is all about: tight, accurate casting; fishing areas that most anglers fear; working tiny lures in imaginative ways and making them look as irresistible as possible.

Sarah was especially thrilled with this bass because it took a popper from the surface at incredibly close range. Thrilling stuff!

Dead Baiting

Dead baiting may not be as satisfying as lure fishing, but when none of your lures seem to be working, a dead bait – which the predator can detect by smell – can be highly effective. When the weather is very cold and/or the water is very cloudy, there's little chance of a fish actually seeing your lure and it may not want to expend valuable energy chasing it. Dead baiting needn't be a static or tedious method. You can, for example, use a dead bait twitched sink-and-draw fashion in very much the same way as a rubber jig or even a plug.

Efficiently struck – Always hit a run at the first indication of a bite. Delay and there's a chance that the dead bait will be snaffled and taken into the throat where unhooking becomes a perilous business.

Preparation and selection

All serious anglers have a few dead baits stored away in a freezer. Freeze baits individually wrapped in cling film. Ensure that they're stored flat – kinked dead baits are difficult to cast any distance, awkward to hook and, being so unnatural, aren't very attractive to a predator. Popular dead baits include sea fish such as mackerel, herrings and sprats. Natural freshwater dead baits are also excellent, so store any that you find freshly dead in the margins. Eel sections are also good. Variety is the spice of life when it comes to dead baiting, and there's always room for exotics such as the horse mackerel – a round, oily fish that gives off a good, strong smell.

Weather conditions

The successful predator angler is the one who can make all manner of successful calculations and come up with the correct answers. You've got to think about the water, its clarity, features, structures,

Cold weather – As autumn turns to winter, you'll find that pike, for example, don't want to expend unnecessary energy hunting a fast-moving bait. It's these first few days or weeks of falling temperatures when a dead bait stands a good chance of being taken. Once predators have acclimatized to the cold weather, slow-moving lures are once again accepted.

Flat calm – There can be times when the water is like a millpond and predatory fish can become very reluctant to move. Obviously, if there's no wind interference, the sound of oars, an engine, casting and even anglers talking is greatly enhanced. As a diver I have experienced this for myself: as you lie in a lake on a calm day, you will hear all sorts of muffled sounds – every sound above and below the surface is hugely exaggerated. For this reason, if you're going after a big, suspicious fish, it sometimes pays simply to cast out a dead bait and wait for the fish to make a move.

heavy rains or high winds, then it could be that dead bait will have a slight advantage over lure fishing. If a predator has to hunt by sight alone, this makes lure fishing in very cloudy water an extremely difficult task. Dead baits work well when visibility is low because, of course, they emit a good, strong scent. Lure fishing is huge fun, but don't become blinkered and refuse to use other methods if the weather conditions scream out for them.

Presentation considerations

A pike has plenty of time to examine a dead bait, as it is either static or very slow moving. Anything suspicious will be ignored. The simplest rig to use is the legered dead bait. I use a float for indication, as this is absolutely immediate and creates little disturbance. Dead bait generally provides enough weight for long casts. Putting extra lead on the line simply pulls it into bottom weed. If weed is a problem, you can 'pop up' a dead bait by inserting buoyant material, such as a balsa wood stick, polystyrene or foam, into the stomach cavity or mouth. Make baits partially buoyant so they will sink very slowly and come to rest at the top of any weed. A totally buoyant bait held a few inches off the bottom by lead weights can be good, but only for limited periods, as pike soon get wise to this approach.

A freeze-up – When the temperatures have really plummeted and the water is largely covered by ice, the lure angler certainly has a hard task. Lure fishing is a roving, mobile way of fishing, and if most of the water is absolutely inaccessible, this method obviously becomes extremely difficult. However, you still want to go fishing, so the best bet in these conditions is a dead bait under a float cast into a hole in the ice. Do make sure, however, that the ice is not too thick to stop you landing a hooked fish.

fish numbers, target species, methods, lure types, shapes, colours, actions and, last but certainly not least, weather conditions. As a very rough rule, if your water has severely coloured up due to very

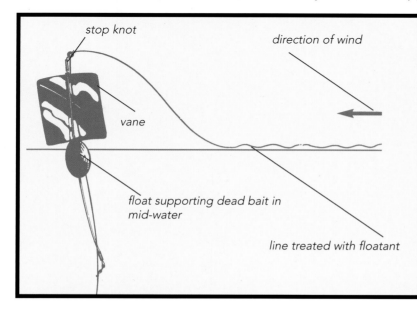

stop knot

direction of wind

vane

float supporting dead bait in mid-water

line treated with floatant

The Drift Float

This rig works particularly well for searching out large waters when there's a decent breeze blowing. The vane catches the wind and will trot before it, providing the line is well-greased, covering huge areas of the water. It is quite possible to drift the float over 137m (150yd) or more, but it's wise to have binoculars with you at these distances so that you can see a take. Once the float disappears, wind down tight and strike immediately to avoid deep hooking.

Added scent – I don't rate trout very highly as dead baits, but they do seem to work in waters where pike are used to feeding on them. I believe that the lack of smell is a big disadvantage, so it's a good idea to inject them with an added dose of fish oils. Do take great care, though, when using a syringe – injecting an air bubble into your own bloodstream will prove fatal – so never dream of injecting a dead bait in a boat if there's a swell on.

Attractive aromas – This shot demonstrates why I like to use dead baits that have a good smell about them: the odours of the dead bait attract increasing numbers of small fish. A feeding frenzy takes place, and these ripples of excitement spread through the water and are picked up by big predators many metres away. Their instincts are aroused and they begin to follow the signals, homing in on the small fish and your bait.

Landing your fish – A well beaten dead-bait caught pike comes to the bank. Look how the trebles are flying free. This is indicative of a well-timed strike, but if a net is used now, a real tangle is almost guaranteed, probably wounding the pike in the process. Far better to lift the pike out of the water by hand. Until you become skilled, use a stout leather glove to save your fingers.

Trolling

At its simplest level, trolling is the act of pulling lures behind a moving boat in order to attract predatory fish. It's a great technique for lake trout, pike, muskies, perch, Nile perch, tiger fish and even, at times, zander. However, because the fishing is comparatively monotonous and the normal skills of casting and bite detection don't really come into play, trolling is frequently depicted as being unskilful. To an extent I agree with this. However, there is a world of difference between an average troller and a good one.

Trolling is one of the best ways to fish for predators from a moving boat. However, it can be boring after a long while. You can liven up the session by doing some fly fishing from the boat as you move along. Remember that safety is paramount, so make sure the fly casting is well away from other anglers.

Getting the boat right

Some trolling anglers are just much more successful than others, so there has to be some element of skill involved. First, your boat must be stable enough to deal with foul weather conditions. It must accommodate two anglers, often with lots of gear. An engine is virtually essential, and it must be able to troll at very low speeds. Reverse gear is also vital, both to retrace steps over snags to free lures and also to chase fish should this prove necessary. Electric motors are particularly useful in still, shallow, bright conditions. Whether petrol or electric, engines should be very reliable, as they can, in certain situations, save your life. Never, ever forget to take oars; there will be times when the engine refuses to fire. Don't forget the rowlocks and do ensure that they fit the boat before setting out on your fishing trip. Importantly, never, and I mean never, forget either the baling bucket or the lifejacket.

Boat rod-rests are essential. Screw them very tightly to the boat's sides – the pressure exerted on them when a fish is hooked or a snag is encountered can be enormous. If the water is too deep and dark to be able to see to the bottom, an echo sounder

Dam right – These two anglers are trolling in Scotland on one of the big hydro-electric lochs in the extreme northwest. Once again, location is paramount and the guys are investigating very deep water – well over 30m (100ft) – near the dam.

of some sort is a great bonus. Without one, you will be fishing blind over large areas of water – never the shortest cut to success.

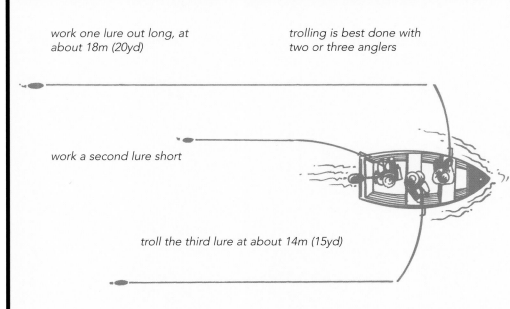

work one lure out long, at about 18m (20yd)

trolling is best done with two or three anglers

work a second lure short

troll the third lure at about 14m (15yd)

TROLLING TECHNIQUES

An angler can troll solo, but there's always a risk of entanglement in heavy winds or when a fish takes. With two or three people, one can work the engine and control the boat while the others work the rods. Take turns, and develop the mentality that any success is a 'boat' capture rather than an individual one. Constantly experiment with different depths and different lures until you find the winning combination.

Trolling tackle

For most general work, the best trolling rods are 9–11ft long, with test curves of between 2–3.5lb. You might want to go shorter and heavier at times, but for big pike and lake trout, for example, this type of rod is ideal. A rod longer than 11ft is an encumbrance in a boat.

The experienced troller will nearly always use a multiplier reel. Depending on the size of the fish being pursued, the depth of the water, the amount of snags and the size of lure being trolled, pick a line to withstand all the stresses and strains thrown at it.

Choose your lures carefully. Decide at what level you want to work them and choose top water, middle water or deep working plugs, spinners and spoons.

The trolling technique

At the start of the troll, let plenty of line out so that the lure is working between 46m and 64m (50yd and 70yd) behind the boat. There are certain species – musky and pike, for example – that will take lures much closer than this, but big trout are very wary if the water is clear.

Vary the trolling speed from very slow, to slow, to quicker, sometimes even to short, fast bursts. Only rarely will you take a dead-straight line. You are more likely to adopt a zigzag course along the preferred depths. Critical moments come when the boat changes direction and the lure rises and falls enticingly in the water, often inducing a take.

Don't troll blindly. Look at what your echo sounder tells you. Troll round islands. Try to find man-made structures such as water towers, dams and boat jetties. Look at the bankside for clues. If the bank is precipitous, then its water shelves are likely steep. If the bank is low-lying and level, the water is likely to be shallow. Look for shoals of small prey fish close to the surface – the predators you are pursuing will likely be close by. There will be commercial fish cages on many trolling waters. Work as close to these as you can, always obeying signposts and minding the ropes and chains that tether these cages to the bottom.

Be prepared to do things differently. For example, if you want to get very deep – over 18m (20yd) – then you will probably need a downrigger. However, depth

---

THE DOWNRIGGER

A downrigger allows you to troll a lure very deeply indeed, way past its normal working depth. You will also play the fish freely, for when it takes, the line reel is snapped away from the downrigger's cable. Operate the downrigger from the stern of the boat, and lower the rig down with the winch provided. A word of caution: don't use a downrigger if you're fishing solo. If the trolling weight snags and you're in a heavy wind, a small boat can be put severely at risk. The downrigger is especially useful on glacial waters, where depths frequently exceed 60–90m (200–300ft).

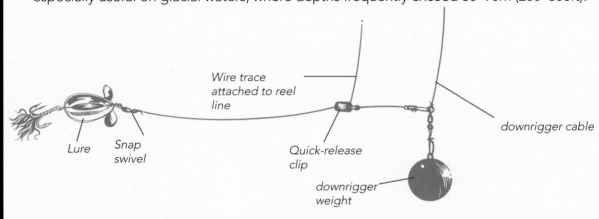

Lure

Snap swivel

Wire trace attached to reel line

Quick-release clip

downrigger weight

downrigger cable

Not all trolling has to be deep. Johnny holds a magnificent Swedish pike taken in a bay no more than a metre deep on a very buoyant, tiny plug trolled just a few rod lengths behind the boat. As it was hooked in such shallow water, it could only run far, not deep, and at times it forced the boat to follow.

is not always an issue; most predatory fish come closer to the surface when they are feeding hard.

On many waters for many species, the best trolling conditions are rough ones, but I can think of many days when flat calm and bright conditions have served very well. If you suspect that fish are wary of the engine, don't hesitate to troll on the oar or on the electric motor. There are many occasions when it is imperative to troll with the same finesse you would use to flick a dry fly or a nymph.

The mists of the west – *This big Irish lough is just the sort of water for which trolling was designed.*

■ CHAPTER 6

SEA FISHING

It doesn't matter whether you are fishing for striped bass off a New York coast, sea bass close to London, bonefish in the Bahamas or skate off Iceland, you have to understand the fish's environment if you're going to succeed. It's easy to think of the sea as a vast, unreadable environment that is impossible to understand or get to grips with, but this is not the case.

Introduction to Sea Fishing

The seas and oceans of the world offer an endless list of angling possibilities, and demand an equally endless list of skills in order to conquer the challenges involved. Beach casting, rock casting, wreck fishing, uptide fishing, saltwater fly fishing, lure fishing, big game fishing, float fishing... enough excitement and complexity here to last a lifetime.

Dusk can be one of the best times to be out on the beach. This particular evening saw shoals of mackerel and bass hunting right in amongst the breakers.

Fathomable features

Skilful sea anglers do not catch fish by accident. They catch them regularly and by design, and they can do so because they know exactly how to read the many features saltwater possesses. Take an experienced sea angler of any discipline to any ocean in the world and he will immediately point out features everywhere. This watercraft is essential and, because of the size of saltwater venues, it is even more important here than in freshwater. In an average-sized lake you can lob in a bait, ignoring all fish-holding features, and the odds are a fish will chance on it sometime in the day. Not so in the sea, where you could be miles from a feeding fish.

Depth and bottom contours play a vital role, especially where shallows drop off precipitously into the deeps. Shoreline irregularities such as inlets, coves, bays and points all attract fish. The make-up of the seabed is vital, as different species are attracted to different geological areas. Rocks, broken ground, sand, shingle and mud all play their part, as do cliffs, estuaries, creeks, marshes, inflowing freshwater streams, reefs and sandbars. Weed beds are home to many fish, as are underwater caves. Man-made structures, too, play a huge role. Fish will always congregate around piers, wrecks, sea defences, harbours, offshore rigs and even anchored boats.

A rugged shoreline like this provides a massive amount of food for all species of fish. There are endless features that you can fish and explore. Cast as close as possible into the rocks and make use of the surging waves to push your bait as close as possible into the crevices. Always be very careful on slippery rocks like these and never take any risks.

Above: Low tide is an excellent time to explore your sea fishing grounds. Look for gullies and areas of weed, gravel and sand. You will sometimes find areas that show signs that fish have been working there, looking for worms or crabs. Always check your tide tables so you are not caught out by rising water.

Below: Sea bass, like freshwater bass, are all about structure. Look for them around rocks, large weed beds, gulleys, drop-offs, breakwaters, boat moorings – anywhere that food is likely to collect.

Time and tide

Seawater is nearly always moving, and it is important to understand the influence of the wind, currents, and the strength and height of the ever changing tides.

Sea bass

Like freshwater fish, sea fish exhibit wildly differing characteristics. Take two of my favourite species – the bass and the mullet. I can walk five minutes from my house to the shingle spit that runs four miles to the west and even further to the east. At the right time of the year, when the weather and the tides are perfect, I'll see the bass at work. They'll be chasing sand eels and any number of species of small fish. They'll even

come into the brackish estuaries to hunt sticklebacks. They'll chase small flatfish and sometimes send up puffs of silt where they're digging for them. You'll see them sometimes in shallow water with their tails waving as they dig for crabs hiding between the stones. These are fish with a big spirit, a big mouth and a big appetite, and providing you can locate them, hooking up isn't that difficult.

Grey mullet

Now let's take the mullet, pretty much the same size and not at all dissimilar to look at. However, these creek mullet behave in a totally different fashion. It's dawn, in June, with an incoming tide. You sit on the marsh head watching the water push across the muds, and soon, when it's only a hands-breadth deep, you will see the mullet appearing. They'll be there in huge shoals following the very furthest fringes of the tide. Some of them are big fish – 4, 5 or even 6 pounds – and they're hungry. Again, you see them on their heads as they feed, their tails and their backs wavering, perhaps catching the first rays of

the rising sun. These mullet should be easy to catch, you think. After all, they're even feeding right there, almost under your rod tip.

You couldn't be more wrong. Back in the 1970s, in the course of three or four years I managed to hook just four – after scores, if not hundreds, of attempts. Why? Because they are feeding on tiny organisms that live in the surface film of the muds. The mullet are simply hoovering up microscopic food particles, and your lugworm, rag worm, bread flake or sweetcorn look to them about as edible and as appetizing as a rock. Now, some 30 years later, I'm just learning to catch them on fly tackle and the tiniest imaginable black and brown goldhead nymphs tied on size 20 hooks – sometimes.

Size 20 hooks! I fished with a mate off the north coast of Scotland for giant skate and up there we used hooks 100, perhaps 200 times the size. And in that one thought lies the wonder of sea fishing. It is simply a sport of never-ending skills to be learned.

Grey mullet can be very difficult to catch out in wild creeks, but they are much more easy in harbours where they are used to eating discarded food.

Beach Casting

This is the rough, tough side of angling skills. Fishing off the shore over rough ground in strong winds and in big tides is physically gruelling, and is demanding for both the angler and his tackle. You could not think of a scenario more removed from the angler fishing a dry fly or flicking out a tiny lure for a black bass. Fishing from beaches like this can call for long walks in atrocious conditions. Beach casting rods are built to be tough, and reels are almost invariably multipliers that work harder for a living than any other reel on the planet.

I love the exhilaration of a big sea like this pounding against the rocks. It is amazing how close bass in particular will come inshore in conditions like these. I'm looking for takes just feet from the rocks. At close range, takes are violent and unmissable.

A range of skills

Fishing like this is virtually always about bait, and that bait is frequently hard come by. The chances are that the crabs will have been individually grubbed up from underneath their rocks and that the lugworm will have been dug in back-breaking circumstances from the muds.

It is likely that the targets will be cod, codling, haddock, flatfish, pollack, bass or any one of a dozen species that in the heavily netted waters of the northern hemisphere are probably scarcer than they have ever been. The big catches that fell to rod and line from the shore years ago are now largely a thing of the past. To catch anything these days over many marks takes a huge amount of skill.

This was brought home to me when I went out fishing for a day with Tony and Ian on the northeast coast as it approaches Scotland. As we walked from the cars with a mountain of gear over perilously slippery rocks, I soon realized that this was a tough man's sport, but equally one demanding a high level of skill. Its 'macho' nature can blind one to the delicacy of it all.

Okay, Tony's rod, reel, line and terminal gear are immensely powerful, but that doesn't mean all these devices aren't used with great skill and consideration. While the bait might look a hideous concoction of peeler crab and worm, it's still threaded onto the hook and tied there with enormous manual dexterity.

Where and how

Of course, fish aren't scattered around the sea like currants in a bun, but have exactly the same territorial requirements as the most aristocratic brown trout. Tony knows exactly the sorts of places that his quarry might live in, and if it means him wading out to some distant and difficult rocks to punch a 100yd cast out into the teeth of a gale, then Tony will do it.

The delicatessen – *One of Tony's secrets is to match the best baits with the season. His baits are always fresh and mounted with great care, to keep them secure during the cast and to withstand the pounding the sea gives them.*

You might well think that a fish in such a wild environment, faced with such a big bait, on such heavy tackle will inevitably give a bone-crushing bite that is impossible to miss. This is not always the case. Watching Tony and Ian stand on their rocks, their rods constantly to hand, fingers on the line, made me realize that this touch legering style of theirs is every bit as sensitive as anything I might employ on a small, clear river. They can feel what sort of ground their bait is fishing over and the very moment a 3lb codling breathes on their bait at a distance of 70m (80yd). This is high skill, often displayed in conditions that want to kill you.

You might also think that when a 5lb or 10lb fish is hooked on gear as gutsy as this, the fight will be a foregone conclusion. Again, not so. At about 1 p.m., Tony felt a quivering on his line and then, at distance, a gentle take. He struck hard – and his rod just walloped over. The strength of the tide was

Armed to the teeth – An investigation of almost any rod stand will show that the multiplier is the 'must have' reel. Keep your multipliers well serviced and avoid getting grains of sand inside the casing of the reel.

Splendid isolation – A shore fisherman like Tony often finds himself in more rugged, isolated places than any angler is ever likely to experience. Take care. Don't take risks with cliffs or slippery rocks. You don't want to be caught injured and on your own, in a dangerous situation with the tide beginning to turn.

On the rocks – Tony is constantly looking for places where the shoreline and the tides work together to produce fabulous fish-holding areas.

enormous, and trying to control the fish in the current proved virtually impossible. The area was strewn with rocks, gullies and forests of tough weed. Again and again, the fish found sanctuary, but Tony was able to guide it out. Just when success looked probable, the fish found an unyielding snag and it was gone. Tony shrugged – 5lb, 10lb perhaps, but a monster in conditions like this.

Right: Fly fishing is one of the most exciting and productive ways of fishing saltwater. The method was pioneered in America and is now common throughout the UK and Europe. Saltwater fly fishing works just as well in cold water as it does in warmer conditions and I have used saltwater flies as far north as Iceland.

Below: This seemingly peaceful scene is actually a scene of carnage! A few metres from the shore, tiny fish are being forced to the surface by hunting bass beneath them. You'll see the birds circling and diving, picking off tiny fish that are in distress and sometimes wounded. Watch the skies carefully and the birds will often give you clues to fish location.

Sea Bass on the Fly

For freshwater bass fishing, you are unlikely to need anything stronger than your general trout-fishing kit. This isn't always the case on the sea. While 6-, 7- and 8-weight rods can work admirably well in calm conditions, most of the time the sea isn't like a millpond, so be prepared to invest in 9- or even 10-weight gear. You also need to be aware that when you are sea fishing there's always a chance of hooking into something much bigger than you might be expecting. For example, a good pollack hooked off the rocks can destroy light gear. If you're in a boat, there's sometimes even the chance, albeit remote, of hooking into a small or medium-sized tope.

In the surf – To get the better of sea bass, you have to be in there with them putting the fly where it counts. First-class waterproof clothing, a buoyancy aid, good balance and a bit of nerve are important ingredients.

Reel and lines

It's as well to have at least two different sized reels – one to take 6- or 7-weight lines and a larger one for boats and heavier water. Floating lines are sometimes all you will need, but there are going to be occasions when you have to get a fly down, so a selection of lines, from intermediate to fast sink, is important. It's a wise idea, therefore, to look for a reel that offers the possibility of a number of cheap spools. It's important to have gear that's sufficient for the job – you don't want to sell yourself short and find yourself struggling on the sea. When fishing from a boat, especially, depth can be critical, so if you're not contacting bass in one zone, then change lines continually until you find where the fish are swimming and feeding. A lazy angler is rarely a successful one when it comes to saltwater bass fishing.

Choosing the right pattern

There are endless fly patterns available today that will land you a sea bass. In essence, bass in the

Rods and reels – A collection of different weight rods and reels (above) can be vital if you are fishing at different depths around different features in rapidly changing weather conditions. Always hose your kit down with freshwater after it has done saltwater work.

Choosing the fly – Sea bass come in close to the shore to hunt the small fish and crabs that are hiding there. Flies should look, therefore, like small, vulnerable, tasty food items fluttering helplessly in the tide.

wild are looking to feed on sand eels, elvers, tiny fish – anything that is silvery and ripples sinuously. Translucent silvers and greens are, therefore, always a good starting point. Each area tends to have its own favourites, so it's wise to listen to local advice. However, you can't go far wrong with clousers, deceivers, bait fish and squid patterns. Alternatively, if you think the bass are feeding deep, over rocks, on crabs, why not try a crab pattern on the end. Sea-bass fishing on the fly is still in its early infancy, and it is this pioneering aspect that makes it so attractive to so many anglers.

Some basic tips

The warning about sun cream and sun block is even more applicable at sea, where the salt exacerbates the burning process. Polarizing glasses and a peaked cap or a hat with a brim are important. If the water isn't warm enough to go bare-legged, breathable chest waders are a must if you're shore fishing. So, too, is a line tray: without this, loose line will simply catch in the rip and soon be all over the place. Pay special attention to clothing: a nice day on shore can easily become wet and freezing cold once you're afloat. Don't take chances and make your day a misery. Look after your catch, too. If you're going to take the odd bass to eat (and why not?), gut it and clean it on the beach, on the boat or, at the very least, as soon as you get home. Don't leave this job and jeopardize wasting a fish. The bounty of the sea is increasingly precious to all of us, and a meal of fresh sea bass that you yourself have caught just hours before is a privilege that mustn't be wasted.

The right fly – *Howard and Juan discuss the right fly for a Spanish sea bass. Notice the use of breathable waders and wading jackets – staying dry all day long will considerably enhance your fishing experience.*

Be mindful of the fish you are taking. Be aware of size limits, and remember that bass take five years to mature, so just occasionally, try to limit yourself to only one for the pot.

Salt and corrosion

Salt, of course, is a big problem, and the last thing you want is your beloved rods, reels and accessories destroyed by corrosion. It makes absolute sense to buy gear that is anodized and saltwater resistant. Check this out carefully before making a purchase. The second great bit of simple advice is to wash everything thoroughly in cold, clean water after a saltwater outing, and that includes estuary fishing. Note, too, that salt doesn't just work its malevolence on rods and reels, but can also rust hooks, forceps, zips and even the studs and eyes of wading boots.

Your waders are expensive, so look after them. Don't allow them to fester, crumpled in a corner. If they remain damp, the salt will work on them and cracks will begin to appear. Rinse them and then hang them upside down to allow the air to circulate and dry then off naturally so that they keep their shape.

It's vital to pay close attention to the state of your line, especially if you've been casting over rocks or abrasive sand. Wipe it down carefully after use to prolong its life.

Finally, even though you've rinsed your rods and reels, it's not a bad idea to dry them down with a soft cloth. Take special care with reel seats, and from time to time use a little light oil on them.

Shore technique

Shore fishing for bass is probably the easiest and cheapest way to get into this exciting sport. A rod, lines, flies and waders are all you need.

Weather and tide

The best conditions for fly fishing for bass from the shore are relatively calm ones. You don't want a big wind, as this makes fly fishing physically difficult and, more importantly, it will stir up the sand and make

Low water clues – At low tide, get out and look for clues to sea bass location. Rocks, gullies and weed beds are all great starters.

the water cloudy, so calm, clear water is ideal. If you can get out early or stay out late, then you'll probably hit the bass in prime feeding mood.

In many places, bassing off the shore doesn't depend too much on the state of the tide. Even in low water, for example, when fish get caught up in estuaries, they will tend to mill around but are still willing to pick up food and take the fly.

Finding features

Bass love to forage amongst big rocks and, generally, the rougher the ground the better. So look for beaches that are mostly rock and boulder with comparatively little sand or gravel. Fissured rocks, large boulders, crevices, weed and all similar features are really attractive to the bass.

Search for areas that will hold passing food items. Walk the beach at low water, making a note of pools still full of water at the lowest of the tide. Note the position of weed beds and big boulders – these are good places to concentrate on once you start

Bass coastline – You'll find bass wherever there are features, because wherever there are features there is food upon which they thrive. The groynes, sea defences and rocky outcrops harbour endless crabs and tiny fish, while the freshwater stream brings all manner of food items from the village just inland.

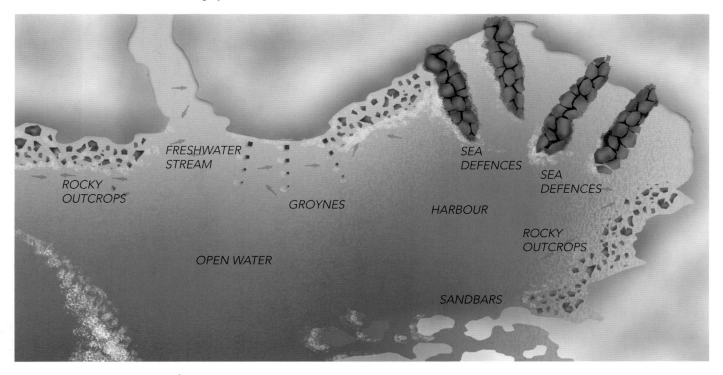

ROCKY OUTCROPS

FRESHWATER STREAM

GROYNES

SEA DEFENCES

SEA DEFENCES

HARBOUR

ROCKY OUTCROPS

OPEN WATER

SANDBARS

fishing. Also, look out for deep gullies amongst rocks, because bass use these as highways from one feeding area to the next. Don't worry too much about depth – bass will be happy in water anywhere between 1– 12ft deep.

Cast and retrieve

You don't have to strain massively to cast huge distances. Very often you will pick up bass just a few metres out in the surf. It's better to cast short distances and approach gently rather than splash around and scare the fish. You don't really need to work the fly much at all in a strong tide because the sea will do it for you. If, however, there's little flow – say you're up a low water estuary – then it pays to give the fly some good tweaks and keep it on the move, simulating a fleeing fish.

Boat technique

A lot of fly-caught bass can be taken from the shore, but there's no doubt that a boat gives more options and allows you to cover far more potential bass-holding features.

Locating bass

The sea is a big place, and finding the bass is the first issue. Just like our black freshwater bass in Spain, you should be looking for features. These can be reefs, wrecks, gullies, drop-offs, weed beds, rocks, submerged islands – anything that harbours the sand eels and small fish that the bass like to feed upon. Also, it goes without saying, look for the gulls. Wherever you see gulls diving, you can be sure that small fish are being pushed to the surface and bass are going to be the most likely culprit, so get yourself there fast.

Inshore waters

There are two distinct types of sport included under this title. Firstly, let's look at fly fishing for bass in the shallower, calmer estuaries. In the estuary, you will have bright, clear water and frequently a very smooth surface. Most of the fish you are pursuing are school bass in the 1–2lb bracket, and they're

often visible. For this sort of work, you can make do very happily with a 5- or 6-weight, 9ft rod – the Hardy Angel TE has won loads of supporters for this kind of task. You're fishing a floating line here and using comparatively small flies – say, tied on an 8 or even a 10. In fact, this is just like stillwater fishing for trout and the same gear will suffice. Leaders don't need to be heavier than 8 or 10lb, but they should be fluorocarbon. As for flies, the smallest possible clousers are hard to beat.

Open ocean

Away from the estuary or the shoreline, it's a completely different ball game. Now, you are fishing over deep water, probably in a swell, possibly catching the wind, and you need to get down deep. You might need 9- or even 10-weight rods and reels. A fast-sink line is probably necessary – a full line probably gets down deeper and more quickly than a shooting head. The tides and the saline content both make it more difficult to sink a fly deep. You are aiming to fish your fly 10ft or even 15ft down, possibly for much bigger fish. A fluorocarbon leader

A hint from the skies – *The sky can give you hints to bass location. If you see gulls swooping down upon small fish on the surface, there's a good chance that there are bass underneath.*

From the shore – When fishing for bass, spinning can be as effective as fly fishing, and you do cover ground a lot faster.

of 10–12lb is a must. You're probably going to be fishing bigger flies – streamers, for example, on a 2/0 or even a 3/0. Dark olive and white are good colours, and anything made of Arctic fox fur really flows in the water. Look for pearly, translucent patterns as the current vogue for dressing flies in the colours of small pollack.

The double haul

If you're serious about taking up one of the most glamorous and quickly developing styles of fly fishing in Europe, then you've really got to set about mastering the double haul technique (see pg. 78). A lot of times you'll be on a pitching boat, in screaming winds, casting big, heavy flies long distances, and this is demanding and potentially dangerous work. Without the ability to double haul, you are both

limiting your fishing and potentially endangering yourself.

Working the fly

Fishing these big flies down deep calls for slightly specialized techniques. You shouldn't always be ripping the fly back to the boat but rather letting it work in the tide. Either cast the fly into the rip or let the current simply pull the line off the reel. Once you think you've achieved the required depth, let the fly rise and fall with the flow of the water. Twitch the fly back, stop. Twitch again. Sometimes give solid pulls of a couple of feet or more and then stop again. In short, you are trying to make the fly dart and flutter like something small and alive.

Don't neglect your poppers, even here on the sea. They can be deadly in shallower, clearer water and at those times when you can actually see the bass hammering into prey on the surface. It's often a good idea to fish your popper on a dropper with a streamer underneath it. Bass frequently chase the popper only to turn away at the very last moment. That's when they will often pick up on the streamer or clouser, even one that's just working enticingly in the current. Again, for excitement, you just can't beat the dramatic, visual take.

The right boat

The perfect boat for sea-bass fishing probably hasn't been built yet, but there are still several things to consider when choosing your boat. It needs to be stable, because a lot of the time you'll be standing up, casting in the swell. You need the side of the boat to reach well up to your thighs. A rail at shin level is neither safe nor comfortable, and you'll find yourself knocking into it a lot of the time.

Decks shouldn't be too smooth, and if they have a slightly adhesive surface, so much the better. Equally, think carefully about your footwear and look for the sole that gives the best grip. You should be looking for a deck that is as open-plan as possible, without cabins or aerials or anything to hamper the flow of line. In fact, a line tray is a good idea in itself.

A boat with a shallow draught is also preferable, because often you'll be hunting bass close-in along the estuaries where there is only a foot or two of water. Of course, think safety and seaworthiness – reliable engines, lifejackets, up-to-the-minute weather forecasts… take no risks.

This is a crucial time in any battle. When a big fish dives close to the boat, keep the rod as high as possible and make sure the clutch can give line. In your excitement, don't get too close to the side of the boat and never lose your balance.

Sea Fishing in Action

Any good sea angler who takes his sport seriously will want to dig his own bait. However, it's a job that demands experience, technique and physical resilience. I should know. For a year after college, I dug worms for a living. That was 30 years ago, but my hands still bear some of the scars inflicted and the small of my back has never been quite the same.

Features like this sandbar make sea fishing very exciting. They attract all types of sea species and if you wear chest waders you can get out there and fish for them in amongst the surf.

Earning every penny

A typical day would see me and my fellow bait diggers meet up three or four hours before the winter dawn broke. We would then walk over the marsh head and out across the mud, sometimes for three or four miles, to arrive at the worm beds just as light was breaking. We'd then have to find our patch, drain it and dig methodically and quickly, an eye always on the tides and for any sign of creeping mist. We'd dig for three or four hours, until we'd found between a 1,000 and 1,500 worms, and then we'd head back for home.

The walk back was always the hardest, thanks to an overwhelming tiredness and the sheer weight of the worms in the bucket swinging against the shoulder blades. At some point in the early afternoon, once the worms have been counted, washed and packed, I'd start thinking about… yes, doing a bit of fishing before supper and going off early to bed.

Understanding the feeding fish

Bait fishers will know all about rag worm, lugworm, prawn, soft crab and bait fish of endless varieties, and which fish are feeding on what at any particular time, but the fly fisher must also know what the fish are up to and what his or her flies are meant to imitate. Out in the Bahamas, our guide, Magnus, would get up well before the rest of the group each and every morning, just as the sun was beginning to rise. We'd wake up to find him invariably at his vice, tying flies for the coming day. The previous day, he'd have been seen peering into pools, looking through weed, lifting stones and rocks, searching for any clues, any pointers as to what the bonefish were eating. His flies were mini masterpieces, imitating crabs or shrimps with breathtaking accuracy. To have complete and utter confidence in whatever you are offering the fish – be it a couple of prime, succulent worms on a hook or a fly tied to perfection – is a bonus beyond words.

Lugworms – Lugs like this (above right) are one of the favourite baits for most sea fish species around Europe. Digging them at low tide, however, can be back-breaking work (right).

389

The world of the sea trout

It's that piece of the world between the land and the open sea that fascinates me most of all. Here, the tide ebbs and flows, sometimes there's water, at other times exposed mud and sand. This is a marvellously exciting, shifting world. You'll find seals, sea otters and more species of birds than you can begin to count. The weather is also massively unpredictable: sometimes you think the mist will never break, then there are fissures of blue above and within minutes the sun is beating down and you need to remove your jacket.

There are several species of fish to target in this world of constant change, but one of the best is surely the sea trout. Sea trout, we know, are browns that have decided in their own swashbuckling way to go to sea and will only really return to freshwater in order to spawn. However, many sea trout won't go that far from their native river, and they love the estuaries, creeks and inshore gullies and sandbanks.

Fun in the estuaries – John Wolstenholme holds a stunning sea trout taken from a southern hemisphere estuary.

Hebridean scene – Sea fishing in the northern hemisphere often gets better the more remote you become. Certainly, the north of Scotland can provide tremendous sport around islands and rocky outcrops.

On the rocks – *Some sea anglers love the rocks, and are quite willing to scale dizzying cliffs to get there. Other anglers know the surf beaches intimately and they'll lure, bait or fly fish there knowing exactly when and where to find the fish. These are skills that come from considerable experience and lessons handed down by fellow anglers.*

There have been times in my life when I have been obsessed with these fish in these places. As a kid, I used to bait or lure fish, but over the last ten years, it has been fly only which, in truth, hasn't changed the rate of my success. What's important is knowledge of the environment and the habits of the fish.

In some places, your best chance lies with the flood tide, in others with the ebb. Sometimes, it's the sea pools at the lowest water that you need to target. You may need to tramp miles and follow runnels of water through an endless wasteland of mud until you reach the long, still, mysterious pool that is your goal. If you're lucky, the sea trout sometimes give themselves away by chasing prey or splashing after an off-course terrestrial cranefly. On other occasions, there will be no visual action whatsoever, and you will retrieve your fly in hope rather than expectation. However, that won't stop you retrieving your fly with all the skill you can muster. You know how a crab works as it scuttles from stone to stone, and

that's how you want to make your fly behave. Your eye is constantly on the water, looking for signs of movement. It's also on your watch face, because you know you don't dare play games with the incoming tide.

Sea trout in the Arctic

The toughest sea fisherman I ever encountered was a man called Geiri who took us to the north coast of Iceland for sea trout. When we failed to catch one in the rivers, he told us he'd walk us out to sea – and he did. As the tide ebbed, we waded the estuary in water nearly up to our armpits. We then walked the north shore of the creek for an hour whilst the sun went down and the stars came out. The night, he told us, was the best time. We stopped when we came to a point where a big, deep, fast channel swirled close in to the shoreline. We waded 18m (20yd) out so we could fish the channel effectively and there began to cast.

The wind was biting. The stars glittered. Although it was after midnight, there was still enough light above the Arctic Circle to see big, big sea trout occasionally thrash themselves out of the water 50 or 100 yards away from us. Just once I had a heavy, electrifying tug, and Geiri got into a fish that ran out virtually all his backing before throwing the fly. Eleven pounds he said, and then cursed. Then, before the tide flowed again, we walked fishless all those miles back home.

The tricky mullet

Perhaps the most difficult fish to catch anywhere in the sea is the mullet. Sometimes, it's true, harbour mullet can be easy when they are weaned onto a diet of bread, chips or whatever the public throw at them. The mullet of the open creeks and freshets, however, are a different matter. Like the sea trout, they come and go with the tides and the seasons but, unlike the sea trout, they are notoriously picky when it comes to food items. Often, they will simply scrape the algae from the surface of the muds and refuse anything offered bigger than a pinhead. What makes it more difficult still, is that they are hugely spooky. With those big eyes of theirs, it seems they can see

The grey ghosts – *Mullet are found almost worldwide and are fascinating to catch. Generally, you've got to pursue them with the tiniest baits to replicate what they feed on in nature.*

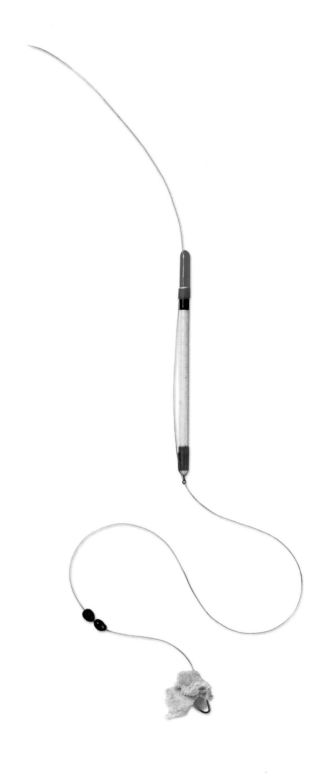

Fishing for mullet – *No fish in the sea is better suited to being fished for by freshwater methods than the mullet. This rig would be at home in the upper reaches of the river, but here in a salty creek, a light float and bread crust work equally well.*

you coming 100yd away in clear water. Murky water doesn't fare much better, as they can feel your boots on the soft mud or crunching over stones and shells. You can't even net them – believe me, I've tried. They'll hit the net, retreat, and then come again and clear it like an Olympic high jumper! If you're lucky enough to hook a mullet – they will occasionally sip in a tiny goldhead fly twitched agonizingly close to their snout – you're into a fish as fast as a bonefish, but with considerably more resilience.

Boat-fishing for sailfish

Then there is boat fishing, perhaps with fly gear, for sailfish. I once went out of Oban, on the west coast of Scotland, and though I had two bites, I missed them both. You'd think with fish this size they'd be easy to hit, but they're not. A guy with me had just one bite, which he hit, and that was skill indeed, but I'm not sure about the rest. It was all heave-ho for the next hour until the fish loomed from the dark water. The guy's pumping technique was tight and disciplined,

Happy days – Our angler is justifiably delighted with this fabulous capture from the Caribbean. The fact that it was fly-caught only increases his pleasure.

and he'd made sure that his gear was sound, so the least we have to grant him is extreme competence.

Sunrise and sunset are the ideal times to fly fish from the shore. Fish will come in close once the light of the day has subsided. In the darkness, they love to hunt in the shallows and a fly that mimics a small fish will be taken savagely.

GLOSSARY

bite: the action of a fish sipping in the bait on the hook.

bivvy: a stout, camouflage tent essential for long-stay carp fishing. There will generally be a bed inside along with a cooker, mobile phone and sometimes even a television set!

boilies: The bait sensation of the 1980s and still going strong into the 21st century, boilies are round, marble-sized baits with a tough outer skin that keeps them from being interfered with by smaller species. Boilies are made out of a base mix such as fishmeal, eggs, flavourings, sweeteners and various colours. The mix is then shaped accordingly and boiled to give the skin. Boilies can be made at home or bought commercially.

bolt rig: a rig incorporating a heavy weight close to the bait. The concept is that the carp picks up the weight, feels the weight of the lead, and bolts, thereby hooking itself.

buzzer: a fly tied to imitate a hatching nymph and fished just in or below the surface film.

caster: a maggot that has changed into a chrysalis prior to hatching out as the fully formed fly. Casters are particularly useful for roach, bream and tench.

controller: the name generally given to a float used when fishing surface baits for carp. The weight of the controller allows you to cast small floating baits greater distances and, of course, the controller gives you visual indication when a carp takes a bait and moves off.

crease: the line between fast and slow water on a river. Fishing the crease is one of the great art forms. Fish will generally hang in the slow water, moving along the crease to intercept food items coming down in the quicker current alongside.

dapping: a common form of fishing, most famously for wild trout on the big loughs in Ireland. Dapping takes place most frequently during the mayfly season when either large artificials are used or the real fly itself. Dapping can also continue throughout the season, often using crane flies as imitations.

downrigger: a device to take lures down deep when trolling from a boat. Downriggers are often used when fishing for large predatory trout, pike or members of the char family, especially in North America.

dry fly: an artificial fly that floats.

feathering: the act of slowing the line down as it comes off the spool when casting. You feather the line by dabbing the rim of the spool with your finger to create a type of breaking action. Feathering allows the terminal tackle to land smoothly in the water.

float: a pencil-shaped object that is made of plastic, feather quill, or reed. The float is attached to the line above the bait. Its purpose is to suspend the bait at different levels in the water, and also to signal when a bite has taken place.

floaters: baits that float, such as bread crust, dog biscuits and so on.

fly line: a plastic or polymer-coated line that gives fly anglers the necessary weight to cast the fly out from the bank.

forceps: Forceps or pliers are very useful for getting the hooks out of the bony mouths of predators – especially pike. Often ones with quite long noses are very useful.

free-lining: A method of fishing rivers, primarily without any weight on the line whatsoever apart from the hook and the bait itself. For this reason, the bait always tends to be a large one and favourites include large pieces of bread flake and lobworms. The trick is to let the bait waft down in the current but to keep a tight line and strike at the first indication of a bite.

groundbait: Bait fishers often use groundbait to attract fish into the area and to get the fish feeding without suspicion. A groundbait can be samples of the actual hook bait. Alternatively, it may be a cloud made of something like breadcrumb, with flavourings and scents added to it.

handlining: the name given to a method of extracting big fish embedded deep in the weed. You point the rod directly at the fish, grasp the line between the reel and the butt ring and pull backwards and forwards in a saw-like motion. The direct pull often brings the fish free.

hook length: Bait fishers generally use a main line,

which can be quite strong, and then a slightly finer piece of line – generally around about 1m (3ft) or so in length – that is attached to the hook. This is known as the hook length.

jigging: the act of moving a little spinner up and down through the layers of water to attract a predatory fish.

leader: a length of nylon line that attaches the heavy fly line to the artificial fly. It is tapered, thicker near the fly line and thinner toward the fly itself. The leader is generally about the length of the rod – longer in difficult situations.

leger weight: a piece of lead that can vary in shape but that is attached to the line to take the bait quickly down to the bottom and keep it there – even in a quick flowing current.

lie: a place where a trout decides to hang, particularly in a river.

lure: a general term given to an artificial creation meant to resemble a natural prey fish.

multiplier: a type of reel used both in sea fishing and in freshwater for large species. A multiplier is often used on salmon rivers for casting lures.

nymphing: using an artificial that looks like a real nymph.

plastic baits: small rubber lures meant to resemble such creatures as frogs, lizards, elvers and so on. They come in many different colours and look and feel fantastic.

plug: a lure made out of wood, plastic, or metal and designed to look like a small prey fish. Some are built to work on the surface, some in mid-water, and some down deep. Nearly all have a violent kicking action in the water that sends out vibrations.

pole: Some bait fishers – especially those looking for large numbers of smaller fish – do not use a conventional rod and reel. Instead, they use a pole. This can be very long – often 9m (30ft) or more in length – and made out of the lightest carbon fibre. The line is simply attached to the top ring, and then the float and bait are flicked out. Small fish are then swung in without being played off a reel.

popper: the name for a largish fly imitation fished on the surface and retrieved in an erratic fashion that creates splash, vibration and noise. Poppers are particularly useful for black bass and other predators.

pre-baiting: Very often bait fishers seeking big, crafty fish will put samples of the hook bait into the swim over a period of several days before actually fishing. The suspicions of the fish are relaxed and they begin to look for samples of the hook bait.

quiver tip: a very fine insert of carbon fibre into the top of a conventional rod. The line from the quiver tip to the bait is maintained under tension so the quiver tip bends just a little. When a fish picks up the bait, the quiver tip either pulls right round or leaps back straight.

rig: the general term given to the business end of the carp tackle – hook, hook length, lead and so on. Carp rigs are constantly being developed, and many shops carry an extensive range of items to make up the rigs of your choice.

rise: the name given to the act of a trout as it comes to the surface film and sips in an insect. The rise is also the name given to that period in the day when large numbers of trout come up to take insects.

run: This is generally a carp fishing term for a carp bite. When a big fish such as a carp picks up a bait, it generally runs off with it – hence the terminology.

side hooking: the opposite of hair rigging. With side hooking, the boily is actually placed onto the hook but with plenty of point still showing.

sight fishing: this means stalking and casting to an individual fish that you have seen.

spinner: a small metal object that rotates through the water, catches the light, and looks like a small prey fish.

split shot: pieces of metal put onto the line beneath the float. These make the float cock in an upright position and also help take the bait down to the required depth. These were originally made out of lead, but they are now made of non-toxic metal, since lead has been shown to be harmful to wildfowl.

spod: a large plastic container that is attached to a very strong rod and line, filled with boilies, pellets, corn or other small particle baits, and then cast a long distance to the chosen fishing area. The spod has a buoyant nose cone that makes it flip end-up in the water to deposit the bait. A cunning way of groundbaiting that is popular with carp anglers.

spoon: a bigger piece of metal than a spinner and made spoon-shaped so that it kicks and rotates through the water, sending out signals to any hungry predator.

strike: the act of lifting the rod and pulling the hook out of the bait into a biting fish.

stringer: a length of soluble PVA string tied to the hook. Several boilies are threaded along this string and the whole rig is cast out. Once in the water, the PVA string quickly dissolves, leaving the boilies around the hook bait. PVA bags are also available, allowing quantities of boilies to be spread around the hook bait.

swim: a particular area of water chosen by the bait fisher to groundbait and fish intensely. A swim is often situated close to a feature such as lily beds or deeper water.

swim feeder: a small container made out of plastic and put on the line – somewhere just above the hook length. It contains samples of the hook bait that then dribble out of the feeder once it has hit the bottom. The idea is to entice fish and lull their suspicions.

swivel: the main line from the rod and reel is attached to a trace by a swivel. This lets the lure rotate without twisting the main line.

throwing stick: a simple device designed for throwing boilies a long distance. Catapulting also achieves this objective, but is probably less accurate.

tippet: the last metre (yard) or so of the cast leading toward the fly.

trace: the length of material – generally 50cm (1½ft) or so – that attaches the lure to the swivel at the end of the main line. This trace is generally made of wire – especially if pike, walleye, zander or muskies are expected. The teeth on these species can cut through ordinary nylon line.

trolling: Trolling is always done from a boat. Anything from one to six rods is used and each has a plug, spinner or spoon attached to the end. The engine is fired up, the boat then sets off, and the lures are trolled around the water. This is a good method for big lake predators.

trotting: allowing the current to take your float along the river, thus exploring a great deal of water and giving you the possibility of covering many different fish. It's possible to trot anything up to 90m (300ft) or more away.

wet fly: an artificial fly that sinks.

zinger: used primarily in the game fishing world to attach tools like scissors, forceps and line cutters to the fly angler's waistcoat.